I0893520

This book was awarded the State Prize of the Republic of Uzbekistan (Science and Technology category), inaugurated in 2007.

Finis libri non finis quaerendi
The book is finished but not the investigation.

This book is dedicated to the history of the civilisations and states of the vast region of Central Asia, and to the interactions between the cultures and religions of the different countries of the Eurasian continent.

This publication is intended for a wide range of readers interested in the historical past of their peoples.

THE LANDS OF CENTRAL ASIA

Millennia-old Central Asian civilisations, from the Neolithic to the early medieval period

EDVARD RTVELADZE

SCALA

CONTENTS

FOREWORD

This book is dedicated to the memory of an exceptional scholar: its author, Edvard Rtveladze.

The Lands of Central Asia has been in preparation for two years. Edvard Rtveladze's untimely death preceded its release, meaning that the great author will not see the publication of his grandiose final work, but its impact will be felt forever.

This publication undertakes an almost-impossible task: describing the vast history of our region, covering ancient times up to the early Middle Ages. Carefully studying numerous sources and artefacts from Uzbekistan and surrounding countries, the book presents vibrant and comprehensive research only possible thanks to the heroic life-long dedication of Rtveladze.

The thirst for discovery moved Rtveladze from a young age. He went on his very first expedition while still a schoolboy. Armed with knowledge drawn from every source available at his local library, he independently studied archaeology and history. Eventually, Rtveladze came to Uzbekistan, where he studied history and archaeology at Tashkent State University. After his graduation, he continued his research at the Institute of Art History of the Academy of Arts of Uzbekistan, where he subsequently worked for over thirty years.

Rtveladze participated in more than eighty expeditions to different parts of the globe during decades of academic research. With his participation, the most important archaeological artefacts of the region were discovered, including the ancient fortress of Kampirtepa in the Surxondaryo Region. Based on his discoveries and collaborations with other researchers, Rtveladze published hundreds of articles and texts. His efforts laid the foundation for understanding the ancient and medieval history of Central Asia, which is now available to readers worldwide.

As well as a historian and archaeologist, Rtveladze was also a member of the Oliy Majlis (parliament) of Uzbekistan. In the last years of his life, Rtveladze supervised the major research project Cultural Heritage of Uzbekistan in the Collections of the

World. Its purpose is to collect all available information about historical monuments, manuscripts and artefacts of Uzbekistan kept in the collections of world museums. Through summarising, analysing and promoting this body of knowledge, Rtveladze provided the general public with access to the history of Central Asia. Throughout his life, he was preoccupied with popularising and carefully preserving the cultural heritage of our country, believing that it is crucial for knowledge to be shared and promoted and to inspire future generations. His death is an irreparable loss not only for the international academic community but for inquisitive minds around the world, driven by the thirst for discovery and ambition to unravel the secrets of history.

This posthumous edition of *The Lands of Central Asia* by the prodigious scholar Edvard Rtveladze marks a crucial achievement for the historical knowledge of Uzbekistan, opening new horizons for readers eager to learn more about the history of our lands.

Saida Mirziyoyeva
Deputy Chairwoman of the Council of the Art and Culture Development Foundation of the Republic of Uzbekistan

PREFACE

This book explores a vast region that stretches from the Caspian Sea in the west to the Pamir mountains in the east; from the Kopetdag and Hindu Kush mountains in the south to the lower reaches of the Amu Darya and Syr Darya rivers in the north.

In geographical and historical academic literature, the name Central Asia, *Srednaya Aziya* in Russian (literally 'Middle Asia'), has long been used to describe this region. In the early 1990s the Russian name to describe the region changed to *Tsentral'naya Aziya*, 'Central Asia', and this usage has since been increasingly common both in academic literature and in everyday life. Often, especially recently, both these designations have been used concurrently, which is very confusing when it comes to understanding exactly what territory is being referred to. In Russian-speaking academia, *Tsentral'naya Aziya* has always been understood to refer to the territory of the Altai, Mongolia, Xinjiang, Western China and Tibet, a region which in European academic literature is referred to as 'Inner Asia' as opposed to 'Central Asia'.

Although this book primarily focuses on *Srednaya Aziya* – Middle Asia, it also covers *Tsentraly'naya Aziya* – Central Asia, China and the Far East – and the historical past and interactions with these regions as well as with Mediterranean countries.

For the purposes of this translation, the designation Central Asia is used to cover the meaning of 'Middle Asian' territories in the senses of the Russian designation mentioned above. 'Inner Asia' is used on occasions where it is deemed necessary to refer to a broader territory covering part of today's Western China, Mongolia, the Russian Far East and Siberia.

Some sections of the book place greater emphasis on the region between the two major rivers of Middle Asia that is referred to as Transoxiana in European literature. This name was first introduced into the academic literature by the French scholar B. d'Herbelot. The Arabs referred to this region as *Mā Warā' al-Nahr* (henceforth Mavarannahr in this publication), 'That Which Lies Beyond the River'. The name 'Turan' was also used, which probably derives from the tribe called Tur mentioned in the Avesta, and was first used by Firdawsi. The border between Turan and Iran was the river Amu Darya. Since medieval times, the name Turkestan has been used to apply to most of Middle Asia, reflecting the dominant role of Turkic peoples since the turn of the 11th century, when the power of the Qarakhanid, Ghaznavid, Seljuk and Anushteginid dynasties was asserted here.

In ancient China, the central and eastern parts of Central Asia, as well as Eastern Turkestan, were called the 'Western Regions'.

The chronological range of this book is from the Bronze Age, 2nd millennium BC, to the 4th and 5th centuries AD, although a number of sections also necessarily cover medieval and modern times, such as in the section on Sogdian seafarers.

The book comprises published and unpublished sections and chapters that I have written over the last 15 years, some of which have been published in hard-to-access publications, often abroad. This information covers a wide panorama of the development of civilisations and states, and the interactions of different cultures, in the vast expanses of the Eurasian continent from the Atlantic to the Pacific Ocean.

I hope that this book will be interesting for the reader and will make a positive contribution to learning about the historical past of Central Asia, especially since such academic literature is very rare.

In conclusion, I would like to express my sincere gratitude to the United Nations Development Programme office in the Republic of Uzbekistan and the leadership of the University of World Economy and Diplomacy, without whose help this book would not have been published.

PART I

CIVILISATIONS

1.1

ORIGINS OF CIVILISATIONS

Prehistoric cultures and archaeological sites from the Neolithic Age to the Early Iron Age

THE HISTORY OF CENTRAL ASIA DATES BACK TO EARLY PREHISTORY. Archaeologists have established that the region was inhabited as early as the Lower Palaeolithic Age. Evidence of primitive human settlement dating back 500,000 to 1 million years ago was discovered in the Selengur cave in Southern Ferghana, in the Sokh river valley. Sites from the Upper Palaeolithic Age (40,000–12,000 years ago) were uncovered in Samarkand, at Amankutan and the Machai and Teshik-Tash caves in the Surkhan Darya region. Studies of the remains of a Neanderthal boy found in Teshik-Tash are further evidence of the existence and evolution of modern humans in southern Central Asia. Rock paintings depicting bull hunting in Zarautsai in the Kugitang mountains in the Surkhan Darya region, and the petroglyphs of the Shakhty cave in Tajikistan, date back to the Mesolithic Age (12,000–5,000 years ago).

During the Neolithic period (6,000–4,000 years BC), three vast prehistoric cultures developed in Central Asia: the Jeitun, Hissar and Kelteminar.

The **Jeitun culture** occupied the strip of the Kopetdag foothills in southern Turkmenistan. Sites here revealed evidence of the oldest Neolithic agricultural settlement in Central Asia, dating from the 6th or 5th millennium BC, possibly around the beginning of the 4th millennium. The name comes from the first fully excavated site, the Jeitun settlement, located 30 kilometres north-west of Ashkhabad. Research was undertaken here in the second half of the 1950s and early 1960s by the STACE archaeological team (the South Turkmenistan Archaeological Complex Expedition) led by V.M. Masson. Jeitun culture bears the hallmarks of the most important period in human history – the transition from an existence based on hunting and gathering to an economy based on agricultural production. The main activity of the Jeitun civilisation was farming based on a primitive form of irrigation known as *liman*. Hunting and gathering continued to play a role in the Jeitun economy. People lived in small village settlements with one-room houses for whole families. For example, archaeologists surmise that approximately 150–160 people lived in Jeitun, which consisted of 30 one-room houses built with loaf-shaped pieces of clay. The site includes a temple like that found at Pessejikdepe with walls decorated with primitive painting. Hallmarks of Jeitun culture include hand-moulded ceramics with a brown and red painted decoration. Tools for work and everyday use were made of stone and bone, and included axes, bone sickles and borers, flint microlithic cores, sickle blades and plates. The most important sites of Jeitun culture are the settlements of Jeitun, Chagalydepe, Choplidepe and Pessejikdepe, among others. In southern Turkmenistan Jeitun culture was followed by the Chalcolithic culture, as evidenced by sites such as Anau, Altyndepe and Karadepe.

The **Kelteminar culture**. In the lower reaches of the Amu Darya, along the Akcha Darya delta and in the adjacent areas of the Kyzylkum desert, are archaeological sites of Neolithic Kelteminar tribes who lived here in the second half of the 4th and the 3rd millennium BC. These tribes relied on hunting and fishing and their settlements were situated within the delta and along its banks. They lived in huge dwellings made of wood and reeds, with conical roofs. The history of Kelteminar culture can be divided into two phases: an earlier phase (covering the second half of the 4th to the first half of the 3rd millennium BC) and a later phase (covering the second half of the 3rd to the beginning of the 2nd millennium BC). The earlier phase is predominantly characterised by microlithoid flint objects: arrowheads, blunt-edged blades, scrapers made from stone flakes or blades and borers. There is evidence of point-bottomed, hand-moulded pottery made with clay mixed with chamotte, crushed stones, crushed shells and fine quartz sand. The firing in the vessels is poor and uneven and the surfaces are decorated by inscribed or wavy lines, chevrons and round impressions. Some of the vessels found have been decorated with red or yellow paint. In the later phase, trapezoidal arrowheads and spearheads, very large knives, wedge-shaped axes and flat-bottomed vessels appear. The most important sites are Janbas-4 and Kavat-7 in the Turtkul district of Karakalpakstan.

The third important Neolithic culture in Central Asia was the **Hissar culture**, named after the first artefacts found in the Hissar valley in Tajikistan. It was the culture of the tribes which inhabited mountain valleys and foothills, which is why the culture is often referred to as 'Mountain Neolithic'. These tribes were mainly concentrated in southern Tajikistan, although isolated finds of their material culture have been found in the Baisun and Babatag mountains in the south of Uzbekistan and also in Kyrgyzstan.

Reliant on cattle breeding and primitive farming, these tribes also engaged in hunting and gathering. Scholars believe the culture to have developed precisely during the transition from a hunter-gatherer economy to a producer economy based chiefly on cattle breeding. The Hissar culture lasted for 3,000 years (from the 6th to the 3rd millennium BC). Major settlements include Tutkaul, Kui-Bul'en and Tepe-Gaziyon, which represent the early, middle and late phases of the development of the culture respectively.

The stone tools produced include polished axes, scrapers, borers and sickle blades. A distinctive feature of the culture is the predominance of pebble tools. Other characteristic features were the coarse hand-made pottery and the remains of dwellings, which survived in the form of open stone surfaces, which had provided the bases for houses with timber frames.

From the above it can be seen that three distinctive regional cultures or historical and cultural communities – the Jeitun, Kelteminar and Hissar cultures – took shape in Central Asia during the Neolithic period. They differed from one another in their economic and cultural features and probably their ethnic character as well.

The Neolithic age is an important period in the history of Central Asia. It was at this time that agriculture based on primitive artificial irrigation emerged, along with the first permanent settlements including the first houses and temples with walls made out of lumps of clay and mud bricks. Pottery from this time is decorated with ornamental painting, and rudimentary art can be seen in the form of wall paintings in temples and primitive clay figurines. All these elements are, however, characteristic of Jeitun culture. Other regions in Central Asia depended on cattle breeding, hunting, gathering and fishing.

Bronze Age cultures and sites

Farming settlements continued to evolve during the Chalcolithic period (4th millennium BC) and particularly in the Bronze Age (3rd–2nd millennium BC), when the use of tools and weapons made of bronze became widespread, farming developed, canals and ditches were dug, and specialised crafts in pottery, metal working and other forms emerged. Large proto-urban settlements such as Altyndepe, Jarkutan and Namazgadepe were built, featuring well-developed structures (fortress plus settlement), often surrounded by walls made of mud brick. As well as dwellings inside the settlements there were monumental structures such as palaces and temples with separate large necropolises. The farming settlement culture from Margiana and southern Turkmenistan began to spread further east and south-east during this period, covering the territory of present-day southern Uzbekistan and northern Afghanistan, i.e. Bactria.

Sites of the Dashly-Sapalli culture are found here; this was a highly developed Bronze Age culture of tribes who settled in present-day areas of northern Afghanistan, southern Uzbekistan and Tajikistan in the 2nd millennium BC. Some historians refer to it as the Oxus civilisation, and it is also often referred to as the Bactria-Margiana Archaeological Complex. The main occupations of the population were irrigated agriculture, cattle breeding and crafts. The settlements were in two parts – the main unfortified area plus a square fortress – and located in small river oases. As the culture developed, proto-urban settlements such as Jarkutan emerged. The dwellings here were built above the ground, with clay and mud bricks, but the settlements also included monumental, multi-room buildings such as temples and palaces. Tools and weapons were made of stone, bone, horn and high-quality bronze.

Agricultural implements, tools for weaving, stone seals, bronze mirrors and pins, often decorated with animal figurines, and beads made of various materials were widespread. High-quality, wheel-turned pottery was fired in two-storey kilns. Ceramics were undecorated and were mostly produced in bright and reddish colours, for example, vases on high hollow legs, conical bowls, vessels with tubular spouts, and so on. Vessels were also made of bronze, leather and wood.

A significant number of weapons are characteristic of the sites, including battle-axes, arrowheads, spearheads and swords. The dead were buried in graves with side chambers, or in catacombs, in a contracted position on one side, accompanied with a range of grave goods, or in chambers under the floors of living areas, or in bespoke necropolises. Cenotaphs and burials of animals are also notable.

The most important cultural sites are Dashly (northern Afghanistan), the settlements of Jarkutan, Mollali and Sapalli, and the Bustan burial grounds 1–5 (Uzbekistan).

Archaeological sites from the same period in other geographical areas in Central Asia reveal evidence of their settlement by peoples of different cultures and modes of existence.

Thus, the north of Central Asia was occupied by the pastoral Andronovo steppe culture, which gradually spread to the Transoxiana region of Central Asia and beyond. Traces of its existence have been found in southern Uzbekistan, Tajikistan, Turkmenistan and northern Afghanistan. The lower reaches of the Zarafshan river and the Mahan Darya valley were inhabited by the Bronze Age Zamanbaba culture. The Bishkent culture was widespread in south-western Tajikistan, with tribes belonging to the Srubnaya culture living in western Turkmenistan.

The Zamanbaba culture was based on cattle breeding and farming. Settlements comprised large houses with a pole-and-frame construction, partly sunk into the ground, and hearths and storage pits within. Archaeological finds include flint tools (arrowheads, borers, sickle blades, stone querns, hoes and spindle-whorls), as well as bronze knives, mirrors, fishing hooks, bone awls, beads and terracotta figurines. Pottery vessels were fired in two-storey kilns and were all hand-moulded, of fine quality, flat- or round-bottomed, undecorated and of various shapes. The dead were buried in burial pits with side chambers, in a contracted position on their sides and accompanied by grave goods. Burials were individual, in pairs, or collective. The Zamanbaba culture developed out of the local Neolithic culture and was influenced by the settled farming cultures of southern Central Asia. The most important sites are the Zamanbaba burial grounds and settlements in the Karakul district, in the Bukhara region.

During the second half of the 2nd to the early 1st millennium BC, the Late Bronze Age Tazabagyab culture was establishing itself in the lower reaches of the Amu Darya, along the Akcha Darya delta. Tazabagyab tribes relied on farming using primitive irrigation techniques and on cattle breeding. Their unfortified settlements were situated within the delta and on the banks of streams. They lived in semi-dugout houses with a frame construction of wood and reeds. Typical finds include bronze knives, tetrahedral awls with bone handles, bronze bracelets, pendants and bronze and carnelian beads. Objects made of stone continued to be used. The pottery vessels are hand-moulded and flat-bottomed and made from clay mixed with crushed stones and crushed shells, and sometimes have burnished surfaces. Many vessels are decorated with geometric shapes, especially cross-hatched triangles. Burials were made in shallow earth pits, with bodies laid on the side in a contracted position and accompanied by grave goods (vessels, jewellery, tools). There is evidence of both individual and double burials. The Tazabagyab culture has some similarities with the Andronovo culture of the Bronze Age. The most important sites are the settlements of Anka-5 and Kavat-3, and the burial site of Kokcha-3 in the Turtkul district of Karakalpakstan.

In the 2nd to the early 1st millennium BC, the southern Akcha Darya delta of the lower Amu Darya was settled by the Bronze Age Suyurgan culture. Two phases in the development of Suyurgan culture, an early (Kamyshlin) and a later (Kounda), have been identified. Suyurgan sites were mainly situated along the banks of water courses. The houses were built above ground with the roofs supported on poles. Early Suyurgan culture is characterised by flint and quartzite arrowheads, knives and scrapers. Cooking vessels were flat-bottomed, hand-moulded and made of clay mixed with crushed stones and crushed shells, often burnished, and sometimes with simple ornamentation.

In the later phase there is evidence of widespread use of bronze objects, such as sickles and knives. Vessels were made with greater care, well-fired, burnished, and decorated with an ornamental band in relief. The Suyurgans relied mainly on hunting and fishing and later on farming and cattle breeding. Suyurgan culture can be traced back genetically to the Kelteminar culture, although it also has some links with the Anau culture of southern Turkmenistan. The most important sites are Kamyshly, Janbas-6 and Kaundy-1 in the Turtkul district.

Suyurgan culture in Khorezm was followed by Amirabad culture of the Late Bronze Age (early 1st millennium BC). This culture relied on irrigated farming, and settlements were located by the side of fairly large canals. The semi-dugout houses with a frame construction had a central hearth and several storage pits. Bronze objects such as sickles, arrowheads, needles and awls were common. Stone moulds for casting arrowheads have also been found. Pottery vessels were flat-bottomed and made of clay mixed with chamotte and crushed stone. Their outer surfaces were often burnished and occasionally decorated with an ornamental band along the neck. There is evidence of a well-developed network of irrigation channels, including main canals several kilometres long and small ditches. The Amirabad culture can be traced back genetically to the late phase of Suyurgan culture. The most important site is the settlement of Yakke-Parsan-2 in the Turtkul district.

The Chust culture of the Late Bronze Age settled in the Ferghana Valley between the end of the 2nd and the beginning of the 1st millennium BC. Chust tribes relied on farming, cattle breeding, and the crafts of metalworking and pottery. The sites included both unfortified and fortified settlements, enclosed by walls of clay and mud brick, and with a citadel erected on natural hills (such as the Dalverzin settlement). Wood and reed frame-houses were partly dug into the ground, but the settlements also had clay dwellings above ground. Bronze objects (daggers, arrowheads, horse bits, knives, sickles, awls, needles and jewellery) and stone objects (mortars and pestles, grinding stones and whetstones), as well as objects made of bone and horn, weaving tools and casting moulds were widely used. Crude kitchen utensils and delicate eating utensils of various kinds were made by hand using cloth templates. Ceremonial dishes were decorated with red slip, burnishing and ornamentation in black paint. There is evidence of several types of burials: individual burials with the dead laid on one side in a contracted position, as well as on their backs, collective burials, disarticulated corpses, and burial in vessels. Burials were made within the territories of the settlements.

Chust culture belongs to the group of painted pottery cultures that were widespread in Central Asia during the Late Bronze and Early Iron Age. The most important sites are the settlements of Chust and Dalverzin in the Namangan region.

The Tashkent oasis, in the valleys of the Akhangaran and Chirchik rivers, was home to the tribes of the Burgulyuk culture of the Late Bronze Age, dating back to the first half of the 1st millennium BC. The main occupation of the population was cattle breeding and farming.

Settlements were located alongside rivers and on natural hills; one of the sites has a defensive wall made of mud brick. The dwellings were partially dug out and of a frame construction. Bronze sickles, celts, arrowheads, awls, knives and toilet spoons (for cosmetic purposes) were all used. Stone objects found include grinding stones, pestles and querns. Pottery vessels were hand-moulded, both flat- and round-bottomed, and included coil pots made with cloth templates. They were unornamented but occasionally decorated with triangles, cross-hatching and dots in red-brown paint. The Burgulyuk culture also belongs to the painted-pottery cultures of the Late Bronze to Early Iron Age, which were widespread in the vast territory of Central Asia. The most important sites are the settlements of Burgulyuk-1 in the Akhangaran valley (Ak-Kurgan district) and Shashtepa in Tashkent.

According to one theory, the middle of the 2nd millennium BC is particularly significant in the history of Central Asia, as this was a period when Indo-Aryan tribes migrated across the territory on their way to India, with the Harappan civilisation dying out following their arrival.

It is possible that during the Late Bronze Age, in the second half of the 2nd millennium BC, the first formations of proto-states began to emerge in the most advanced regions of Central Asia – rather like the city-states of the ancient Egyptian *nome*. A state, as a unique form of social organisation, generally emerges in certain regions where a civilisation (in the widest meaning of the word) reaches a particularly high level of development in its social evolution.

The first kinds of state-like entities are the earliest cities, which became the economic, political and religious centres of extremely small 'states' (in terms of the territory they occupied), to become what are now known as city-states. Later, for various reasons, these city-states united to form single, relatively large kingdoms, and some grew into vast empires. This was the fundamental process for the evolution of such state entities, and they emerged in locations in the Near and Middle East.

The development of early forms of states in southern Central Asia followed a similar evolutionary path, but there were many differences too, for specific historical reasons. For example, in the south, in the agricultural oases of Bactria and Margiana, in the second half of the 2nd millennium BC, the proto-states that emerged were more like fully fledged city-states in terms of their structure. This was true of places such as Altyndepe, Namazgadepe, Jarkutan and other major settlements, which were tied to a particular area through a water-management system and had many features of a city-state or city-oasis.

Oasis states of this kind, particularly in Bactria, subsequently merged into kingdoms under a single state authority. This assumption is based on an analysis of archaeological data, and supported by the accounts of the Greek historian Ctesias of Cnidus (5th century BC), who referred to a mighty Bactrian kingdom led by King Oxyartes that fought against the powerful Assyrians.

Later than the ones in Bactria, some form of proto-state grouping began to emerge in Sogdia. At any rate, even in pre-Achaemenid times, large settlements with citadels like Koktepa, Uzun-Kyr and Er-Kurgan were already in existence here, perhaps constituting the capitals of such groupings.

A different route to the formation of states was underway in the north of Transoxiana, in Khorezm, on territory inhabited by the Sakas. It appears that as early as the beginning of the 1st millennium BC confederative alliances became established here, the core of which was probably Khorezm, based on the principles of military democracy, and led by an elected king or queen such as Tomyris or Zarina.

Central Asia in the first half and beginning of the second half of the 1st millennium BC

At the beginning of the 1st millennium BC, the nature and substance of cultures in Central Asia underwent significant changes. During this period, most of southern Central Asia was occupied by the Yaz I culture or the East Khorasan culture. Communities associated with the Yaz culture were Eastern Iranian tribes of the Late Bronze Age and Early Iron Age who occupied a vast area in the south of Central Asia, extending from the Kopetdag mountains in the west to the Pamirs in the east. Their economies relied on irrigated farming and cattle-breeding settlements.

Two-part settlements with a fortified citadel built on a high brick platform were typical. Dwellings were made of mud brick and clay, but also included houses that were partly dug out with a frame construction. Tools and weapons were made of stone and bronze (grinding stones, bell-shaped pestles, sickles, and arrowheads with sockets or tangs). Later came objects made of iron, and the large irrigation channels were also created. Hand-moulded vessels, both decorated and plain, were made using clay mixed with chamotte and crushed stone. Pottery was typically decorated with concentric ornamental triangles, obliques and straight lines in brown and red paint. Wheel-turned pottery was used as well. Striking finds from this period include the head of a male in stone from Mashhad and an assemblage of ritual objects. The largest and most thoroughly studied settlements of this period are Yaz I in Margiana, Kuchuktepa and Bandykhan I in Northern Bactria, and also Tillyatepa in Southern Bactria.

Today, dozens of settlements of Yaz I culture have been found throughout the territory from the Caspian Sea in the west to the Pamirs in the east and from southern

Afghanistan to the middle reaches of the Amu Darya in the north. Scholars believe the origins of Yaz I culture are connected to the migration and settlement of Eastern Iranian tribes starting out, in the opinion of V.I. Sarianidi, from a single centre in eastern Khorasan. Hence the name proposed for this culture – the East Khorasan culture. V.M. Masson believed that the origin of this Bronze Age culture can be explained with reference to a number of historical factors.

The emergence of this culture may also be linked to the movement of the Chust tribes, with which it shares many features such as hand-moulded, painted pottery and stone cult objects. However there are also considerable differences between them.

The question as to how long this culture lasted is no less complex. V.M. Masson dates it to the period from the 9th to the mid-7th century BC. At present, several scholars, particularly European ones, date the Yaz I culture to the middle of the 2nd millennium BC. However, such a date would contradict the dates for the subsequent cultures – Yaz II and Yaz III – and give rise to large chronological lacunae.

The Yaz I culture was succeeded by the Yaz II culture dated to between the 7th and mid-5th century BC (650–450 BC, according to V.M. Masson). The sites of this culture occupy the southern parts of Central Asia, especially Bactria and Margiana, but they need further and closer investigation. This culture reflects the pre-Achaemenid and early Achaemenid periods in the history of Central Asia. The culture had evolved and wheel-turned, painted pottery began to predominate; while the types of settlement had also begun to change. One of the most remarkable settlements – Bandykhan II – consisted of three parts, with a fortress and an extensive non-fortified area.

This period was one of the most important periods in the history of Central Asia, during which the first states took shape, historical and cultural regions emerged as definitive entities, and the first monotheistic religion appeared – Zoroastrianism. It was also marked by the emergence of the first cities such as Bactra, Maracanda, Koktepa, Uzun-Kyr and Er-Kurgan, each spanning over a hundred hectares and surrounded by strong fortified walls.

1.2

HISTORICAL AND CULTURAL AREAS: THE FOUNDATIONS OF CENTRAL ASIAN CIVILISATIONS

Throughout antiquity and early medieval times, Central Asia was home to several large and small historical and cultural areas. The names of some of these regions survive to this day, for instance, Khorezm and Ferghana. The development of these regions probably began in the 2nd millennium BC but the earliest information about some of these areas, namely, Bactria, Parthyene, Sogdia and Khorezm, can be found in accounts of geographical areas mentioned in the *Videvdat* (of the Avesta) texts, the inscriptions of Achaemenid kings (the Behistun inscription), and works of ancient Greek authors (Herodotus, Ctesius and others), and these date back to the 6th and 5th centuries BC.

The largest of these regions were Bactria (present-day northern Afghanistan, southern Uzbekistan and Tajikistan), Parthyene (the foothills of the Kopetdag in southern Turkmenistan), Sogdia (the present-day Kashka Darya, Samarkand and Bukhara regions of Uzbekistan), Dayuan/Ferghana (the Ferghana valley of Uzbekistan), Margiana/Margush (lower Murghab in Turkmenistan) and Chach/Chachan (the present-day Tashkent region of Uzbekistan). In the early medieval period (5th–8th centuries AD) there was also mention of other historical and cultural areas of Central Asia, including Chaganian (the Surkhan Darya basin in the south of Uzbekistan), Shuman, Akharun, Khuttal (southern Tajikistan), Ustrushana (the Jizzak region of Uzbekistan and the Khodjent region of Tajikistan), Kesh and Nakhshab (the Kashka Darya region of Uzbekistan) and many others.

Unlike regions established on the principles of state and administrative rule, the historical and cultural areas emerged over an extended period of time as the result of a variety of factors such as territorial and geographical location, as well as economic, cultural and ethnic commonalities. For a number of reasons, particularly socio-economic and political ones, as well as natural, geographical factors, the ethnic groups that originally settled in a small area near a source of water gradually spread out over a larger area, and this then often retained the name of the former, smaller area. Large historical and cultural regions such as Bactria, Sogdia and Khorezm began like this and later developed into larger states.

Within each such region, smaller territorial units formed, and initially these also became established for historical and cultural reasons rather than administrative ones. These units occupied a small, geographically limited area, mainly in river valleys or mountainous regions. All these areas appear to have been inhabited from the beginning of the 1st millennium BC by ethnically homogeneous populations speaking Eastern Iranian dialects. However, although these areas shared extensive ethnic affinities and economic and cultural commonalities, they also exhibited local differences.

Bactria (known as Bactriana in Ancient Greek; Bahlika – Sanskrit; Bactrish – Old Persian; Bahdi – Avestan; Bakhlo, Balkh, Bactrian, Farsi), originally a small area in the Balkhab valley, refers to a historical and cultural region that straddled both banks of the Amu Darya, from the Hindu Kush (in Afghanistan) to the Hissar Range (in Uzbekistan, Tajikistan). The capital city was Bactra, later known as Balkh in northern Afghanistan. According to the data from a range of ancient sources, it was originally called Zariaspa ('having golden horses'), then renamed Bactra after the name of the river on which the city was situated. Hence, the name Bactria is of riverine origin. The etymology of the word 'Bactria' is unclear. Some scholars believe it to derive from the Avestan word *baxta, baga* – meaning 'a share, portion'. Still others believe it comes from the word *bahtar*, which means 'the East' in Persian, or *Bahtar Zamin*, i.e. 'the Land of the East'. It is possible that the word Bactria is of Indo-European origin, the second component of the name is clearly present in the Indo-European word *gotrá* meaning a 'shelter' – a place where people live together. Compare the names of Bactrian cities cited by Ptolemy (Ptolemy, *Geogr.* VI, 11, 6) – Marakodra, Alikodra. Human exploration of the area dates back to the Palaeolithic and Neolithic periods. The beginning of the 2nd millennium BC, perhaps a little earlier, saw extensive development of the Amu Darya plain in the south and north by tribes of agricultural settlers (Dashly-Sapalli culture) arriving from the Murghab valley and southern Turkmenistan.

Small oases existed in the river valleys with several settlements with fortified centres. There is evidence of advanced agricultural techniques using artificial irrigation, and also specialised craftsmanship, for instance pottery and metalwork.

Architecture, construction and trade were greatly developed, with monumental buildings and palaces being built in this period (at Dashly-3 and Jarkutan).

The second half of the 2nd millennium BC saw the emergence of proto-cities in this region. Soon after, perhaps as part of an early combining of states, an ancient Bactrian kingdom emerged.

From the middle of the third quarter of the 6th century BC until 330 BC, Bactria, as a satrapy, was part of the Achaemenid state. Between 329 and 327 BC it was conquered by Alexander the Great. From 306 BC to the middle of the 3rd century BC it was under the control of Seleucid kings. In the middle of the 3rd century BC the Graeco-Bactrian kingdom established itself on the territory of Bactria, and lasted for more than a hundred years. This period saw the emergence of many cities in Bactria, and significant local, economic and cultural development with strong Hellenistic influences.

The most outstanding monuments of this time are the site of Ai-Khanum and the Temple of the Oxus at Takht-i Sangin. In the second half of the 2nd century BC, Saka and Yuezhi (or Tokharian) tribes arriving from the north and north-east settled in Bactria. It is possible that Bactria began to be called Tokharistan from this time onwards; the name was first recorded in AD 386 after one of the tribes that conquered Bactria – Tokharians. In the first half of the 1st century AD, Bactria was part of the Kushan kingdom. In the middle of the 3rd century AD, it was conquered by the Sassanians. From the middle of the 5th century until the second half of the 6th century AD Bactria/Tokharistan was one of the main locations of the Hephthalites.

From the second half of the 6th century AD until its final surrender to the Arabs at the beginning of the second half of the 8th century AD, Tokharistan was a confederation of many small feudal estates under the yoke of the Turkic *yabghu*.

The population of the region during the 1st millennium BC and the beginning of the first centuries AD mainly consisted of Bactrians who spoke one of the Eastern Iranian languages. It seems that scripts of foreign origin (cuneiform, Aramaic writing) appeared here as early as the middle of the 1st millennium BC, and Greek script from the end of the 4th and 3rd centuries BC. Under the Kushan king Kanishka or his predecessor Kadphises II, Bactrian script, based on the Greek alphabet, was introduced and used here up to the 8th and 9th centuries AD. In antiquity and early medieval times, other scripts were also used in Bactria/Tokharistan: Kharoshthi, Brahmi, Pahlavi, Aramaic, Sogdian and the so-called unknown or undeciphered script. The contribution of advanced Eastern and Hellenistic civilisations to the formation and development of Bactrian/Tokharistan culture was considerable.

Dayuan (in the Ferghana valley) was a separate state that probably existed in the last centuries BC. The earliest information about Dayuan can be found in the accounts of

Zhang Qian (128 BC). The capital was the city of Guishan, now identified as today's Kasan or Kokand.

At the head of the polity was a ruler (some rulers' names are known – Mu-Kua, Meicai and Chanfeng). A council of elders played a major role in the management of the state, replacing and appointing rulers at their own discretion. According to Zhang Qian, Dayuan had a population of several hundred thousand and more than 70 towns and cities. Agriculture, especially alfalfa farming, viticulture and winemaking, played a significant role in Dayuan's economy. Wine was produced in large quantities and successfully stored for several decades without spoiling. Rice and wheat were also cultivated, and specialised horse breeding was widespread in Dayuan/Ferghana, especially that of a special breed of 'glorious Argamaks who sweat blood' and of 'heavenly horses' derived from this breed, over which the Han–Dayuan War of 104–102 BC was fought. After establishing nominal rule over Ferghana and placing a ruler on the throne, the Chinese troops withdrew. After their departure, the people of Ferghana overthrew the ruler appointed by the Chinese and installed their protégé, Chanfeng. Dayuan remained an independent state, however, and it established regular diplomatic relations with China.

Margiana (Margav=Mouru – Avestan; Margush – Old Persian; Margiana – Ancient Greek; Marv – Arabic) was a historical and cultural area that spanned the middle reaches of the Murghab river and Merv oasis. The etymology of 'Margiana' lies in the word *marg* meaning a 'meadow' or 'ground grassed over'. It began to be inhabited by humans during the Neolithic and Chalcolithic periods. At the beginning of the 2nd millennium BC, an ancient agricultural oasis (the land of Margush) emerged in the very north of the Murghab delta, with large settlements surrounded by walls with towers, and also a fortress (Keleli). The capital of Margush was the settlement of Gonur, where V.I. Sarianidi investigated a fire temple, a palace and a large necropolis, where he discovered gold jewellery, stone statuettes and sealstones with various mythological scenes, high-quality ceramics, bone objects and other articles. Monumental temples, probably of proto-Zoroastrian origin, have also been excavated here. Of these, Togolak-21 is particularly distinctive – its monumental structures and other archaeological finds here attest to a highly developed civilisation in Margiana, representing one of the advanced centres of the ancient East, in the 2nd millennium BC. Further settlement of the area dates back to the early Iron Age at the beginning of the 1st millennium BC. Large irrigation systems were developed during this period, along with settlements with citadels on tall artificial platforms such as at Yazdepe and Arvalidepe – the centres of small estates. In the middle of the 1st millennium BC, the centre of the region moved south to the sites of Erk-Kala and Gyaur-Kala, where the capital city of Margiana (or ancient Merv) was established near the present-day city of Bairam-Ali. The conquest of the region by the Achaemenids prompted a widespread popular revolt, the Frada uprising, which was brutally suppressed in the early years of Darius I's reign (522–486 BC). At the end of the 4th century BC Margiana was conquered by Alexander the Great, who founded the city of Alexandria in Margiana on the site of Gyaur-Kala. From the end of the 4th century BC to the middle of the 3rd century BC, Margiana was part of the Seleucid state with its centre at Antioch in Margiana.

After the establishment of the Graeco-Bactrian kingdom (mid-3rd century BC) Margiana became part of the Parthian state. From the second half of the 1st century AD until the beginning of the 3rd century AD, the local dynasty of the descendants of King Sanabares ruled here. From the second quarter of the 3rd century AD until the middle of the 7th century, Margiana was part of the Sassanian state until it was conquered by the Arabs in AD 651.

Sogdia was an ancient historical and cultural area originally covering only the Zarafshan valley but later also encompassing the territory of the present-day Kashka Darya and Bukhara regions of Uzbekistan. Most early Arab and Persian geographers and historians took Penjikent to be Sogdia's eastern border, and Carmania (near Navoi) to be its western border. However, some writers included Bukhara and Kashka Darya as part of Sogdia, as do some Chinese accounts where Kesh is referred to as part of Sogdia. After the 10th century, the name Sogdia as the designation of a country and region gradually fell out of use, surviving only in the time of Amir Timur (also known as Tamerlane) as the name of two small *tyumen* (provinces) west of Samarkand.

The etymology of the word Sogdia remains unclear. Beginning with W. Tomaschek, scholars believed that it derived from the Iranian **suxta*-meaning 'to burn, sparkle or shine'. According to V.I. Abaev, the name of the land and people of Sugd/Sogdia means 'clean and light', while O.I. Smirnova believes that Sogdia stands for 'a land of fertile valleys'. The earliest use of this toponym is found in the Behistun inscription of Darius I, in the *Mihr-Yasht* hymn in the Avesta (first half of the 1st millennium BC). The Sogdians who populated this area were of Eastern Iranian stock. Human exploration of Sogdia dates back to the Upper Paleolithic Age (40,000–12,000 BC) as indicated by Amankutan and the Samarkandskaya Palaeolithic site. The upper reaches of the Zarafshan valley were farmed by the ancient Sarazm tribes in the 4th millennium BC. From the end of the 6th to the 4th century BC Sogdia was part of the sixteenth satrapy of the Achaemenid state. In 329–327 BC Sogdia was conquered by Alexander the Great, who encountered defiance from local tribes led by Spitamenes. In the 3rd to mid-2nd century BC, Sogdia was alternately part of the Seleucid and Graeco-Bactrian kingdoms. In the 2nd to the 1st century BC several independent dominions emerged on its territory, headed by nomadic tribal leaders of Saka and Yuezhi origin. In the last decades BC, Sogdia became part of the Kangju confederation. This was a time of intensive migration to the east by Sogdians, to Semirechye, Xinjiang and China. Numerous Sogdian settlements sprang up along the Silk Road. Sogdian script was widely used in the 2nd and 1st centuries BC. In the mid-7th century AD, the powerful Sogdian dominion of the Ikhshids emerged, which was destroyed by the Arabs in the mid-8th century AD. From AD 670 onwards, Arabs began to raid Sogdia, but encountered fierce resistance from the Sogdians, particularly from Devashtich. From the middle of the 8th century AD, Sogdia was part of the Abbasid Caliphate. Archaeological sites on Sogdian territory, such as Afrasiab, Varakhsha, Penjikent and Sarazm have given up remarkable objects and monuments of the material and artistic cultures of the region.

Khorezm (Uvarazmas – Old Persian; Chorasmia – Greek; Khwarazm – Arabic) was an ancient historical and cultural area situated in the lower reaches of the Amu Darya. The etymology of the name Khorezm is not entirely clear. According to some researchers, the word *Khorezm* means 'the land of the sun'; according to others, it stands for 'fertile land'; according to a third point of view, it means 'the good gift of the land' or 'land with good gifts', i.e. good towns. The Soviet archaeologist and ethnographer S.P. Tolstov proposed a completely different interpretation with 'land (country) of the hvari people' (or *harri*), which according to him reflected the name of the Hurrian people who established the state of Mitanni in Asia in the 2nd millennium BC.

Khorezm has a long and ancient history. During the Neolithic period, Kelteminar culture, dominated by hunting and fishing, was widespread in the region between the second half of the 4th and the 3rd millennium BC. During the Late Bronze Age, in the second half of the 2nd millennium BC to the beginning of the 1st millennium BC, it was followed by the Tazabagyab culture, whose main occupations were farming and cattle breeding, and the Suyurgan culture, which initially relied on hunting and fishing, and later on farming and cattle breeding. At the beginning of the 1st millennium BC, the Amirabad culture, more highly developed than its predecessors, was spreading across Khorezm.

According to one theory, based on the writings of Hecateus of Miletus (late 6th century BC) and Herodotus (5th century BC), Khorezmians lived in the Murghab and Tejen river basins. This, somewhat confusing, information contributed to the hypothesis of 'Larger Khorezm', a state with its centre in the region of Merv and Herat, which allegedly existed as early as the pre-Achaemenid period, i.e. in the 7th–6th centuries BC. Advocates of another hypothesis believe that the Khorezmians came to these territories from their original habitat further north.

The earliest, most reliably dated mention of the name Khorezm is in an inscription made on the orders of King Darius I on the Behistun rock between 518 and 521 BC. In the 540s BC Khorezm was possibly conquered by the Achaemenid king Cyrus II (*c.* 600–530 BC), and under Darius I this area, along with Sogdia and Parthia, became part of the 16th satrapy of the Achaemenid state. The emancipation of Khorezm from the Achaemenids and the establishment of the Khorezm kingdom dates back to the second half of the 4th century BC. Greek sources make reference to the king of Khorezm, Pharasmanes, arriving in Samarkand in 329 BC to propose an alliance with Alexander the Great.

Shaushafan, ruler of Khorezm. Coin

In the 2nd or possibly 3rd century BC, Khorezm became an independent part of the large Kangju confederation. As early as the 2nd–1st centuries BC, it began issuing its own coins in imitation of the Graeco-Bactrian coins of Eucratides, first with a distorted Greek inscription, and then with a legend in Khorezmian script. The iconography of the coins was also changed, with the local ruler appearing on the obverse and a horseman and *tamga* (seal) on the reverse. These symbols then appear on all Khorezmian coins up to the middle of the 8th century AD and are testament to the dynastic succession of Khorezmian rulers for more than 800 years. The study of Khorezmian inscriptions by V.A. Livshits and B.I. Vainberg made it possible to establish the names of the Khorezmian kings (Khorezmshahs) Artav, Vazamar, Bravik and others, which differ significantly from the list of names of the so-called Afrighid dynasties provided by al-Biruni.

In the first centuries AD, Khorezm was a powerful independent state with a capital located in the Toprak-Kala settlement. Khorezm retained its independence until the second half of the 8th century AD, when it was incorporated into the Abbasid state.

The civilisation of ancient Khorezm is one of the most distinctly original and vibrant in Central Asia and home to many outstanding monuments such as Koi-Krylgan-Kala, Toprak-Kala and Ayaz-Kala among others.

Chaganian (Saganian – Arabic) was a historical and cultural area in the middle and upper reaches of the Surkhan Darya (Chagan-Rud). The region is first mentioned by Xuanzang (around AD 650). The earliest traces of habitation in the area date back to the Mesolithic and Neolithic periods. In the second half of the 2nd millennium BC, the first farming settlements (Mullolitepa) appeared here, and in the middle of the 1st millennium BC, the early town of Kyzyltepa came into being. Between the 1st century BC and the 3rd century AD Chaganian was part of the Kushan state. During this period, the region's economy and culture evolved considerably, and many cities and settlements emerged, along with the development of commodity and money relations and irrigated agriculture, while many different kinds of crafts, and fine and applied arts, especially applied monumental clay and plaster sculpture (for example in Khalchayan and Dalverzintepa), flourished. Towards the end of the 3rd and in the 4th century AD, Chaganian came under the rule of the Sassanian Kushanshahs. In the second half of the 5th and the first half of the 6th century AD, this area was alternately ruled by the Hephthalites and the Sassanians. From the second half of the 6th to the second half of the 8th century AD, Chaganian was governed by a local dynasty of Eastern Iranian origin, who were only nominally subordinate to the supreme rulers of Tokharistan, the Turkic *yabghus*. The names of some Chaganian Hidevs or Chagankhudats (rulers) have been determined on the basis of written, epigraphic and numismatic data, i.e. Faganish, Sashr, Zarin, Turantash, Tish and Hnar. In the second half of the 7th century AD, Arabs raided Chaganian and they overthrew the local dynasty at the end of the 8th century AD. From the middle or second half of the 9th century until the beginning of the 11th century AD, Chaganian became the hereditary domain of rulers from the Muhtajid dynasty, who were among the most powerful semi-independent vassals of the Samanids. The amirs of this dynasty, Abu Bakr Muhammad ibn Muzaffar (died AD 940/41) and especially Ahmad ibn Abu Bakr Muhammad, also known as Abu Ali Chagani (died AD 955/56), played a prominent role in the Samanid state, holding the most important administrative positions as deputies of Khorasan and the *sipahsalars*. Under the Muhtajids, in addition to the territory that corresponds to the present-day Surkhan Darya region, Chaganian also comprised the Shuman and Akharun regions in north-west Tajikistan. The capital city of Chaganian had the same name and was located at the site of the ancient settlement of Budrach, 6 kilometres south-east of Denau at the confluence of the Kyzylsu and Syr Darya rivers. At the time, the city of Chaganian (or Saganian) was one of the most significant economic and cultural centres in Central Asia, with an area of about 6 hectares. The Chaganian amir Ahmad ibn Muhammad became famous in the East as the patron (*mamduh*) of many renowned poets, such as Dakiki, Farruki and Manjuki. In the first half of the 11th century AD, Chaganian depended to some degree on the Qarakhanids, at times becoming a short-lived sovereign domain. In the second half of the 11th to the first half of the 12th century, Chaganian was absorbed into the Seljuk state. During the period from the second half of the 12th to the early 13th century it was ruled at different times by the Qarakhanids, Karluks, Gurids and Khorezmshahs. After the Mongol conquest in the mid-13th century, Chaganian became the hereditary possession of Chagatai's grandson Yesun-Tuva and then his son Borak. A new city was established during this period on the site of a former *rabad* (a suburban district for crafts, commerce and trade) and existed until the beginning of the 16th century, when the province of Chaganian was conquered by Shaibani Khan. The main centre then moved to Dih-i Nau (present-day Denau).

Chach (Shash – Chachan, Arabic) was a historical and cultural area situated on the right bank of the Syr Darya river, in the Chirchik and Akhangaran river basins, in the present-day Tashkent region.

The earliest use of the name Chach is in King Shapur I's inscription (AD 241–272) on what is known as the Kaab-i-Zoroaster, which lists the borders of his states. The name Chach also appears in Sogdian script in early inscriptions on bronze coins issued in this region, possibly from the 3rd century AD onwards. Dating from this period (i.e. 3rd century) or thereabouts are also the Sogdian inscriptions on bricks and stones found at Kultobe (southern Kazakhstan), which mention a leader of the army of Chachannap, meaning literally 'the people of Chach'. The full name of the area was probably Chachan, as this name appears in some inscriptions on ancient and early medieval coins, and Chach is most likely a truncated form like Kesh (Kish) for Keshan and Chagan for Chaganian.

Arabic written sources refer to Chach as Shash, with 'sh' used to denote the sound 'ch' since Arabic has no letter for it. Similarly, in Arabic, the name of Chaganian, another region in the Surkhan Darya valley, becomes Saganian.

Ancient Chinese sources refer to this region as Yuni, and later in the 5th–6th centuries AD, as Shi. The ancient form of the name Chach, Arabised as Shash, has survived until today in its Turkic form – Tashkent.

Human exploration of ancient Chach territories began in the Stone Age. The stone-working shafts in Kulbulak and the settlements on the banks of the Bozsu and Karakamysh rivers date from the Lower and Upper Palaeolithic periods. During the Bronze Age (3rd to 2nd millennium BC), this area was inhabited by Andronovo-like steppe tribes who gradually transitioned to farming here.

In the 9th to the 7th century BC a significant part of this area was occupied by tribes of the Burgulyuk culture who relied mainly on farming, cattle breeding, metal working and weaving. One of the Burgulyuk settlements, Shashtepa, was located on the site of modern Tashkent. During this period, one of the many Saka tribes may also have settled in this area. The end of the Burgulyuk culture in the 3rd century BC can probably be attributed to the spread of the Sarmatian tribes coming from the Aral Sea region to the lower reaches of the Syr Darya. These tribes brought to the Tashkent oasis traditions of urban culture and skills in building mud brick and *pakhsa* (tamped earth) houses. Early cities emerged here at this time, notably on the Kanka and Shashtepa sites.

From the last centuries BC to the first centuries AD, Chach was a separate territorial area known as Yuni, and part of the vast Kangju confederation of states. In the 3rd and early 4th centuries AD, Chach (or Shi, in Chinese sources) became an independent entity. This is evidenced, in particular, by independent coinage depicting a portrait of the ruler, a *tamga* (seal) and a Sogdian inscription, indicating the name of the king – Vanvan ('victorious') or Vanun, his title – *hvab* ('ruler'), and the name of his dominion – Chachannap. These inscriptions are in fact the earliest mention of the name Chach, as these coins were issued earlier (perhaps even as early as the 2nd century AD) than the AD 262 inscription of Shapur I on the Kaab-i-Zoroaster, usually considered to be the earliest record of the name Chach.

The continued production of bronze coins based on an ancient model, albeit of poorer quality, show that before its incorporation in the Great Turkic Khaganate at the beginning of the second half of the 6th century AD, Chach had maintained its independence up to the second half of the 5th or the 6th century AD. Chach may also have been under the aegis of the Hephthalites.

Between the 7th and the first half of the 8th century AD, Chach was probably a confederation of small territories under the aegis of Turkic rulers bearing the titles of *tudun* and *tegin*. Numismatic data has helped to establish the names of some of these rulers (Turkesh, Shanibag and Kaviradn, among others) as well as the names of territories apart from Chach, for instance, Kabarna and Tunukand. In addition to these names and those found in written sources, the names of rulers of ancient Chach origin which are similar to Sogdian names appear along with Turkic names. In the 7th–8th centuries, Chach was an economically developed area with many towns and villages, boasting advanced agricultural techniques and crafts, and commodity-money relations. The Chach mines were especially famous. The region remained similarly prosperous under the Abbasid Caliphate, to which it belonged in the second half of the 8th century AD. In the 9th and 10th centuries, the name 'Chach', but in its Arabised form, was being used for the territory of the Chirchik valley, as well as for yet another region: Ilak in the Akhangaran valley. In later years the name 'Chach' gradually fell out of use.

1.3

HISTORICAL CIVILISATIONS, STATES AND ANCIENT CITIES

Even in distant antiquity, as far back as the 2nd to the early 1st millennium BC, the process of the formation of distinct and unique individual civilisations was taking place in Central Asia; these included the civilisations of Bactria, Margush, Sogdia, Khorezm and Ferghana-Chach, among others. They were each characterised by stages and features of historical and cultural process, local trends and particularities of development arising from a highly complex genesis of culture, ethnicity and statehood. They were essentially river-dependent civilisations based on irrigated agriculture, and therefore also urban, since cities and towns were an inseparable part of their existence at all stages of their development – from embryonic proto-urban forms to the most developed conurbations such as Alexandria, Balkh, Merv and Samarkand. Pastoralism, both domestic and nomadic, played a huge role in this region, but it did not determine its fundamental character.

The states that emerged from the foundations of these civilisations, and as an expression of them, developed in parallel, providing the civilisations with sustainability and longevity and, in some periods, political, economic and cultural cohesion.

If we consider writing to be the most important factor for the development of advanced forms of statehood, then it follows that civilisations emerge simultaneously alongside states, since writing is also one of their most important elements (albeit not the decisive one).

But if a civilisation, and above all a historical civilisation, is a stadial phenomenon that can be observed at all the chronological stages in the development of human society, starting with the Stone Age, then statehood is a secondary phenomenon, a derivation of civilisation, which emerges at a particular stage in the development of society, namely in the Bronze Age, when the first embryonic forms of the state – the so-called city-states – emerged in the historical civilisations of Mesopotamia, the Eastern Mediterranean and the lower reaches of the Nile.

Ethnic groups shaping a particular type of civilisation have played a huge role in the formation of historical civilisations. However, an equally important role in this process has been played by migrations of peoples from one civilisation to another for given geographical, political, military and demographic reasons, and because of the overwhelming desire of human beings to explore 'unknown territory'. This has been the case since the Stone Age, when the first cultural exchanges took place. In fact, the entire ethnic history of humanity has been a history of the migration of peoples from one environment or geographical area to another, and of their assimilation.

In the course of long migrations, first spontaneously and then permanently, historical civilisations have changed, ethnic substrates have been assimilated and autochthonous populations have mixed with the migratory ones. As a result new, mixed ethnic and linguistic communities have been created that retained their autochthonous basis to some extent. Indeed, both historical and modern peoples were not and are not homogeneous ethnic groups (historical peoples less so, especially in the early stages of history), but are in fact multi-ethnic communities, that is to say communities of heterogeneous, mixed ethnicities whose anthropological, glottogenic and psycho-ethnic characteristics are combinations of inclusions and borrowings entering the aboriginal ethnos and autochthonous culture at each stage of historical development. In the study of history, and not only in this field, the term 'autochthonous people' is often used for a number of speculative reasons. *Autochthon* is a word of Greek origin meant to designate an indigenous person, the original inhabitant of a territory or country – as with the Latin word *aborigines*, derived from *ab origine* which means 'from the beginning'.

However, are there any criteria for defining the idea of an 'aboriginal people' in terms of the chronology and stages of evolution? It would appear that there are not, apart from a very variable territorial one, which, after careful analysis, may classify such people as secondary, tertiary, following on from 'aboriginal', etc. In other words, modern peoples living in a particular territory have been able to change their territory, environment and even language several times during the course of historical evolution. A classic example is that of the Bulgarians, who changed their original habitat three times before settling in present-day Bulgaria – this people migrated from Inner Asia, to the lower Don, and then to the Balkans, and their language changed with them from Iranian to Turkic to Slavic. Essentially, what we call an autochthonous population could only have been one in the very early stages of development, during the Stone Age. Subsequent epochs are characterised by constant migratory ethnic 'injections' and mixing at each new stage of migration. Ethnic groups moving to new territories were themselves already the bearers of the multi-ethnic characteristics that they had acquired in their former habitat, along with the corresponding elements of cross-breeding.

In this way, the resettlement of peoples, including the so-called 'great migrations', is essentially the spread of heterogeneous communities – of communities made multi-ethnic and heterogeneous through migration and mixing – in a constant state of renewal that precludes ethnic homogeneity. In effect, globally speaking, there are no ethnic groups for whom it would be possible to trace a single line of ethnic development from the Stone Age, without evidence of multiple multi-ethnic injections, except for those tribes and ethnic groups who have inhabited the 'fringes of the ecumene' – whether isolated mountain valleys or isolated areas of plains – but even they will have arrived there from somewhere else, having already been cross-bred in their former territories of habitation.

Evolving in stages, multi-ethnic societies created particular kinds of symbiotic cultures, which at every stage of development were complemented by new ethnic migrations, by the bearers of new cultural elements, and less frequently through trade and other forms of cultural exchange. In other words, each migratory ethnos carried with it its own culture, which in the new territory collided with the culture of the people who were already living there, acquired new features and developed a different type of culture in which autochthonous and newly introduced features were shaped and developed in parallel, in symbiotic unity.

Cultural objects or phenomena introduced many centuries ago acquired a fixed (sustainable) form of existence, moving from one stage of development to the next in such societies. At the same time, their original source was completely forgotten and they came to be considered as 'their own', belonging to their society. A classic example of this is the *piala* (a bowl-shaped cup for drinking tea), which could be said to embody the national identity of Central Asian peoples, who, with rare exceptions, are unaware that this vessel, like its name, was introduced as a result of Hellenic migration to this region, in the 3rd to the 2nd century BC.

Civilisation, as a permanent and all-encompassing material and spiritual form of human society, has been characteristic of all peoples without exception at all times in their history, differing only in the stage of development reached at a given point, and in ethnic, typological and hierarchical characteristics. The civilisations at the highest levels of the hierarchical ladder (so-called high-order civilisations) are defined by the dominant and advanced forms of existence and achievements attained in the course of long-term historical development. These include, in particular, towns and cities which are the focal point of political, economic, cultural and other attributes that largely determine the course of development of advanced civilisations; this is something that applies to both ancient and modern times. It does not follow that towns and cities have created civilisations. On the contrary, the pre-eminence of civilisation is clear. At first, a certain type of civilisation with its own culture emerges. Then economic development accompanied by the refinement of social institutions and cultural developments leads to the creation of the first towns and cities, which in turn define the key features of civilisations. The original urban cores of civilisation, which determined the oldest but at the same time the most permanently developing form of a civilisation, played an essential role in this process: it was here that the range of key achievements and elite forms of material and spiritual culture developed.

There were three such original urban centres in Central Asia – Samarkand/Marakanda, Merv/Maru/Bairam-Ali and Bactra/Balkh – which emerged as cities in the early 1st millennium BC. They have an uninterrupted, almost 3,000-year history, spanning different eras with various evolutionary periods, social systems and cultural manifestations. These urban centres of civilisation subsequently determined the course of development of the historically earliest and most advanced Central Asian civilisations: those of Bactria, Sogdia and Margush. It is not surprising that the Arabs, who travelled vast distances and had seen hundreds of cities in the ancient East, declared Bactra/Balkh to be *U'm-al-bilad* – the Mother of Cities, thereby acknowledging the historical role it played as the progenitor of cities.

The same was true, but perhaps to a lesser extent, of other early urban centres of Central Asian civilisation, such as Sogdian Kesh, whose original site, Sangirtepa, dates back to the 10th century BC. It was then gradually transformed into the large city of Uzun-Kyr, and then, from the 3rd century BC onwards, into the ancient city of Kitab. The Northern Bactrian cities of Sherabad (the ancient name is unknown, the modern name is from the 18th century) and Dih-i Nau (known as Denau from the 15th century) are possibly the oldest cities of Central Asia. They emerged as cities as early as the second half of the 2nd millennium BC and have been in existence continuously for over 3,000 years, changing their location only within a limited radius, mainly in the early stages of their existence, and later developing in the same place.

Essentially, these kinds of cities should be seen as huge conurbations, and as ethnically, typologically and chronologically heterogeneous composites, parts of which, for reasons given above, have moved spatially over time within a limited area.

Some cities correspond to a type of state, whose origin as a form of political, administrative and legal organisation of society is a city, but it later develops into a state. These are the so-called city-states, or *nomes,* as they are often referred to by historians, (based on the example of ancient Egypt, whose history is well documented in textual sources). They consisted of a major urban centre with an adjacent rural district that controlled the water-management system or river. The union of several

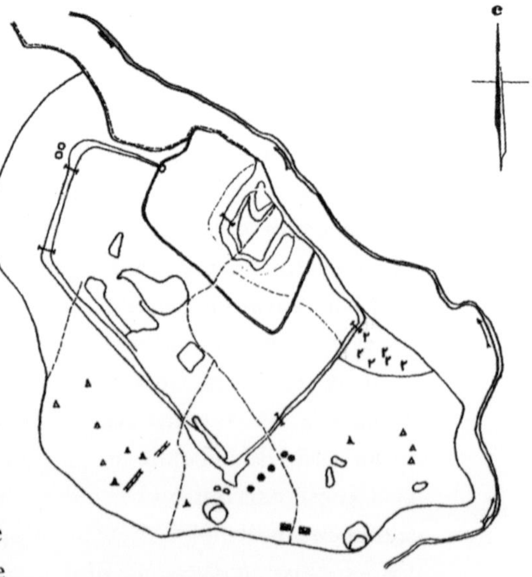

Site of Kanka with a rabad (a suburban district for crafts, commerce and trade)

such *nomes* led to the creation of the first states in ancient Egypt and Mesopotamia.

This type of proto-town and proto-state organisation emerged in the middle to the second half of the 2nd millennium BC in the south of Transoxiana, in the present-day Surkhan Darya region of Uzbekistan. An example is Jarkutan (near the city of Sherabad), a huge conurbation covering an area of over 100 hectares. It consisted of several settlements merged into a single complex, with the fortified residence of the ruler and the temple at its heart making up the ideological core. This was not, however, the only way that the cities of Transoxiana arose. There were other kinds of towns as well. For example, many of the cities grew out of the progressive development of small settlements with a citadel that appeared in the early 1st millennium BC and gradually became large cities. Others were originally built as a *refugium* – a shelter consisting of a large, mostly undeveloped area with a citadel, where the surrounding population could take shelter along with their chattels and livestock in times of conflict. Later on, these areas became inhabited, and various buildings were built, with the *refugium* turning into a city with all its associated functions.

There were also cities that were built in accordance with a king's wishes and to a well-thought-out plan. This kind of development of a city was typical of the Hellenistic world from the time of Alexander the Great and his successors. We know about this from Arrian's description of such a city being built within 20 days on the banks of the Syr Darya river on Alexander's orders (it may well be the Kanka settlement in the Tashkent region); it became inhabited by veterans of his army and the local population.

How long ancient cities survived depended on natural, geographical, political and economic factors. Some of them rose and developed only to die suddenly (often as a result of a military invasion) or were gradually abandoned and never resurrected. This was true of many ancient Transoxiana settlements, which ceased to exist in the 4th and 5th centuries AD. Others evolved steadily and grew into medieval and then modern cities. There are many such cities in Transoxiana, but only a few of them go back 2,500 years or more (Samarkand, Bukhara, Khiva, Kitab, Karshi, Termez), and beyond Transoxiana, Merv and Sarakhs.

There were other reasons for the demise of cities too, especially the issue of taboo. A sacred prohibition existed against settling on the former dwelling place of another people, if they followed a different religion, for example, or for fear of demonic forces that may exist there. Examples of such taboos forcing a population to leave an area they had previously occupied, never to return, are well known to historians all over the world. The spiritual world of ancient societies was much richer and more complex than we can imagine on the basis of the few written sources and archaeological artefacts available to researchers. After all, archaeologists can merely interpret the materials available but cannot be sure of their true meaning.

Central Asia has many examples of abandoned ancient sites that were deemed to be home to demonic forces by local people, for instance Devkesken and Devkala, among others. Visiting or living near such sites is considered *haram* or taboo. The name of a city in Northern Tokharistan, Hashemgird, reflected the presence of demonic forces. The word 'Hashemgird' is derived from an Avestan demon's name – Aesma, a demon of anger, malice and fury, so Hashemgird was regarded as 'the city of Aesma'.

We have touched on the genesis of cities above, but what is more important is the chronological relationship between the evolution of a city and a state. We need to consider the significant manifestations of both, especially in the Near and Middle East, along with such factors as the presence of written language, commodity-money relations, legal institutions, monumental art, administrative systems, and so on. It is essential to bear in mind that the existence of a state as such is unthinkable without the existence of a written language that makes it possible to create and manage an administrative system. When the city-states of ancient Sumer, Akkad, Elam and Egypt emerged, many different writing systems were already in use. The same was true of ancient China, India and Hellas, where writing systems emerged at the time of the Harappan and Cretan-Mycenaean civilisations.

The analysis of all available data suggests that the most substantial evidence of the endurance of an ancient city and its status as such is the existence in it of thick habitation layers from various dates, sometimes reaching a depth of up to 20 metres or more in total, and the gradual transition from one stage of the development of the urban entity to another, following a particular pattern: an initial settlement or group of settlements; a proto-town; an early city; a developed city of antiquity (of two or three parts), including a citadel or *ark*; the city itself, with emerging suburbs, religious and funerary buildings and a rural hinterland. The medieval city was even more complicated in structure. It consisted of a citadel or *kuhendiz*, the city itself (*madina* or *shahristan*), and often an inner city, the *madina-dahil* or *shahri-darun,* and an outer city, the *madina-harij* or *shahri-birun,* as well as a district for crafts, commerce and trade on the outskirts, the *rabad* – or sometimes even two *rabads,* an inner and an outer one. Each stage of a city's development (except for the earliest one) has distinctive features which characterise it: a strong fortification system for every or almost every part, monumental buildings for public, civil, religious and memorial functions, well-developed craft production, commodity-money relations, administrative and fiscal services.

Only when these crucial features are present and when there is a gradual development from one stage to the next can we speak of an extended history of a functioning city and the ancient nature of its existence. Historical data tells us that only a few of the cities in Central Asia that currently exist meet these criteria. These include Bukhara, Samarkand, Khiva, Merv and Sarakhs, as well as Sherabad, Denau, Termez and Kitab/Shahrisabz.

1.4

MIGRATION: A DRIVING FORCE IN THE DEVELOPMENT OF CIVILISATIONS

In Soviet scholarship, the phenomenon of migration was not always recognised as a distinctive form of movement of ethnic groups, which in most instances contributes to cultural and economic progress and often results in the creation of hybridised and mixed populations, or indeed in the total replacement of the population of a region. Instead, the historian and linguist N.Y. Marr proposed a theory of 'autochthony' and the progressive stages of the development of society, and this theory at one time had a significant influence on the direction taken by Soviet historical study. After the theory was heavily criticised by Stalin in his article 'Marxism and Problems of Linguistics', N.Y. Marr was soon forgotten and his works were banned for many years and withdrawn from libraries. Since then, a fresh look at historical development worldwide has demonstrated that the phenomena of autochthony and migration are in fact closely related and cannot exist independently of each other. Throughout history, the evolution of ethnic, autochthonous peoples has always been subject to additional stimuli from migrations of other peoples, and this has been reflected not only in changes in anthropological appearance and language, but also in the development of civilisation in its broadest sense, which has ultimately led to the progress of society as a whole. There is hardly anywhere in the world today where we are likely to find an ethnic group whose individual members can claim to have preserved the purity of their language and appearance from the earliest times.

Autochthonous peoples not influenced by the migrations of other peoples either became extinct, or led an unenviable existence.

Textual sources, legends on coins and epigraphic information have all provided strong evidence for the very earliest dates for the presence of one or another ethnic group and their linguistic identities in Central Asia.

While the value of different hypotheses in scholarship can be acknowledged, nevertheless, they will not be discussed here, because any scholarly conclusions based on unproven hypotheses, especially in relation to as important a subject as ethnic history, frequently lead to all kinds of speculations about the ethno-genesis of this or that nation in Central Asia. In any case, the subject of focus here is not ethno-genesis, but rather is mainly the migrations that occurred in Central Asia, starting from early periods of its history and up to the 18th century. Moreover, the focus will be on the earliest periods of existence of different ethnic groups in Central Asia, as documented by the relevant sources. Problems concerning their subsequent existence in this region are not discussed here.

Academic knowledge about the history of this region has been gathered since the 17th century and was developed particularly in the 20th century, during the Soviet era, when extensive archaeological, anthropological and ethnographic research was undertaken. This has made it possible to apply a confident approach to a description of the ethnic history of Central Asia. Due to its geographical location, not only has this region been the recipient of successive waves of ethnic migration, it has also been an area of transition. Tribes and peoples of different language families have migrated through its territory to the south, west and east of the continent of Asia.

Based on available data and textual sources, we can speak about six main waves of ethnic migration to Central Asia in ancient and medieval periods (before the 18th century) – Indo-Aryan, Iranian, Graeco-Macedonian, Semitic, Turkic and Mongol – representing four language families, Indo-European, Semitic, Altaic and Mongol. Migrations of speakers of languages from other language families, such as Finno-Ugric and Chinese, are also likely to have taken place, but these were insignificant in terms of size and they did not leave any prominent traces in the ethnic composition and languages of Central Asian peoples. For example, in a text dating from about AD 630 the famous pilgrim Xuanzang mentions a small town located in the south of present-day Kazakhstan as being inhabited by the Chinese.

A hypothesis from the mid- to second half of the 20th century suggests that the population of the south of Central Asia could have been speakers of a Dravidian language. This possibility had already been proposed by S.P. Tolstov in 1948, and supported by the historians and archaeologists B.A. Litvinsky and V.M. Masson. The philologist V.V. Ivanov also believes that the substrate language in Central Asia could have been a Dravidian one.

According to Litvinsky, more recent archaeological evidence supported this hypothesis. He was referring to the Shortugai site which was discovered on the left bank of the Amu Darya in north-eastern Afghanistan and has been linked to the Harappan civilisation (whose population may have spoken a Dravidian language). However, the settlement was apparently the only north-western outpost of the Harappans – there are no sites associated with this culture in Central Asia itself. Proponents of the Dravidian hypothesis do not cite anthropological data, which would have been very revealing. The Dravidians, according to many experts, originally inhabited the Eastern Mediterranean in the 5th–4th millennia BC. Subsequently, they migrated through southern Central Asia and Afghanistan to what is now Pakistan and India, where they mixed with the aboriginal population.

The anthropology of the population of southern Central Asia has been studied in considerable detail thanks to the excavations of Bronze Age burials, revealing numerous series of skulls. Of these, skulls of equatorial origin are extremely rare, and this fact seems to negate the hypothesis that the Bronze Age population of southern Central Asia was Dravidian-speaking.

Anthropologists who have researched this area claim that during the Bronze Age, the population of this area, from southern Turkmenistan up to and including the Pamirs, had Eastern Mediterranean origins with close connections to Western Asia. This is what many scholars believe, in particular V.V. Ginzburg, T.A. Trofimova, L.V. Oshanin, V.P. Alekseev, T.K. Khodjaiov, and others. We should probably also be looking in the same direction for answers to questions relating to the linguistic background of early farming cultures from the Bronze Age.

The easternmost limit for recorded finds of ancient Eastern inscriptions dating from 2000–3000 BC runs along the southern shore of the Caspian Sea and the north-eastern shore of the Persian Gulf, running roughly through the centre of Iran. It is notable that Hurrian texts and proper names have been found in inscriptions in the north, closer to the Caspian Sea and Lake Urmia, while in the south and in the centre, Elamite inscriptions have been discovered just a few hundred kilometres from the south-west of Turkmenistan. Thus, in terms of linguistics, it is reasonable to assume that the population of the southern part of Central Asia at that time was very probably related to a Hurrian ethnic group or one which had a language close to Hurrian.

In this regard, it is worth highlighting the significant similarity between the folkloric motifs of the populations of the Aral Sea area and Western Asia, as established by L.S. Tolstova. There are also parallels with the name of one of the Uzbek tribes – the Mitans – and 'Mitanni', the name of the Hurrian kingdom which occupied territory in north-western Iran near Lake Urmia and north-eastern Turkey in the middle of the 2nd millennium BC.

There may well be a genetic link between some Central Asian toponyms and the name of the Hurrians – *hr, huru*. For example, the name for the two-part settlement Urmitan or Hurmitan in the Bukhara oasis, which was recorded as early as the 8th century and consisted of two words: *hur maethana* (Old Iranian for 'staying place', 'house', 'homeland'), i.e. the place of Hurri or Hurrians. S.P. Tolstov also believed the name Khorezm was of similar origin. It is rendered as *Hvarazm* in Arabic script and may be read as *Khvarazm* or, possibly, *Khuarazm*, 'the land of the Hurri'. According to Herodotus (5th century BC), the Khorezmian settlement was near Tejen, i.e. in present-day southern Turkmenistan. According to I.M. Dyakonov, the mass migration of Semitic Arameans to territory previously inhabited by Hurrians, as well as the advance of Armenian-Phrygian tribes at the end of the 2nd millennium BC, resulted in the 'scattering of the Hurrian population into separate areas'. However, this could also have caused Hurrian tribes to migrate further east to Central Asia, where their language was subsequently Iranised.

Archaeological evidence does not contradict this view and suggests that the development of the ancient agricultural civilisation of Khorezm was connected with cultural innovations brought there from the south. The hypothesis expressed here is an attempt to draw together anthropological, archaeological and ethnographic evidence in order to solve a most vexed historical question: the ethnic affiliation of the substrate language of southern Central Asia.

Some studies have provided information about the specific ethnicity of the Central Asian population but only dating back to the Early Iron Age (6th–5th centuries BC). However, earlier than this, perhaps in the middle and second half of the 2nd millennium BC, the first wave of migration of Indo-European peoples moved across Central Asia, with the collapse of the Harappan civilisation following in its wake. However, the reasons for the collapse of the Harappan or Indus Valley Civilisation are as yet unclear.

The Indo-European language family

Throughout its ancient past, Central Asia has witnessed the migrations of many different peoples associated with the Indo-European language family including Tokharians, Indo-Aryans, Iranians, Greeks and Armenians.

The Tokharian migration was probably the earliest. The philologists and historians V.V. Ivanov and T. Gamkrelidze believe that the Tokharians originated in Western Asia and migrated across Iran and Central Asia in the 4th and 3rd millennia BC to the territory of present-day Xinjiang. However, another hypothesis suggests that the Indo-European Tokharians were the aboriginal people of this region.

Graeco-Roman texts (Strabo, Justin and Pompeius Trogus) first mention the Tokharians only in the second half of the 2nd century BC when, according to these accounts, they, together with other tribes such as the Asii, Pasiani and Sakarauli, crushed the Graeco-Bactrian kingdom. In historical studies, the Tokharians are often referred to as the Yuezhi mentioned in Chinese texts.

In the early centuries AD, Ptolemy writes that the Tokharians were the largest tribe in Bactria (Ptolemy, VI, 11, 6), so it is no coincidence that this country later came to be known as Tokharistan ('land of the Tokhars'), as first recorded in texts from the end of the 4th century AD and more widely used in early and later medieval periods.

Examples of Tokhar language are preserved in manuscripts dating from the 3rd to 7th centuries AD in Niya and Kucha in the Tarim basin in Xinjiang. There are two variants – an early Tokharian A and the later Tokharian B. There is evidence to suggest that the language of the manuscripts belongs to a distinct branch of the Indo-European family, sharing many affinities with Western European languages.

It is also possible that an 'unknown script' recently discovered in a vast area stretching from Kabul to Lake Issyk-Kul may belong to the Tokharian/Yuezhi; the earliest evidence for this script dates from the 4th to the 3rd century BC and the most recent from the 7th to the 8th century AD. However, the script has yet to be deciphered.

While some scholars believe that Indo-Aryans migrated from the north through Central Asia, and were responsible for the destruction of the Harappan civilisation of the Indus valley in the middle of the 2nd millennium BC, more recent evidence suggests that the collapse of this civilisation is attributable to climate change.

However, a different view holds that the Indo-Aryans travelled through the Caucasus and present-day Iran and Afghanistan to reach Central Asia. Their presence in the north-west of Iran as early as the second half of the 2nd millennium BC is documented in written records originating from the state of Mitanni, which also mention the Indo-Aryan deities Indra, Varuna and Nasatya. L.S. Tolstova's hypothesis is noteworthy in this regard: she associates the word *mitan*, encountered frequently in toponyms and ethnonyms in Uzbekistan, with the name of the state of the Mitanni. However, there are no documented traces of an early wave of Indo-European tribes in Central Asia. It is also worth noting that in his list of tribes inhabiting Bactria, Ptolemy, in particular, mentions the Skordai, whose name has a clear analogy with the name of the Celtic tribe of Skordisci who lived along the banks of the Danube (Ptolemy, VI, 11, 6).

Ptolemy also mentions two cities in Bactria, Marakodra and Alikodra; the second component of the names is clearly present in the Indo-European word *gotrá* meaning a 'shelter' – a place where people live together.

The migration of Iranian tribes

The question of when Iranian-speaking tribes appeared in Central Asia is a matter of debate. Some scholars believe this to have taken place during the second half of the 2nd millennium BC when tribes of the Bronze Age Andronovo culture, whose ethnicity has been defined as Iranian, also arrived here (traces of these peoples have even been found in sites in northern Afghanistan). Another assumption is that the Andronovo tribes were Turkic-speaking.

However, these views, although interesting, remain unproven, as there is no evidence relating to the language spoken by the Andronovo tribes. It would be just as reasonable to suggest that they spoke a Finno-Ugric language, or some other unknown and dead language that was absorbed by the languages of other ethnic groups in the process of assimilation.

A much more likely hypothesis is that the Yaz I culture is of Iranian origin. This culture dates back to the 9th–early 7th centuries BC and was dispersed across almost all of southern Central Asia, from the Caspian Sea to the Pamirs, including northern Afghanistan.

Objects of material culture found at Yaz I sites are significantly different from those associated with the Late Bronze Age Namazga VI and Dashly-Sapalli cultures. If we follow the logic of historical science, this would suggest either a distortion and regeneration of the preceding culture in the process of culturogenesis or a change in ethnosphere. The latter seems more likely, since, according to textual sources, the areas where Yaz culture had been widespread were somewhat later settled by Eastern Iranian tribes.

According to information in the Avesta and the accounts of ancient Greek authors (Herodotus, Ctesias of Cnidus, Pseudo-Scylax and others), as well as in the inscriptions of Achaemenid kings, many regions had emerged in Central Asia between the 6th and 5th centuries BC, i.e. Bactria, Parthia, Margiana, Sogdia and Khorezm, and were inhabited by Bactrians, Parthians, Sogdians and Khorezmians respectively.

Texts found in these regions dating back to the last centuries BC and first centuries AD (further details are listed below) provide conclusive evidence that the language of these peoples belonged mainly to the East Iranian language group as opposed to the Parthian language, which is considered a Western Iranian language. The *Ch'ien Han Shu* – 'The History of the Former Han Dynasty' – describes events that took place up to AD 25. According to this account the languages spoken from Dayuan (Ferghana) to Anxi (Parthia) were very similar and mutually intelligible, although there were many differences between dialects. There are useful parallels between the information given in the *Ch'ien Han Shu*, about the commonality of the languages and differences between dialects, and texts that have been found in Central Asia and the languages of these documents for the periods in question. In the last 50 years, many documents in a number of local scripts based on Aramaic and Greek scripts have been discovered between Ferghana and the Caspian Sea. Among them are:

1 Northern Parthia. An archive of Parthian documents from New Nisa dating from the 2nd to 1st centuries BC; legends on coins and inscriptions on clay potsherds (ostraca).
2 Legends in Sogdian script on coins, the earliest of which date back to the 2nd to 1st centuries BC; documents from Mount Mugh from the 7th to 8th centuries AD; inscriptions on potsherds and gemstones.
3 Khorezm. An archive of Khorezmian documents from Toprak-Kala from the 3rd century AD; legends on coins from the 1st to 8th centuries AD; inscriptions on potsherds, the earliest of which (from Aibugir-Kala and Koi-Krylgan-Kala) date from the 4th to 3rd centuries BC.
4 Northern Bactria. A large number of Bactrian inscriptions from the 2nd to 3rd centuries AD on a variety of materials (clay, stone and plaster). Among them is a six-line inscription on the base of a sculpture from Airtam.

Studies of these written remnants and materials have revealed that they are in Parthian, Khorezmian, Sogdian and Bactrian, which, despite some dialectal differences, nonetheless belong to the same Eastern Iranian language group.

The data from these materials and from the *Ch'ien Han Shu* complement each other, and together provide convincing evidence that between the last centuries BC and the first centuries AD most of the peoples inhabiting Central Asia were speakers of a range of different East Iranian languages.

In the 4th–5th centuries AD, ethnic homogeneity in Central Asia began to be disrupted by migrations of Chionites, Kidarites and Hephthalites, whose linguistic identities have yet to be established. For example, there are several theories regarding the origin of the Hephthalites in this region. Were they Mongol, Turkic or Iranian? The first mention of the presence of Turks in Central Asia is in textual sources from the second half of the 6th century AD. The 6th–8th centuries AD saw the most intensive wave of migration of Turks into Transoxiana, where they gradually began to put pressure on the Eastern Iranian population, both in terms of political dominance in some areas, and in terms of territory for settlement.

The expansion of the Arabs and the incorporation of Central Asian regions into the Abbasid Caliphate in the middle of the 8th century AD led to the spread of Arabic, which then replaced local languages in the domains of religion, politics and science and, to a certain degree, in that of everyday communication.

In the 7th and 8th centuries, the Eastern Iranian languages – Bactrian, Sogdian and Khorezmian – were widely spoken in Transoxiana, but in the south-west of Central Asia the language spoken was Middle Persian. In the 8th century, New Persian – Farsi – began to spread here, and the earliest texts in this language, dated by the linguist W.B. Henning to the mid-8th century, are recorded on the tombstones of an ancient Jewish cemetery near Herat. Scholars believe that the modern Tajik language is based on this language, which spread out from south-west Fars, and that it therefore belongs to the Western Iranian group of languages.

By the 9th and 10th centuries AD, the language of Farsi, or Farsi Dari, gradually displaced the indigenous Eastern Iranian languages, which were then only being used in rural outskirts and the mountain regions of the Pamirs. The earliest literary works written in Dari also date from the 10th century AD. Some scholars believe that a people known as the Tajiks emerged in Transoxiana at the turn of the 11th century. It is at this time that the most important changes were taking place in the ethnosphere of Central Asia. The first is connected to the extensive spread of Turkic-speaking peoples, and the second to the displacement of Eastern Iranian languages (one of which – Sogdian – has survived until today only in the Yagnob valley in Tajikistan), and their replacement with the New Persian language – *Zaboni Farsi e Dari.*

Hellenic migrations

The earliest evidence of Greek presence in Central Asia dates back to the reign of the Achaemenid king Xerxes (486–465 BC), a time when priests of the Temple of Apollo, the Branchidae, were resettled there after fleeing from the city of Miletus in Asia Minor. They built their own city, which many scholars believe was located at the site of Kalif in Turkmenistan or in the Kashka Darya province in present-day Uzbekistan.

According to the annals of Arrian and Quintus Curtius Rufus, during Alexander the Great's campaign to Central Asia in 329–327 BC, the Hellenic Branchidae had already become so assimilated that they spoke a form of Greek mixed with the local language (Strabo, XI, 11, 4; Curtius, VII, 5, 28). The arrival of the Branchidae in Central Asia could be said to constitute the first, though small, wave of Greek migration to the region.

The second migration of Hellenes and Macedonians to Central Asia was considerably larger than the first and is associated with Alexander's campaign. There is no information about the number of Hellenes who came and settled here, but there are likely to have been several thousand at least. Alexander founded several cities in Central Asia, including Alexandria in Oxiana, Alexandria Eschate and Alexandria in

Margiana. According to the testimony of Arrian, the population of these cities was mostly made up of Hellenic mercenaries and Macedonian veterans no longer fit for military service, as well some 'barbarians' who wanted to settle there (Arrian, IV, 4). In addition to cities, military cantonments were probably also established in Central Asia and inhabited by Hellenic settlers. Greeks and Macedonians remained in Central Asia even after Alexander's death and the collapse of his empire. A further influx of Hellenes into Central Asia, mainly to Bactria, is associated with the Seleucid era and especially with the Graeco-Bactrian kingdom (mid-3rd to mid-2nd century BC).

Here, on the southern bank of the Oxus, the Amu Darya, the Greeks established their own city of Ai-Khanum, with typically Greek elements – a gymnasium, a propylaeum, a theatre, a *heroon* (a funerary monument), and so on. It is clear that the majority of the city's population was Greek, although it has been established that its citizens also included Bactrians.

This was probably a time when the process of interethnic mixing increased significantly, as a result of marriages between Greek and indigenous people, starting with the marriage of Alexander the Great to the Bactrian beauty Roxana.

According to the 15th-century Persian historian and geographer Hafiz-i Abru, a Greek town at the 'Greek' crossing also existed in Northern Bactria – which we assume was at the city-site of Kampyrtepa, where the only ostraca with Greek inscriptions ever found in Central Asia were discovered.

By the second half of the 2nd to the 1st century BC, the Greek population of Inner Asia had largely been absorbed as a result of invasion by North Iranian tribes: first the Sakas, then the Asii, Pasiani, Sakarauli and Tokharians or Yuezhi (the latter, however, may well have been an Indo-European tribe).

The most recent archaeological findings suggest, however, that some pockets of Greek communities with Greek rulers – judging by their names – continued to govern themselves in Bactria and Southern Sogdia even after the collapse of the Graeco-Bactrian kingdom, in places such as parts of present-day India. The latest textual data on the Greeks in Central Asia relates to a certain Palamedes, possibly an architect, whose name appears in an inscription from Surkh Kotal. Even though the Greek ethnos did not make a significant impact on the composition of the population in Central Asia (although folk legends link the origin of some of the Pamir population with Alexander's Greek-Macedonians), elements of Greek culture persisted for many years in pre-Islamic Central Asia.

Migrations of the Indian subcontinent's peoples

There is still no clear timeline for the arrival of Prakrit-, Sanskrit- and Dravidian-speaking peoples from the Indian subcontinent into Central Asia. As we mentioned above, historical scholarship has suggested that the Bronze Age population of Central Asia was Dravidian-speaking. Archaeological confirmation of this otherwise wholly unsupported thesis has come from the discovery of the Shortugai settlement on the left bank of the Amu Darya, founded by the Harappan culture, whose population was most likely Dravidian-speaking.

It is possible that representatives of peoples from the Indian subcontinent entered Central Asia during the Achaemenid period (6th–4th centuries BC), when Central Asia and the north-western regions of the Indian subcontinent were also part of the Achaemenid state. The same can be said about the Central Asian peoples of the time of Alexander the Great, who began his campaign to India from the territory of Bactria. His army included Bactrian soldiers.

When the powerful Indian state of Maurya was at its height, its north-eastern borders nearly reached Central Asia, as evidenced by an edict of King Ashoka (273–236 BC) found in Kandahar (south-eastern Afghanistan). It is precisely to this time that the eminent Indian scholar P.C. Bagchi dates the arrival of Buddhism in the southern part of Central Asia, and the bearers of this religion at that time were without doubt peoples from India.

The influx of people from the Indian subcontinent into Central Asia and vice versa intensified after the conquest of the north-west Indian subcontinent by the Graeco-Bactrian king Demetrius the Great (200–185 BC). This meant that the Bactrian population had continuous contact and familiarity with Indian scripts and languages, as testified by a significant number of Demetrius' coins bearing inscriptions in Sanskrit written in Kharoshthi script found at Kampyrtepa, Termez and Takht-i Sangin.

The fragmentary inscription written in Kharoshthi script on the gates of the citadel at Kampyrtepa, probably dating to the 2nd century BC (the exact date is yet to be determined), is particularly significant in this regard. Its importance lies firstly in the fact that it is the earliest known inscription in an Indian script in Central Asia. Secondly, in contrast to all other inscriptions, which are predominantly of Buddhist content, this inscription is related to non-religious, state matters. Its presence on the gates of the citadel shows that Kampyrtepa was inhabited by people familiar with Sanskrit and the Kharoshthi script, i.e. people from India. The especially large influx of peoples from the Indian subcontinent to the south of Central Asia, into Bactria, occurred during the period of the Kushan state (in the 1st to the mid-3rd century AD). It is connected with the spread of Buddhism and the erection of a great number of Buddhist structures in this region, especially in Tarmita, Airtam, Dalverzintepa and other cities of Northern Bactria.

The size of the Indian population in this area was very large, and it is possible that they even constituted the majority in one of the cities.

Among the cities located between the Oxus (Amu Darya) and Jaxartes (Syr Darya), and at a certain distance from them, Ptolemy mentions the city of Indikomardana (Ptolemy, VI. 12, 6), whose name, as I.V. Pyankov reasonably suggests, can be translated as 'city of Indian people'. In all probability, this city was situated in Old Termez, where a large number of Buddhist monuments have been discovered, including the grandiose monasteries of Karatepa and Fayaztepa, along with several inscriptions in Brahmi and Kharoshthi scripts. It was here that, by all available data, a large number of Buddhist priests as well as laymen from India resided.

In the first centuries AD, people from India, apparently mainly from Gandhara, migrated to Central Asia, not only to Bactria, but also to Margiana, where two large Buddhist monuments have been found on the site of Old Merv. The existence of a major trade route from India to the countries around the Black Sea and the Mediterranean also contributed to this. This route is described by ancient Greek authors, in particular by Pseudo-Scymnus, according to whom, on the River Phasis, the Rioni river, was a 'Greek city of Milesian origin, where men of sixty nations come together, speaking different languages: men of barbarian origin from India and Bactria would meet there' (*Ad Nicomedem regem*, 934 [F 20]). The trade route that ran from India to the northern parts of Central Asia through Bactria and the Iron Gate, a mountain pass, served the same purpose.

Migrations of Indians continued during the early and late medieval periods, and were facilitated by the unification of several regions of Central Asia and the Indian subcontinent within a single state or empire.

The Semitic language family

Three ethnic groups of this family, Jewish, Arab and Aramean, are known to have migrated to Central Asia. The earliest evidence of Semitic presence in Central Asia (Bactria) dates back to the 330s BC. There is evidence of a temple dedicated to the Semitic god Bel in Bactria recorded in recently discovered Aramaic inscriptions from the Khalili collection in Bactria, deciphered by S. Shaked and J. Naveh.

The migration of Jews

Some researchers believe that the resettlement of Jews from Babylon to Transcaucasia and Central Asia may have already begun during the period of the Achaemenid kingdom, after 559 BC. This view is based on a passage from the Book of Esther, compiled a few decades before 78–77 BC, according to which Jews settled in all the provinces of Persia. However, to date there has been no evidence to support this view.

According to the scholar M. Zand, the first reliable evidence of the presence of Jews in Central Asia dates back to the beginning of the 4th century AD. The evidence is a story from the Babylonian Talmud about the sojourn at *MRGW'N* (Merv) of Samuel Bar Bisena, an *amora* (scholar) and member of the religious academy in Pumbedita (or Peroz or Shadur – a city in Mesopotamia). According to the story, during a visit to Merv, Samuel refused to drink alcohol with his fellow men, because he doubted its ritual purity. According to M. Zand, this indicates that Jews had been living in Merv for several generations, as they had begun to forget the ritual rules regarding alcoholic beverages. The belief that Jews lived in Merv before the 4th century AD has been confirmed by the discovery of an unfired clay vessel in Merv's citadel, the Erk-Kala, the top of which has a Parthian inscription in black ink with *tamga*-shaped signs below. The stratigraphic conditions of the discovery of this vessel allowed the archaeologist Z.I. Usmanova to date it to the 1st–3rd centuries AD. According to the Iranist V.A. Livshits, the inscription consists of four words that read: 'Property of Pacores, son of Yosa', in which the name 'Yosa' is an ancient Hebraic diminutive, a hypocorism of 'Joseph'.

The second Parthian inscription, made in black ink on the body of the vessel, dates from the 2nd to 3rd centuries AD, but only the name *MYLK* has been preserved. However, according to V.A. Livshits this inscription is in fact Semitic and not Parthian.

These two inscriptions are now considered to be the earliest evidence of the presence of Jews in Margiana and Central Asia in general. M. Zand, as well as other researchers, attribute their appearance in this region to trade on the Silk Road. This is entirely plausible, although there were probably other circumstances that prompted the migration of Jews to other lands, and especially to Central Asia. An example is the uprising of the Jewish people led by Bar Kokhba (AD 132–135) against the Romans during the reign of Marcus Aurelius and the subsequent brutal suppression and annihilation of Jews, which prompted them to flee their home.

According to the scholar J. Neusner, Jews played an active role in the Parthian kingdom in the early centuries AD and according to the historian B.N. Mukherjee this was also true of areas adjacent to north-west India. Many of them were involved in trade between China and Rome.

Recently, Mukherjee revealed a gem from a private collection with a Prakrit inscription in Kharoshthi and Brahmi script, which according to him reads as *Yudevadanu* and which he interprets as a phrase meaning 'sanctuary of the Jews' (an interpretation of this phrase as 'belonging to the teachings of the Jews' is also possible). According to Mukherjee, this gemstone is evidence of the presence of Jews in north-west India in the 1st or 2nd century AD.

The excavation of a synagogue at Dura-Europos (in present-day Syria), celebrated for its frescoes, suggests that the city was a major Jewish centre in the first centuries AD.

It was connected to Parthyene, Margiana and Bactria by a road via Hatra, Ecbatana and Hecatompylos. It seems it was along this road that Jews entered Central Asia and north-west India. The earliest and most extensive settlement was probably in Merv. As we know, during excavations of the necropolis in 1954–1956, ossuaries from the 6th to 7th centuries AD were found here bearing inscriptions in Hebrew square script; they were published by the historian A. Kelvan.

It would appear that it was from Merv that Jews set out to settle in Bactria/ Tokharistan, Sogdia and Khorezm. This migration may also have been facilitated by the fact that the Jewish academy in Pumbedita, began to actively propagate Judaism in north-western Iran, as well as in Khorasan and probably other neighbouring areas, at the end of the 6th century AD.

Jews settled in Balkh, the capital of Tokharistan, probably long before the Arab conquest of the city, which took place in AD 709. According to the *Faza'il-i Balkh* ('The Merits of Balkh'), a 13th-century local history of Balkh, and *Bahr ul-Asrar* ('The Ocean of Secrets in the Accounts of the Noble', an encyclopaedic work), one of the gates of Balkh was known as the Yahudiyyah (Jewish) gate. It appears this gate was near a Jewish suburb of Balkh called Yehudanak (Jahudanak), literally 'a small Jewish place'. This suburb is mentioned by the 9th-century historian and geographer Yaqubi and had probably become established in pre-Arab times. North-west of Balkh, in Jozjan province, an entire town called Yahudiya or Jahudan al-Kubra ('Jewish town') is mentioned in Yaqut al-Hamawi's *Mu'jam al-buldan*, a geographical dictionary, which suggests that this town was either founded by Jews or substantially rebuilt in the early medieval period. Later, between AD 988 and AD 1031, it was renamed Maimana – as it is still known today.

Early medieval Jewish cemeteries with tombstones containing texts in Ancient Hebrew and New Persian have been found near Herat and other regions of Afghanistan. W.B. Henning believes the inscriptions on these tombstones date back to the middle of the 8th century AD and that they are the earliest surviving examples of text in New Persian.

Unfortunately, no textual sources relating to the presence of Jews in Samarkand and Bukhara in the early medieval period have been found, but there is little doubt that Jews were living in these cities during this period. A Samarkand legend in the *Qandiya* by the well-known historian Umar ibn Muhammad al-Nasafi (died AD 1142) tells the story of a lead water pipe – the Jui Arziz – dating back to pre-Arab times, which had allegedly been built by a Jewish sage.

There is some evidence that Jews had come to Khorezm long before the Arab conquest of the area in the first decade of the 8th century AD. According to the Pahlavi account *Shahrestan-i Eranashah*, the founder of the capital city of Khorezm

– Kath – was Narseh, the son of a Jew. According to yet another medieval legend, a second city in Khorezm, Khiva (medieval Haivak), was also founded by a Jew – the biblical Shem, son of Noah. However, the information in these accounts may be far from reality, as archaeological evidence suggests that Khiva and Kath were both established long before the first century AD, but there is undoubtedly some truth in these stories. An account by the Persian historian At-Tabari mentions the presence of *ahbars* – an Arabic term for Judaic priests – among the counsellors of a Khorezmshah during the Arab conquest of Kath in AD 712.

Jews made their way through Sogdia, Chach and Ferghana to East Turkestan (the present-day Uigur Autonomous Region of Xinjiang in China). A Persian document from the 8th century, written by Jewish merchants in a Hebraic script, was found at Dandan-Oilik.

To all this information can be added an ancient Hebraic inscription from the 5th to 6th centuries AD, from Gilgit in the upper Indus, and fragments of ancient Hebraic inscriptions on stucco from the 6th to 7th centuries AD (still unpublished), found recently in southern Kazakhstan in the Chimkent region (reported in a personal communication from V.A. Livshits). This is the sum of all the information scholars have to date regarding the settlement of Jews in pre-Islamic Central Asia and its neighbouring regions.

Arab migration

The Arabs seized Merv in AD 651 when pursuing the remaining troops of the Sassanian Shah Yazdegerd and made it their base. From here they embarked on a series of aggressive raids into Transoxiana, accounting for the Arabic name for the region Mavarannahr (Arabic for 'what lies beyond the river').

Early campaigns by the Arabs were characterised by short pillaging raids to seize property and take captives. The first Arab commander to cross the Amu Darya was the 'standard bearer' of the Prophet, al-Hakam ibn Amr al-Gifari. In the account of al-Balazuri, he was also the first to recite a Muslim prayer beyond the Jayhun river, in present-day Uzbekistan. This event must have taken place somewhat earlier than AD 670, the year when al-Gifari died in Merv. According to the historian H. Gibb, al-Gifari crossed the Jayhun in AD 667 before going on to invade Chaganian.

From AD 670 onwards, Arab troops led campaigns against Bukhara, Paikend, Samarkand and Termez several times a year, with each campaign involving not only soldiers but often entire families as well. Thus, during Salma ibn Ziyad's march on Bukhara in AD 676, his wife Umm Muhammad accompanied him, and became the first Muslim woman to cross the Amu Darya. This was also the first time the Arab army wintered in Mavarannahr instead of returning to Merv for the winter as usual.

In AD 689, an Arab commander from the Qays tribe, Musa ibn Abdallah, captured and held Termez for 15 years.

By the beginning of the 8th century AD, Arab tribes were already widespread throughout Sogdia and Northern Tokharistan. This process intensified after AD 704, when Qutaiba ibn Muslim led military campaigns against Mavarannahr, from Chach to Khorezm. These were inevitably accompanied by the destruction of monuments and cultural artefacts, the spread of Islam and the establishment of Arab towns and settlements in Mavarannahr. By the middle of the 8th century, the Arabs had succeeded in subjugating almost all of Central Asia, which had become part of the Abbasid Caliphate.

We know nothing of the size of the Arab populations that arrived and lived in Khorasan and Mavarannahr from the mid-7th to the mid-8th century AD, but there is little doubt that they were considerable in number. Textual sources tell us, for example, that the following Arab tribes moved here partially or in entirety with their families or participated in the campaigns: al-Atik, al-Mahrah, Amir, Amr, Anazzah, Anbar, Asad, Azd, Bahila, Bajila, Bakr, Bal'am, Banu Khuza'ah, Banu Laith, Banu Murra, Banu Sa'd, Barzan, Dabba, Darim, Disar, Duba'i, Fazara, Ghani, Ghatafan, Gudana, Hakami, Hakifa, Hamdan, Hanzala, Hilal, Himiyar, Huzail, 'Ijl, Jahdar, Ju'fa, Jundub, Ka'b, Kalb, Kilab, Kindah, Ma'n, Malik, Mudar, Najiya, Nasr, Nizari, Numayr, Qays, Quray, Quraysh, Rabi'ah, Shayban, Suhayb, Sulaym, Taghlib, Tammim, Tayy, Utar, Uvafa, Wa'il, Yahmad, Yemeni, Zahran and Zalim. Among them, the largest migrations were from the Sahili tribes of Yemeni, Qays, Quraysh, Mudar, Rabi'ah, Tammim, Hanzala and al-Huza'iy tribes.

The Arabs in Central Asia established settlements consisting entirely of one or another tribe, for instance in the al-Lin and Fenin settlements of the Khuza'ah tribe in the Merv oasis (see Tabari, pp. 313, 321), or they occupied separate quarters of cities, as in Bukhara, displacing the previous population.

Thus, Arab migration to Central Asia in the second half of the 7th to the 8th century had a very significant impact, but it probably began to subside gradually as early as the 9th century AD, marking the end of the era of Arab conquest. From that time onwards, the cities of the region began to be settled by representatives of Arab families, including religious figures, scientists, doctors, and so on.

Arab influence in Central Asia was reflected primarily in the acceptance by the population of this region of the new religion, Islam, in a language that became not only the language of religion but also the everyday and literary language of Central Asian peoples. Over time, the Arabs became an organic part of the diverse peoples of Central Asia, preserving their ethnic identity in specific parts of the Bukhara, Samarkand and Kashka Darya regions of Uzbekistan.

The Altai language family

Historically, ethnic groups speaking the following languages have migrated to Central Asia: Turkic, Mongol and to some extent, Manchurian, represented by the Kidans (or the Kara-Khatai or Kara-Kitai, as they were also known) who invaded the region in the middle of the 12th century AD.

The migration of Turkic tribes

The migration of Turkic speakers was the earliest. Three main waves of Turkic migration into Central Asia took place: in the 6th–8th centuries AD, the 10th–12th centuries AD, and in the 15th–16th centuries AD.

The earliest written evidence of the presence of Turkic-speaking tribes in Central Asia dates back to the second half of the 6th century. As we have already noted, there is no evidence of a single Turkic word, title, name or toponym in the numerous forms of written evidence (such as coin legends and inscriptions) from the first half of the 1st millennium AD. This would not be the case if large numbers of Turkic people had lived here at that time.

The original homeland of the Turks was the Altai mountains of southern Siberia, where they emerged as a community in the 5th century AD. The Turks, or Turkuts, established their state – the Great Turkic Khaganate – in AD 551 and began to advance west and south-west from here. In the same year, under Ishtemi Khan they conquered Khorezm and Semirechye, where the Dulu and Nushibi tribes (related to the Turkic tribes) lived. In the early 560s the Turks penetrated the territory of Transoxiana, Chach, Sogdia and Bukhara, and between AD 563 and AD 567 they inflicted a crushing defeat on the Hephthalites near Bukhara, thereby ending Hephthalite domination in the region.

Around the same time, the Turks reached the Iron Gate, which was the main route from Sogdia to Tokharistan and India at the time. The first incursions by Turks into Tokharistan took place in AD 589. The Turkic-Sassanian military conflicts at the end of the 6th and beginning of the 7th century ended under the West Turkic Khagan Tun-Shekhu (AD 618–630) when the Turks achieved a final victory by securing Tokharistan, which was entrusted to Tun-Shekhu's son, Tardush-Shad. The Turkic incursion into Tokharistan was very significant. According to Xuanzang (in about AD 630), Turkic dynasties had already consolidated their positions in many parts of Tokharistan. At the beginning of the 6th century AD Turkic rulers were ruling separate domains of Sogdia and Chach. The first numismatic evidence of Turkic presence in Transoxiana comes from silver imitations of Peroz coins (AD 459–484) using the Turkic titles *tegin* and *khagan* and dating from this time, as well as copper coins bearing the name of Tun-Shekhu.

Thus, the period from the mid-6th century AD to the beginning of the 7th century AD is the earliest stage of Turkic infiltration into Transoxiana. In the second half of the 7th to the 8th century AD this process intensified even further: in some areas of Sogdia, Chach and Ustrushana, Turkic dynasties had already become firmly established, and Transoxiana was itself part of the West Turkic Khaganate. Turkic coinage proper began to appear with Turkic names and titles (for example, Turgesh coinage bearing the title *Khagan*, or Chach coinage bearing the title *Tegin* or *Il-tegin*); the first Turkic runic inscriptions in Semirechye and to some extent in Chach and Northern Tokharistan date from this period; and Turkic sculptures – *balbals* – also became widespread.

Beginning in the 10th century AD and over the next two centuries, incursions by various Turkic tribes into Transoxiana continued, and from the 11th century AD onwards these apparently became widespread, resulting in the final replacement of Eastern Iranian dynasties by the Turkic dynasties of the Ghaznavids, Seljuks, Qarakhanids and Anushteginids throughout Central Asia, from the Caspian Sea to the Pamirs. Among the various Turkic tribes that migrated to Central Asia in the early and later medieval periods (6th century AD to the beginning of the 8th century AD), the most important role was played by the Turks, Oghuzes, Karluks, Kyrgyzes, Kipchaks, Tukhli, Chigils and Yagma; these were probably also the largest tribes.

Around this time, the term Turkestan (meaning 'land of the Turks') was increasingly applied to Central Asia. According to Fahr ad-Din Mubarak-Shah Merverudi, '...no country in the world can compare in size or breadth to Turkestan. To the east of the vilayat of the Turks lies the land of Chin [China], to the west the border of Turkestan touches Rum [Byzantium], in the north it runs along the wall of Gog and Magog, and in the south it extends along the snowy peaks of the mountains of Hindustan.' He also provides a list of 50 tribes that settled in the region at this time.

Among the Mongol tribes that arrived in Central Asia in the 13th–14th centuries were Turkic tribes such as the Jalair, Sunit, Tatar, Merkit, Kurlat, Torgut, Uirat, Tumat, Bulgachin, Telenggut and Urengit. However, these tribes only came to be identified as Mongol under Chinghis Khan, whereas hitherto they had been known as Turks.

The last major influx of Turkic-speaking tribes into Transoxiana took place during the 15th and 16th centuries AD, and according to B.A. Ahmedov, the collective term 'Uzbek' had come into use for the Turkic-Mongol population of the eastern part of Dasht-i Kipchak long before the accession to the throne of Uzbeg Khan (1312–1340/41).

Based on his analysis of written sources, B.A. Ahmedov has proposed possible numbers for the Turkic-speaking tribes that came here from Dasht-i Kipchak. According to him, at the beginning of the 16th century there were some 24 to 26 of these tribes, by the mid-16th century their number had grown to 40 and by the start of the 17th century there were more than 50 of them.

The migration of Mongol tribes

The question as to when the Mongol tribes appeared in Central Asia remains open. It is possible that some of their groups and even individual tribes may have migrated here long before the main migration in the 13th–15th centuries. According to one theory, the Mongol-speaking people were the Huns (Xiongnu), who played an active role in Central Asia between the last centuries BC and the first half of the 1st century AD.

According to anthropologists, the earliest inclusions of Mongol elements into the Caucasian population in Central Asia were in the middle of the 1st millennium BC.

T.K. Khodjaiov distinguishes three phases of an intensive influx of Mongol peoples into Central Asia: the middle of the 1st millennium BC; the 10th–12th centuries AD; and the 16th–17th centuries AD. However, there could be both Turks and Mongols among the Mongol migrants. For this reason, it was only the incursion by Mongol troops into Central Asia in 1219–1221 under their leader Chingis Khan that we can say with historical certainty was the first migration of Mongol ethnic groups to this region. Rashid al-Din recorded the names of several Mongol tribes who settled here, however it is well known that a significant number of Chingis Khan's troops were members of Turkic, Manchurian, Tangut and Tungus tribes.

The main areas of settlement for the Mongol tribes in Central Asia were between the Amu Darya and Syr Darya rivers, and also the Semirechye. The largest tribes occupied strictly defined territories here.

For example, the Jalairs settled in the modern Tashkent region and in the Khodjent area. The Barlas settled in the Surkhan Darya valley and northern Afghanistan, while the Kauchins settled in the Ferghana valley and southern parts of the Kashka Darya. Other Mongol tribes who migrated here included the Alchin, Duglat, Suldus, Ming, Manghit and Qunghirat, among others.

However, the number of Mongol tribes who came here was probably insignificant, and over time they met the same fate as the Mongols of the Golden Horde, and were turkicised by the indigenous population who outnumbered them. Nonetheless, these turkicised Mongols continued to strictly observe Mongol customs and rules for a long time. None other than Amir Timur (the founder of the Timurid dynasty) provides a striking example. Till the end of his life, in spite of all the power he possessed, and not being a 'Chingisid', a descendant of Chingis Khan, he refused to accept the highest title of the Turks and Mongols – Khan – and referred to himself as 'Küregen – Khan's son-in-law', a title he cherished. Moreover, in coin legends he used only Mongol words.

Over the course of time, great differences were established between the turkicised Mongols of Mavarannahr, who by the mid-14th century considered a Turkic language to be their native tongue, and the Mongols of Semirechye, who had preserved their language, old customs and rites.

The Mongols of Semirechye scornfully referred to the turkicised Mongols of Mavarannahr as *Qaraunas*, i.e. 'mixed, Métises', while the latter called Semirechye Mongols *jete* meaning 'robbers'. It is fair to assume that during the 14th–15th centuries the Mongols became absorbed by the indigenous Turkic population. Similarly, the nomadic Uzbeks who came from Dasht-i Kipchak together with Shaibani Khan at the beginning of the 16th century had also become turkicised by this time.

The last wave of migration by Mongol tribes to Central Asia in the 17th–18th centuries is linked to the Kalmyks, but it only affected the north-eastern regions of Central Asia (Tashkent) and some areas of inner Mavarannahr.

The above-mentioned data allows us to conclude that there were regular migrations of different ethnic groups to Central Asia. Thus, it has been established that from the middle of the 2nd millennium BC the main migrations took place from west to east: Indo-Aryans, Iranians, Graeco-Macedonians, Semites (with the last Semitic migration, the Arabs, taking place in the second half of the 7th–8th centuries AD). The first known migration of Yuezhi/Tokharians, which we know about from textual sources, marked the beginning of ethnic movements from the east, which later occurred regularly throughout the medieval period: Huns (Xiongnu), Turks, Khitans, Mongols and Kalmyks. Only in the second half of the 19th century, with the conquest of Central Asia by the Russian empire, did ethnic movements from the west – from Europe (Russians, Ukrainians, to a lesser extent Belarusians, Poles and other Slavic peoples) – resume.

The impact of migration on the ethnic composition of the Central Asian population was varied. The most important role in this respect was played by the migrations of Iranian- and Turkic-speaking peoples.

The migration of East Iranian peoples initially led to the formation of several ethnic groups who shared closely related Central Iranian languages – the Bactrians, Sogdians, Parthians and Khorezmians. The migration of Turkic-speaking tribes, in several strong waves at different times, since the 6th century contributed (if we accept the evidence of textual sources, epigraphic and archaeological data) to the spread of the Turkic language throughout Central Asia. It also led to the assimilation of the local East Iranian peoples and an ethnic symbiosis that would later shape the development of the Turkic-speaking peoples of Central Asia, such as the Uzbeks and Turkmens. They were mainly Caucasian in anthropological terms, while the other Turkic-speaking peoples of Central Asia – the Kazakhs, Karakalpaks and Kirgizes – were Mongol.

PART II

STATES

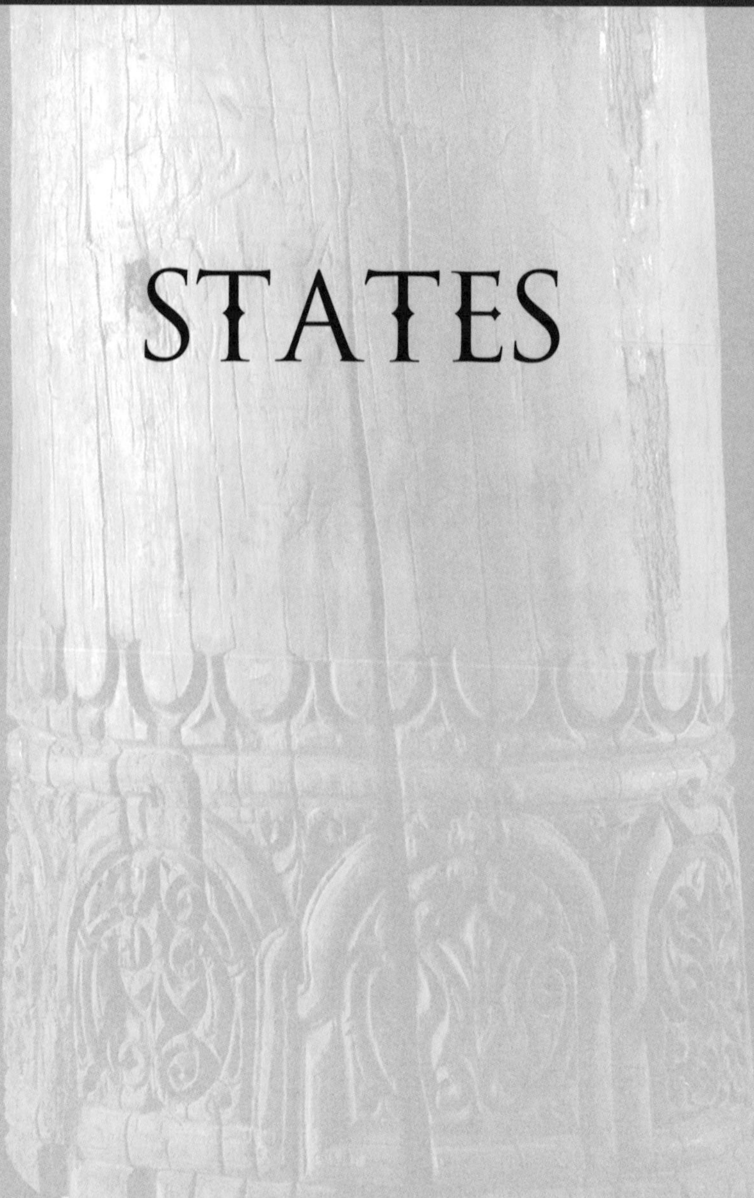

2.1

PERIODS IN THE DEVELOPMENT AND TYPOLOGY OF EARLY STATES IN CENTRAL ASIA

HISTORICO-LEGAL AND ARCHAEOLOGICAL SCHOLARSHIP SHOWS US THAT WE can only really begin to speak about the emergence of statehood when civilisations have reached the point of sufficiently developed economies built on irrigation-based agriculture, metalworking, crafts and trade, with the latter initially based on barter but subsequently on money and ingots. Further, such civilisations are characterised by a differentiation of property ownership, with the formation of corresponding social groups and classes and a complex social hierarchy with a monarch at the head, a state-administrative apparatus, the right of inheritance, and a writing system, which facilitated the drafting of all kinds of legal documents for the management of the state.

These are the main features, but by no means all of them, that characterised the earliest forms of states in Lower Mesopotamia (Sumer and Akkad), Egypt and the Eastern Mediterranean, which emerged at the end of the 4th millennium and beginning of the 3rd millennium BC.

The first type of state entities to emerge were very ancient cities, serving as the economic, political and religious centres of very small 'states' in terms of the territory they occupied. Thus, an area of just 1,000 square kilometres in Lower Mesopotamia had several city-states: Uruk, Larsa, Lagash and Ur, with Uruk and Lagash just 24 kilometres apart. Later, as a result of invasion and conquest, such city-states were – often forcibly – merged into one relatively large kingdom covering up to several hundred square kilometres with an established system of despotic rule. These early kingdoms eventually turned into monarchies, mostly through the violent subjugation of neighbouring territories, sometimes occupying vast areas.

This logic of the development of states, when combined with particular conditions, transformed some of them into vast global empires spanning several continents. The most obvious example of this was the Achaemenid empire, which included territories in Asia, Europe and Africa. This was how state-like entities evolved in the regions where they first emerged in the Near and Middle East.

The process of the genesis and evolution of state entities in Transoxiana was considerably different, however. Nonetheless, for particular historical reasons, these territories were also part of the Achaemenid and Seleucid empires at certain points.

Transoxiana is a distinctive, historical, geographical and cultural area, whose civilisation flourished for many thousands of years thanks to two great rivers: the Amu Darya (ancient Oxus) and the Syr Darya (ancient Jaxartes). The states that emerged here differed from states in other parts of Central Asia in many ways, both in antiquity and in medieval times, even though they also shared some common features. Even within the territory of Transoxiana, the northern (Khorezm) and southern provinces (Bactria) were notably different from one another, especially in antiquity. They differed considerably in their ethnic composition and cultures, their languages and writing systems, as well as their polities. This situation stemmed from the cultural and genetic particularities of each region, and the rivalry between settled and nomadic peoples, the extent of which varied in different regions.

The periodisation of the development of ancient statehood proposed here is based on selecting those features of statehood which are most characteristic and important for each period and which are new in comparison to the preceding period.

It is based on the main findings of national and international research into the history and archaeology of Central Asia. Given the huge number of publications that in one way or another address these or other issues and problems of statehood, this author's approach has been to reduce these references to a minimum so as not to overload the main text.

Periods in the development of early states

With regard to the evolution of ancient statehood/early states in Transoxiana, it is possible to single out six main periods spanning the second half of the 2nd millennium BC to the second half of the 3rd or beginning of the 4th century AD, i.e. until the time of transition from ancient to medieval states.

The emergence of early forms of statehood in this region took shape on the basis of the economic and cultural achievements of the settled farming civilisations, which had been developing in the territory of southern Uzbekistan since the Late Bronze Age. The end of this process more or less coincided with the decline of the Kushan and Parthian kingdoms in the first half of the 3rd century AD. At about the same time, the Kangju state also ceased to exist.

The **first period** covered the second half of the 2nd millennium BC. Initial forms of statehood in Northern Bactria may have included a voluntary association of several cultural oasis areas headed by an elected ruler and council of elders, which may have been a part of a larger association formed on the territory of Bactria at that time.

The state-like nature of such associations is suggested by evidence of a relatively developed economy, including irrigation-based farming, several types of crafts (pottery, metalwork), trade between districts and regions, and especially by the appearance of dominant settlements such as Jarkutan, which, judging by the presence of several necropolises, consisted of a number of 'settlements' united under the common authority of an elected ruler. The presence of a temple and a palace at this site indicates a sufficiently developed administrative apparatus and the establishment of temple officials. The recently discovered site of Tillya-Bulak in the Kugitang foothills, situated near mines of various metals and iron ore, points to the deliberate extraction of mineral wealth by the rulers.

However, the absence of a writing system, seen as the hallmark of statehood even at the earliest stages of development of early states (such as Sumer, Akkad, Egypt and China), means that we cannot assume that the ancient Central Asian agricultural societies of the Bronze Age had evolved into states as such.

The **second period** spanned the early part of the 1st millennium BC through to the year 539 BC. The historical and cultural areas of Bactria, Sogdia and Khorezm emerged during this time, along with initial forms of states with extensive hierarchical systems of political power. Evidence of this can be found in the Avesta, and its details about social structure, for example, it lists the following: *nmana* (house-family), *vis* (clan, clan settlement), *zantu* (tribe), *dahyu* (province, country) and the various leaders in the state, including the ruler of the country, and of a province (*dahyupati*), other rulers, lords (*sastar*), and so on.

It is also possible that it was during this time that larger territorial accumulations, such as the kingdoms of ancient Bactria and ancient Sogdia, began to take shape or confederations of tribes, usually headed by a queen, as with the Sakas of the northern part of Transoxiana and their queens Zarina and Tomyris.

In the **third period**, 539 BC–330 BC, the Achaemenid conquest and the incorporation of Central Asian regions into the Achaemenid state interrupted the development of local state entities. For 200 years the whole or almost all of the territory of Transoxiana was under the control of the Achaemenid (ancient Persian) system of statehood, which amounted to an absolute monarchy, under the despotic and unlimited power of the 'King of Kings'. The entire territory of this kingdom, often referred to in historical literature as an empire, was divided into satrapies, which paid tribute in specific weight units of silver (talents) into the treasury of the Achaemenid kings. Three of the Central Asian satrapies – Bactria, Sogdia and Khorezm – were situated wholly or partially in what is now Uzbekistan.

At the same time, according to textual sources, small regions, such as Nautaca, Xenippa and Paraetacene, which were probably part of larger satrapies, maintained their autonomy under the rule of Bactrian and Sogdian aristocrats (Oxyartes, Chorienes, Sisimithres, Catanes, Austan) who preserved some degree of independence in their own possessions (fiefdoms). These regions had well-fortified centres and temporary shelters – *petraes*. In Khorezm, where the Sakas had played an important role, they were able to establish an independent kingdom in the second half of the 4th century BC after a prolonged struggle with the Achaemenids.

The arrival of Alexander the Great, who defeated the main forces of the Achaemenids in 330 BC, caused the collapse of the Achaemenid empire. Alexander's pursuit of the last claimant to the Achaemenid throne, Bessus, a satrap of Bactria, cleared his path to Central Asia. The conquest of Central Asia took three years (330–327 BC), during which time Alexander's armies met with fierce resistance, especially from the Sogdians led by Spitamenes.

The **fourth period** spanned the end of the 4th century BC to the beginning of the second half of the 2nd century BC – from the conquests of Alexander the Great to the end of the political domination of the Hellenes and the fall of the Graeco-Bactrian kingdom. This was a period of the coexistence of two different systems of statehood: the Hellenic in Northern Bactria and to some extent in Sogdia, and the Khorezmian-Kangju in other parts of Transoxiana. The appearance of Hellenic statehood is connected with the campaigns of Alexander the Great in Central Asia in 330–327 BC, which covered all of Sogdia and Northern Bactria. However, its formation and consolidation took place after Alexander's death in 323 BC, at first under the aegis of the Greek satraps who were appointed in those regions during the so-called War of the Diadochi. Then, from 306/305 BC, Bactria and Sogdia became part of the Seleucid state. However, as early as the middle of the 3rd century BC, Diodotus, a Seleucid satrap in Bactria, rebelled against the centre and created a separate state, known in scholarship as the Graeco-Bactrian kingdom and sometimes as the Greek state of Bactria.

Greek notions and norms of statehood seem to have been introduced in the regions that were part of these states. It is possible that some of the major cities were governed by systems used in the Greek city-states (*poleis*). Greek political rule in the south of ancient Uzbekistan lasted for about 200 years, and for a somewhat shorter period in Sogdia, up to the second half of the 2nd century BC.

At the same time, in the northern and central regions of Transoxiana – in Khorezm, Sogdia and Ferghana – an autochthonous type of statehood was emerging, which we could refer to as the 'Khorezmian-Kangju' type.

Khorezm, which broke free from Achaemenid domination in the 4th century BC, was the first to form its own independent state. As early as 329 BC, in Maracanda, Alexander the Great received the Khorezmian king Pharasmanes, who offered Alexander peace and an alliance. According to the Khorezmian king, his state extended as far as that of the Colchians (a people of Georgian descent, who at that time had their own state in western Georgia) and the Amazons in the north.

Even taking into account some exaggeration in this information (given by Herodotus), we can nevertheless assume that the Khorezmian kingdom at that time constituted a fairly extensive state stretching westward to the Caspian Sea, where its peoples could have come into contact with the Colchians. A recent study of the site of Kalalygyr II in historical Khorezm suggests that trade relations with the regions bordering the Caspian Sea did indeed exist.

At the turn of the 3rd–2nd century BC, the independent states in Bukhara and Sogdia emerged. Their rulers minted coins in imitation of Antiochus I and Euthydemus, with legends in distorted Greek, later followed by those in Sogdian. At the same time, a type of state was being established in Dayuan (Ferghana).

The confederative Kangju states were also formed at this time, and included central and northern parts of Transoxiana.

The **fifth period** spanned the second half of the 2nd century BC to the beginning of the 1st century AD. The Graeco-Bactrian kingdom fell under pressure from the Saka or Sarmatian tribes (Asii/Asiani, Pasiani, Sakarauli) as they advanced from northern and central regions of Transoxiana and then from the Tokharians (Yuezhi) who came to Sogdia and Bactria fleeing from Inner Asia to escape the Huns (Xiongnu).

This period is distinguished by the existence throughout the territory of Transoxiana of a type of statehood that we can define as the 'Kangju-Yuezhi' type. It combined nomadic principles of governance with the traditions of statehood that were already present here. Yuezhi/Tokharians gradually settled in Sogdia and Northern Bactria, later capturing the whole of Northern Bactria and establishing their capital in Bactra (present-day Balkh in northern Afghanistan). They created a distinctive confederative state consisting of five independent principalities. These principalities had the right to mint their own coins, which were mostly silver.

Somewhat earlier, Kangju, a state of a similar type, had been established in the central and northern regions of Transoxiana. In addition to the territories on the Jaxartes river, it also included five possessions located in Khorezm, Bukhara, Sogdia and Chach. These possessions also had the right to mint their own coinage, initially in imitation of the Graeco-Bactrian coins of Eucratides and Euthydemus, and later using their own variants.

Tamgas or dynastic signs constituting a kind of state symbol appear to have been used for the first time in Central Asia on the coins minted in Kangju and its subject territories. From this time on, they appeared on coins almost everywhere in Transoxiana until the region became part of the Abbasid Caliphate in the middle of the 8th century AD.

The emergence and widespread use of Sogdian and Khorezmian writing systems based on the Aramaic alphabet is a significant indication of the political stability in the region.

In the second half of the 2nd century BC, the missions of Zhang Qian opened up the Western Regions (i.e. the territories of Central Asia) for Han China for the first time. From the end of the 2nd century BC onwards, regular diplomatic and trade relations were established between China and the Western Regions. The notable result of these relations was the formation of the Silk Road – the first transcontinental road in the history of civilisation – to connect the countries of the West and the East.

The **sixth period** spanned the beginning of the 1st century AD to the mid-3rd century AD, and was a period of the rise and growth of ancient statehood in the territory of what is present-day Uzbekistan, but was also the time of the final stage of its development.

The most notable phenomenon of this period is the emergence of the powerful Kushan kingdom, established in the early 1st century AD by Kujula Kadphises, one of the leaders of the Kushan clan of the Yuezhi tribes. His successor, Wima I Takto, incorporated the south of present-day Uzbekistan into the Kushan kingdom, a situation that endured until the middle of the 3rd century AD. This territory, a border region, headed by the Bactrian *karalrang/karalraggo* (meaning 'head of a border region or 'margrave'), played a key role in the history of the Kushan kingdom. To the north-west of this area, in the Hissar mountains, a powerful defensive wall was erected to protect the area from raids by nomadic tribes from the north. This period in the south of Uzbekistan was a time when cities, settlements and the economy flourished, along with commodity-money relations and all the other attributes of a developed state.

To the north of the Kushan kingdom was the confederative Kangju state, parts of which had become hereditary and acquired even greater independence. Thus during this period Khorezm became a very powerful, independent state and the Afrighid dynasty assumed power. The tradition of dynastic succession found expression in, among other things, the use of state symbols on the reverse of the Khorezmshah's coins – that of a horseman and the Kangju *tamga*, which continued to be used for 700 to 800 years, until the Arab conquest.

During this period, states that were strong enough to pursue independent domestic and foreign policies existed in Bukhara, in south-western Sogdia (the Hyrcodes dynasty), in Samarkand Sogdia (the Kan rulers), in Southern Sogdia/Kesh (the Artat dynasty), in Ferghana and in Chach.

At the same time, with the exception of Khorezm, whose rulers were referred to as *MR'Y MLK* ('lord king') and 'shah', and those of Northern Bactria, which was part of the Kushan kingdom, none of the rulers of other dominion-states in Transoxiana had used the equivalent of a royal title. Judging by the inscriptions on the coins, in most cases they were referred to by the Aramaic title *MR'Y* ('ruler' or 'lord').

Coins from this period suggest that there were two centralised states on the territory of ancient Uzbekistan – the Kushan kingdom and the state of the Khorezmshahs, while Kangju was a conglomerate of independent possessions united into a state through a system of confederative administration.

Thus, this period is one of the most important in many respects in the history of the development of ancient statehood on the territory of Uzbekistan. Its features included:

- The use of state symbols – dynastic signs – on coins;
- The appearance and widespread use of a writing system;
- The emergence of independent coinage and the development of commodity-money relations;
- The formation of separate dominions, with all the functions of a state;
- The development of extensive diplomatic relations between these dominions;
- The emergence and functioning of the Silk Road, which facilitated extensive exchanges of goods, international contacts and the spiritual enrichment of peoples and states.

This period also marks the final phase in the development of the ancient statehood of Uzbekistan.

The collapse of the great Kushan and Parthian kingdoms and of the Kangju state in the first half of the 3rd century AD, followed by invasion by nomadic tribes and decline in various spheres of the economy and social life, are probably connected to initial changes in the ancient social structure, i.e. the collapse of kingdoms led to the formation of many possessions-states in Transoxiana and consequently to a new political situation and new administrative practices. Iconography and the content of coin legends reveal that the replacement of old dynasties and the coming to power of new ones took place in Bukhara, Kesh and Nakhshab, Tokharistan and Chach. However, as Chinese textual sources tell us, the power in possessions of Transoxiana was hereditary and passed from one generation to another. If this was the case, then dynastic changes were reduced to the transition of power within 'one royal house', and the rulers of the new dynasties came from the same Kangju and Yuezhi families.

This transitional period, from antiquity to the medieval period, is one of the most important in the history of statehood in ancient Uzbekistan and in Central Asia as a whole.

2.2

TYPES OF STATE ENTITIES

Different kinds of state entities existed throughout antiquity in Transoxiana. In terms of their organic structure we can distinguish autochthonous states, i.e. state associations that emerged and progressively developed on a local basis (such as the state of Kangju and the kingdom of Khorezm), and foreign ones, i.e. states that incorporated Transoxiana through invasion, conquest and subsequent subjugation (such as the Achaemenid empire and the Graeco-Bactrian kingdom). It is also possible to distinguish state associations that emerged as a result of symbiosis with foreign invaders, who settled and to a certain extent blended with the local population. Such 'mixed' states existed, for example, in Sogdia and Northern Bactria, founded by the Yuezhi who moved out of Inner Asia between the late 2nd century BC and the beginning of the 1st century AD. According to the 7th-century chronicles, the *Beishi* ('The History of the Northern Dynasties') and *Sui Shi* ('The Book of Sui'), the rulers of the dominion of An, an area identified with Bukhara, and Kan (Samarkand Sogdia) were both descended from the house of Zhaowu, i.e. Yuezhi, who originally lived in the north of the Qilian mountains, in the modern Chinese province of Gansu. But after resettling in Sogdia, all the dynasties of Yuezhi origin who had established themselves there, including in the cities of Samarkand and Bukhara, 'retained the name Zhaowu'. These dynasties ruled here until the 7th–8th centuries AD. In a letter to the Tang emperor Taizong in AD 627, the Bukhara ruler Alinga claimed that 'his royal house had already been in power for twenty-two successive generations'. If we assume an average of 20–30 years for each reign, it would appear that the Yuezhi house of Alinga had reigned here about 400–600 years, i.e. since the beginning of the 1st century AD.

The dynasty of the rulers of Khorezm, who, according to the same sources, also stem from the house of Zhaowu, was a stable one as well. According to numismatic data, the dynasty ruled Khorezm from the 1st to the 8th century AD inclusive. The evidence for this is provided by state symbols: a rider, a horse and a *tamga* are all present on coins from ancient and medieval Khorezm from the time the coins were minted until they stopped being issued. This phenomenon is unique to all the dynasties that ruled not only in Central Asia, but in other states of the East as well. These are the main typologies of the organic structure of the dynasties that ruled in pre-Islamic Central Asia. Now let us consider the typology and arrangements of state formations.

Types of early states in the territory of present-day Uzbekistan

1. Kingdoms with an absolute monarchy

In the ancient history of Uzbekistan there were several periods when it was part of a kingdom ruled over by an absolute monarch.

From 539 BC to 330 BC, almost the entire territory of Transoxiana, with the exception of Ferghana and Chach, was ruled by Persian Achaemenid kings. This included Khorezm, Sogdia, Bactria and even the lands of the Sakas, which constituted special administrative units or satrapies governed by satraps appointed by the Achaemenid kings, and obliged to contribute to the state treasury.

Another absolute monarchy with a system of governors who enjoyed a certain amount of independence was the Graeco-Bactrian kingdom. This kingdom was established in the middle of the 3rd century BC and continued until the second half of the 2nd century BC. During this period, Northern Bactria and, at certain points, Sogdia, were also part of this kingdom. However, royal power in this state was not always hereditary: its first kings, Diodotus I and Diodotus II, were overthrown by Euthydemus, who was not a blood relative.

From the end of the 4th century to the middle of the 3rd century BC, Northern Bactria and Sogdia were part of another Greek kingdom – that of the Seleucids. However, the second ruler of this dynasty, Antiochus I (281–261 BC), was half

Parthian kings coins.

Sogdian: the son of Seleucus and Apama, daughter of the Sogdian leader Spitamenes. Consequently, all the subsequent members of this dynasty, which lasted until the middle of the 1st century BC, had Sogdian blood.

Likewise, the Kushan kingdom, which lasted from the 1st century AD to the middle of the 3rd century, was an absolute, and more than that, a pronouncedly theocratic monarchy. Throughout this period, with the exception of the reign of the first king, Kujula Kadphises, the southern regions of Transoxiana were part of the Kushan state. It was divided into distinct satrapies whose rulers were completely dependent on the Kushan kings. In addition, the Kushan kingdom included specific border regions akin to margravates, headed by *kanarangs/karalrangs*, military leaders, known as *karalraggo* by Bactrians. The present-day Surkhan Darya province in Uzbekistan was probably one of these regions.

The Khorezmian kingdom, which emerged in the second half of the 4th century BC before the collapse of the Achaemenid state, appears to have been a similar type of state. From the 1st century AD onwards a new hereditary dynasty was established here with coinage issued by a centralised mint.

From the middle of the 3rd century AD until the end of the 4th century, Northern Bactria was part of the Sassanian kingdom, with Bactria enjoying special rights within it. Bactria was ruled by Sassanian princes with the title 'Kushanshah', who were descended from different branches of the dynasty and were entitled to mint gold, silver and copper coins. Some of them later became kings of the entire Sassanian state.

2. *Confederative kingdoms*

The form of government in confederative kingdoms was a kind of limited monarchy. The Kangju and Yuezhi states or the Great Yuezhi state in the first, pre-Kushan period of its existence can be classified as confederative kingdoms. These kingdoms usually consisted of several independent dominions ruled by tribal leaders or heads of clans, who minted their own coins.

For example, the Kangju state had at least five such dominions: Bukhara and its environs, whose rulers issued imitations of the coinage of Euthydemus, with inscriptions of their own names and titles; the south-east of Bukhara Sogdia and north-west of Samarkand Sogdia, ruled by leaders from the Hyrcodes dynasty; Samarkand Sogdia, which issued coins with the names of different kings; and Southern Sogdia, which also had an independent mint. No Kangju coinage was shared by these dominions at this time. Khorezm was a completely independent kingdom whose rulers bore the highest title – *MR'Y MLK'* ('lord king' – *MR'Y* means 'lord', *MLK'* means 'king').

The Yuezhi state during the first pre-Kushan period was a similar confederative kingdom. Like the Kangju state, the Yuezhi state consisted of five dominions headed by representatives of different Yuezhi clans. These possessions – Hsiu-mi, Shuang-mi, Kuei-shuang, Tu-mi and Hsi-tun – were located in different parts of Bactria, and apparently subordinate to a nominally supreme Yuezhi leader.

Five different coin mints can be identified for this period: the coins of Sapadbizes, Pseigacharis and Kushan (Heraeus), and imitations of the coinage of Heliocles and Eucratides. This demonstrates the virtual independence of the various Yuezhi clan leaders who minted the coins.

Some years later, the descendants of one of these, Kushan, founded the great Kushan kingdom – which was in fact the same state as the Great Yuezhi, as ancient Chinese texts accurately referred to it, at a new stage of its historical evolution.

3. *Dominions*

Other types of states, governed by hereditary tribal leaders or heads of clans, consisted of small dominions. In Transoxiana, the 'dominion' was the most ancient type of state formation and was established on the basis of historical and cultural regions. These types of state had already been mentioned in the Avesta, by the classical Greek authors (Herodotus and Arrian among others), and in ancient Chinese chronicles. Zhang Qian, who visited Bactria after the fall of the Graeco-Bactrian kingdom in 128 or 126 BC, reported that Bactria consisted of many small independent dominions 'where almost every town had its own ruler'. The Chinese chronicles mention the presence of 55 dominions in the territory of Transoxiana, all of which enjoyed a certain degree of independence and pursued their own external policies – in particular, the establishment of diplomatic relations with China.

This type of state, which was common for the region had probably been established for the first time in the late 2nd and early 1st millennium BC, and seems to have been still in place when similar kinds of dominions governed by elected chiefs and a council of elders appeared. It continued even during the Achaemenid period, and is clearly alluded to in textual sources. Such dominions include, in particular, the dominions of Sisimithres in Nautaca, of Xenippa and Nikhshapa, and the dominions of Chorienes and Oxyartes, which probably enjoyed a degree of autonomy.

This kind of state acquired particular importance during transitional periods: for example, between the second half of the 2nd century BC and the 1st century AD, after the collapse of Hellenic statehood; or in the 3rd–4th centuries AD after the downfall of the Kushan and Kangju states, when independent possessions, such as Kesh and especially Chach, were established on the basis of historical and cultural regions. This period was characterised by the emergence of 'Khwabs' (Khwab = *χwβ* on coins – 'ruler'), sometimes entirely independent rulers (as was the case with Chach) of relatively small dominion-states.

2.3

TITLES OF RULERS OF STATES AND DOMINIONS IN CENTRAL ASIA FROM EARLY IN THE 1ST MILLENNIUM BC TO THE 3RD–4TH CENTURIES AD

The political significance of a particular state can to a large extent be determined by the title or honorary rank of its leader, as well as a number of other factors. These titles were inherited or acquired through power struggles with other persons who had initially borne equally important titles. As a state expanded and became increasingly powerful, its initial leader, who may have held a title of modest importance, would acquire all sorts of glorifying titles, as would his state. In many states, leaders were placed on a par with deities, with the Chinese referring to a ruler as the 'son of god', the Indians using the equivalent title *devaputra*, and the Bactrians the title *bagopouro*. Of course, there are also examples throughout history where the rulers of small and politically insignificant domains assumed the title of 'king' or 'king of kings', but this was the exception rather than the rule.

The titles of the kings and rulers of Central Asia have long been a subject of interest for historians, and much research has been undertaken, especially by the scholars V.A. Livshits, B.I. Vainberg, I.M. Dyakonov, E.V. Zeymal, S.P. Tolstov, O.I. Smirnova and W.B. Henning. However, most studies have concentrated on the titles of rulers of individual states, for example of Khorezm or the Kushan kingdom, and the main focus has been on the identification of the origin of the titles, of their meaning and of their ethnic history. However, there are no studies examining the titles of pre-Islamic rulers in Central Asia, the nature of their development, or how they changed over time.

An analysis of available data reveals that the titles of Central Asian rulers changed regularly throughout the period in question, depending on the languages used in the dominant states, or on historical and cultural factors. The scarcity of data makes studying this process difficult. The primary sources include Chinese and Graeco-Roman historical records, supplemented by literary texts, numismatic and sometimes epigraphic data. We can distinguish four periods in the evolution of the titulature of Central Asian rulers for the period in question: first, the Avestan (first half of the 1st millennium BC); second, the Achaemenid (mid-6th to late 4th century BC); third, the Hellenistic (late 4th century BC to the beginning of the second half of the 2nd century BC, although this period lasted until the 2nd century AD in Bactria); and the fourth, the Aramaic-Kushan period (beginning in the 2nd century BC and ending in early medieval times). Aramaic-Kushan titles continued to be used in several provinces of Transoxiana up to and including the 8th century AD.

This by no means implies that there were no titles emanating from within other cultural groups or other languages in Central Asia, for example the language of the Sakas, ancient Khorezm or Kangju, but, unfortunately, to date we have no data about these. Nor do we know what titles were used by leaders of settled farming tribes in Central Asia when statehood was emerging in the Late Bronze Age. Attempts to link these with Avestan titles are not justified, as there is no direct evidence that the Avestan language was already in use throughout Central Asia in the 2nd millennium BC.

The earliest title used by Central Asian rulers that we know of today was probably *kavi*, believed by scholars to have been used to signify the kings of Bactria or Drangiana in pre-Achaemenid times. It was at the court of one such *kavi*, Kavi Vishtaspa, whom the Zoroastrian tradition persistently associates with Balkh (Bactra), that Zarathushtra first gave his sermons.

The historian and linguist I.M. Dyakonov believed that originally the designation *kavi* was a name that meant 'poet or prophet', and that it only later came to be used as something akin to a royal title. According to the Iranist V.A. Livshits, the title *kavi* was predominantly used by nomadic tribal leaders hostile to the Zoroastrian community. In his opinion, this title, mentioned in the Gathas, dates back to the time of the Indo-Iranian community, i.e. at least to the 2nd millennium BC.

The designation *kavi* was also used to denote the high priests of tribes, thus combining religious and secular power. This suggests that, in the earliest stages of their development, the first state entities were probably theocratic in nature, at least in southern Central Asia. This tradition was continued in later times, for example in the state of Kushan, and is reflected in the iconography of coins, on which the king is depicted before an altar of fire, as if performing priestly functions. According to V.A. Livshits, in Iranian mythology, a *kavi* is a 'good prince', a patron of Zarathushtra and Zoroastrianism. He also believed that the title *kavi* had a higher status than that of simply a tribal leader.

The name of the second legendary dynasty of the Eastern Iranians – the Kayanians, founded by Kavi Kavata (referred to as Kay Qobad in the *Shahnama*) – is derived from the word *kavi*. The name combines the title *kavi* with the name Kavata.

Is it possible, however, that the rulers of Central Asia in the first half of the first millennium BC used the title 'king'? The information we have from local sources, including the Avesta and ancient Iranian epos, is not well substantiated in this respect. Nevertheless, we can extract interesting details from ancient Greek texts describing events from the 7th to 6th centuries BC, i.e. in the pre-Achaemenid and early Achaemenid periods.

Thus, according to Ctesias, 'the Sakas remained outside the satrapies' and were led by the king (βασιλεύς – *basileus*) Cydraeus, the husband of the legendary Zarina, who probably ruled in the 7th century BC. Amorges, who led the Sakas in the war against Cyrus, i.e. in the second half of the 6th century BC, and Amoraeus the leader of the Derbices, also bore the title *basileus*.

Basileus was also used for the Bactrian ruler Oxyartes. We can tell that the Greeks were well aware of the different nuances in the hierarchy of the titles used by rulers of Central Asia by the fact that the ruler of Parthia, Mermerus, was simply referred to as a dynast (δυνάστης) and the ruler of the Barcani tribe, Astyages, was called an *archon* (ἄρχων), i.e. titles used for them were, from the hierarchical point of view, lower down the scale than *basileus*. We could therefore argue that in pre-Achaemenid times, the rulers of the Sakas and Bactria at any rate, did bear a royal title and that their states may have been referred to as kingdoms. It follows that the title *kavi* was in use at this time and was equivalent to the Greek title *basileus*.

The title of *kavi* continued to be used in later times, for example on the so-called 'Turan series' of copper coins depicting an altar, dating from the 4th to 5th centuries AD, used in the Bukhara oasis; the word *kavi* is inscribed on them to the right of the image of the altar. Bukharkhudat coins from the 5th to the 7/8th centuries AD bear the inscription *pwx'r xwβ k'w'* next to the portrait of the king. This is usually translated as 'Lord of Bukhara, Kavi' or 'Lord of Bukhara, King', where the letters *xwβ* represent the title 'lord' and the letters *k'w'* mean 'king'. Thus the title *k'w* (= *kavi*), was in use in some areas of Central Asia for almost 1,500 years.

Titles of rulers are also cited in the Avesta, the oldest parts of which, the Yashts and Gathas, pertain to the beginning of the 1st millennium BC. In particular, among the most significant titles mentioned is *sastar* – a ruler of a region and its centre, perhaps the type of oasis with a central settlement that was typical in Bactria in the beginning of the 1st millennium BC, such as the Bandykhan oasis with the central settlements of Bandykhan I and II (9th–6th centuries BC). The same ruler also functioned as a military leader. The title *Sastar* was used to designate the ruler of a region or province.

The Avestan word *dahyupati* may also be synonymous with the ruler of a province, and may have designated the rulers of small regions uniting oases such as those mentioned in descriptions of Alexander the Great's campaign to Bactria and Sogdia: Nautaca, Xenippa, Gabaza, Paretacene and Bubacene. Small possessions like these were headed by rulers such as Oxyartes, Sisimithres, Chorienes and Catanes. It is possible that rulers of a similar status existed here in earlier times as well, as the traditional oasis-based system dating back to the Bronze Age was still in place in the 5th and 4th centuries BC. Such rulers may well have held the title of *dahyupati*.

V.A. Livshits and many other scholars believe that the title '*Dahyupati* of all *dahyus*' meant 'lord of all provinces', and designated the ruler of a particular territorial and tribal group. In all probability the title was held by the rulers of large territories such as Bactria and Sogdia, which incorporated smaller territorial units, such as the above-mentioned provinces and oases (Gabaza, Bubacene, Paraetacene, and others).

On the basis of information from the Avesta, the historian and linguist I.M. Dyakonov suggested that linked areas such as 'Mauru Hariva', i.e. an alliance of Margiana with Aria (Herat), may also have existed in Central Asia. These were loose military federations resembling the federations of Mesopotamian cities of the first dynasties of Kish and Uruk (27th–26th centuries BC).

Hence, many sources appear to indicate that in the pre-Achaemenid period, i.e. before the second half of the 6th century BC in Central Asia, two titles were being used for rulers with the highest status – *kavi* and '*dahyupati* of all *dahyus*'– which ancient Greek writers regarded as equivalent to the title of *basileus*.

It is possible that all of these titles denoted equivalent status in the hierarchical structure of the confederative-type state associations that existed in the central and western areas of Central Asia in the first half of the 1st millennium BC. This type of statehood emerged locally and subsequently, after the period of Achaemenid and Hellenistic states, became one of the main types of state here. The Kangju, Yuezhi and Hephthalite states were similar confederative states, although more highly developed.

Between 539 and 529 BC the regions of Central Asia were conquered by the Achaemenids, and for almost two centuries (until 329 BC, when the army of Alexander the Great invaded Central Asia), the ancient Persian royal titles were prevalent here: *shah* for 'King' and *shahanshah* for 'King of Kings'.

Central Asia itself was divided into special administrative units – satrapies – corresponding to the historical and cultural regions of pre-Achaemenid times:

Bactria, Parthia and Khorezm. They were headed by satraps appointed on the personal instructions of the Achaemenid 'king of kings'. The largest of these satrapies was Bactria, whose satrap was usually a son of the king, confirming its unique and very important role.

During the Achaemenid period, besides satrapies, smaller administrative units ruled by rulers from the local aristocracy, such as Sisimithres, the ruler of Nautaca province, or rulers of the small provinces of Paretacene and Gabaza also existed in Central Asia. However, the local titles for these rulers are not available in written sources.

With the conquest of the southern regions of Central Asia by Alexander the Great and the installation of the Seleucid and then Graeco-Bactrian kings here, from the mid-3rd century BC until the end of the 1st or the early 2nd century AD, exclusively Hellenic titles were being used: *basileus* for 'king' and *basileus basileon* for 'king of kings'. With regard to the local titles of rulers, it appears that at this time in Central Asia there were no states, apart from those of Greek origin mentioned above, whose status corresponded to that of kingdom-like states. The only exception seems to have been Khorezm, whose ruler, Pharasmanes, or Phrataphernes as he is also known, came to Maracanda to see Alexander the Great with a proposal of friendship and cooperation. In Greek texts he is referred to as *basileus*, i.e. 'king' (Arrian, IV, 15, 4).

Freed from Seleucid domination in the middle of the 3rd century BC, the Parthian kings nevertheless retained the Greek title for 'king' and corresponding epithets, at least on coin legends.

The creation of titles in other historical and cultural areas of Central Asia, in particular in Transoxiana, which had broken free from Greek domination, followed a different process. Some, regions, like Sogdia or Bukhara, had probably already broken free by the beginning of the 2nd century BC. Others, like Northern Bactria, did so at the beginning of the second half of the 2nd century BC. However, the titles used to designate their rulers evolved differently, depending on the prevailing role of particular cultural influences or on ethnic factors.

The main source of information for this period is coins minted in imitation of Graeco-Bactrian coins from the 2nd–1st centuries BC, with legends in the language of Khorezm, Bactria and Sogdia appearing at a particular point bearing the titles of rulers of various possessions in Transoxiana. The most distinctive features of these titles are of Aramaic and Yuezhi-Kushan origin, and hence this phase in the development of rulers' titulature can be described as the Aramaic-Kushan period. For example, the linguist W.B. Henning discovered that the coin inscription on imitations of Euthydemus tetradrachms, which had been circulated and minted in Bukhara as early as the 2nd century BC, contained the Aramaic ideogram *MR'Y* (pronounced *mrai*). The original meaning of this ideogram was 'master', but given that it applied to the rulers of Central Asia it is usually taken to refer to a ruler, but not one of royal status.

It follows that the possessions governed by rulers with the title *MR'Y* were not kingdom-like states, in the true sense of the word. The title *MR'Y* also appears on Southern Sogdian silver coins depicting Heracles and Zeus. These coins also bear the name of the ruler, which the archaeologist E.V. Zeymal has read as *'ywnwn MR'Y*, whereas the author of this work, using a restored prototype of the inscription, believes it reads *rtt MR'Y*. Judging by the archaic rendering of the letter *aleph*, similar to the *aleph* on the imitations of the tetradrachms of Euthydemus, it is probable that these coins began to be minted in the second half of the 2nd or in the 1st century BC.

Around the same time, ancient Khorezmian B- and C-group coins dating from the 1st century BC to the 1st century AD are inscribed with a different, higher-status title, in Aramaic. The coins are inscribed with *MLK'*, the title of a supreme ruler (king) of state entities varying in their political relevance, but of significantly higher status than of those state entities headed by rulers with the title *MR'Y*. The double title of Aramaic origin *MR'Y MLK'* meaning 'master king' or 'lord king' appears on the D-group coins which began to be minted in the 4th–5th centuries AD.

A similar dual title, *xwβ k'w*, of Iranian origin, denotes 'lord king', where the title *xwβ* is equivalent to *MR'Y* ('master'), and *k'w* is equivalent to *MLK'* ('king'). These appear, as has been said above, on Bukharkhudat coins from the 5th century AD and continued to be used until the 7th–8th centuries AD.

This suggests that unlike other dominions in Transoxiana in the first centuries AD, Khorezm was a state entity with a higher status – except for Bactria, which was part of the Kushan kingdom, and so its rulers had a much higher status than the rulers of ancient Khorezm.

It is therefore fair to assume that in the period from the 2nd–1st centuries BC to the first centuries AD, the rulers of Khorezm, Bukhara and Kesh (Southern Sogdia) held titles of Aramaic origin. Unfortunately, there is no clear information about this relating to Samarkand Sogdia, as the legends on the coins minted there at that time show only names, but no titles. However, based on Chinese texts showing that the rulers of the land of Kan (Samarkand Sogdia) belonged to the house of Zhaowu, i.e. Yuezhi, we can assume that these titles were of Yuezhi origin. Hyrcodes, apparently the founder of this house, as well as other rulers of Sogdia who issued coins, in particular, with the image of an archer, could, like his Yuezhi brother-in-arms Kujula Kadphises, use the title of a tribal leader, *yabghu*, which was possibly of Yuezhi origin. In any case, the Yuezhi (Kushan) chief Kujula Kadphises was the first ruler to have this title appear on coins.

The reasons why titles of Aramaic origin appear on coins from large areas of Transoxiana, except Bactria, remain unclear. It is possible that this is related to the spread of the Aramaic alphabet and language, which became the official language and writing system for the administration of the state and for record keeping (as it did in Achaemenid Iran). At any rate, according to V.A. Livshits, the first examples of texts in ancient Khorezmian script, which is related to Aramaic (or perhaps it is still Aramaic), that have been found so far date back to the 4th–3rd centuries BC.

The creation of titles in Southern Transoxiana followed a different process and was strongly connected to the emergence and development of the Kushan state. Titles of the rulers of this state were of Saka-Khotanese, Yuezhi, Greek, Bactrian and Chinese origin. According to Chinese records, the rulers of five Yuezhi possessions, which included Guishuang (Kuei-shuang, i.e. Kushan), used the title *hsi-hou* (*xihou*) or *hi-heu*, which, some scholars believe, is equivalent to the title *shanyu*, used by Hun (Xiongnu) and other rulers of nomadic tribes in Inner Asia. However, many scholars consider it equivalent to the title *yabghu* – a leader of nomadic tribes.

Coins of Kushan (or Heraeus, as some scholars believe the issuer's name to be) have the Greek title *tyrannos* (tyrant), comparable to the Etruscan *turan* ('mistress, lady'), and therefore equivalent to the Aramaic *MR'Y*, which had the same meaning – 'master', 'lord'. At the same time, the title *MR'Y*, as we have demonstrated above, was used by the rulers of Bukhara and Southern Sogdia (and much later by Khorezmian rulers as well).

Thus, the rulers of the different dominions that emerged in the 2nd–1st centuries BC in Transoxiana bore almost the same titles in terms of political significance, but the titles had different ethnic origins – Aramaic and Greek (*MR'Y*, *MLK'* and *tyrannos*, *basileus*).

According to J. Kennedy, the title *tyrant* found on the so-called Heraeus coinage reflects the vassal condition of its bearer, but in the Greek tradition, a tyrant was someone who forcibly seized power in a *polis* to establish sole rule, and the fundamental characteristic of tyranny is one-person rule. In Greek history, alongside tyrants of small, insignificant territories, are examples of tyrants who ruled large territories and possessed unlimited power. Examples are Peisistratus in Athens, Dionysius I and II and Hieron I and II of Syracuse, and the tyrants of Samos and Corinth.

If this title was used for Kushan (Heraeus), then we can assume that the first Kushan ruler known to historians came to power by force and by subjugating other Yuezhi rulers. It would also suggest that the process of Yuezhi unification under Kushan rule began earlier than is recorded in Chinese texts, and also that it was not Kujula Kadphises who tried to create the first state of Kushan, but Kushan himself. The area of distribution of the Heraeus coins does not contradict this assumption; they were widespread throughout most of Bactria, especially in the east, and also in Gandhara. Kushan's successor in the rise of the Kushan state, Kujula Kadphises, bore other titles. On all of the four earliest types of coins with Kharoshthi legends he is referred to as 'Kushana Yavuasa/Yavugasa', which means '*yabghu* Kushan'. This title, written in Greek on his coins, is rendered as *Zaooy*, which also means leader or chief of nomadic tribes.

There is some disagreement about the interpretation of the ethnic origin of this title. Some scholars consider the title *yabghu* to be Turkic, others believe it to be Saka-Khotanese, i.e. originally of East Iranian origin before it became incorporated in Turkic languages.

Later, apparently during the second period of the reign of Kujula Kadphises, royal titles of Indian origin *maharaja* and *rajatiraja* ('great king') and 'king of kings' appeared on his coins. The next king, Soter Megas, who is now identified with Wima I Takto or Sadashkana, bore the Greek title *basileus basileon*, 'king of kings'. The same Greek title was retained by his successors, Wima Kadphises and Kanishka.

The titles of Kushan kings start to become more grandiose and significant under Wima Kadphises, when the Kushan state included vast territories of northern and central India. The titles of Kadphises II are mainly of Indian origin, although the traditional Greek title *basileus basileon* was still being used. At the same time, the Iranian title *shahi* was used for the first time in relation to a Kushan king in the Mathura inscription. Later, in the Bactrian form *shao* or in the combined form *shaonano shao*, this title was used by all Kushan kings from Kanishka I to Kanishka III inclusive.

On his coins, Wima Kadphises is referred to as '*maharaja rajatiraja, sarvaloga ishvara, mahishvara*', i.e. 'the king of kings, lord of the world' (Maheshwara is one of the epithets of the Hindu god Shiva). Furthermore, a number of epigraphic inscriptions ascribe to Wima Kadphises yet another title – *devaputra* – 'son of god', which, according to some scholars, beginning with E. Thomas, is a borrowing from Chinese practice whereby Chinese emperors of the Han dynasty were called 'sons of heaven'. B.N. Mukherjee, however, does not rule out the possibility of some Greek and Arsacid influence here.

Unlike his predecessor, Kadphises II, who favoured Indian traditions, Kanishka I based his administrative, religious and linguistic policies on Bactrian practices. In particular, he introduced a language reform, something which has long been confirmed by coin legends and more recently by the Rabatak inscription. In coin legends, the Greek title *basileus basileon* was replaced by the equivalent Bactrian title *shaonano shao*, which was a borrowing from the Saka language and which replicated the Old Persian formulation *kshayathiyanam kshayathia* – 'king of kings'.

Indian titles disappeared from the coin legends while epigraphic inscriptions used other Bactrian titles, such as *xoadēo* (in Surkh Kotal and Dilberzhin) originating from Old Persian **xwatāwya*, i.e. autocrat or sovereign, used just like *shao* as a synonym for the word 'king'. The same title, but in the form *xdeo,* was widespread in Bactria and Tokharistan up to the 8th century AD.

An inscription from Surkh Kotal also uses other Bactrian titles of Kanishka, emphasising his divine origins in titles such as *bagoshao* ('god-king') and *bagopouro* ('son of god'), equal to the Indian *devaputra* and Chinese *tien-tzu.*

From around the end of the 3rd century or beginning of the 4th century AD, after the collapse of the Kushan state, titles such as *shao* and *xoadēo* appeared in a somewhat modified form, sometimes *shayo* and *xdeo,* and though preserved, they had lost their former significance. The rulers who bore these titles were often rulers of small territories, such as Shao Goboziko in the Termez area or Shao Rogoz(iko) in Chaganian. This process of losing the former significance of the titulature continued into the early medieval period.

In the 3rd and 4th centuries AD, the old Aramaic titles *MR'Y* and *MLK'* were used to designate rulers throughout almost the whole of the Central Asian interfluvial area, and sometimes used in the combination *MR'Y MLK',* as in Khorezm. The only exceptions were Bukhara and Northern Tokharistan. Copper coins from Bukhara dating from the 4th century AD include an image of an altar along with the extremely ancient title *k'w.*

In Tokharistan, conquered by the Sassanians, probably under Shapur I (241–272), Middle Persian was used for the titles of rulers. At this time, Tokharistan was a separate province under the Sassanians, and on Kushano-Sassanian coins its rulers are referred to in the legends as *kws'n MLK'* ('King of the Kushans'), *RB'kws'n MLK'* ('Great King of the Kushans'), and *RB'kws'n MLK'n MLK'* ('Great King of the Kings of the Kushans').

Sassanian Kushan coins use the same titles, but in Middle Persian: instead of *shaonano shao koshano* they have *oozorko koshano shohono shoho* or *oozorko koshano shoho* ('Great King of Kings of Kushan' or 'Great King of Kushan').

This analysis of the evolution of the titulature of the rulers of Transoxiana demonstrates that the title 'king', if this is what the title *kavi* implies, was being applied to rulers as early as the beginning of the 1st millennium BC. There then followed a big gap in its use until the 5th century AD, when its use was revived on Bukharkhudat coins. From the middle of the 6th to the end of the 4th century BC, Transoxiana was incorporated into the Achaemenid kingdom, whose rulers bore ancient Persian royal titles *Shah* ('King') and *Shahanshah* ('King of Kings'). After Alexander the Great's conquest and with the creation of the Seleucid and Graeco-Bactrian kingdoms, the ancient Persian titles were replaced by the equivalent Greek titles *basileus* and *basileus basileon,* which continued to be used here until the late 1st and early 2nd century AD.

The rulers of the remaining territories in Transoxiana (in Sogdia, Bukhara, Chach) – to judge from coins found there – were using the title *MR'Y,* which was hierarchically below the title 'king' as represented by *MLK'*, starting in the second half of the 2nd century BC, i.e. after the collapse of the Graeco-Bactrian kingdom and after the establishment of rulers of Yuezhi origin.

This situation continued throughout antiquity until the early medieval period, i.e. up to the 4th century AD. Only rulers of two regions in Transoxiana in antiquity had a title of the highest rank. These were the rulers of Khorezm, referred to on coins as *MLK'* ('King'), and the rulers of Bactria/Tokharistan, which was a part of the Kushan state. The elevated status of these kings meant that their titles were comparable only with those found in the most significant states of the ancient world – China, Parthia and Rome.

As regards Kangju, this apparently confederative state did not have a single confederate mint producing a uniform coinage, and so we have no idea of what title or status its ruler possessed.

It should be noted that the Chinese textual sources mention five Kangju possessions. However, there are doubts over their locations, including the claim that some of them were supposedly located within Sogdia, Bukhara and Khorezm. The same Chinese sources claim that rulers from the 'house of Zhaowu', i.e. of Yuezhi origin, were the heads of these possessions. It is possible that the view of the archaeologist A.N. Bernshtam, who placed these possessions along the Syr Darya, is more reliable. It would seem that the south-eastern edge of this state was Chach and the north-western one the lower reaches of the Syr Darya. Coins of this period from different regions of Transoxiana and the titles found on them suggest a high degree of political independence for these dominion-states. This is particularly the case with Khorezm, whose ruler bore a royal title.

If we construct a hierarchical ladder for the ancient states of Transoxiana, its highest point undoubtedly belongs to the Kushan kingdom (the state of the Great Yuezhi). On the rung below was the Khorezmian kingdom, and on the lower rungs dominions (but not kingdoms!) like Bukhara, Samarkand, Kesh and Chach.

The linguistic roots of the titulature of the ancient states and possessions of Transoxiana varied, depending on different circumstances, notably the political domination of particular states, and on cultural traditions. Aramaic, Greek, Old and Middle Persian, Indian, Saka-Khotanese, Bactrian and Sogdian were all used for these titles, illustrating how varied the historical process of the formation of states and dominions in Transoxiana was, and how many different ethnic groups were involved in them during the stages of their development.

2.4

THE EVOLUTION OF ARTISTIC CULTURE AND THE DEVELOPMENT OF STATES

THROUGH THE AGES, ART, LIKE MANY OTHER ASPECTS OF POLITICAL, PUBLIC and cultural life, has also reflected the features and patterns of the development of states. We can see this most clearly in ancient Egypt, Mesopotamia and Western Asia, where the development of statehood and culture, especially art, followed parallel courses, as states evolved from primary, rudimentary forms of city-states to despotic, powerful monarchies. Similarly, artistic and cultural expression developed over time from rudimentary forms to the grandiose monumental art designed to impress lesser mortals with the greatness and divine nature of the pharaohs and *shahanshahs* who commissioned them.

In other words, a given stage in the development of a state corresponds to a particular level of development of the arts: an embryonic stage of statehood corresponds to primitive forms of art, usually more decorative than fine arts, while a more evolved stage of statehood goes hand-in-hand with more developed forms of art, at times of a very high level. During so-called 'transitional phases', which generally followed the collapse of great empires and were usually accompanied by socio-economic and other upheavals, artistic expression seems to have reverted to primitive forms again, although there are sometimes exceptions to this pattern.

The development of official art has to a large extent been determined by state policy. This was true in antiquity and largely remains true today, although at times artistic consciousness leads artists to seek and realise new artistic directions that are independent of official policy.

Unlike in the case of the Near and Middle East, until recently, we had no written evidence from Central Asia of the dominant role played by state politics in the arts. However, the discovery of the Rabatak inscription, in which the Kushan king

Kanishka gave his governor Shafar instructions to build a temple and erect statues of previous kings – of his great-grandfather Kadphises, his grandfather Wima I Takto and father Wima Kadphises – now allows us to argue that in Central Asia too, at any rate in the Kushan kingdom, the development of monumental art was largely determined by the will of kings.

Archaeological investigations in Bactria, Sogdia, Khorezm and Margiana have afforded new insights into the material and artistic culture of this vast region, which stretches from the Caspian Sea in the west, to the Pamirs in the east, and is bordered by the steppes of Kazakhstan in the north and the Hindu Kush mountains in the south. The new discoveries provide ample evidence of the main developmental stages of ancient Central Asian art, covering three major historical periods: the Achaemenid (second half of the 6th century BC to 330 BC), the Hellenistic (late 4th to second half of the 2nd century BC) and that of local antiquity (1st century BC to the 3rd–4th century AD).

In line with this argument, let us now consider the evolution of art in ancient times in the territory of Uzbekistan. The heart of its development was in the Surkhan Darya region, where a non-nomadic farming civilisation of the ancient Sapalli culture emerged in the middle of the 2nd millennium BC. At the same time, a number of forms of arts and crafts were developing, reflected in the continuous refinement of earthenware, from small bowls to the finest vases on tall, fluted legs, and in the increasing range of pottery and jewellery made with all kinds of semi-precious stones and forms of ornamentation.

Representational art, manifested in metalwork and glyptics (engraved stones), in bronze hairpins decorated with miniature animal figures and in relief depictions of mythical animals and human figures on stone and clay seals, was also typical of this period. Rudimentary monumental art also emerged in this period, in the form of small, clay, human sculptures painted in slip, yet schematic in form, as found in the Jarkutan burial grounds.

Thus the art of this epoch developed alongside and in synch with the evolutionary stages of the emerging rudimentary forms of statehood.

Art from the Achaemenid period

Ancient Greek textual sources point to the existence of well-developed and complex cities in Bactria, Sogdia and Margiana in the late 4th century BC, i.e. during the Achaemenid period.

Archaeological studies have not only confirmed the existence of these cities and settlements, but have also provided important insights into their features, structure and fortifications, as well as their material cultures. The most interesting findings have come from explorations of Erk-Kala, the ancient core of the city-site of Old Merv in Margiana, the city-sites of Afrasiab (ancient Maracanda) and Koktepa in Sogdia, the sites of Uzun-Kyr and Sangirtepa in Southern Sogdia, Kyzyltepa in Northern Bactria and Elkharas in Khorezm, as well as from several other smaller settlements of this period. There is both direct and indirect evidence about the development of monumental representational art in this region. For example, that the well-known romantic tale by the 4th-century BC writer Chares of Mytilene about Zariadres' love for Odatis, 'the most beautiful woman in Asia', which was extremely popular in Central Asia, was 'depicted in temples and palaces, as well as in private homes'.

Thus it is fair to assume the existence of monumental wall painting in both pre-Achaemenid and Achaemenid times. Evidence supporting such an assumption is provided by the fragments of multi-coloured wall painting found in Elkharas in the palace building and the associated temple dated by L.M. Levina to the late 6th–early 4th century BC. Fragments of anthropomorphic clay sculpture were also found there. Finds from Isfara in the Kanibadam district of Tajikistan are evidence of the existence of sculpture. Two three-dimensional, life-size, hollow ram heads weighing 8.1 and 14.8 kilograms and cast in bronze, dating from the 5th to the 3rd century BC, were found here. They may have been part of a single sculpture, or of a sculptural composition decorating the interior of a building, or the ornamentation of a zoomorphic throne, a feature that was widespread in Central Asia and Iran in pre-Islamic times. Another discovery, in the mountains of Sultan Uiz Dagh (Khorezm), of a stone capital decorated on its different sides with polymorphic figures of animals lying with their legs bent under them and with faces of bearded men looking in opposite directions is further evidence of the development of monumental sculptural forms. It has close similarities to the art of Achaemenid Iran.

Ceramic art of this period is notable both for its variety and for standardised vessel shapes, as well as high-quality manufacturing techniques, the use of slip for painting, and a lack of ornamentation. Painted motifs in red and brown on the surfaces of vessels, which were widespread in the pottery of the 1st millennium BC, all but disappeared in this period.

The ceramic art of this period is characterised by the refinement of vessel shapes, usually cylindrical-conical, a form that dates back to the ceramics of the preceding 7th–6th centuries BC. Cylindrical-conical ceramics were widely distributed over almost all of Central Asia from Khorezm to Bactria. Other forms of decorative art are evident in glyptics – several Achaemenid-style gems (from the collection of the History Museum of Uzbekistan in Tashkent) were apparently found on the site of Afrasiab.

Outstanding amongst this meagre range of artefacts of the Achaemenid period from Central Asia's settled agricultural areas are the numerous objects of artistic culture (small artistic objects – round metal plates, toreutics and jewellery) from the Amu Darya hoard or Oxus treasure and from the Oxus Temple treasure in Takht-i Sangin. However, if we follow a strictly academic approach, with few exceptions these objects cannot be regarded as reliable historical sources for describing Achaemenid art in Central Asia. They can only give us an idea of the kinds of treasures, and of the countries from which they came, before they accumulated in Bactrian temples over a period of several centuries. If we go by the dates when these hoards were hidden – which was much later than even the end of the Achaemenid period, and is connected to the time of Alexander's conquest of Bactria in 329 BC – we can date the artefacts to a period covering 200 years. The Amu Darya hoard was most likely concealed in the 4th century BC, and the Oxus Temple hoard on the eve of the Yuezhi invasion, i.e. at the beginning of the second half of the 2nd century BC. The objects may have been brought to the temple (or temples?) as votive offerings at any time and could have come from anywhere.

There is no question about the historical authenticity of the objects from the Temple of the Oxus in Takht-i Sangin, as the find was documented following proper archaeological methods. However, doubts about the authenticity of the Amu Darya hoard (the Oxus treasure) remain. Strictly speaking, it is a collection of items obtained in various circumstances in Rawalpindi (Pakistan). Some of them do indeed belong to the Amu Darya hoard, and were possibly found at the Takht-i Qobad site. Other objects, however, most likely have been collected together at Rawalpindi but consist of possible finds from Gandhara or Kabulistan.

There is also some doubt about the provenance of coins that make up part of the treasure, as these were 'added' (i.e. described as belonging to the hoard) by the academic E.V. Zeymal from various museum collections (whose find-spots are unclear). All the more so because, to date, no coins from the Greek cities and Achaemenid satraps of Asia Minor dating from the 5th to 4th centuries BC have been found in the territory of Central Asia, including Bactria. Only recently, apparently, a hoard of Achaemenid *sigloi* was found in southern Turkmenistan, and some of these have ended up in private collections in Tashkent.

Naked youth. Silver. 5th–4th century BC.

Examination of the early part of the Amu Darya hoard has made it possible to identify five groups of gold and silver objects according to their place of origin:

1. Pre-Achaemenid objects from Media and Lurestan;
2. Objects from the Achaemenid period, from Western Iran, which may have belonged to kings or satraps;
3. Objects made in accordance with traditions in Asia Minor dating from before the end of the 4th century BC;
4. Objects of local Bactrian origin from the same period;
5. Objects made in accordance with Scythian-Siberian traditions.

Only the last two groups of objects can be said to reflect the distinctive features of Central Asian art in Achaemenid times, and then only the development of the art of toreutics and jewellery. As regards the objects in the first three groups, one hypothesis suggests that they were brought to the Bactrian temple when Alexander the Great's troops were stationed there, or as trophies of war captured by the Macedonian army from major Iranian cities and then given as offerings to the temple. But this is only one possible hypothesis of many that might be put forward, provided that it can be proved that the Temple of the Oxus (to which the archaeologist I.R. Pichikyan linked the Amu Darya treasure) had already been built at the time of Alexander the Great. The absence of habitation layers with the cylindrical-conical pottery characteristic of the 5th–4th centuries BC at Takht-i Sangin is significant, and suggests that the temple was built later, namely in the Seleucid or Graeco-Bactrian periods.

It is unlikely that the Amu Darya hoard is composed of some of the precious metal objects selected from the treasure of the Temple of the Oxus. It is clear that we are dealing with two different 'collections' from different times. The first, the Amu Darya hoard, is from an earlier period, namely the 6th–4th centuries BC, with an almost complete absence of objects from Hellenistic times (3rd–2nd centuries BC). This hoard was probably hidden between the late 4th and the early 3rd century BC, as the scholar R. Ghirshman justifiably surmised. The second, the treasure of the Temple of the Oxus, is more recent and dates from the 3rd century to the beginning of the second half of the 2nd century BC and includes a small number of objects from Achaemenid times but mostly objects from Hellenistic times.

The very existence of two temples located close to each other (in this case 5 km apart), even assuming that they functioned simultaneously, is a common phenomenon in religious practice. The assumption that the Amu Darya hoard belongs to the temple treasure is questionable. Even though most of it consists of religious, votive objects, the hoard also includes many domestic objects. The suggestion that it may have belonged to a Bactrian aristocratic family is also doubtful. E.V. Zeymal believes that the Amu Darya hoard is simply not big enough to be considered a part of the temple treasure or even the treasure of an entire family. It could have belonged to one rich and noble person, as for example is the case with the Dalverzin hoard, found in the house of a noble Kushan town-dweller. The gold in the entire Dalverzin hoard weighed more than the gold in the Amu Darya hoard – one gold bar alone from the Dalverzin hoard was greater than the entire amount found in the Amu Darya hoard.

It is clear that part of the Amu Darya hoard dating from the Achaemenid period and part of the treasure from the Temple of the Oxus that also dates from the Achaemenid period reflect art from countries distant from Central Asia. First of all, the artefacts have all the ideological hallmarks of Achaemenid Iranian art, with its firmly established canon, complex religious symbolism and unified but nonetheless diverse range of artistic styles: specifically Iranian and Irano-Mesopotamian, styles from Asia Minor, and Scythian-Iranian styles. The objects of Bactrian origin mainly include unfinished artistic objects such as the horse head and more than 30 thin gold plaques with the profile of an upright figure holding a bundle of staves. The many pieces of decorated jewellery could also be of Bactrian origin: there are rings with different images on their panels, bracelets finished with animal heads, pendants in the form of birds, gold plates and plaques with images of animals – horses, camels and lion-griffins. Another category of items of local origin is believed to be in the Scythian animal style. Not only the artistic objects from the Amu Darya hoard that are fashioned rather primitively, but also other – highly artistic – items could have been made in Bactria itself, which was highly developed during the Achaemenid period. Account should also be taken of the deep-rooted traditions of Bactrian fine and decorative art which can be traced back to the Bronze Age.

Art from the Hellenistic period

Hellenistic art is represented insufficiently as yet since the habitation layers of this period discovered at a number of archaeological sites, namely Afrasiab, Er-Kurgan, Old Termez and Dalverzintepa, which are all covered by thick habitation layers from later periods, are almost inaccessible to exploration. However, as in many parts of the Near and Middle East, art in these areas developed in keeping with Hellenistic traditions. At any rate, this is evident in the composition of the Amu Darya hoard found in southern Tajikistan, and objects from Takht-i Sangin, many of which were brought to these places from the Hellenistic Near East or were made in the style of Hellenistic art. These objects attest to the development in Northern Bactria of such artistic forms as monumental clay and plaster sculpture, glyptics, toreutics, jewellery, bone carving and many others. Along with Hellenistic traditions, some of these objects bear the imprint of the artistic techniques of the Scythian animal style.

Medal engraving and particularly monetary iconography were highly developed in Bactria at this time. In terms of artistic design, the coins of the Graeco-Bactrian kings were among the best in the world. The portraits on the obverse of the coins are very distinctive images of the kings, while the figures of the deities on the reverse are copies of famous Greek sculptures.

Flask. Mustahara. 2nd–1st century BC.

Art of the Yuezhi period

In the third quarter of the 2nd century BC Northern Bactria was conquered by the Yuezhi (Tokharians according to Graeco-Roman sources), who, under pressure from the Huns (Xiongnu), migrated here from an area that corresponds to the present-day Gansu province of China. Later, the Yuezhi/Tokharians conquered Southern Bactria and established a confederate Yuezhi state with Bactra as its centre, which continued to exist until Kujula Kadphises established the Kushan kingdom in the first half of the 1st century AD.

A building in Khalchayan and its unique sculptural compositions and remnants of monumental painting, surveyed by the Uzbekistan Art History Expedition in 1959–1963, can be regarded as an example of monumental works of art of the Yuezhi period. There is little agreement among scholars about the date and interpretation of this building, however. According to G.A. Pugachenkova, the building was a small palace erected at the end of the 1st millennium BC/beginning of the 1st millennium AD, and which survived for about two centuries. Over time, the main hall of the palace became a hall of deified ancestors. By contrast, the scholars B. Rowland, B.J. Stavisky and A.V. Sedov attribute the construction of the Khalchayan building to the early Kushan period, from the 1st century AD to the beginning of the 2nd century. Stavisky and Sedov both believe that this building was originally erected as the temple of a dynastic cult. However, their views on the dating and interpretation of the building are not supported by any substantial facts, as already pointed out by Pugachenkova, whose analysis of this issue is more credible.

The interpretation of the content of the sculptural scenes and of particular images is a different matter altogether. The palace at Khalchayan was a small building (35 × 20 m) made of mud-bricks with a deep six-column portico or *aiwan* on the main façade, followed by a reception hall, and a throne room with two columns; to the right and left of the central hall were lesser rooms, a guard room, and so on. The *aiwan* and the palace hall were decorated with a diverse range of sculptural compositions, with those in the main hall better preserved and those in the *aiwan* less so. The clay sculptures ranged along the walls were painted mostly in red, and sometimes in white and black. The background against which the sculptures were placed was also painted. The heads of the sculptures were fully rounded, with the lower parts to the waist in three-quarter or half-volume, and the rest descending to the feet in bas-relief. The sculptures were placed at a height of 2 metres in the form of a wide frieze, continuously passing from one wall to the next.

Pugachenkova's reconstruction consists of three distinct scenes depicting several individual human figures, riders on horseback and figures of deities. The main composition was on the throne wall, the central place with figures of the ruler and his wife seated on thrones, with sculptures of family members and local nobility on either side, and above them sculptures of a 'primitive' Athena, Heracles and Nike. The composition on the northern wall shows the ruler sitting on a low bench, with sculptures of his kinsmen and close associates from the 'Heraeus clan' to his left and right. The sculptural composition on the south wall includes a dynamic scene of a battle between lightly armed archers and heavily armed warriors – cataphracts – as they gallop towards each other on their horses.

Another panel on the walls above these compositions shows dancers, costumed entertainers and nude youths carrying heavy garlands, with sculptures of musicians, satyrs and jesters in the loops. Together, the figures depicted here reflect a range of Dionysian motifs widespread in Hellenistic art.

The images of people in the sculptural compositions are very individual and are clearly portrait-like, reflecting artistic norms of expressive realism in the visual art of Bactria, typical of the period from the 2nd century BC to the early 1st century AD.

Analysis of the Khalchayan sculptures demonstrates that although the style of art retains Hellenistic features and images of Greek deities, its main subject matter comes from another ethno-cultural environment which influenced both the form and substance of artistic expression. In Pugachenkova's interpretation the main series of sculpted scenes were dedicated to the glorification of the 'Heraeus clan'. These depict triumphal celebrations with military victories or banquets with musicians, entertainers and figures in masquerade under the protection of the gods Athena, Nike, Heracles and possibly Cybele. The interpretation that these sculptures represent the glorification of 'Heraeus clan members' is based on the predominance of a particular group of sculptures that share typological and ethnic features: thick black hair tied and held up by a headband, thick sideburns, small moustaches, square faces with large, slightly slanted eyes. These features of this group of sculptures have strong similarities with the depiction of the ruler on Kushan coins from this period known as 'Heraeus'.

However, the attribution of the name Heraeus to this group of sculptures may be incorrect because the legend depicted on these coins has itself been misinterpreted. The legend on the tetradrachms consists of four words: *ΤΥΡΑΝΝΟΥΝΤΟΣ ΗΙΑΟΥ ΣΑΝΑΒ ΚΟΡΡΑΝΟΥ*, which translates as 'Of the supreme ruler (Tyrant) "Heraeus" Sanab Kushan', where the first word of the legend has been generally interpreted as a title, the second as a personal name, the third as a personal name or name of a region, and the fourth as the name of a tribe or dynasty in the genitive.

Taking into account more recent numismatic data, this legend should be read and understood as follows: the first word is a Greek title, the second is also a title, but not a local one and possibly Yuezhi, the third word is a nickname (on some coins it is Greek *ΑΝΤΕΙΧ*, on others it is Iranian *ΣΑΝΑΒ*, but has the same meaning – 'repeller of the enemy'), and the fourth word is the personal name 'Kushan'.

In all likelihood, the ruler who issued the tetradrachms and oboli and founded the new Yuezhi dynasty was Kushan and not 'Heraeus' (which seems somewhat far-fetched). Subsequently, all rulers of the Kushan kingdom, put their founder's name on their coins as a mark of respect, just as for many centuries the rulers of the Parthian state, descended from the nomadic Parni tribe, retained the name of the founder of the Parthian dynasty – Arsaces – on the legends of their coins.

The combination of two titles can already be found on coins from Khorezm from the first centuries AD, containing *MR'Y MLK'* ('lord king') in the inscription, and later on Bukharkhudat coins as *xwβ k'w*, which stands for 'ruler-king'. The first two words in the legend on the tetradrachms of Kushan can be interpreted in the same way.

Another point to consider is that the legends on the coins minted in the ancient states of Central Asia up to the 3rd–4th centuries AD did not carry ethnic and dynastic names, but only the title plus name, and occasionally an honoured nickname, as on Graeco-Bactrian and Parthian coins, plus name of the founder of the dynasty, as on Parthian and, as it now turns out, Kushan coins.

Yuezhi head. Clay. Khalchayan. 1st century AD.

Thus, it is fair to assume that the Khalchayan building was indeed a palace, later transformed into a temple of deified ancestors. Its principal sculptural compositions were devoted to the glorification and accession to power of the new Yuezhi dynasty, the Kushan. The sculpture of the ruler in the reception scene most probably depicts the founder of the new dynasty, Kushan. The main figures in the Khalchayan sculpture depict a generalised ethnic Yuezhi type, rather than the representatives of any particular clan. The sculptural compositions from the Khalchayan palace could only have been created after this part of Northern Bactria was incorporated into the Kushan kingdom, which, judging by numismatic data, happened under the reign of the son of Kujula Kadphises – Wima I Takto. Clearly the Khalchayan sculptures are an integral part of the genesis of dynastic art of the Kushan state, or the Great Yuezhi state, as it is referred to in ancient Chinese texts. Other forms of art from the Yuezhi period have yet to be discovered. However, we can mention the development of terracotta as reflected in some of the types of terracotta statuettes that have been found.

Ancient art from the territory of Uzbekistan reached its peak of development in antiquity, the time when the powerful Kushan and Kangju states came into being. This was a time when cities flourished in a dense network, along with smaller towns, across the territory of Transoxiana. The Silk Road flourished too, promoting intellectual and cultural exchange between the East and the West. Central Asia played the role of both an intermediary and a transmitter of many of its own cultural achievements, and Sogdian colonies emerged along the length of the eastern part of the route, all the way to the capital of Han China, Chang'an. The economy, based on agriculture, and crafts developed intensively in parallel with commodity-money relations.

All this could not but have an impact on the development of art. Representational art evolved and developed rapidly in this period, along with new forms of art such as three-dimensional, wall-mounted, monumental clay and plaster, painted sculpture, as can be seen in the diverse compositions in Khalchayan, Dalverzintepa, Fayaztepa, Karatepa and Toprak-Kala. The interiors of many palaces and temples were decorated with monumental wall paintings using a rich palette of colours and a range of secular and religious themes. Terracotta artefacts made from moulds, as well as glyptics and jewellery, were widespread. Local craftsmen were well acquainted with the art of working metal and stone, as

Kushan head. Clay. 1st century BC–1st century AD.

is reflected, in particular, in the sculptural reliefs of the Airtam frieze. In addition to Hellenistic and Gandharan influences, the artistic techniques of all these forms of art reflect local traditions dating back to ancient times.

Art of the Kushan period

Southern Central Asia became part of the Kushan state under the reign of the great king Wima I Takto in the middle or early second half of the 1st century AD and remained part of it until the conquest by the Sassanians under Shapur I (AD 241–272). The Hissar mountain range formed the northern boundary of the Kushan kingdom and here they built a strong fortification system, which separated Bactria from Sogdia, and the Kangju state from the Kushan kingdom. As a result, Kushan art found here represents the Bactrian art of the period.

Art from this period originating in the Surkhan Darya province of Uzbekistan and northern Afghanistan is richly varied and distinctive and includes examples of monumental sculpture, wall painting, architectural decoration, terracotta, pottery, bone carving, glyptics, jewellery and artistic metalwork. Kushan art developed along two main lines – Indo-Buddhist and local Bactrian, which was largely Hellenistic – with some of influences of nomadic art traditions, especially in the decorative arts.

Monumental sculpture is a particularly notable art form of the region, with a tradition dating back to Seleucid and Graeco-Bactrian times, as the excavations of the Temple of the Oxus have revealed. The main materials used were clay, plaster and stone, although metal sculpture or sculptures combined with metalwork may also have existed in the area, as evidenced by the statuette of a man made of wood with a thin silver overlay found at Kampyrtepa. Clay sculptures were made by hand, using a technique whereby several layers were applied to an inner shell with the overall shape of the figure then being defined, followed by a carefully sculpted layer of the same clay or plaster and painted in the colours of the body and face. Stamps were often used to impress individual facial details and ornaments. As a rule, clay sculpture in front of walls or mounted on walls was worked in high relief. Stone sculpture was rendered in friezes (as in Airtam) or in separate sculptural groups of seated (also in Airtam) or standing figures (as in Surkh Kotal). Bactrian sculpture was generally monumental and had a strictly frontal perspective. However, judging by the images of kings and deities on coins, which are apparently copies of monumental sculptures, profile and three-quarter images were clearly not unknown.

In Bactria, monumental sculpture, designed primarily to be installed in temples, embodied two main areas of thematic and ideological content: religious and secular. No mythological images have been found to date. The Buddhist religious sculptures are numerous: they include works from Airtam, Dalverzintepa, Karatepa, Fayaztepa and other less significant sites. The Bactrian religious sculptures are represented by far fewer samples: they include works from Dalverzintepa, Surkh Kotal and other sites. Evidence for how widespread the use of Bactrian deities was comes from the inscriptions of Surkh Kotal and especially Rabatak, giving us the names of the statues of the Zoroastrian deities in the temple of Kanishka: Umma, Nana, Ahura Mazda, Mazdovan, Sroshard, Narasa and Mihr. There is no doubt that other Bactrian temples also had sculptures of local deities, but so far the only evidence of their existence is the sculpted head of a goddess from the temple at Dalverzintepa. It is probably the goddess Nana, depicted as an older woman wearing a band around her head.

Secular art also became widespread in the Kushan period, with 'dynastic art' assuming particular importance. The Rabatak inscription also makes it clear that alongside the statues of patron deities installed in the temples of Bactria were statues of kings. The statues were not just of the ruling king such as Kanishka but of all his predecessors: his great-grandfather Kujula Kadphises, his grandfather Wima I Takto and his father Wima Kadphises. The stone statue found at Mat of a king on a throne, since established as Wima I Takto by the numismatist J. Cribb, is another example of this phenomenon.

The stone statue from Surkh Kotal of a standing, richly attired figure is probably that of a king (perhaps Kanishka) and is notable for its size and frontal pose. It is possible that the sculpted block from Airtam bearing a Bactrian inscription and showing a (seated?) male figure with a female figure standing next to him also depicts a king (perhaps Huvishka).

Secular preoccupations are also reflected in the clay and plaster depictions of donors from the rural Buddhist shrine of Dalverzintepa. The most impressive sculpture here is the head of a 'Kushan prince' with noble features and a high conical hat, apparently decorated with gold plaques. G.A. Pugachenkova compared this sculpted head with the head of King Antiochus from the Commagene shrine, noting their stylistic similarity. In addition, a careful comparison of images of King Vasudeva I of Kushan on gold coins with the head of the 'Kushan prince' from Dalverzintepa also reveals a close similarity in their facial features and the

Terracotta figure. Parthian. Kampyrtepa. 1st century BC–1st century AD.

shapes of their headdresses and jewellery. It is possible, therefore, that the sculpted head of the nameless 'Kushan prince' is that of the Kushan king Vasudeva I. Bactrian monumental sculpture is clearly an outstanding artistic phenomenon, embodying Hellenistic, Indo-Buddhist and Bactrian features.

The earliest examples of wall painting in Central Asia are the paintings from Pessejikdepe dating back to the Neolithic period of the 6th millennium BC. After a break of several millennia wall painting reappeared in Central Asia in the period we know as antiquity. The earliest examples are fragments of murals from Khalchayan from the early 1st century. Wall paintings from the 1st–2nd centuries AD are thought to be from temple murals of Bactrian deities, from palace buildings at Dalverzintepa, the Buddhist cave complex of Karatepa, and the Buddhist monastery above ground in Old Termez. Paintings from this time were also found at Zartepa. Beyond Bactria, monumental wall painting from the Kushan period has been found in Toprak-Kala (2nd–3rd centuries AD).

Judging by the locations of finds, monumental wall paintings were probably part of the interior decoration of both religious and secular buildings. Paintings covered the walls of *aiwans*, halls and individual rooms. They were painted with mineral paint on an adhesive mortar applied to the surface of dry clay-plaster or a thin layer of alabaster. The paintings were ornamental (and perhaps also narrative), featuring secular, religious or mythological motifs.

Small fragments of images with secular themes found at the palace in Khalchayan show heads of two boys – one with Hellenistic features, the other with possibly Inner Asian features. A fragment of another painting, probably also secular, from the palace of Dalverzintepa shows a helmeted Bactrian soldier with the muzzle of an armoured horse.

Religious paintings depict two religious trends – Buddhist and local Bactrian. The surviving fragment of a wall painting from Fayaztepa of a scene, which had depicted many figures, shows ten remaining individuals: the Buddha with local deities walking towards him with halos above their heads. An inscription bearing the name of the fire deity Pharro can still be seen above the head of one of them.

Paintings from Karatepa have also survived only in a highly fragmented state. One of the fragments depicts a scene with the Buddha with a halo above his head and in a mandala, sitting under a Bodhi tree with monks. Another fragment shows the Buddha sitting in the *dhyana-mudra* pose. Another fragment, somewhat strangely for a Buddhist shrine, probably depicts the Zoroastrian rite of the purification of bones before burial in a *naus* – a Zoroastrian funerary structure.

The fragment of a wall painting discovered on the floor of the temple of the goddess Nana at Dalverzintepa reflects the indigenous Bactrian religion. The reconstructed scene shows the goddess seated on a zoomorphic throne being approached by a priest dressed in white with an infant child raised above his head, together with a priestess with two infants in her arms. The meaning of the scene remains unclear, but it clearly relates to some kind of religious ritual – perhaps the offering of the infants to the goddess for blessing or for a ritual of sacrifice.

There is no unpainted space in the temple painting: the figures are all depicted on a red background filled with plant tendrils and six-petalled flowers. The palette is quite extensive: black, blue, brown and yellow are all used. The skin of the infants and female figures is painted in pale pink, while the male figures are red. The figures have fine black outlines. An effect of three-dimensionality is achieved through the use of light and shade and frequent red hatching at the edges of the outlines. The paintings have an unusual style of portrayal: all the characters have expressive and finely traced faces, but no attempt has been made at an anatomically correct reproduction of the hands and fingers of the infants. It is possible that this was a deliberate attempt to convey their helplessness and total submission. The temple paintings are vibrant, dynamic and expressive, and without the hieratic characteristics of religious art.

The entire composition is framed by ornamental borders with either a combination of plant tendrils (two- or three-leaved) and geometric patterns (white circles on a black background) or simple bands of red, black and brown. The upper part of the wall of the room was decorated with paintings on alabaster of a running wave motif that was widespread in Hellenistic art.

Several frescoes have also been found in a room used for worship in a craftsman's house in Dalverzintepa. One of these is a scene with several figures and a horse with a man standing next to it and women looking down at them from a two-tier balcony. The whole scene may well be mythological. The monumental painting of an enormous bird in one of the buildings at Zartepa may also have mythological content.

Thus, while preserving Hellenistic features in the use of colour, technique, manner and ornamental motifs, Kushan wall paintings are filled with new content and artistic styles. Despite the small number of examples found, the paintings point to the existence of a large and distinctive school of mural painting in Bactria, and its significant impact on the development of painting in Khorezm and Serindia (Miran) is borne out by the style and painterly techniques used.

2.5

FINANCIAL SERVICES AND MONEY IN ANCIENT STATES IN CENTRAL ASIA

Tax (revenue collection) systems

THE VERY EXISTENCE OF A STATE IS DETERMINED BY THE PRESENCE OF various kinds of institutions, including tax-collection systems. We have information about the existence of tax-collection systems within Central Asia, and ancient Uzbekistan in particular, only from the time it was incorporated into the Achaemenid kingdom. Around 518 BC, King Darius I (522–486 BC) began to introduce reforms to reorganise the state's administrative and financial systems. According to Herodotus, the entire territory of the Achaemenid kingdom was divided into 20 satrapies, of which Bactria, Sakasthana, Khorezm, Parthia, Sogdia and Haraiva were within the limits of Central Asia.

Each of these satrapies had to contribute a certain amount to the royal treasury measured in a unit of weight – a talent. One talent was equivalent to 25.92 kilograms. Thus, Bactria paid 360 talents of silver (9,331 kg); Sakasthana and Caspiane paid 250 talents (6,480 kg); Khorezmia, Parthia, Sogdia and Haraiva paid a total of 300 talents (7,776 kg).

This means that the Achaemenid kingdom received annual revenues amounting to 910 talents, or about 23,587 kilograms of silver, from the whole territory of Central Asia. Judging by the total amount of the tax collected, Central Asia clearly occupied a leading position in the Achaemenid kingdom, surpassed only by the satrapies of Mesopotamia (1,000 talents) and Asia Minor (more than 1,000 talents).

The well-known account by Herodotus about the river Akes (the modern Tejen river), indicates that taxes for the use of water were also levied in the form of money for the treasury of the Achaemenid kings (III, 117). 'I have heard and know that he exacts great sums, over and above the tribute, for the opening of the gates,' writes Herodotus.

In addition to monetary taxes, the satrapies of the Achaemenid kingdom, including those in Central Asia, also had to pay taxes in kind. Thus, gold was brought from Bactria, lapis lazuli and carnelian from Sogdiana and a blue gemstone (perhaps turquoise) from Khorezm to build the palace of Darius I in Susa. The famous reliefs in the Persepolis palace depict representatives of various satrapies paying tribute to the Achaemenid king. Specifically, Bactrians are depicted with containers and two-humped camels; Sakas as leading horses and carrying objects of some kind; the Sogdians have cups in their hands and are accompanied by two two-humped camels; and the Khorezmians are shown with swords, bracelets and horses. These objects and the kinds of animals depicted on the walls of the Persepolis palace reflect the specific tributes paid by each province to the treasury of the Achaemenid kingdom.

Tax collection was the responsibility of satraps, nomarchs, town governors, village elders and tribal chiefs. Special royal tax collectors and tax inspectors also existed. According to some scholars, in certain satrapies of the Achaemenid kingdom taxes due from the population were not collected directly from the citizens, but with the help of tax-farmers. A tax-farmer was an individual who would pay taxes to the royal treasury in advance, thereby obtaining a monopoly from the state for tax collection. He would then collect taxes from the local population, while increasing the amount of tax collected. There is no clear information about the tax-collection system in Central Asia, but it is likely that it resembled one of the revenue-collection systems that were in use in other parts of the Achaemenid kingdom.

After the conquest of the southern provinces of Central Asia by Alexander the Great and their subsequent incorporation into the Seleucid and Graeco-Bactrian kingdoms, a revenue-collection system typical of the Hellenistic world was established there, but possibly adapted to local conditions. Until recently, however, we had no information about the nature of the administration of taxes and the system of taxes levied on the population of these territories. The discovery, in recent decades, of ostraca with Greek inscriptions in Ai-Khanum (northern Afghanistan) and at the site of Kampyrtepa (southern Uzbekistan) has shed some light on the issue. For example, two ostraca with Greek graffiti were found at Kampyrtepa, 30 kilometres west of Termez on the banks of the Oxus river. One of them indicates a monetary unit or measure of weight, 15 drachmas, and the other a measure of liquid, 7 *hoi* (*hoi* is an ancient Greek liquid measure equivalent to 3.28 litres). These two small examples of Greek graffiti are important in helping to understand aspects of the taxation system in Northern Bactria during the Hellenistic period, as aside from these two graffiti no other inscriptions indicating units of money and weights have been found there so far, or indeed, anywhere else in Central Asia.

As is well known, several vessels found in the treasury of the Ai-Khanum palace have inscription-labels with references to drachmas and ancient Indian stamped coins ('karshapana'). According to the archaeologist C. Rapin, these containers, intended for storing revenues from taxpayers, were collected by special tax officials for subsequent transfer to the royal treasury, where they were kept. The inscriptions even mention the names of the officials guarding this treasury: Zenon, Timodem, Strabo, Philiskous, Nikerat.

The Ptolemaic ostraca, which originated in Egypt, were a different method of recording financial documents used in the Hellenistic world. They are a form of receipt issued by bankers and tax collectors on receiving levies.

Owing to the brevity of the inscription and its uniqueness, it is difficult to determine what kind of financial record the Greek graffito from Kampyrtepa, on which drachmas were recorded, represents. It is clear, however, that it is a different kind of record to the ones suggested by the Ai-Khanum inscriptions, as the latter usually include the names of several officials, while the Kampyrtepa graffito is anonymous. Moreover, the graffito does not cover a whole vessel, but only a fragment of one, suggesting it was not used for storing deposits. In all likelihood, the graffito was an ostracon used as a receipt similar to the aforementioned ostraca of Ptolemaic Egypt.

The second example, the graffito designating 7 *hoi*, is a similarly unique document. Seven *hoi* are equivalent to 22.96 litres, although this inscription was found on a vessel that would have contained barely a litre even when full. Hence, the ostracon with this inscription was probably a kind of receipt given to record the amount of some liquid received, most probably wine. Documents or records of this kind were typical of Parthian Nisa.

The finds at Ai-Khanum and, to some extent, at Kampyrtepa all point to the existence of an advanced system of tax collection and accounting in southern Central Asia in Graeco-Bactrian times and therefore, of some kind of institution for revenue collection. This is confirmed by a remarkable tax document on parchment dating from the early 2nd century BC which was acquired in north-west Afghanistan and subsequently by the Ashmolean Museum in Oxford. It has been published in English and French. The document, drawn up in Bactria under King Antimachus Theos, mentions a certain Menodotus, a tax collector, and Diodorus, an inspector of state revenues, i.e. the person who supervised the collection of taxes. According to C. Rapin, the toponym Asangorna mentioned in the document corresponds to the medieval Sangaran, later Sangaraka – a small town or district situated in the upper reaches of the Balkhab river in Western Bactria.

The presence of a tax collection system in another Central Asian state, the Parthian kingdom, is evident from ostraca with Parthian inscriptions found at the New Nisa site. Studies have shown that inscriptions on ostraca from Nisa reflect a system of taxation of vineyards located around this first capital of the Arsacids in the 2nd–1st centuries BC. The inscriptions include the names of vineyards on which taxes were levied, such as Nakbakan, Natpak and Kashashi, as well as the word *khum* – the word for a large vessel used to store wine. Finally, the inscriptions detail the amount of tax, the year of payment and, most significantly, the name of the official who drew up the document, along with his title *marubar* ('accountant').

For example:

1. 'According to this receipt (?) from the vineyard due to be taxed … 10 (?) *khums* were delivered. Vahuman, accountant. Paid for the year 141 (or 140).'
2. 'According to this receipt (?) from the vineyard due to be taxed (?) (from the locality) called Htrk (?), 8 (or 7) vessels, paid for the year 133 were delivered. Mihrdat, accountant (?).'

A detailed study of the content of the inscriptions on the ostraca from Nisa by the scholars M. Masson, I.M. Dyakonov, M. Dyakonov and V.A. Livshits led them to the following conclusions:

1. The tax collected was recorded on a special document, a type of a tax receipt.
2. There were two categories of land – taxable and non-taxable. The term (*a*)*baz* was used to denote the land tax.
3. The amount of tax paid was measured in large vessels called *khums*, which had a standard size and served as measures of capacity.
4. The tax was not levied on any particular individual, but on the community, as indicated by the nature of the formula 'delivered'.
5. The collection of the tax involved strict record keeping by the state and the tax was paid annually.
6. The person who collected or received the tax was an official or accountant – a *marubar* or *madubar* (?).
7. Taxes were delivered from the district to the administrative centre of Mithradatkirt (Nisa).
8. The ostraca were copies of the receipts kept in the revenue office, while the originals were given to the owners of the land or produce to avoid a repeat collection.
9. Comparison of tax documents dating from similar periods but from

different states – Graeco-Bactrian and Parthian, which included the southern regions of Central Asia – suggests that at least two kinds of taxes were levied: a monetary one and one paid in kind.

10. There was a well-developed administrative apparatus for tax collection, employing officials of different ranks who ensured revenue collection, accounting and the inspection of revenues.

It is probable that the same systems of administration, the nature of tax collections and sources of taxation were also in place in the ancient states of Central Asia in the first centuries AD, but there is little information about this so far.

Economic documents relating to the palace of the Khorezmshahs in Toprak-Kala, dating from the 3rd century AD, provide a list of what would appear to be tax revenues from individuals, taxes that were paid in flour, wine and livestock in specific quantities, deposited in the king's 'treasury'. Documents of a similar type were found in a room of a large family residence at the city-site of Kampyrtepa, in a layer dating from the first half of the 2nd century AD, but they are in very poor condition.

The hoard of gold objects from Dalverzintepa, believed to have been buried in the early 3rd century AD, may provide important material for study, although some of the objects in it (jewellery) are undoubtedly from an earlier period. Among other objects, the hoard contains 21 gold bars making up two groups: Group 1 has bars measuring 85 x 24/5 x 20 millimetres, weighing between 876.2 and 877.8 grams. Group 2 has bars measuring 68 x 16 x 16/17 millimetres, weighing between 358.1 and 449.7 grams. Ten of these bars have inscriptions in Kharoshthi which, according to the scholar M. Vorobyova-Desyatovskaya's reading, indicate the weight of each of the bars in staters, drachmas and dhane, as well as proper names and possibly the titles of official positions, and also the word *shramana*, which denotes a Buddhist monk. Here is a translation of the three clearest examples:

1. 51 staters, 1 drachma, 2 dhane. Given by Mithra.
2. 25 staters, half a drachma. [From the] chief. Given by Mithra.
3. 50 staters. From Kalyana. [Delivered by] *shramanas.*

Several suggestions have been made about the interpretation of the content of the inscriptions and the purpose of the bars themselves. According to Vorobyova-Desyatovskaya, given the specific nature of the Dalverzin inscriptions, the name Mithra must have belonged to one of the officials of the Kushan treasury. At the same time, E.V. Zeymal suggested that the formulation 'Mitrena dite' used in the inscription had a sacred meaning, and that this reading of the inscription is confirmed by the name of the god Mithra and that it is associated with the main function of this deity – a guarantor of contract and obligation. However, Vorobyeva-Desyatovskaya disagrees. Referring to the use of the word *shramana* in inscriptions on the four bars, she suggests that the Dalverzin bars were part of the property of the Buddhist community of that city, and could have been intended to cover the costs of building Buddhist stupas, as well as the production of golden Buddha figurines, and for the ornamentation of temple sculptures, as stipulated by Vinaya rules.

G.A. Pugachenkova thought the Dalverzin hoard was military booty captured in north-west India by the owner of a large house, DT-5, who, in her opinion, belonged to the Kushan-Bactrian military nobility.

Another supposition, and perhaps a more likely one, is that the bars, both with and without inscriptions, may have constituted tax revenues in the form of gold bars of a certain weight, and in this case of groups of different weights, with the first group of bars weighing between 358.1 and 449.7 grams, and the second weighing between 876.2 and 877.8 grams. As already noted, this kind of levy had existed in Central Asia from the middle of the 1st millennium BC, and was collected for the treasury of the Achaemenid king. This would suggest that the formulations of the inscriptions on the bars 'given by Mithra, or, by Mithra given', or 'the *shramanas* (delivered)' should be seen as denoting the individuals making the tax payments: in the first and second cases the rich landowner or merchant Mithra, and in the third representatives of the wealthy Buddhist community of the city (Dalverzintepa) that owned two temples there.

The inscriptions were made using a punching technique, by a special tax official in charge of recording tax revenues, who would have been similar to a *madubar*, an accountant in Parthian Mithradatkirt or an accountant of tax revenues in Graeco-Bactrian Ai-Khanum.

In Ai-Khanum, receipts were kept in special vessels in the treasury of the city governor's palace, from where they were transferred to the king's treasury. It is possible that the DT-5 building at Dalverzintepa was the palace of a Chaganian satrap, where tax revenues from the entire region were delivered before being transferred to the royal treasury. G.A. Pugachenkova and V.M. Masson had already suggested the possibility of regarding this building not as a nobleman's house but as a palace.

Another important document was found at Dalverzintepa – an ostracon with a Pahlavi inscription dating from the mid-3rd century to the mid-4th century AD. According to V.A. Livshits and A. Nikitin, the inscription translates as 'Year 12. Navbun (?) let him pay denars 100 (?)...'. The scholars believe that this refers to a payment of 100 or even 1,000 (this reading is plausible) gold coins, connected to the monetary transactions conducted by Persian merchants who came to Dalverzintepa from Iran. It is probably only the draft of a document, as final financial records were made on leather. However, in this case too, the ostracon could have been a tax document, a reminder to pay a debt to a certain person (Navbun?), or a tax accounting memorandum kept by a special official.

Dalverzintepa, like the whole of Northern Bactria, was apparently conquered by the Sassanians in the mid-3rd century AD, and there is nothing surprising about the presence of the Sassanian administration, in addition to merchants arriving from Iran.

The evidence cited is still sparse, but it reflects the existence of an established revenue-collection system in ancient Central Asia, which was further developed in the early and late medieval period.

Money

Two main centres from which metal money originated have been identified.

Firstly, the **Graeco-Lydian centre**, which unified the Greek cities on the Ionian coast of Asia Minor, ruled by Lydian kings at the time, and Aegina island. The Milesian monetary system is thought to be the earliest among four monetary systems: Milesian, Euboean, Corinthian, Phocaean, dating from the 7th and even 8th century BC. Recent evidence suggests that Lydian coinage did not emerge before 640–630 BC and the oldest surviving coins were minted around 615 BC.

The first coins were minted from electrum, a natural alloy of silver and gold. The obverse of the coins was stamped with a lion's head and a bull's head, verifying that the coins had the correct weight and were of good quality. This made it possible for the first time to trade without needing to weigh the metal.

Secondly, the **Chinese centre**. Here, curious knife-shaped and spade-shaped coins first appeared in the small kingdom of Shu, in north-eastern China, in the 7th or early 6th century BC. Circular coins with a hole in the middle were also occasionally produced at this time. Later, from the early Han era onwards, a traditional type of Chinese coin with a square hole and with hieroglyphs on both sides emerged. All early Chinese coins were bronze, and cast in moulds of stone and clay. Gold and silver coins were not produced in either the early or the later stages of the Chinese coinage system.

Ancient Persian and Ancient Indian coinage systems are cited as other examples of independent centres of the creation of metal money, but they probably both originated under the influence of Greek centres.

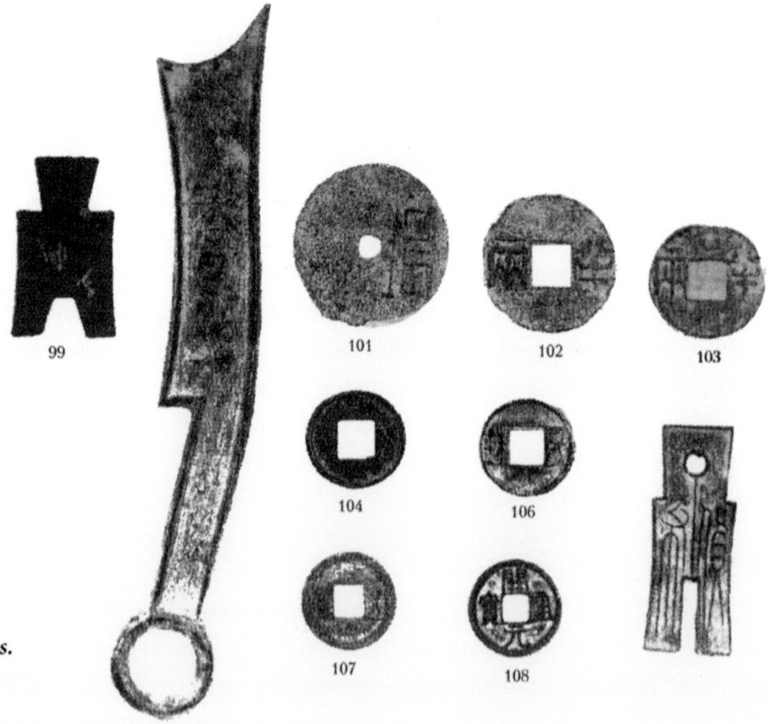

Chinese coins.

In Achaemenid Iran the minting of gold (daric) and silver (siglos) coins began under Darius I, probably in 518 BC, soon after the conquest of Asia Minor by the Persians. However, some scholars believe that coins were issued in Iran even before the reign of Darius I, and the earliest of these were silver sigloi. In India, the minting of what are known as 'punch-marked coins', made of much-alloyed silver, started under Achaemenid or Greek influence in the 5th century BC. These coins, known as 'karshapanas', were first minted in Gandhara in north-west India, and later spread into the interior of the Indian subcontinent. Later, an independent type of coinage was developed here, featuring rectangular silver and bronze coins.

Coinage in the Phoenician cities of the Eastern Mediterranean emerged very early, between the 6th and 4th centuries BC. At the same time, the Graeco-Lydian and Chinese coinage systems had a decisive influence on the emergence and subsequent development of coinage in different territories of Eurasia: the Chinese systems influenced coinage in the Far East and South-East Asia and also in Central Asia during the 7th–8th centuries AD. The Graeco-Lydian systems influenced coinage in the Mediterranean countries, the Near East and the Middle East, as well as in Central Asia, especially between the last centuries BC and first centuries AD.

The emergence of money, that 'commodity of commodities', was the logical outcome of the socio-economic development of advanced ancient civilisations. The long and complex process of commodity exchange and the development of retail and international trade in the 2nd and early 1st millennium BC, after passing through stages when commodities were used as money, followed by the use of metal ingots of different standard weights, eventually led to the appearance of metal money.

Early coins differed from metal ingots in that they were stamped on one or both sides to authenticate their weight. Initially these stamps were a combination of various geometric figures and images of animals, birds and fish, such as a lion, a turtle, a seal, an owl or a tuna fish. Ancient Indian karshapanas were similar to the stamped coins, but local features such as astral symbols were more commonly used for these. Inscriptions and images of deities appeared on the coins only sometime later. Then, in the middle of the 4th century BC, under Alexander the Great, portraits of rulers began to appear on coins.

In Lydia, the first coins were minted in electrum and later in silver. Only under King Croesus (561–546 BC) did a coinage system based on bimetallism (the simultaneous use of gold and silver) begin to spread, and went on to become widespread in ancient Persia.

Even the most ancient monetary systems, such as those of Miletus, Phocaea, Aegina and Euboea, had coins of different denominations, designed differently for each weight standard. A single norm for coinage was introduced in the time of the rise of Macedonia and the establishment of the kingdom of Alexander the Great. Silver coins came to be based on what is known as the Attic system, with a tetradrachm weighing 17.44 grams, a drachma 4.36 grams, and an obolus 1.6 grams. For several centuries after this period, the Attic system prevailed in all the countries that fell under the influence of the Hellenistic world, including the southern regions of Central Asia, with some variations in the weight of the main denominations of coins.

Central Asia was not one of the first areas in which metal money appeared, the main reason for this being an insufficiently high level of socio-economic development. For many centuries before the appearance of coins, various forms of barter and possibly circulation of ingots had been used here, although no concrete examples of the latter have as yet been found in the region.

Until recently, the question of the origin of independent coinage in Central Asia was only considered in chronological and territorial terms, that is, where and when coins first began to be used as a means of payment. Theories and more concrete ideas concerning the nature and characteristics of the early stages of the formation of coins have been documented by E.V. Zeymal in a number of recently published studies based on extensive numismatic material.

In his view, the emergence of monetary circulation and independent coinage in Transoxiana began with foreign coins making their way here as 'treasure'. This was followed by the minting of local imitations of foreign coins that were most 'familiar' within a particular area. These not only constituted an initial form of coinage, but also the initial form of money circulation in regions and countries adjacent to the states which already had developed mechanisms of money circulation. The final phase of this process was the issue of independent coinage in some areas of Transoxiana. However, even if we accept this hypothesis, the question remains unclear as to whether Seleucid and especially Graeco-Bactrian coins can be seen as 'foreign' in Sogdia and Northern Bactria, or whether they were circulating here because both these areas were part of the Hellenistic states. This question is connected with the political history of Transoxiana in the 3rd–2nd centuries BC. However, information from textual sources and numismatic data at present remains sparse.

It is unlikely that Seleucid and Graeco-Bactrian coins functioned only as 'treasure' rather than as a means of currency, especially since copper chalkoi often turn up in finds, and these coins were very rarely used outside the states where they were minted. It is possible, however, that Achaemenid daric coins and sigloi (specimens have probably been found, although the circumstances of these finds are unclear) or coins from the 6th–5th centuries BC, such as the staters of Achaemenid satraps of Asia Minor, imitations of Athenian coins, and coins of Macedonian kings from the Amu Darya hoard, were imported into Central Asia.

A hoard of silver Achaemenid sigloi was recently discovered somewhere in southern Turkmenistan. However, the number of Achaemenid coins in a world of barter probably amounted to a mere sprinkling: there is no trace of them in the subsequent history of coinage in Central Asia, and they did not become the basis for the development of later coinage, whereas by contrast, Seleucid and especially Graeco-Bactrian coins were to determine the formation and development of money circulation and coinage in Central Asia for several centuries. They were the basis for the first imitations of coins that were minted here and for the independent coinages that followed.

Clearly, the model proposed by E.V. Zeymal was not universal, and this is borne out by an analysis of numismatic data. As we have already demonstrated, the emergence of independent coinage followed different patterns in the different historical and cultural areas of Transoxiana.

An enormous amount of numismatic material has been accumulated to date, making it possible for the first time to produce a fairly detailed and meaningful timeline of the development of money circulation in Transoxiana (but of course, not limited to its geographical area) up to the 3rd–4th centuries AD. Unfortunately, the almost complete absence of textual sources and epigraphic data makes it difficult to clarify many issues about money circulation related to such things as rates of exchange, financial policies, and so on.

The first period (second half of the 2nd millennium BC to the first half of the 1st millennium BC). This period was characterised by exchange and barter and the use of commodities and, possibly, of metal ingots as a means of monetary exchange. There is little information about the specific items used for barter and exchange, but if we go by what we know of other countries, these items could include such things as grain, cattle, a range of handicrafts, shells and so on. It is worth noting the presence of round, ceramic objects similar to coins discovered at archaeological sites from the first half of the 1st millennium BC. Some scholars believe these are counters used for games, but it is possible that they could have been used as coin equivalents or units for counting.

The second period (5th century BC to the end of the 4th century BC). In this period the population of Central Asia became acquainted with coinage, and the period is characterised by the use of metal ingots and the first Achaemenid coins. The Achaemenid coins included local counterstamps.

Although there is evidence of coins from this period, we need to approach this data with caution, as not a single coin from this time has been found in archaeological excavations. According to some reports, Achaemenid daric coins have allegedly been found at the site of Afrasiab, in Old Termez and in Kerki.

A treasure trove of silver Achaemenid sigloi depicting an archer in a tiara on the obverse, and with all kinds of counterstamps, is said to have been recently discovered somewhere in southern Turkmenistan, or, according to some reports, in Khorezm. Two coins from this hoard were published by D.V. Biryukov, who believed they justified wondering whether southern Central Asia was part of the monetary system of the Achaemenid kingdom. At any rate, the presence of counterstamps on these coins does make it possible to consider them as examples of the first form of money in Central Asia. Achaemenid darics and sigloi are believed to have been part of the Amu Darya hoard, but the circumstances surrounding both the discovery and subsequent additions to the hoard are problematic.

This hoard also included other coins dating from the 6th and 5th centuries BC: tetradrachms and drachmas from Greek cities and Achaemenid satraps in Asia Minor, imitations of Athenian coins, and coins of the kings of Macedonia. However, even if these coins originated from the Amu Darya hoard, they were most likely used as treasure rather than circulated as money.

It is likely that ingots were also circulated here. In Central Asia, regions divided into three satrapies paid taxes in silver into the treasuries of the Achaemenid kings. The weight unit of the tax was a talent, equivalent to 25.92 kilograms. For example, Bactria was paying 360 talents annually, equivalent to approximately 9 tonnes (Herodotus, III, 93).

It is entirely possible that this tax was not paid as an amorphous mass of silver, but in weighted ingots, and in all probability they were stamped. Thus, in Achaemenid times (mid-6th century to late 4th century BC) initial forms of money circulation were already being used in the most developed regions of Central Asia, in the form of ingots and coins, including gold and silver coins, but not as yet in a very developed form.

We should not overlook another aspect related to the acquaintance of Central Asian peoples with coinage and indicating a possible route for its early introduction to Central Asia. A well-established practice existed of Bactrians, Sogdians and Khorezmians serving in the army and living in different parts of Achaemenid Iran, Greece and Egypt. They may have brought in Achaemenid coins themselves or transferred them to their homelands in Central Asia by using the appropriate banking houses that existed at the time (such as that of Murashu in Babylon).

However, the fact that actual discoveries of coins from this period in Central Asia are extremely rare, suggests that this was a time when the population of the region first became acquainted with coins and their possible use, especially of counter-stamped sigloi. These coins would have been used for some commercial transactions, while barter would have had an active role in trade, and precious and semi-precious metals of certain weight standards would have been used for payment of taxes.

The third period (late 4th to late 2nd century BC). Generally, this period is characterised by some regions of Central Asia (Bactria, Sogdia, Parthia) joining the Hellenistic coinage system; the establishment and development of actual commodity-money relations; the penetration of money relations into the sphere of small-scale market trade, which has been determined by finds of copper (or bronze) coins at many sites; and the multi-functional use of coins as money, treasure, and so on. It was in this period that the first coins were minted in Bactria under Seleucus I and possibly in Sogdia in the Graeco-Bactrian period. It was also the time when the first coins were minted in the name of a local ruler (i.e. the coins of Vakhshuvar in Bactria in the late 4th century BC) as well as when the first local imitations of the Seleucid coins of Antiochus I (in Sogdia in the early 3rd century BC) and imitations of the coins of Alexander the Great were issued. The whole period can be divided into two phases: 1) from the end of the 4th century to the mid-3rd century BC; 2) the middle of the 3rd century to the end of the 2nd century BC.

The first phase is distinguished by the emergence of money circulation, and is borne out by the (admittedly rare) findings of coins of Alexander the Great (336–323 BC), Seleucus I (311–281 BC) and Antiochus I (281–261 BC) in Northern Bactria and Sogdia.

Thus, drachmas of Alexander the Great or Seleucus I (early issues of these coins do not differ from each other) have been found near the *kishlak* (a Central Asian term for 'village') of Darband, near Old Termez (Northern Bactria) and at the Kunya-Fazli site (Southern Sogdia). A rare type of Seleucus I drachma was discovered at the site of Shahr-i Munk (Northern Bactria) and a Seleucus I dichalkous coin was found at Afrasiab. A large number of coins (47 specimens of Seleucus I tetradrachms and drachmas) made up part of the Amu Darya hoard.

Under the reign of Antiochus I, commodity-money relations expanded and developed more intensively in Northern Bactria and Sogdia. Antiochus I coins have been found at Takht-i Sangin, including six chalkoi (weighing between 0.72 and 3.12 g), three drachmas and one chalkous at Old Termez, two chalkoi at Kampyrtepa, one chalkous at Denau (Northern Bactria), chalkoi at Samarkand and one obolus at Kurgantepa (Sogdia).

The prevalence of chalkoi among these finds indicates a sufficiently well-developed money-based economy and, in particular, the existence of small-scale retail trade. It should also be noted that Seleucid coins from Seleucus I to Antiochus II (261–246 BC) were found in an area immediately adjacent to Transoxiana, at Ai-Khanum. This find included 67 specimens, among them 62 Antiochus I coins, one specimen of Seleucus I coins, three specimens of joint-issue Seleucus I and Antiochus I coins, and one specimen of Antiochus II coins.

The most important event of this period was the emergence of the Bactrian coinage of the Seleucids under Seleucus I and Antiochus I. Under Seleucus I, silver coins of high value (tetradrachms, drachmas, hemidrachms) were minted at Bactra with the head of Zeus on the obverse and the image of Athena in a chariot pulled by two elephants or four horses on the reverse. They were struck according to Attic weight standards (whereby a drachma was equivalent to 4.27 grams).

An exception is one series bearing the name of Seleucus and Antiochus, struck according to the ancient Indian karshapana weight standard, which in practical terms is 3 grams. Under Antiochus I, Bactrian coinage became even more versatile: gold staters and silver tetradrachms and drachmas were produced, also struck to the Attic standard, with the bust of Antiochus shown on the obverse and the head of a horned horse on the reverse. Copper chalkoi were probably also issued for use in retail trade.

It is quite possible that drachmas of Antiochus I were also minted in Sogdia, as can be seen, in particular, by the issue at the end of the 3rd and during the 2nd century BC of Sogdian imitations of Antiochus I drachmas depicting a horned horse head.

During this period, the first coins in the name of a local Bactrian ruler rather than in the name of a Greek Bactrian king were also issued. These are coins of the ruler Vakhshuvar, as can be seen in the legend in Aramaic on the obverse: there are specimens of gold staters (depicting the bust of a man wearing a *κυρβăσίā*, a type of headdress, on the obverse and a man on a quadriga facing right on the reverse); and there are also double staters (depicting the head of Alexander in an elephant helmet on the obverse and a standing figure of Nike facing left on the reverse).

There is little consensus among scholars about the place and period of issue of the Vakhshuvar coins, although E.V. Zeymal and I.M. Dyakonov believe them to be early Parthian (Arsacid), like Andragoras coins, dating from the middle of the 3rd century BC. However, I.R. Pichikyan believes that these coins are of Bactrian origin and are the coins of Vakhshuvar Oxyartes, whose daughter Roxana married Alexander the Great and who, according to Arrian, became a satrap of Paropamisadai following the death of Alexander. However, it is possible that in addition to Paropamisadai, he also controlled Northern Bactria, the core region of his possessions. It is in this area, in Northern Bactria, in the Baisun mountains, but north-west of Denau, that a *kishlak* called Vakhshuvar is situated, i.e. with the same name as on the above-mentioned coins. We have also noted a similar place name in the Babatag mountains on the road to Chagam.

According to V.A. Livshits, the word Vakhshuvar itself (of which the Greek derivative is the name Oxyartes) means 'chosen by (the god) Vakhshu' (or 'believing in the god Vakhshu / protected by the god Vakhshu'). Surveys carried out by this author in Vakhshuvar village found the site of Sartepa here, the lower layer of which dates from the first half to the middle of the 1st millennium BC. It is possible that this very place, which has retained its ancient name for more than two thousand years, was the main residence of the Bactrian aristocrat Vakhshuvar-Oxyartes, and the Rock of Oxyartes was also located here.

The second phase of the third period is characterised by further development of money relations in Transoxiana, along with expansion of the area in which they were established and the incorporation of new areas, in particular Bukhara, into money relations; expansion of the sphere within which coins were used; the appearance of the first coin hoards, testifying to the existence of large amounts of money owned by specific individuals; and the appearance of the first Sogdian and Bactrian imitations of Seleucid and Graeco-Bactrian coins as the first stage in the emergence of independent minting in Transoxiana.

The variety of weight standards used for silver and copper coins in circulation (tetradrachms, drachmas, oboli, chalcoi, dichalcoi) minted under the Attic system is an indicator of the apparent progress of commodity-money relations, the use of coins as means of payment and circulation, and probably also as treasure. Large-scale trade transactions, including international and interregional ones, were conducted using silver coins of high value. In Northern Bactria, and partially in Sogdia, money relations were also used for small-scale trade between cities and small settlements. Evidence of this comes from the finds of coins at many sites and settlements in the southern and central regions of Transoxiana.

Northern Bactria. Nearly 100 silver and copper Graeco-Bactrian coins of various denominations have been found here. They include coins of Diodotus, Euthydemus,

Antimachus, Agathocles, Eucratides, Demetrius and Heliocles, i.e. all the great Graeco-Bactrian kings. The bulk of the finds of Graeco-Bactrian coins (over 70 specimens) have been concentrated in this area near the Amu Darya river (for example, 27 specimens were found at Takht-i Sangin, more than 30 at Old Termez, and another 15 at Kampyrtepa). Yet another area where finds of such coins were clustered (15 specimens) is in the valleys of the Surkhan Darya and Kashka Darya rivers (at Dalverzintepa, Denau, Regar, Khaitabadtepa and Shahr-i Nau). There have also been isolated finds of these coins at other sites and settlements, namely:

Sogdia. A total of more than 10 individual coin finds have been recorded here, as well as two coin hoards.

Kesh and Nakhshab. Three Antimachus oboli were found at Shahr-i Sabz, a Diodotus chalkous at Sangirtepa, as well as a hoard including Eucratides oboli, drachmas and tetradrachms.

Samarkand Sogdia. About 10 coins have been recorded from this area, including drachmas of Euthydemus, tetradrachms of Demetrius, Antimachus and Heliocles and oboli of Eucratides, found at Afrasiab, near Samarkand and in Penjikent.

Bukhara. In the eastern part of Bukhara, a hoard of 56 tetradrachms of Diodotus, Euthydemus (about 50 specimens) and Agathocles were found at Takhmachtepa. Tetradrachms of Demetrius and Euthydemus have also been found on the outskirts of Bukhara (in Khoja and Obon).

Khorezm. There is no evidence of money circulation in this area during this period. Only three finds of Graeco-Bactrian coins are known. These coins probably found their way to this area as foreign coins, as Khorezm was not a part of the Graeco-Bactrian kingdom. These finds include a Eucratides tetradrachm from Janbas-Kala, a Euthydemus tetradrachm from Khiva, and a chalkous from Yakke-Parsan.

To date, no Graeco-Bactrian coins have been found in other areas of Transoxiana. This suggests that money relations existed only in the two most developed areas of this region – Northern Bactria and Sogdia, which were under the jurisdiction of Graeco-Bactrian kings. Further, in Sogdia (however, with the probable exception of large cities such as Maracanda, Er-Kurgan and Bukhara) a bartering system would have been predominant in some areas.

The fourth period (the end of the 2nd century BC to the beginning of the 1st century AD). After the collapse of the Graeco-Bactrian kingdom in the late 2nd century BC, under pressure from the Sakas and Yuezhi, the political situation in Transoxiana underwent a fundamental change. A confederative Yuezhi state emerged in Bactria, while Sogdia remained under the nominal rule of the (also confederative) Kangju state, which consisted of several relatively independent dominions ruled by Yuezhi dynasties. Meanwhile in Khorezm an ancient dynasty seems to have survived.

The most important feature of this period is the widespread circulation of imitation Graeco-Bactrian coins in almost all regions of Transoxiana, except for Ferghana and Chach. Initially, these imitations were almost identical to their prototypical Graeco-Bactrian coins. Later, the Greek legends were altered and new symbols of deities were used. Ultimately, transitional imitations of coins emerged with a mixture of Greek and Aramaic legends and bearing images of local rulers.

According to E.V. Zeymal, this was the first stage in the development of independent coinage in Transoxiana. What is more, each province of this region produced specific images, which were unique to it. For instance, in Northern Bactria Yuezhi imitations of coins of three Graeco-Bactrian kings were issued – those of Demetrius, Euthydemus and Heliocles.

Two groups of Bronze imitations of Heliocles coins of several weight standards (23–26, 10–16, 3–5 grams) were distributed over the widest area. A large variety of types of these coins were produced and they were minted with the greatest intensity. The first group included copies of Heliocles coins with minor alterations, while the second group featured a local ruler and a horse.

In the south-east of Northern Bactria, silver imitations of Eucratides oboli weighing 0.3–0.6 grams were in circulation (they were in effect hemi-oboli). At a certain point of their development they included a 'portrait' of the local ruler. Small bronze and silver imitations of Demetrius coins were also part of the money-based economy of this area.

The Yuezhi rulers of Northern Bactria did not mint silver coins of high value, but the shortage of these was replaced by Graeco-Bactrian silver, which, as E.V. Zeymal has demonstrated, were apparently still in circulation up to the beginning of the 1st century BC.

The stock of coins circulating in the different regions of Sogdia during this period was even more varied. For example, small imitations of Antiochus I coins weighing 0.3–3.2 grams (oboli, hemidrachms and drachmas) were widespread in the Samarkand region and were probably minted from the end of the 3rd to the 1st century BC. J. Lerner identified these imitations as Sogdian Euthydemus coinage dating from the period before he usurped the Graeco-Bactrian throne. Judging by their discovery at the site of Er-Kurgan, they, along with imitations of Demetrius coins, must have been in circulation in the western part of Southern Sogdia. During the same period, large silver imitations of Euthydemus tetradrachms weighing 13–16 grams were issued in the Bukhara area.

Between Bukhara and Samarkand Sogdia, probably in the second half of the 2nd century BC, small silver coins weighing 2–3 grams, with an image of the ruler's head on the obverse and the standing figure of a deity on the reverse side accompanied by the

Greek legend *ΟΡΔΗΤΡΟΥ ΜΑΚΑΡΟΥ*, were issued by the Yuezhi *Hyrcodes* or Urkod dynasty. During the same period, Khorezm minted its own coinage for the first time. These were large silver imitations of Eucratides tetradrachms weighing 13–16 grams.

Each of these groups of coins had a strictly local circulation and, judging by the topography of their finds, circulation was limited to the area where they were minted. This meant that local money markets developed and the demand for coins was met by locally minted coinage. There were at least four such local markets within one large area, like Sogdia.

Coin systems in the different regions of Transoxiana also varied. Silver and bronze coins of different denominations were minted and circulated in Northern Bactria. In Sogdia and Khorezm only silver coins were in circulation, and in Khorezm only large denominations were in circulation, while in Sogdia both small and large denomination coins were being used. The 'tetradrachms' in circulation here were probably imitations of Euthydemus coins, which, judging by the topography of finds, were in circulation throughout Sogdia.

The monetary system in Sogdia and Khorezm was clearly a departure from the Attic system based on the drachma, which had survived despite the change in the government of Bactria. The obolus and tetradrachm became the main units of currency in Sogdia, and in Khorezm it was the tetradrachm. The shortage of small change in Sogdia was apparently remedied by numerous issues of small silver coins – oboli and fractions of them – while in Khorezm, several types of trade were probably still dominated by barter.

The weight standards of the coins were also changing and began to deviate from Attic standards. Thus, the weight of imitations of Euthydemus and Eucratides tetradrachms ranged from 13 to 16 grams, while the Attic tetradrachm weighed 17.26 grams.

The fifth period (1st century AD to the first half of the 3rd century AD). The money-based economy of this period in different parts of Transoxiana changed radically along with the new political situation. In particular, there was a further departure from Hellenistic traditions of coinage both in weight standards and coin metals. The iconography and symbolism used also changed and were replaced by local Asian norms and traditions. From the second half of the 1st century AD, with the reign of Wima I Takto, the son of Kujula Kadphises, the southern part of Transoxiana became part of the dominion of this powerful Kushan king.

Throughout the reigns of Wima I Takto and Kanishka II, the money-based economy of this area and the make-up of the coin supply followed the official minting policy of the Kushan kings. Political stability contributed to the rapid growth of towns and villages, and crafts, agriculture and trade flourished, resulting in the intensive development of commodity-money relations. For example, according to our calculations, several thousands of Kushan coins have been found in the territory of Northern Bactria in both individual finds and in hoards. Moreover, the number of coins in some of the hoards is estimated as including several hundred specimens, which suggests that individual people had accumulated considerable amounts of money. Commodity-money relations were developing rapidly in rural settlements as well as in remote mountainous areas. Although bartering may have continued during this period, it appears that it became much less important.

It is possible to distinguish three stages in the money circulation of this period in Northern Bactria. In the first stage, two different denominations of bronze coins were in circulation during the reign of Wima I Takto (Soter Megas). Large coins weighing 8–9 grams and small coins weighing 2–3 grams were in circulation. Specimens of these coins have been found in large quantities at all Kushan sites in Northern Bactria.

The weight standards, iconography and symbolism of the coins of Wima I Takto differ from those of his predecessor Kujula Kadphises, suggesting that Wima I may have undertaken small-scale monetary reform during his reign. There is no information about any gold and silver coins minted by him, however, and it remains unclear what denominations were used for large-scale trade transactions: it is possible that Graeco-Bactrian silver was used for such transactions, as well as Kushan ('Heraeus') coins, whose tetradrachms and oboli have been found in sufficiently large quantities.

The second stage of the fifth period relates to the fundamental monetary reforms undertaken by Wima I Takto's successor Wima Kadphises, which completely changed the Bactrian monetary system, based on the use of silver and copper, which had been in use since Hellenistic times. The new monetary system introduced by Wima Kadphises, apparently under Roman influence, was based on gold and bronze. The main unit of currency was the gold coin, called a 'stater' for the sake of convenience, weighing 8.3 grams – almost exactly the same weight as the Roman aureus, 7.6–8.1 grams, but less than the weight of the Attic stater which weighed about or slightly more than 8.6 grams. A double stater weighing 16.07 grams and a quarter stater weighing 2.01 grams were also introduced into money circulation.

Although the use of the term 'stater' for these coins was introduced as a convention in scholarship, as the contents of the Dalverzin hoard demonstrate, it was in fact in use. The hoard contained ten gold bars with inscriptions in Kharoshthi bearing notations of weight standards – stater, drachma, dhane. A comparison of the weight of the bars and the indication of a stater's weight in the inscriptions revealed that the latter ranged from 17.08 grams to 18.03 grams, while the calculated average weight was 17.53 grams. For this reason, G.A. Pugachenkova believes that although the inscriptions use the word 'stater', they are actually referring to a double stater, because the weight of a stater was 8.3 grams. However, it is equally possible that the inscriptions indicate the true weight of an ordinary stater, otherwise they would refer to two staters in relation to drachmas and dhane – the local units of weight. According to the information in the inscriptions, one stater was equal to four drachmas, with an average weight of 4.4 grams, and one drachma was equal to 5 dhane with an average weight of 0.77 grams.

The use of the terms stater and drachma in the inscriptions suggests that in Kushan times, the practices from Hellenistic times of using Greek designations for the main units of weight were still in use. They were probably also used to denote units of value, as in Niya and Kroraina, for example, according to Prakrit documents found here.

The iconography and weight standards of bronze coins gradually changed. Large chalkoi weighing 16–17 grams were introduced into circulation and large quantities of these coins have been found in many archaeological sites in Northern Bactria.

The third stage is the period of the reigns of Vasudeva II and Kanishka III, the last of the Kushan kings who ruled Northern Bactria. A comparison of the metrological data of the coins shows that they underwent noticeable changes towards the late Kushan period, decreasing in diameter and weight. Under Huvishka, bronze coins had already gradually begun to decrease in weight, while under Vasudeva I and Kanishka III further reductions in the weight of the main bronze denomination took place.

In the reign of Vasudeva I bronze coins were apparently minted in two denominations: 6–8 and 9–11 grams, while under Kanishka III only one denomination of 6–8 grams was minted. Accordingly, the ratio of bronze and gold coins seemed to change as well, along with the composition of the metal used for bronze coins, which, unlike the coins of early Kushan rulers, were being minted from bronze with two or three component metals.

This data leads us to assume that further monetary reform took place in the late Kushan period, which primarily affected the bronze denominations: its main characteristic was the replacement of bulky, heavy coins with coins of lower weight and smaller diameter that were easier to use in the domestic market. Available data (the quantitative ratio of coin finds) reveal that during the late Kushan period, the scale of commodity-money relations remained at a high level in the towns and settlements of Northern Bactria.

An analysis of coin hoards provides us with a similar picture. The hoards from the first stage contain only Soter Megas (Wima I Takto) coins and no other coins from earlier times, such as coins of the 'Barbarian Heliocles'. They appear to have been buried in the initial period of the early Kushan era.

Seven of the hoards relate to the second stage: six of them contain coins of Wima Kadphises and Kanishka I, and only one, the hoard from the Temple of the Oxus, contains Soter Megas coins. In fact, this suggests that the coins of earlier periods, from the reigns of Wima Kadphises and Kanishka I, either did not have a significant role or had disappeared from money circulation.

The hoards of the third, late Kushan stage, indicate the same tendency to completely replace old coins with new ones. There are five hoards from this period, four of which contain only Vasudeva I and Kanishka III coins, with one hoard containing Huvishka coins (from the Kyzyl-Ketman hoard). Analysis of the hoards' composition seems to indicate that the Huvishka period can be regarded as a transitional stage from the advanced stage of money circulation to the Late Kushan stage, since only a small number of these coins have been found in hoards from either the preceding or the subsequent period (the hoard of Huvishka and Kanishka coins from the Temple of the Oxus and the hoard from Kyzyl-Ketman). Not a single coin from the early Kushan rulers Soter Megas (Wima I Takto), Wima Kadphises and Kanishka I has been found in the hoards of the late Kushan kings. Since all hoards, as we can see from their composition, are the result of short-term accumulation, they provide a snapshot of money circulation at any given stage. This allows us to conclude that the replacement of old coins with new ones in Kushan Bactria took place at a much faster pace than was previously thought, and that the circulation period for old coins was of limited duration. In other words, it is reasonable to argue that the old coins may have been withdrawn from circulation and then gradually replaced by new ones.

In Sogdia the denomination of coins and their metal composition remained unchanged during this period ('tetradrachms' and 'oboli'), but new issues and minting centres appeared. For example, in Southern Sogdia small silver coins weighing 0.4–0.9 grams (hemi-oboli) with the images of Heracles and Zeus were minted, but with an as yet not fully deciphered Sogdian legend consisting of two words, where only *MR'Y* / 'ruler' is legible. Apparently, these coins were in circulation throughout the region from the middle of the 1st century BC right up to the 4th century AD, when they were replaced by bronze coins depicting a scene of single combat. Whereas previously only isolated specimens were recorded (over 20 specimens in all), a hoard of these coins has now been found in Talimardzhan.

The following groups of coins were in circulation in different parts of central Sogdia. In Samarkand, Penjikent and adjacent areas, small silver coins were in circulation depicting the image of an archer and a Sogdian legend conveying the names of various rulers: *a'st'm βγwrty, hprwmh, kyδr, twrak*.

In the lower reaches of the Zarafshan river, in Bukhara, and to some extent in Samarkand Sogdia, small silver coins of the Hyrcodes group were still in circulation. These had an image of the ruler on the obverse and a protome of a horse on the reverse, along with a Greek and Sogdian legend. The weight of these coins varies between 0.6 and 3.0 grams, which apparently points to the existence of different denominations (hemi-oboli and oboli).

In Bukhara itself and in adjacent areas, large silver coins – 'tetradrachms' weighing 9–11 grams – were being minted, indicating a departure from comparable prototypes both in terms of weight standards and iconography: the 'portrait' of Euthydemus was replaced by the image of a local ruler, and the Greek legend by a Sogdian one.

Thus, throughout this period, Sogdian markets were well supplied with both small silver coins in various denominations and larger ones. Moreover, the smallest silver coins weighing 0.3–0.6 grams replaced bronze coins that were not found here and were used for small change, while large commercial transactions in Sogdia were undertaken with 'tetradrachms' imitating Euthydemus coins.

The reasons for the absence of bronze coins in Sogdia, both in this and earlier periods, remain unclear. The increasing number of discoveries of coin hoards containing only 'tetradrachms' or only small silver coins points to the accumulation of large sums of money by a particular segment of the Sogdian population.

The makeup of the coin supply in Sogdia and in Bactria during this period was quite different in every respect, suggesting fundamental differences between the dynasties and the polities of these regions. Bactria was a part of the Kushan kingdom, while Sogdia was ruled by four independent dynasties during the same period, and this was reflected in its coinage (imitations of Euthydemus tetradrachms, Hyrcodes coins, coins depicting an archer, coins depicting Heracles and Zeus).

Important changes to coinage were also taking place in Khorezm, which was experiencing a shift from the use of imitation coins to that of fully independent coinage. The earliest stage of development of coin minting in Khorezm is represented by Group A coins. The coins belonging to this group clearly reflect the introduction of new elements, such as the use of a Khorezmian royal *tamga* and the image of a horseman instead of one of the Dioscuri on the reverse, with an image of the ruler on the obverse. Altogether there are three sequential stages, which reflect the development of Khorezmian coinage. The first stage of Group A coins – Group A I – includes the earliest coin shown by V.M. Masson, which differs from the Eucratides tetradrachm in such details as the image of a face on the obverse and the presence of a royal Khorezmian *tamga* on the reverse. The next stage – Group A II coins – is represented by the coins from the Samarkand Museum, which – according to B.I. Vainberg – were minted using coins from Group A I as a model. Finally, coins from Group A III contain some of the features of the previous groups, but they include fundamentally new changes: the bust of a beardless king on the obverse, behind whom is a schematic image of the goddess Nike crowning the king, and the image of a horseman riding off to the right on the reverse. The Group A coins are made of silver and they have a similar weight to tetradrachms. They date from the second half of the 1st century BC to the beginning of the 1st century AD.

However, the question about where the coins from Group A I were minted remains open. V.M. Masson believed them to have been minted in the Syr Darya region, while S.P. Tolstov maintained that they were of Khorezmian origin. B.I. Vainberg was unsure about their place of origin: they may have been minted in Southern Transoxiana, but they could equally well have been minted in Khorezm after this area was conquered by nomadic tribes responsible for the defeat of Graeco-Bactria. Nonetheless, Vainberg is confident that the coins from Groups A II and A III were minted in Khorezm.

The coins of Group B are of many types, including depictions of a bust of the king on the obverse with, on the reverse, a horseman followed by a distorted Greek legend and a Khorezmian inscription with the king's name and title. During the same period, shortly before the reign of King Vazamar (Group B V), copper Khorezmian coinage emerged and, during his reign, the use of a more stable type of copper coin was established.

Coins from Group B I, which B.I. Vainberg dates to the middle or third quarter of the 1st century AD, testify to a new and fundamentally important stage in the coinage of Khorezm – they depict a *tamga,* which became customary in the coinage of Khorezm until the late 8th century, and a legend in the local language giving the name and title of the king. Group B I coins represent a complete break with Hellenistic traditions: altered Greek legends are no longer present on the coins, while they do appear on all coins from earlier groups.

Throughout this period, Khorezm had well-developed money relations that ensured a supply of silver and bronze coins for large and small retail trade. However, unlike in Sogdia, no small silver coins were produced here.

Thus, from the 1st century AD to the first half of the 3rd century there existed in Transoxiana three large 'numismatic provinces': three local areas of money circulation using different weights, standards and metals:

1. Khorezm, where only large silver and bronze coins of different denominations were minted;
2. Sogdia, which only minted large silver coins of one denomination and small silver coins of different denominations;
3. Northern Bactria, which was part of the Kushan monetary system based only on gold and bronze coins.

We can tentatively propose a fourth area – Ferghana, where the currency included Chinese wu-zhu bronze coins. It is possible that Chach also entered the sphere of money relations and had begun minting its own coins during this period, but there is not enough data to support this assumption.

Analysis of the information we have indicates that all of the coins issued in Transoxiana had a narrow, localised sphere of circulation within the areas where these coins were minted. They did not penetrate into neighbouring provinces and dominions or beyond the borders of Transoxiana. Their use was limited to local markets and trade. By contrast, Kushan, Parthian and Roman coins were probably used as international currency on the routes of the Silk Road passing through this region. Specimens of these coins have been found well beyond the borders of the states in which they were minted – in India, Central Asia, Eastern Turkestan and China.

The nature of monetary relations in the second half of the 3rd–4th centuries AD (a kind of period of transition from ancient times to early medieval times) differs significantly from the previous period and needs to be considered in its own right.

The collapse of the great ancient kingdoms of Kushan and Parthia had an impact on the overall political situation in the area and paved the way for the transition to a new social system. The most significant events of that time were the large-scale movements of nomadic peoples – Kidarites, Chionites and Hephthalites; the emergence of new, smaller dominions; the change of dynasties in the former dominions; and the political domination of Sassanian Iran in Transoxiana. All these events led to a change in the composition of coinage and the nature of monetary relations, the emergence of new centres of minting and the disappearance of Hellenistic traditions from the iconography, metrology and epigraphy of coins.

2.6

INTERNATIONAL RELATIONS IN ANCIENT STATES IN CENTRAL ASIA

The history of the formation and development of diplomacy in states and possesions of Inner Asia in ancient times has not been adequately covered by historical scholarship to date. There is a lack of both general monographs and specialised publications on this most important subject. Without going into the history of the study of the subject, it is worth noting that, although it has been most thoroughly examined by B.A. Litvinsky in some chapters of *History of the Tajik People*, this in fact complicates our understanding and overview of the topic. Given this, our goal here is to present the history of the formation and development of this region's diplomatic relations with a range of other states in the ancient world, stage by stage, in chronological order. Graeco-Roman and Chinese texts are useful sources of information, allowing us to describe the issue both briefly and in more detail.

The Avesta, which was probably written in the first half of the 1st millennium BC, provides information about the beginnings of early forms of diplomatic relations. The god Mithra was the main guardian of inter-tribal agreements and of the settlement of disputes and military conflicts, and his function as the deity of agreement and accord was the most important aspect of his role.

Thus, in the *Mihr Yasht* (hymn to Mithra), one of the oldest hymns of the Avesta, the Supreme Lord Ahura Mazda addresses the prophet Spitama Zarathushtra and gives the following warning (5, 17–21):

> If the master of a house lies unto him, or the lord of a borough, or the lord of a town, or the lord of a province, then comes Mithra, angry and offended, and he breaks asunder the house, the borough, the town, the province; and the masters of the houses, the lords of the boroughs, the lords of the towns, the lords of the provinces, and the foremost men of the provinces. On whatever side there is one who has lied unto Mithra, on that side Mithra stands forth, angry and offended, and his wrath is

> slow to relent. Those who lie unto Mithra, however swift they may be running, cannot overtake; riding, cannot ...; driving, cannot ... The spear that the foe of Mithra flings, darts backwards, for the number of the evil spells that the foe of Mithra works out. And even though the spear be flung well, even though it reach the body, it makes no wound, for the number of the evil spells that the foe of Mithra works out. The wind drives away the spear that the foe of Mithra flings, for the number of the evil spells that the foe of Mithra works out.

The Avesta also provides other details about inter-tribal treaties made under the auspices of the god Mithra.

International relations between Central Asian peoples and Media and Assyria

Iranian tribes had probably been migrating into the territory of contemporary Iran through the Caucasus and Central Asia from the 9th century BC onwards. Here they formed several tribal alliances, and occupied particular regions, the largest of which were Media in the north-west and Parsua in the south-west of Iran, and took the first steps towards the creation of actual states.

The Kingdom of Media, founded by Deioces, was the first to emerge, but only became a true power under the reign of King Cyaxarea (625–585 BC). Under Cyaxareas, the Medes conquered Assyria, Northern Mesopotamia, Hyrcania, Parthia, Aria and, possibly, part of Sogdia, i.e. the southern regions of Central Asia.

According to Ctesias of Cnidus, Cyaxareas also ostensibly conquered Bactria, but this is extremely unlikely. It is more likely that the borders of the Median kingdom in the north-east were confined by the Amu Darya river, where the Medes encountered the Saka tribes.

According to Ctesias, during the reign of the Median king Astibaras, identified with Cyaxareas, the Parthians had rebelled and broken with Media. They called on the help of the Sakas, led by Queen Zarina (Zarinaea), and the war between the Sakas and Medes that had dragged on for some years ended with a peace treaty, under which the Parthians, though nominally subjugated to Media, in fact retained their former possessions (Diodorus, II, 34, 1–4). This treaty, dating from the end of the 7th century to the beginning of the 6th century BC, constitutes the first international treaty in the history of Central Asian diplomacy known to scholars.

Another account by Ctesias which has survived tells of the war of the Parthians and Sakas against the Medes. After the death of her husband Cydraeus, Zarina married

Mermerus, a dynast of Parthyene, and this started a war with the Medes, headed by Stryangaeus. During the battle, the Saka army was defeated and Zarina was herself wounded and taken prisoner, but Stryangaeus, struck by Zarina's beauty, spared her. Mermerus then defeated Stryangaeus' troops and took him prisoner, resolving to kill him. However, Zarina not only freed the prisoners but also killed Mermerus. Zarina then concluded a peace treaty with the Median king, giving him control of Parthyene.

In spite of all the mythical overtones of these colourful accounts by Ctesias and other authors, and the tales of the romantic love between the Median leader Stryangaeus and the Saka queen Zarina, we can nevertheless deduce that some forms of diplomacy for peace treaties existed in Central Asia in the pre-Achaemenid period, in the 7th and 6th centuries BC.

Diplomacy in the Achaemenid period (mid-6th to the end of the 4th century BC)

Relations between the Saka and the Achaemenid Empire. The western regions of Inner Asia became part of the Achaemenid kingdom in the second half of the 6th century BC. Cyrus (559–530 BC), the founder of the Achaemenid kingdom, conquered Bactria, Parthia, Sogdiana, Margiana and Khorezm in his early campaigns. The advance of the Achaemenids to the north-east inevitably led to confrontation with the powerful Saka-Massagetae confederation of tribes. So, to secure the borders of the Achaemenid kingdom during the last years of his life, Cyrus organised a military campaign against the Saka-Massagetae, who at that time occupied the territory between the lower reaches of the Syr Darya and the Amu Darya. The campaign was preceded by an exchange of oral diplomatic messages between Cyrus and the Massagetae queen, Tomyris, which have survived in the accounts of Herodotus.

In fact, Cyrus tried to stage a diplomatic manoeuvre by proposing marriage to Tomiris via his ambassadors. However, Tomyris realised this was a ruse and she 'would have none of his advance, well understanding that he wooed not her but the kingdom of the Massagetae' (Herodotus, I, 205). Having understood that the ruse has failed, Cyrus initiated military operations against the Massagetae, once he had crossed the river Araxes [Amu-Darya – E.R.].

In response to these moves Tomyris sent a verbal message to Cyrus through a special messenger with the aim of ensuring that the Achaemenid king stop his campaign and leave the Massagetae alone. She also proposed that if Cyrus did not want to follow that advice and was intent on war, then she and her people would withdraw a three-days' journey from the river and allow his army to get across safely before giving battle; or if Cyrus preferred to meet her forces on his own ground /on his side of the river, he should withdraw his troops into their own territory for the distance of a three-days' journey, and allow her and her army to safely cross the river before attacking them (Herodotus, I, 206). Cyrus and the military council of the Persian army considered the message, and Cyrus decided to follow the advice of the Lydian king Croesus. Croesus suggested that Cyrus cross the river and advance forward as far as the enemy withdrew, and then abandon the weakest part of his army there, leaving various meats and wine in the camp, with the rest of the army returning to the river.

Croesus' ploy worked: the vanguard of the Massagetae army led by Spargapises, son of Tomyris, crushed the part of the Achaemenid army that had been left behind and then arranged a feast, during which the Massagetae indulged in excessive drinking and fell asleep. Taking advantage of this, Cyrus attacked them, killed many and took prisoners, including Spargapises (Herodotus, I, 210–211).

These insidious actions by Cyrus provoked a second message from Tomyris, which she also sent verbally through a special messenger (Herodotus, I, 212). In this message Tomyris importuned Cyrus to return her son, and for him and his army to leave the land of the Massagetae: 'But if you will not do this, then I swear by the sun, the lord of the Massagetae, that for all you are so insatiate of blood, I will give you your fill thereof.'

The events that followed show that Cyrus did not follow Tomyris' advice and Spargapises committed suicide, unable to endure his disgrace. In the ensuing, brutal battle, the Massagetae won a decisive victory, most of the Persian army was destroyed, Cyrus himself was killed, and his severed head was placed by Tomyris in a bag with human blood (Herodotus, I, 212–214). Only many years later did the Achaemenid king Cambyses manage to retrieve Cyrus' remains and bury them in a proper tomb in Pasargadae.

These accounts suggest that during the Achaemenid period, diplomacy as a specialised form of negotiating relationships between different states and tribal associations in Inner Asia was becoming more usual: exchanges of diplomatic messages took place, although these were still all conveyed orally, as the Saka-Massagetae did not have a written language. It is probable that the people responsible for transmitting messages had a specialised role, and had to learn the messages by heart.

Diplomacy in the Hellenistic era (late 4th century BC to the second half of the 2nd century BC)

The political domination of the Hellenes in Central Asia, beginning with their conquest of most of the region by Alexander the Great in 330–327 BC, lasted for almost two hundred years, until the fall of the Graeco-Bactrian kingdom at the beginning of the second half of the 2nd century BC.

We can distinguish two periods of diplomatic relations at this time: the first concerns Alexander the Great's relations with the peoples of Central Asia, and the second relates to the time when the southern regions of Central Asia became part of the Hellenistic Seleucid and Graeco-Bactrian states.

The first period. According to Arrian, in 329 BC, when Alexander arrived in Maracanda (Samarkand) he received envoys from the Abian Scythians (Abii) and also from the European Scythians. Under the pretext of a treaty of friendship, Alexander sent them his own envoy; his real purpose, however, was to learn about the nature of the Scythian land, and discover details about the size of its population and their weaponry (Arrian, IV, 1, 1–2; Curtius, VII, 6, 12).

The following year, Alexander marched to Ustrushana, where he built the city of Alexandria Eschate, on the banks of the river Tanais (Syr Darya), apparently the site of present-day Khodjent. A battle with the Scythians followed on the right bank of the river, ending in their defeat. Following this, ambassadors from the Scythian king came to Alexander with an offer of a peace treaty and an apology for the actions of certain groups of Scythians – but not the king himself, who was willing to submit to Alexander. Alexander graciously replied that he trusted the king, but that he would not cease hostilities until he had achieved a complete victory. In 328 BC a new envoy from the European Scythians arrived in Maracanda, accompanied by Alexander's earlier envoy. The Scythian envoys conveyed their king's proposal for a peace treaty and presented him with gifts. The Scythian king offered his daughter in marriage to Alexander, and the daughters of Scythian nobles to Alexander's 'loyal friends'. In a cordial reply, Alexander nonetheless declined the Scythian proposals (Arrian, IV, 15, 1–4). In the same year, an envoy from King Pharasmanes came to Maracanda, accompanied by a cavalry of 1,500 from Khorezm, the first sovereign state in Central Asia, apparently established after liberation from the Achaemenid kingdom in the 4th century BC.

Pharasmanes told Alexander about his kingdom, which bordered the territories of the Colchis and the Amazon women, and offered him a military alliance and assistance in a campaign against these peoples and other tribes living near the Euxine (Black) Sea. Some details in this account are questionable, in particular the suggestion that the Khorezmians lived in territories neighbouring the Colchis, who inhabited Western Georgia. This implies that the borders of the Khorezm kingdom extended all the way to the Caucaus mountain range.

Alexander thanked Pharasmanes, but in his response indicated that such a campaign would be ill-timed and better postponed until he had conquered India and had returned to Hellas, from where he planned to undertake a campaign to the Black Sea coast. After his stay in Maracanda, Pharasmanes returned home accompanied by the satrap of Bactria, Artabazus (Arrian, IV, 15, 1–5).

The first period is therefore characterised by increased diplomatic activity by Central Asian states and tribal associations, and manifest in the conclusion of various kinds of peace treaties and military alliances with Alexander the Great. It is possible that during this period, or perhaps even earlier, some people began almost to specialise in engaging in diplomatic activities.

The second period. This period is characterised by the incorporation of part of southern Central Asia into the Hellenistic Seleucid (late 4th to mid-3rd century BC) and Graeco-Bactrian (mid-3rd to early second half of the 2nd century BC) states and the widespread dissemination of Hellenistic culture. At the same time, in the middle of the 3rd century BC the Parthian state was established in the south-west of Central Asia by Central Asian nomads. In the 2nd century BC a number of independent states were created in Transoxiana, including Kangju and Dayuan. Judging by coins that have been discovered, it is clear some local possessions also existed in Bukharan and Samarkand Sogdia. During this period, the kingdom of Khorezm possibly emerged at the end of the 4th century BC, after freeing itself from Achaemenid domination, and continued to maintain its strength and independence.

Thus, during this period, local state entities were actively being formed while the Hellenistic state of the Graeco-Bactrian kingdom continued to exist. There is no doubt that all these states maintained some form of diplomatic relations as well as alliances between themselves, but unfortunately there is no information about this in textual sources.

For example, we know about the Parthian-Graeco-Bactrian military treaties and alliances, in particular those made between Diodotus II and Tiridates, probably after 237 BC (Justin, XLI, 4), against their common enemy Seleucus II, who tried to reconquer Central Asia. We also know about other treaties made by Graeco-Bactrian kings. For instance, in 208 BC, the Seleucid king Antiochus III (223–187 BC) undertook a campaign against the Graeco-Bactrian king, Euthydemus (230–200 BC), whose troops he defeated at the Battle of the Arius (Tejen) river. In 206 BC, negotiations between the two kings began, resulting in a peace treaty whereby Euthydemus retained his royal authority in exchange for giving up his martial elephants and to a certain extent accepting the authority of Antiochus III, although he was soon released from this obligation.

Between 141 and 129 BC the Graeco-Bactrian kingdom was attacked by the Saka and Yuezhi tribes, and at the same time Hellenic rule in the south of Central Asia collapsed – although, as we have only recently discovered, their small possessions in

Northern Bactria and Southern Sogdia continued to exist for many years following these events.

Northern, and later Southern Bactria, was occupied by the Yuezhi who migrated there under pressure from the Huns (Xiongnu). Subsequently, one of the Yuezhi clans, the Kushans, formed the great Kushan state, and it was the Yuezhi who prompted the Chinese discovery of the Western Regions, as they referred to Central Asia at that time.

Diplomatic relations between Inner Asian countries and China during the Han dynasty (206 BC– 220 AD)

First period (end of the 2nd century BC to the first half of the 1st century AD). From the time of its establishment, the Han Empire pursued an aggressive, expansionist policy, striving to extend its reach beyond its small territory between the Huang he (commonly known as the Yellow River) and Yangtze rivers. This policy was vigorously pursued under the Emperor Wudi (140–87 BC), who was particularly interested in the western territories.

Zhang Qian's mission. The Western Regions, i.e. Central Asia and Eastern Turkestan, are thought to have remained unknown to the Chinese until Zhang Qian's journey. However, this does not mean that they were completely unaware of the vast land inhabited by numerous peoples that existed to the west. There are accounts suggesting that even before Zhang Qian's journey, an envoy was sent from the Kangju region to China.

However, it is also highly likely that active attempts to establish diplomatic relations with the peoples inhabiting this territory, as well as exploration of the caravan routes with a view to its colonisation and a further move westwards, were undertaken only under the Han emperor Wudi.

The main reason for China's diplomatic contacts with the Western Regions was the war that broke out in the first half of the 2nd century BC between the two most powerful tribes of Inner Asia, the Huns and the Yuezhi – or Tokharians, as they are referred to in Greek texts. The Yuezhi suffered a terrible defeat and were forced, for the most part, to move from the territory of present-day Gansu province, where they originally lived, to the Semirechye region. However, the Huns pursued the Yuezhi even here and killed their leader, and turned his skull into a lacquered drinking vessel. The Yuezhi moved to the south of Central Asia, to Bactria, where, along with other tribes, they contributed to the collapse of the Graeco-Bactrian kingdom. Many years later their descendants were to create the great Kushan state.

Fearing the Huns, the Yuezhi were looking for allies to fight them. In turn, Han China, also suffering from the attacks of aggressive Huns and having heard about the Yuezhi, began to look for ways to establish such an alliance. Zhang Qian, a native of Han-Chung province (present-day Hanzhong) and the chief of the gate guard, volunteered to undertake this difficult and responsible mission. He was apparently favoured among other candidates on account of his valour.

The story of Zhang Qian's mission is recounted in the historical account known as the *Shiji* or ('Records of the Great Historian'). Zhang Qian set out on his journey to the west, taking with him a surrendered Hun guide called Ganfu or Tangyi Fu. However, on the way, he was captured by Huns who took him to their prince, who quite justifiably asked Zhang Qian what right the Chinese emperor had to send an envoy to the Yuezhi through Hun territory. Zhang Qian was held by the Huns and remained in captivity for about ten years, and was even married to a Hun woman, with whom he had a son. However, taking advantage of the comparative freedom granted to him, he fled westward with his companions and, after several tens of days, arrived in Dayuan, an ancient historical and cultural area that corresponds to Ferghana.

The ruler of Dayuan told Zhang Qian that he wished to establish diplomatic relations with the House of Han. Zhang Qian replied that if he were escorted to the Yuezhi, the emperor would reward the leader of Dayuan with copious gifts when he returned to China. In his message to the emperor, Zhang Qian wrote about how the people of Dayuan engaged in agriculture, cultivating rice and wheat, and how many vineyards and wines they possessed. There were as many as 70 large and small towns and cities in Dayuan, but the main attraction of the region was the 'blood-sweating' *argamak* horses, which were supposedly descended from the famous 'heavenly horses'. Another historical Chinese account, the *Ch'ien Han Shu* ('History of the Former Han Dynasty'), tells of the horses in the high mountains of Dayuan which are impossible to catch, and that 'this is why five coloured, i.e. bright dams are chosen and let out at the foot of the mountains to mate with the mountain stallions. The colts out of those dams "sweat with blood" and are therefore called a celestial breed of horses'. In the first mission from Dayuan, Zhang Qian was first escorted by specially assigned guides and interpreters to go to Kangju, a confederation of tribes spanning the vast territory of the northern and central part of Transoxiana and the lands to the right of the Syr Darya river. From Kangju, in 128 or 126 BC, Zhang Qian and his companions set out for the state of Great Yuezhi. At that time the Yuezhi had suffered new defeats at the hands of the Huns, who had slain the Yuezhi ruler and placed his eldest son on the throne. He then decided to abandon his homeland for fear of new wars with the Huns, and left with his tribe to go south, conquering the territory north of the Guishui river (the Amu Darya), which was roughly within the borders of the present-day Surkhan Darya province in Uzbekistan and south of Tajikistan. He also conquered the area south of this river, which Chinese sources refer to as Daxia, the local population call Bactria, and which was known to the Greeks as Bactriana.

In the middle or early second half of the 2nd century BC, Bactria was conquered by the nomadic tribes of the Sakarauli, Asii, Pasiani and Tokharians. Some scholars believe that the name Daxia may be derived from a Chinese rendering of the name for the Tokharian people. It is worth noting that later sources refer to this area as Tokharistan, meaning 'country of the Tokhars'. According to the *Shiji*, 'Daxia lies more than 2,000 li southwest of Dayuan, south of the Gui river. Its customs are the ones of sedentary people. There are fortified cities and solid dwellings.' By this time the Yuezhi ruler had decided against taking revenge on the Huns, instead choosing a peaceful way of life in the new territories populated by his tribe.

From the court of the Yuezhi Zhang Qian travelled on to Daxia (Bactria). He remained in Bactria for more than a year, and, having been unable to achieve a military alliance with the Great Yuezhi against the Huns, began to journey back to China by way of the southern route, as he wished to avoid the Huns. Nevertheless, he was recaptured by them. A year later, together with his guide Ganfu, Zhang Qian finally managed to escape from captivity, taking advantage of infighting among the Huns caused by the death of their ruler, and managed to reach China. His first mission to the Western Regions had lasted 13 years, and of the original delegation of over a hundred companions, only two returned – Zhang Qian himself and his guide Ganfu.

Upon his return to China, Zhang Qian gave detailed reports to the emperor about the countries he had visited and heard about from the local populations. In particular, he provided early knowledge of the Western Mediterranean, the countries of Tiaozhi (Asia Minor or the Eastern Mediterranean), and Likan, probably Egypt or ancient Rome, which the Chinese also called Fu Lin or Da Qin.

In his report, Zhang Qian gave detailed information about the Inner and Central Asian possessions of Dayuan, Wusun, Kangju, Daxia, Yancai and Great Yuezhi, about their locations, capitals, roads and distances, occupations, customs, numbers of people and troops. In particular, he wrote that the Kangju and Great Yuezhi possessions had strong armies that could be recruited into service, and if there was a way of persuading them to citizenship, it would be possible to extend the Chinese possessions by almost 10,000 li.

After returning to China, Zhang Qian and his companion received noble rank, and later, for his achievements in the war against the Huns, he was awarded the princely title of *Bo Wang Heu* or *Po Wang Hou* ('Noble of Po-wang'), and the military positions of *Xiao-yu* and *Wei-yu* (commander of a particular contingent of troops).

However, Zhang Qian lost all these ranks and honours in 122 BC, when his troops arrived too late to a battle between the Chinese and Huns, as a result of which a large part of the Chinese army was surrounded and killed. Zhang Qian himself was sentenced to be beheaded, but was pardoned.

Zhang Qian remained out of favour for several years, during which time the Chinese defeated the Huns in several battles, ultimately reaching the Salt Marsh (Lop Nor), which opened up a direct route to Central Asia for them. In connection with this, the Han emperor once again took an interest in states and possessions of the Western Regions, in particular in Daxia and Wusun, and the possibility of their incorporation into China. Zhang Qian was summoned to meet the emperor, and he prepared a detailed report for him describing the state of Wusun. In particular, he described the Wusun *kunmo* or *kunmi* (leader) who had managed to break free of Hun control, and suggested that if they pursued the right policy, they could incorporate Wusun, and then Daxia and other Central Asian possessions, into China.

The report decisively influenced the appointment of Zhang Qian as grand messenger, making him among the nine highest ministers of the government. He was given 300 troops with two horses each and as many as 10,000 head of cattle and sheep, and a large number of gifts to take with him. When he set out for Wusun, Zhang Qian also had a large staff of aides 'bearing their insignia' so that they could be sent to neighbouring states along the way.

However, negotiations with the Wu sun *kunmo* did not yield the desired results for China, as the Wusun domain was divided into three parts, with rulers who pursued almost totally independent policies. Nevertheless, while in Wusun, Zhang Qian managed to dispatch his deputy envoys to Dayuan (Ferghana), Kangju (Sogdia, Khorezm), Daxia (Bactria), Great Yuezhi (Northern Bactria) and Anxi (Parthia). He then returned to China accompanied by a small contingent of envoys whose leader had been instructed by the Wusun *kunmo* to collect as much information about the Chinese court as possible. Zhang Qian died a year after returning to China, in 104 or 103 BC, at which time he held an important government post.

Another year later, envoys sent by Zhang Qian with various tasks to the above-mentioned domains returned to China accompanied by envoys sent from those domains. These were in fact the first diplomatic envoys sent from Inner Asia. This marked the beginning of an era of intensive contacts of various kinds between the Inner Asian and Chinese states, which continued for many centuries, and was another important outcome of Zhang Qian's missions. He had spent 14 years of his life among the peoples of Inner Asia, gaining significant prestige. According to the *Han Shu* ('History of the Former Han Dynasty') '(Zhang Qian) inspired the trust of others and the barbarians liked him.'

Han–Ferghana relations

The first country in the region with which China established diplomatic relations, which at first were quite tense, was Dayuan/Ferghana. One of the main reasons for hostilities between the two countries was the famous 'heavenly horses' of Ferghana, about which Emperor Wudi learned from Zhang Qian.

According to the *Shiji*, Wudi sent a special envoy to the ruler of Dayuan with 1,000 pieces of gold and a golden horse and a request to exchange these gifts for Dayuan's *argamaks*. However, the Dayuan ruler refused the Han envoy's request, not wanting to send the horses and believing that the long distance from China would prevent the Han from sending troops to Dayuan. This angered the envoy and he retaliated by being rude to the Dayuan ruler. To put it in modern terms, there was a scandal, and the envoy was killed and his belongings were confiscated by the Dayuan ruler.

The Chinese emperor responded by sending to Ferghana an army of thousands of men, led by commander Li Guangli. The Han–Dayuan War thus broke out, and lasted four years, culminating in the defeat of Dayuan. A Dayuan elder called Meicai was appointed to replace the former Dayuan ruler Wugua, who was killed by the nobles of Dayuan. The Han took 20 or 30 of their best horses and 3,000 ordinary stallions and mares and set out on their journey home. A year later, Dayuan elders murdered Meicai because of his pro-Han stance, and installed Wugua's younger brother Chanfeng on the throne. Chanfeng established a peace treaty with China (this was the first treaty between this country and a Central Asian country), and sent his son as a hostage, as well as promising to send a pair of 'heavenly horses' to China every year. The imperial court responded by sending an envoy with gifts to cement peaceful relations with Dayuan. On his way back, the Chinese envoy gathered grapes and seeds of the *mu-su* plant (alfalfa – E.R.), which were later cultivated on a large scale alongside the imperial residences, lodges and pavilions. This was how important crops such as grapes and alfalfa were introduced to China for the first time.

Chinese diplomatic activity in the Western Regions increased rapidly after the end of the Han–Dayuan War. According to the *Han Shu*, under Emperor Wudi as many as ten missions were sent annually to various Inner Asian states.

Chinese–Parthian diplomatic relations

According to the American sinologist H. Dubs, at the end of the 2nd century BC, between 111 and 105 BC, and on the initiative of Emperor Wudi, China first established diplomatic relations with the Parthian kingdom, referred to in Chinese sources as Anxi. A Chinese envoy was solemnly welcomed at the eastern border by commanders and a cavalry of 20,000 troops and escorted to the Parthian capital.

The brilliant result of these missions and the opening up of the Western Regions was the beginning of the Silk Road, the first transcontinental route in the history of civilisations, connecting the countries of the West and the East. The peoples of Central Asia, in particular Sogdians, played a major role in its creation. Sogdian trading posts sprang up along the entire eastern route of the Silk Road from Samarkand to Chang'an, and the Sogdian language became the lingua franca for the people living along the route.

Chinese–Kangju diplomatic relations

The diplomatic relations between Han China and another Central Asian state, Kangju, were somewhat different. Having considerable military power (at one time it included Khorezm, Sogdia, Chach and other Transoxiana possessions), Kangju pursued an independent policy from China, and did not recognise the superiority of the Chinese in its diplomatic relations. Thus, according to the *Han Shu*, at receptions with the Kangju ruler, Chinese envoys were seated below Wusun ones, and dinner was served to them later than to Wusun princes and elders.

However, China, which greatly valued the reputation it had built up in the Western Regions, was trying to hold on to its position here at all costs, and therefore tolerated the situation. Despite not recognising China as a suzerain, as the Wusun did, the Kangju ruler nevertheless sent his sons to serve at the Chinese imperial court. The Chinese believed this was a cunning pretext to promote Kangju trade with China.

Chinese–Yuezhi diplomatic relations

Even though the Yuezhi apparently rejected a proposal for a military alliance with China against the Huns when Zhang Qian visited Bactria, diplomatic relations continued to develop between these two states. One of the most significant outcomes of that relationship was the introduction of Buddhism into China, which was greatly facilitated by Yuezhi envoys to China and Chinese envoys to Bactria.

The period is distinguished by the establishment of diplomatic relations between Han China and the countries and possessions of Inner Asia, by the regularity of diplomatic activity, and by the signing of various kinds of treaties. The diplomatic activity of Han China in Inner Asia, and probably also the war with Dayuan, led to the recognition of some of the various states of the Western Regions as vassals that were dependent on Han China. According to Chinese accounts, there were originally 36 states in the Western Regions, and by the beginning of the 1st century AD their number had increased to 55. Some of them had purely nominal dependence, while others, like Kangju, did not recognise China's supremacy in any way, even treating its envoys in a humiliating fashion.

According to these Chinese accounts, the office of the Protector General was established to run the various states of Western Regions on both the southern and northern routes of the Silk Road, but this seems unlikely. One account in the *Shiji* is typical in this respect. It states that if the Chinese ambassadors 'did not hand out silks or other goods they were given no food, and unless they purchased animals in the markets they could get no mounts for their riders. This was because the people considered the Han too far away to bother about.' If the provinces in question had indeed been so dependent on China, the officials of the imperial service, in this case of the Han Empire, would not have found themselves in such a position.

It is more likely that the so-called Protector General was in charge of diplomatic relations but did not actually have anything to do with the administration of the various states of the Western Regions. An important result of the establishment of diplomatic relations between Han China and Central Asia was the development of trade and cultural relations, as evidenced by both written sources and archaeological evidence.

For example, according to these sources, Dayuan received silver and gold from China and used it to produce various goods, but not coins. From Dayuan (Ferghana), along with the famous 'heavenly horses', the Chinese sent back crops such as grapes and alfalfa, which were then widely cultivated in China for the first time. Lacquerware and silk fabrics started arriving in Central Asia from China.

The Chinese introduced cast-iron technology to Inner Asia, which was promoted by conscripts who had deserted from the Han missions and fled to Dayuan where they lived and taught the locals the techniques.

We know from archaeological finds that Chinese wu zhu bronze coins came from China to Central Asia, especially to Ferghana and to some extent to Sogdia, apparently initiating the development of money relations in Ferghana. Several types of the famous Chinese bronze mirrors have been found in considerable quantities in Central Asia, along with occasional finds of jade objects.

In AD 7, Wang Mang (AD 9–23), viewed as a usurper in Chinese historical tradition, seized power in China, and diplomatic relations between Central Asia and China were interrupted.

The rise to power of the Eastern Han dynasty in AD 25 did not initially help to re-establish these relations, although a number of envoys were sent to China from some states of the Western Regions during the reign of Emperor Guangwu, asking if they could submit to the Middle Kingdom (China) and have a Protector General. According to the *Hou Han Shu* ('History of the Later Han Dynasty'), relationships with the Western Regions were fractured for 65 years, and it was not until AD 73 that a range of relationships were re-established.

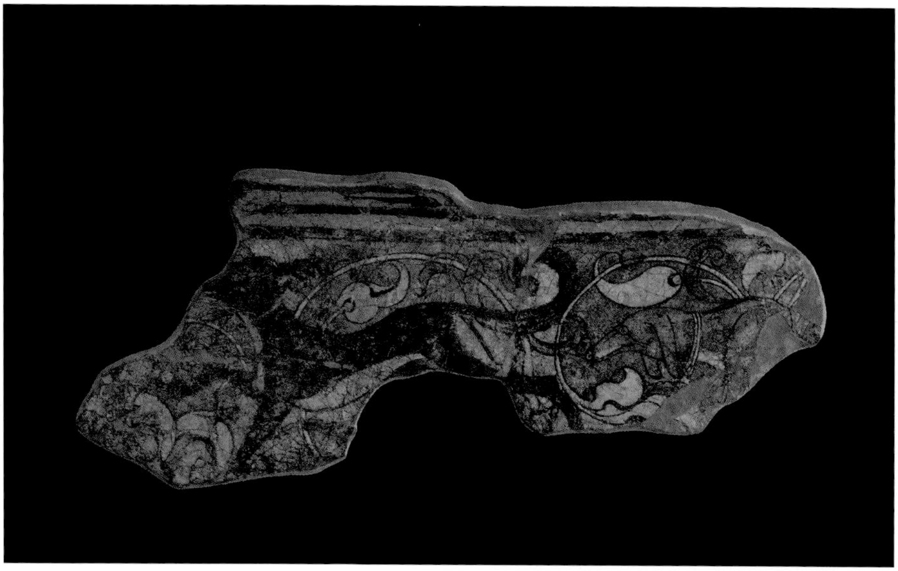

Two hunting dogs ***(top)***
Afrasiab, 11th–12th century
Wall painting, 85 × 35 cm
Samarkand, Historical Museum of Afrasiab
BpKP-429

Panel with a simurgh ***(above)***
Afrasiab, 11th–12th century
Wall painting, 75 × 75 cm
Samarkand, National Centre of Archaeology
95/159 165

Western wall of the Ambassadors painting
Afrasiab, 7th–8th century
Wall painting, 670 × 250 cm
Samarkand, Historical Museum of Afrasiab
КП-6251

Door
Gur-i-Mir, Samarkand, 15th century
Wood, 225 × 106 cm
Samarkand, State Historical, Architectural and Art Museum-Reserve
A-559

Column with capital
Oburdon, 9th century
Wood, 100 × 160 cm
Tashkent, State Museum of History of Uzbekistan
179/2

Wall painting
11th–12th century
51 × 36 cm
Samarkand, Institute of Archaeological research named after
Gulyamov Institute of Archaeological Studies

Head of a bearded man
Khalchayan, 1st century AD
Clay, H. 25 cm
Tashkent, State Museum of Arts of Uzbekistan
28 KTI-36994

Head of a male Mongolian
Khalchayan, 1st century AD
Clay, H. 19 cm
Tashkent, State Museum of Arts of Uzbekistan
17 KTI-36987

Prince in armour
Khalchayan, 1st century BC–1st century AD
Clay, H. 53 cm
Tashkent, State Museum of History of Uzbekistan
40 KTI-37006

Head and shoulders of a Buddha with three eyes ***(top)***
Kuva, Ferghana, 7th century AD
Clay, 76 × 79 × 34 cm
Tashkent, State Museum of Arts of Uzbekistan
82

Head of a bearded man ***(above)***
Khalchayan, 1st century AD
Clay, H. 25 cm
Tashkent, State Museum of Arts of Uzbekistan
28 KTI-36994

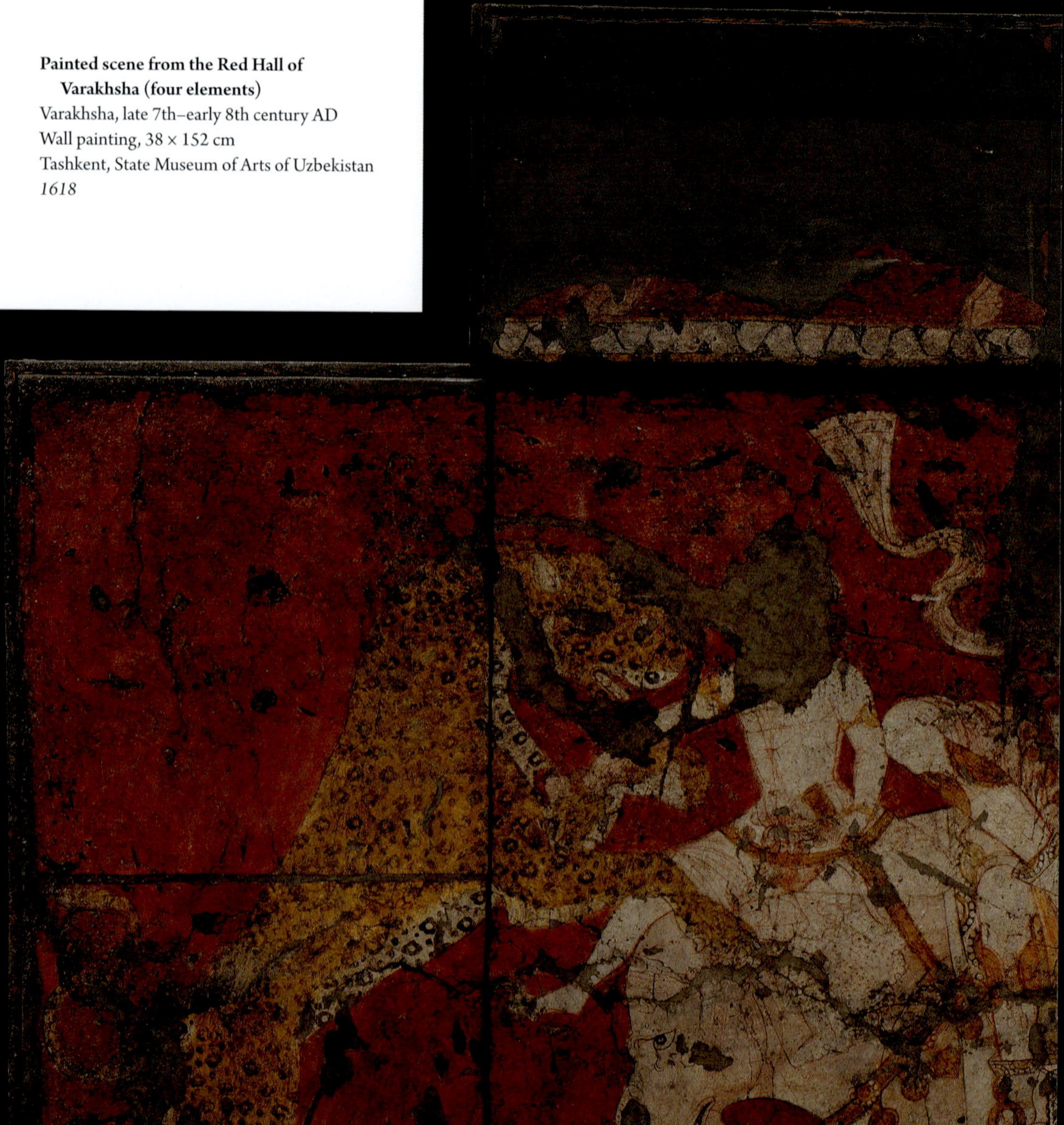

Painted scene from the Red Hall of Varakhsha (four elements)
Varakhsha, late 7th–early 8th century AD
Wall painting, 38 × 152 cm
Tashkent, State Museum of Arts of Uzbekistan
1618

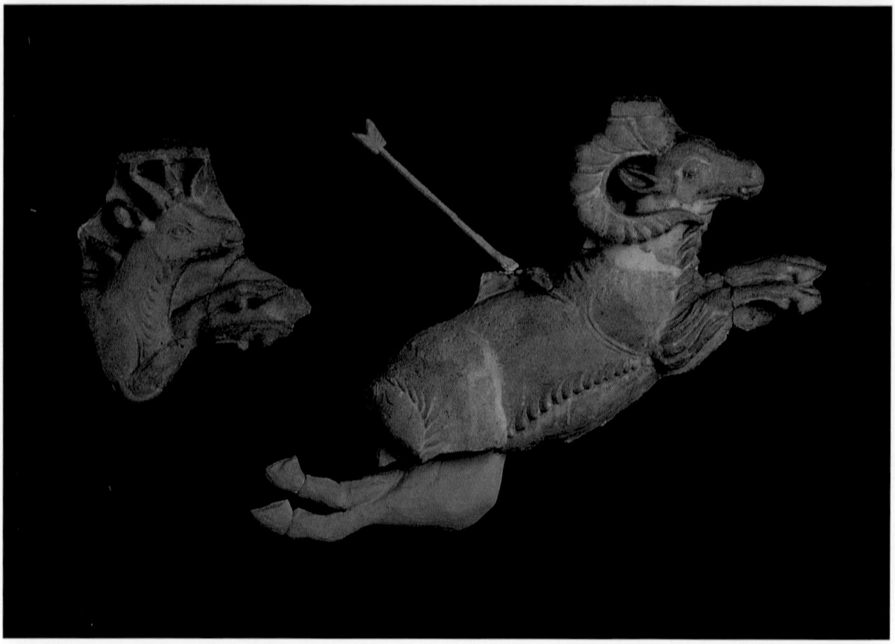

Fragments of architectural decoration: hunting scene (six fragments)
Varakhsha, late 7th–early 8th century AD
Stucco, 30 × 56 cm; 23 × 57 cm
Tashkent, State Museum of History of Uzbekistan
27/6 27/7 27/25 27/8 27/53

Buddha with monks
Termez, Surkhan Darya, 3rd century AD
Stone, 75 × 63 × 28 cm
Tashkent, State Museum of History of Uzbekistan
274/1

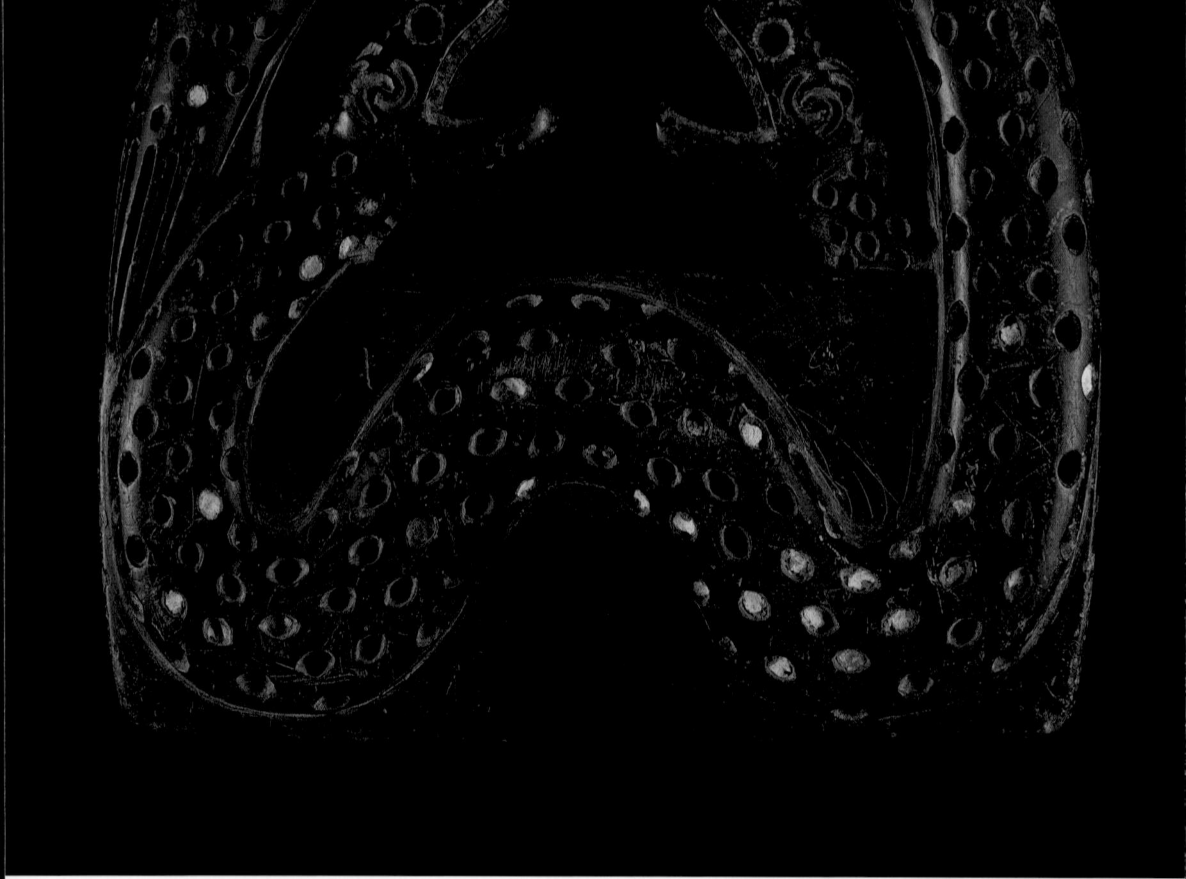

Stone sculpture with two snakes
Sokh, Ferghana valley, 3rd millennium BC
Crystal, 27 × 24 cm
Tashkent, State Museum of History of Uzbekistan
207/1

Unlike its predecessors, the Eastern Han dynasty initially pursued a somewhat different policy in its relations with the Western Regions. The rulers of this dynasty believed that ties with these regions involved too much financial expenditure for China, and for this reason they became erratic.

Various expeditions and missions by the Chinese general Ban Chao to the Western Regions contributed to the establishment of stronger diplomatic relations between Inner Asia and China. According to the *Hou Han Shu*, Ban Chao and his army crossed all of Central Asia and even reached the 'Western Sea' (Mediterranean Sea). After this, envoys from Central Asian kingdoms came to the emperor's court bearing tributes. However, these were probably isolated cases because, according to the same source, while some possessions in the Western Regions resumed contacts with China, others broke them off. This probably refers to relations with Kangju, which at that time consisted of five main possessions: Chi [Ji] (probably referring to Bukhara), Su-hsieh [Suxie] (to Kesh), Fu-mo [Fumo] (to Samarkand), Yü-ni [Yuni] (to Chach) and Yü-chien [Aojian] (to Khorezm), and a number of other, smaller possessions.

Diplomatic relations with Anxi (Parthia) and the powerful Kushan state that emerged in the 1st century AD, which included Northern Bactria and territories as far as the Hissar mountains, were, evidently, a special case.

At any rate, Parthia continued to maintain diplomatic relations with China, which were, however, confined to sending an envoy and gifts in the form of rare animals. For example, during the reign of Emperor Zhangdi in AD 87 a messenger was sent to China with lions and *fuba* (Persian gazelle) as a gift, and in AD 101 the Parthian emperor Manqu (perhaps Pacorus II) sent gifts of lions and ostriches to the imperial court. It should also be noted that Gan Ying, the subaltern of Ban Chao, was the first of the Chinese to reach the Mediterranean Sea, travelling via the territory of Parthia in AD 97, and he described the countries located around it in detail.

Diplomatic relations between Inner Asian states and China in the 3rd–5th centuries AD

Analysis of Chinese texts shows that diplomatic relations between Inner Asia and China during the Cao Wei (AD 220–265), Jin (AD 265–420) and Northern, Eastern and Western Wei (AD 386–556 / 557) dynasties collapsed completely, largely owing to the military and political situations of the periods, as outlined below. The great ancient realms of Kushan and Parthia collapsed; a number of independent provinces were formed in the territory of Northern Bactria, which was a part of the Kushan kingdom, and Sassanian power was established in the south-western region of Central Asia after the fall of the Parthian state. The Kangju confederation probably also split into a number of small independent kingdoms during these times and the tribes of Chionites and Kidarites invaded Transoxiana from the north-west and north-east.

In China, these times were also characterised by unstable political situations and dynastic struggles, aggravated by invasions by the Huns and Zhuzhans. It is notable that for the period from the second half of the 3rd century AD to the beginning of the 5th century no information exists about any form of diplomatic relations between Inner Asia and China. Moreover, according to historical records, they did not receive any ambassadors from the Western Regions at all during the reign of Emperor Mingyuan (AD 409–423).

The resumption of relations is associated with another emperor of the Northern Wei dynasty, Taiwu (AD 424–452), who sent a large contingent of envoys to the Western Regions headed by Dong Wan, the Gentleman Cavalier Attendant, and Gao Ming, together with many gifts, including large quantities of brocade silk.

Dong Wan's mission entered Inner Asia by the northern route, having initially reached the state of the Wusun, whose king received them with much courtesy. The Wusun king told Dong Wan that the states of Poluona (Ferghana – E.R.) and Zheshe (Chach – E.R.) 'longed for the virtue of Wei, and wanted to swear fealty and pay tribute, but were worried there was no road to reach Wei'. This comment should not be understood as referring to a general lack of roads, but to the fact that the Zhuzhans and Huns had closed the roads, cutting off China's communication with Inner Asia to a great extent, if not completely. From Wusun, Dong Wan went on to Ferghana while Gao Ming went to Chach, where treaties were concluded recognising these dominions as vassals of China and gifts were also presented.

The significance of Dong Wan's mission, which restored diplomatic relations between Inner Asia and China after many years of interruption, may be equated to some extent with the impact of Zhang Qian's mission, which had opened up the Western Regions for China.

On the return journey, Dong Wan took with him envoys from 16 Inner Asian states and, as the *Beishi* ('History of the Northern Dynasties'), testifies, from that time on envoys arrived one after another, and not a year passed without the appearance of several state envoys. The considerable intensity of diplomatic and other kinds of relations between Inner Asian states and China, surpassing all previous ones, continued during the Tang dynasty in China (AD 618–907) until the second half of the 8th century AD, when the Chinese advance into Inner Asia was halted by the Arabs.

As we can see, as a special form of international relations, diplomacy emerged in Inner Asia as early as the first half of the 1st millennium BC, but its establishment and development continued from the first centuries BC to first centuries AD.

In the early stages in the development of diplomatic relations in the countries of Inner Asia, due to certain political reasons, these were mainly fostered with Iran and the Hellenistic states of the West, while China became the central focus from the end of the 1st millennium BC.

The nature of diplomatic relations with the various dynasties that ruled China was mixed, however. While considerable diplomatic activity took place under the Western Han dynasty, it declined at the outset of the Eastern Han dynasty, but then resumed, albeit sporadically, at a later stage.

The military and political situation in Inner Asia, raids by the nomadic tribes of Zhuzhans, Huns, Chionites and Kidarites, and dynastic struggles in China all led to the almost complete cessation of these relationships.

They were only fully renewed in the second quarter of the 5th century AD, and were evidently connected with China's search for allies against nomadic tribes in Inner Asia, and also to a change in its state policy towards international relations with Inner Asian states, and to the renewal of its traditional policy of expansionism in this region.

It is entirely possible that at this time Inner Asian states already had dedicated bodies responsible for international relations, and that a cadre of individuals specialising in this area was being formed. At any rate, there is evidence of envoys, aides and interpreters being active at this time.

Clearly, diplomacy in Inner Asia has a long and centuries-old tradition.

PART III

CULTURAL AND SPIRITUAL DEVELOPMENT

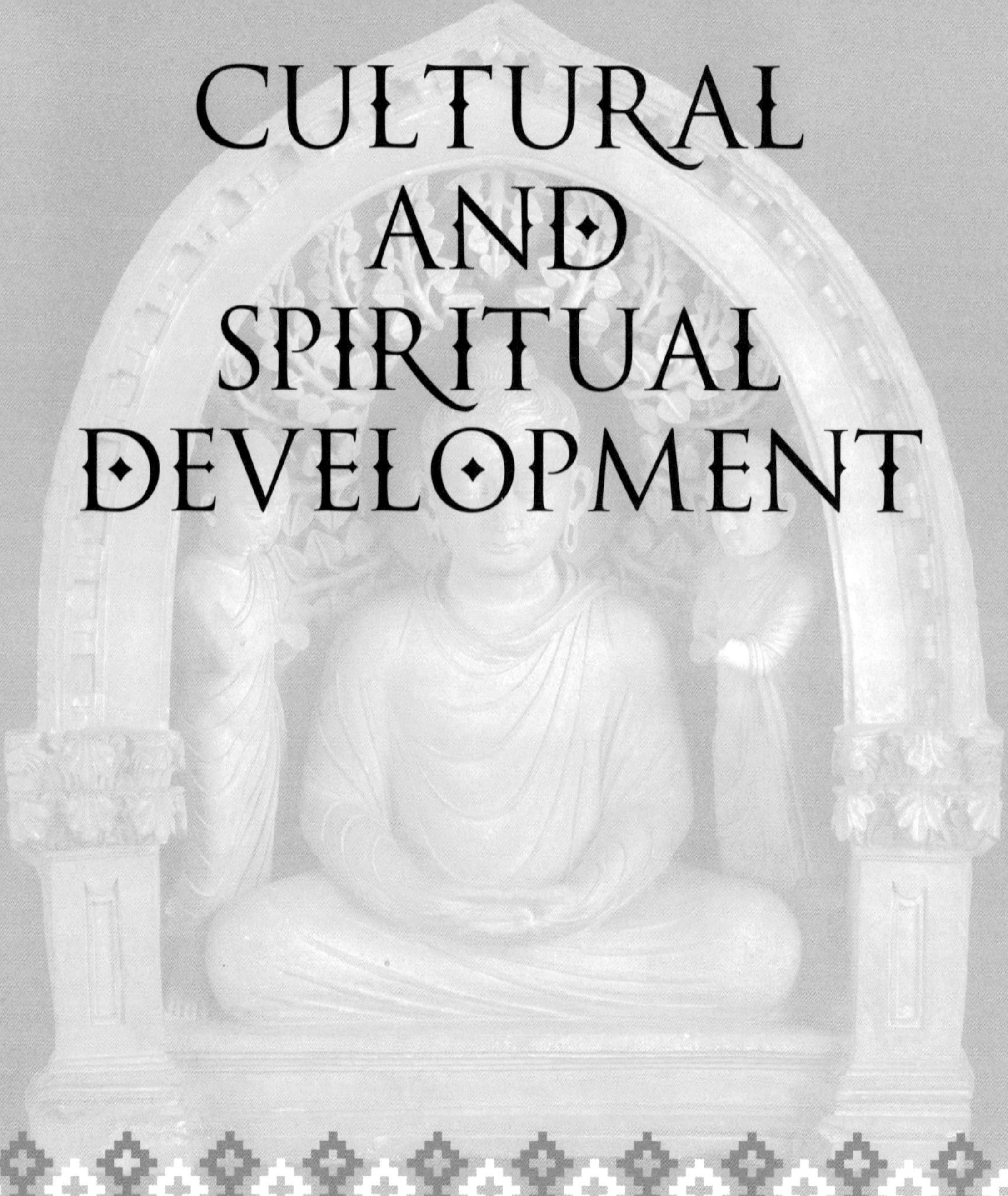

3.1

WRITING AS A KEY FACTOR IN THE LEVEL OF DEVELOPMENT OF CIVILISATIONS AND STATES

The creation of a writing system is generally regarded as one of the greatest achievements of civilisation, and is therefore a determining feature of a people's culture. The most important function of written language is its capacity to preserve in the memory of new generations the achievements and deeds of their ancestors. Writing systems have emerged in parallel with state entities; after all, a state cannot exist without a writing system, as it is fundamental to ensuring the functioning of a range of state and legal institutions.

For example, in ancient Egypt, a writing system (in the form of Egyptian hieroglyphics) emerged at the beginning of the 3rd millennium BC, the time when a unified kingdom developed here. Even earlier, at the end of the 4th and beginning of the 3rd millennium BC, the creation of writing systems began in Mesopotamia, in the earliest Sumerian states, first in the form of pictograms, and then in cuneiform. Both these early writing systems consisted of determinative signs and symbols, initially representing words and later, syllables.

Later, at the end of the 2nd millennium BC, a Semitic alphabetic script was created, most probably in Phoenicia, representing the sounds rather than the semantic meaning of words. This was a true revolution in the history of mankind, as a system consisting of just over 20 signs had now replaced cumbersome hieroglyphs and cuneiform comprising hundreds of graphically complicated signs. Owing to the unique features of Semitic languages, the original alphabet conveyed only consonantal sounds (however, later, it did include some vowel sounds as well).

According to scholars, the most ancient inscription made using an alphabet is a Phoenician inscription from around 1000 BC on the sarcophagus of King Ahiram of Byblos. The inscription was made on the orders of his son and contained a curse on anyone who should try to open the sarcophagus. The final part of it reads: '…if a king from among kings or a governor from among governors, or commander (of an army), should come up against Byblos and uncover this coffin, may the scepter of his rule be broken, may the throne of his kingship be overturned, and may peace flee Byblos, and (as for) him, may his writings be effaced (from) before Byblos.'

Still later, probably in the early 1st millennium BC, the Semitic alphabet was adopted by the Greeks, who refined it considerably, adding letters for vowels to convey both the sounds and written forms of words more accurately.

It was these two writing systems – the Semitic, through Aramaic, and Greek – that were the basis of the local, pre-Arabic writing systems of Central Asia. It should be noted that at a certain time, presumably from the beginning of the 1st century AD to the 8th century AD, the Chinese hieroglyphic script was becoming widespread in Central Asia and that it had emerged independently as part of the evolution of this great civilisation of the Far East. It is well known that in the first half of the 8th century AD, Sogdia even minted coins with a double legend in Sogdian and Chinese.

Going back a little, we should note that Central Asia was not one of the regions where writing first appeared. We cannot trace the early stages of the development of writing on its territory – from primitive forms of writing, so-called object- and picture-based writing (using pictograms and ideograms), to logosyllabic systems, syllabaries and, ultimately, alphabetic scripts. Images on ceramics from the 2nd millennium BC from southern Turkmenistan include separate groups of symbols, which are so systematic and consistent, and follow a particular order in combination with drawings, that they may well be rudiments of pictographic writing. To date, no specimens of Egyptian hieroglyphs have been found in Central Asia, nor any of cuneiform – the main type of writing used in the Achaemenid state and hence in many ancient countries of the Near and Middle East.

At the end of the 19th and beginning of the 20th century, some travellers and local historians reported having seen cuneiform inscriptions in the extreme south of Central Asia. These reports have not been corroborated by contemporary academic evidence; however, the existence of such inscriptions in Central Asia and the familiarity of the population of the region with cuneiform should not be completely ruled out, as Central Asia was part of the Achaemenid state for almost 200 years (from the mid-6th century BC to 330 BC). However, at that time, cuneiform was used by the Achaemenid kings for particularly solemn occasions, such as recording military victories on rock inscriptions. An example is the Behistun inscription of

King Darius I, carved in three cuneiform script languages – Old Persian, Elamite and Akkadian – describing the king's exploits in Central Asia and accompanied by a relief depicting representatives of conquered peoples, the Sakas, Bactrians and the people of Margiana, among others.

Clearly, these images and inscriptions indicate that the peoples of Central Asia were familiar with cuneiform. Some of them must have mastered another script that was widespread in the Achaemenid state – Aramaic.

The Arameans, a people of the North Semitic group, originally lived in Syria, and from the end of the 2nd/early 1st millennium BC migrated to Central Mesopotamia. Arameans adopted and refined the Phoenician alphabet, slightly changing the forms of graphemes (base units of a writing system), and introducing spaces and vowel signs. The Aramaic alphabet was an abjad-type alphabet (all letters were primarily consonants, although some could also represent vowels). Vowels were usually indicated with specific marks such as dots and the like, which were often left out. As a rule, vowels were marked at the beginning and at the end of a word. In the middle of a word, a letter could express either just a consonant or a whole syllable (consonant plus vowel).

Over time, Arameans began to use vowel signs, most often long ones, in the middle of a word as well, but they did this very inconsistently. The most ancient specimens of Aramaic script from the 9th to 8th centuries BC have been found in Syria (the inscription of Bar-Hadad) and south-eastern Turkey (at Zincirli).

In the 7th–6th centuries BC, the Aramaic script, which was easy to learn (it had only about 20 letters) was effectively replacing a number of cumbersome systems of cuneiform that had previously prevailed in Western Asia, namely Akkadian, Elamite and Urartian cuneiform. In the vast and multi-tribal Achaemenid kingdom, in almost all satrapies from Asia Minor to north-west India, including Central Asia, the Aramaic language became the main means of communication and the language of the administrative apparatus and record keeping.

According to Herodotus, every satrap in the Achaemenid kingdom had royal scribes who used to read documents sent by the king. Moreover, nobles who were close to the king could also read and write. When King Darius decided to send a noble Persian called Bagaeus to Oroetes, a satrap of Lydia, Bagaeus wrote up several documents on behalf of the king and on his arrival in Sardis, the capital of Lydia, gave them to the royal scribe to read (Herodotus, III, 128). Aramean scribes often prepared to write documents dictated by local officials (Persians, Medes, Parthians, Bactrians and Sogdians) by first making a mental translation into Aramaic. The same process was followed when a document was received by the chancellery of the satrapy it was intended for: the scribe would orally translate it from Aramaic into the local language. As a result of this practice, a system of local lexical and grammatical correspondences with Aramaic gradually developed. At the same time, the Aramaic language used for documents became heavily influenced by the local languages, with borrowed words (mainly administrative terms) and whole expressions from the local languages becoming incorporated; Aramaic word order was changed as well.

It would appear that at this time, the inhabitants of Central Asia had already mastered the Aramaic script. A papyrus in Aramaic found, along with other papyri, on the island of Elephantine in the lower reaches of the Nile bears witness to this. The document, dated 464 BC, relates to a property dispute between a Khorezmian, Dargaman, who served in the military garrison on the island of Elephantine in the detachment of Artabanus, and a Jew, Mahseiah, from another detachment of the same garrison. This document, which begins 'Dargaman, son of Harshin, a Khorezmian from Artabanus' detachment in the Elephantine fortress said to Mahseiah…', shows that Dargaman, a native of Khorezm who lived on Elephantine with his family, knew the Aramaic language and script.

A few years ago in northern Afghanistan, documents written in Aramaic (in Official Aramaic) were discovered which then came to London to the famous collector of antiquities Nasser D. Khalili. Among them are 30 documents on leather and 18 on wood, written in ink. One document dates from the 5th century BC, but all the others are from the 4th century BC. In general the documents cover the period from 353 to 324 BC, corresponding to the reign of the Achaemenid kings Artaxerxes III, Darius III, Bessus (Artaxerxes V) and Alexander the Great. A preliminary reading of these documents was published in French by the Israeli scholar S. Shaked in 2004.

The documents contain important information about the economic life, political events, administrative apparatus and historical geography of Bactria, along with names of important persons (Akhvamazda, Bagavant). The documents also include promissory notes and business letters. These documents, in particular, mention cities of Southern Sogdia, Nikhshapaya (Nakhshab) and Kish, as well as the Artadatana 'desert', probably a desert in northern Afghanistan. The documents indicate the widespread use of Aramaic script in Bactria in various spheres of activity, about which, previously, we were only able to guess.

The oldest example of Aramaic script found in Central Asia is a short inscription that has survived on a storage jar, a *khum*, found during excavations of the site of Great Aibugir-Kala (Northern Khorezm) by the archaeologist M. Mambetullaev. The inscribed letters and archaeological data suggest that it dates from the 5th or 4th century BC. A few other inscriptions on pottery have been found at other sites in Khorezm, but their brevity (as a rule they contain only Khorezmian proper names) makes it impossible to say whether they are Aramaic or Khorezmian texts written in almost the same script. This is also the case with some inscriptions from Koi-

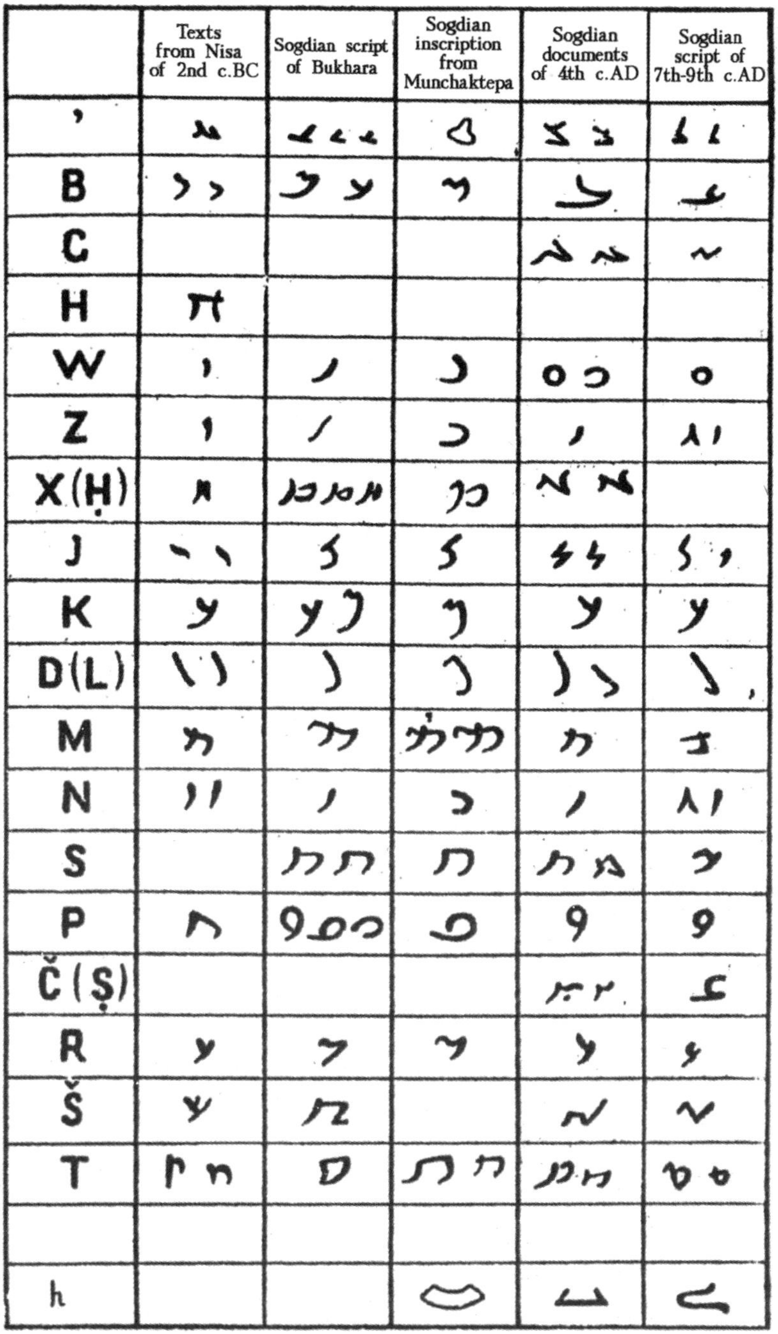

A table illustrating some of the ancient alphabets of Central Asia (based on Aramaic).

Krylgan-Kala, a site that archaeologists believe belongs to the period between the 4th/3rd centuries BC and the 1st century AD.

There are two further examples of the earliest Aramaic inscriptions dating back to the 4th and 3rd centuries BC. One of them is an inscription on a seal ring from the Amu Darya hoard. It consists of four signs engraved over a depiction of the human-headed bull known as Gopatshah and gives the name of the god of the Amu Darya river, Vakhshu. The second specimen is an Aramaic legend on gold coins, with the name Vakhshuvar (Oxyartes in Greek transliteration).

A large series of Aramaic inscriptions on objects made of greenish-blue stone – mortars, pestles and vessels, which had an important role in the ritual preparation of *haoma*, revered as a sacred drink by the Zoroastrians – has been found in the area of ancient Arachosia (southern Afghanistan), neighbouring Central Asia. In particular, these inscriptions include names of Arachosian craftsmen, which are very similar to Bactrian, Sogdian and other ancient Eastern Iranian names, and they represent the oldest collection of such names in Eastern Iran and Central Asia.

After the Achaemenid state succumbed to the armies of Alexander the Great, Aramaic continued to be used for official purposes in Central Asia, even though the Greek language and script were also used for administrative purposes. In the Parthian kingdom, Aramaic was used alongside Greek for some time, while in the newly formed Graeco-Bactrian kingdom, Greek was the main language of administration.

An ostracon found at the site of Ai-Khanum with an inscription in Aramaic dates back to the first half of the 2nd century BC. The text of the inscription is brief – it consists of just three incomplete lines and a postscript (or an earlier but still visible text) made by another hand, and the content appears to relate to accounting. According to P. Bernard and V.A. Livshits, the language is probably Bactrian rather than Aramaic. The find at Ai-Khanum suggests that throughout Graeco-Bactrian history, Aramaic-Bactrian was used alongside Greek for administrative purposes in the kingdom, primarily serving the local population.

As a rule, written language tends to be relatively conservative and traditional. This is because one of its most important functions is to preserve cultural heritage in the memory of several generations. It is therefore no wonder that the tradition of Aramaic writing in Central Asia and Eastern Iran, including Bactria, endured even under Hellenistic rule.

Bactrian-Aramaic script existed in Termez in the Kushan period of the first centuries AD. As V.A. Livshits has established, this is evidenced by a brief one-word inscription on a potsherd discovered by L.I. Albaum during the excavation of the Buddhist complex at Fayaztepa.

The Aramaic script, but not yet Sogdian, was used for coin legends on imitations of Euthydemus tetradrachms that were in circulation in Bukharan Sogdia. The earliest specimens of these are from the 2nd century BC. Aramaic script, along with Greek, was used on imitations of Antiochus coins that were minted in Samarkand Sogdia in the late 3rd or early 2nd century BC. Some scholars believe that these legends are in fact in Sogdian script and language, but it is impossible to determine this because they are so short.

Coin legends usually give the name of the king and his title, which was in fact usually conveyed, not in Sogdian, but by the Aramaic ideogram *MR'Y*, just like the second title found on the coin legends, *MLK'*, which was also in Aramaic. It is therefore premature to speak of the replacement of the Aramaic script by the local Sogdian and Khorezmian script in the last centuries BC. However, it is a well-known fact that somewhere around the 3rd to the 2nd century BC, previously uniform Aramaic writing became fragmented into a number of varieties: 'Jewish square script', Palmyrene and Nabataean. In Central Asia, local written languages based on Aramaic emerged and replaced both Aramaic and Greek scripts only later.

We can trace this process by studying the evolution of the language of coin legends found in the ancient regions of Transoxiana. Evidently, Greek was the dominant script on the coins of Bactria and, partly, of Sogdia in the 3rd–2nd centuries BC. This is not surprising, since from the end of the 4th century BC and up to the beginning of the 2nd century BC or the second half of the 2nd century BC, Sogdia was subject to political and military domination by the Greeks.

However, there have been few discoveries of Greek inscriptions in the territory of Transoxiana. Among those found are six inscriptions from Northern Bactria: a dedicatory inscription dating from the 3rd–2nd centuries BC on a votive altar from Takht-i Sangin that reads: 'Atrosokes dedicated [his] vow to Oxus'; inscriptions dating from the 2nd century BC on fragments of a few vessels from Kampyrtepa, indicating measures of weight and liquid – 15 drachmas and 7 *hoi*, as well as a Greek word/name, *ΚΛΕΘ[...]*; and an inscription on the fragment of a *khum* from the Kushan period found during excavations in Garav-Kala.

Numerous inscriptions in Greek dating from the 3rd–2nd centuries BC have also been found on different items such as potsherds, papyri and stones at the site of Ai-Khanum. The two inscriptions found in the mausoleum of the city ruler or of a highly venerated person are also especially notable. The first one declares that Clearchus, a younger pupil of Aristotle, inscribed the sayings copied by him from reliefs in the temple of Apollo, and the second one actually contains fragments of these philosophical sayings.

It is interesting to note that during later excavations of another structure at this site – the palace – papyrus manuscripts from the 3rd–2nd centuries BC were found. These are the oldest such specimens to have been found in Inner Asia. According to the scholar C. Rapin, they are philosophical manuscripts in Greek relating to the teachings of Aristotle.

Two short Greek inscriptions were also found at Afrasiab in Sogdia. One of these, found in the habitation level from the late 4th to early 3rd century BC, was carved on a ram's astragalus bone (possibly a game piece) and consists of the four letters *ΚΤΗΣ*. According to K. Akhunbabaev, this inscription is most likely an abbreviation for the Greek name of the owner of the game piece – *ΚΤΗΣ[ΙΟΣ]*, meaning 'he who guards the home'.

The Greek language and script were preserved in Bactria even after the fall of the Graeco-Bactrian kingdom, as can be seen in the legends on the coins of Yuezhi rulers of Northern Bactria: imitations of Heliocles, Eucratides and Demetrius coins, coins of Pseigacharis and Sapadbizes, and tetradrachms and oboli of the founder of the Kushan clan, Kushan ('Heraeus'). These legends still feature typically Greek titles (*basileus, tyrannos*). However, although their lettering in the legends was often considerably distorted, they nonetheless indicate that the engravers were acquainted with developments in Greek palaeography. Thus, in keeping with the general change in its appearance on later imitations, the letter sigma acquired a new form, the C-like 'lunate' or square form, losing the normal, crooked back of the classical form (Σ).

Greek writing and language, in particular titles and epithets such as *basileus basileon* ('king of kings'), Soter Megas ('Great Saviour') and the names of Greek gods (Helios) are still preserved on the coins of the early Kushan kings Wima I Takto, Wima Kadphises and Kanishka I. However, during the reign of the greatest of the Kushan kings, Kanishka I, in the first half of the 2nd century AD, a radical change in state policy took place, namely the transition to the Bactrian language and script, although this was still based on the Greek alphabet with the addition of one letter known as *sho* or *san*. The third line of the Rabatak inscription provides clear evidence of this: '... And he [i.e. King Kanishka] issued a Greek edict (and) then he put it into Aryan.' The legends on his coins, where the Greek title *basileus basileon* is replaced by the Bactrian equivalent *shaonano shao* ('king of kings'), are further evidence of this.

At the same time, but probably at a much faster pace, the transformation of Greek legends into local Sogdian and Khorezmian legends on the coins of the rulers of Sogdia and Khorezm was taking place.

Coins of Yuezhi rulers of Sogdia from the so-called Hyrcodes or Urkod group, demonstrate this process especially vividly. On the earliest coins of this group (probably from the 2nd–1st century BC), which contains two issue types depicting a standing figure with a spear, and later a protome of a galloping horse, the legends on the obverse and reverse sides are still entirely in Greek but convey local names and titles: *ΥΡΚΩΔΟΥ* and *ΟΡΔΗΤΡΟΥ ΜΑΚΑΡΟΥ*.

3.1

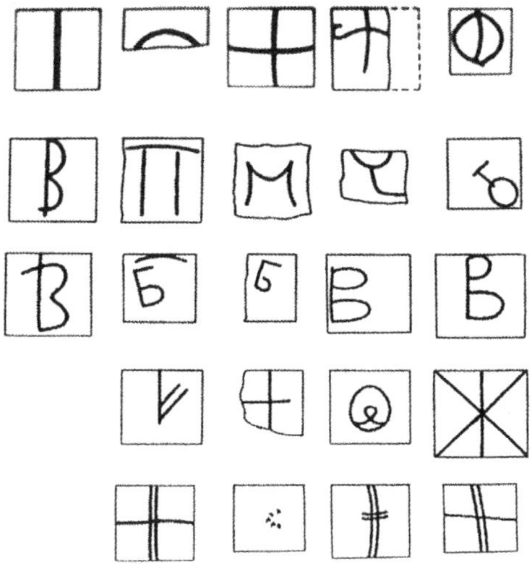

Stamps on mud bricks from the defensive walls of the citadel. Dalverzintepa.

Coins from the same group, which date from a later time (1st–3rd century AD) have legends that are only in Sogdian script. The legends on the coins of Southern Sogdia and Samarkand Sogdia, depicting an archer and Heracles and Zeus, first minted in the 1st century AD, were also written solely in Sogdian.

Around the same time, a similar process of replacing Greek legends took place in Khorezm. The earliest coins from this area are imitations of Eucratides tetradrachms with a partially distorted Greek legend from Group A, and date from the second half of the 2nd to the 1st century BC. Only Group B coins have a short Khorezmian or even Aramaic legend, and these probably began to be issued in the 1st century BC–1st century AD, or according to B.I. Vainberg, in the mid-1st and beginning of the second half of the 1st century AD. The letters of these legends are not very different from the original Aramaic letters. Moreover, the titles in the inscriptions on these coins are only the Aramaic *MR'Y* (*mrai*) for 'ruler' and *MLK'* (*mlka*) for 'king'.

Thus, legends on coins suggest that Greek and Aramaic writing was replaced in Sogdia and Khorezm by local writing systems (based on the Aramaic alphabet) in the 1st century AD. The same was true of Parthia, where, with the rise of the junior Arsacids in the middle of the 1st century AD, Greek legends on coins were replaced by Parthian. This process took place in Bactria somewhat later, where Greek inscriptions on coins were replaced by those of Bactrian language and script only in the first half of the 2nd century AD.

However, we can assume that the process of the substitution of Aramaic script and language with local writing systems occurred over a long period and probably began in the last centuries BC. It is difficult to establish exactly when these changes took place because no examples of any extensive texts in, for example, Sogdian or

Khorezmian scripts or languages have been found. In fact, the earliest specimens date from the 2nd–3rd centuries AD (the Khorezmian texts of Toprak-Kala) or the early 4th century AD (the Sogdian 'Ancient Letters'). Brief legends on coins available to scholars show that lettering on them is still close to Aramaic, and among the inscriptions from the 2nd–1st centuries BC it is difficult to distinguish Parthian inscriptions from Khorezmian or Sogdian ones, for example.

Now, let us take a closer look at the scripts that existed in Transoxiana in the pre-Arab period. The **Sogdian script** was one of the most widespread and probably emerged in the 1st century BC – 1st century AD. In ancient times, and especially in the early medieval period, it was used in the vast expanses of Eurasia, from Old Merv to the Altai mountains, Mongolia, China and Tibet, and the Sogdian language was the primary means of communication, especially for trade between different peoples. In addition to discoveries in Sogdia, elsewhere in Central Asia examples of Sogdian script have been found in Chach, the Ferghana valley and the Semirechye region. The widespread use of Sogdian script can be ascribed to the active trade by Sogdian merchants on the routes of the Silk Road and to the Sogdian settlements that developed well beyond Sogdia. This explains why so many of the Sogdian manuscripts we know of today have been discovered in Xinjiang. Sogdian colonies copied translations of Buddhist, Manichaean and Christian texts, as well as original works of Sogdian secular literature, of which, unfortunately, only a few fragments have survived. In Xinjiang and Mongolia, where Sogdians had especially close contacts with the Turks, Sogdian script was adapted to record the ancient Uigur language, giving rise to the great relay of Inner Asian script being passed from Sogdians to Uigurs and further on to Manchurians.

When and where Sogdian script first appeared has yet to be established with any certainty. The earliest specimens appear to be the brief inscriptions on silver imitations of tetradrachms issued by the Graeco-Bactrian king Euthydemus in the Bukhara region between the 2nd and 1st century BC. At the same time, or somewhat later, Sogdian legends replaced Greek ones on other coins (imitations of Antiochus coinage, coins from the Hyrcodes group and others) that were minted in different parts of Sogdia. Several early Sogdian inscriptions have also been found on gemstones – precious and semi-precious stones with images.

There is also a group of remarkable Sogdian documents known in the scholarship as the Sogdian 'Ancient Letters'. Some scholars date them to the beginning of the 4th century AD while others date them as even older, from the 2nd century AD.

Recently Sogdian inscriptions have been found in an even larger area. The Sogdian legend on the coins of Chach rulers, which reads 'Chach country ruler/sovereign Wanwan', dates back to the middle of the 3rd century AD.

Sogdian inscriptions on the bricks and arches of gateways found at the site of Kultobe in the Chimkent region of southern Kazakhstan date back to the first centuries AD. The British scholar N. Sims-Williams translated the inscriptions. They contain crucial information about the erection of the city (an outpost) for protection against nomads by a coalition of rulers from Sogdian areas of Samarkand, Kish, Nakhshab and Nawakmethan (Bukhara) under the command of the leader of the army of 'Chachannap', to whom this city belonged. Interestingly, in this inscription, as in the legends on coins and inscriptions on silver vessels from Kerchevo and south-east China, the name 'Chach' is rendered as *č'č'n'p* – Chachannap (lit. the 'Chach people/community/country'). This author believes that this is not just a term denoting 'belonging to the Chach people', but the official name of the state: Chachannap.

Many more Sogdian manuscripts have been found in Xinjiang. These are translations into Sogdian of Buddhist, Manichaean and Christian religious texts written in black ink on leather, birch bark and other materials. The few fragments of literary works in Sogdian are of particular interest. Among them is a manuscript fragment of 16 incomplete lines describing an episode in which the epic hero Rustam fights the daevas, and several fragments of manuscripts with Sogdian translations of tales about a merchant, a pearl borer and three fish.

Rock inscriptions left by Sogdian pilgrims on their journeys to holy places as well as those of merchants and messengers are distinctive examples of Sogdian writing. These travellers often inscribed their names on cliffs, sometimes including a date, as if to prove that they had visited the places. Such inscriptions have been found in Mongolia, Semirechye, Tibet and India. For example, Noshfarn, a Sogdian Christian from Samarkand, left an inscription on a rock in Ladakh on the border of Tibet and Kashmir.

A remarkable discovery was made by the German archaeologist K. Jettmar in the upper reaches of the Indus. Here, near the Shatial Bridge, along the Karakorum Highway, are steep cliffs with numerous short inscriptions in Sogdian, which were made by 'visitors' to the area. Studies by H. Humbach and N. Sims-Williams have demonstrated that these were made either by Sogdian pilgrims on their way to India to worship at Buddhist shrines, or by Sogdian merchants from different regions of Central Asia. Scholars have dated some of these inscriptions to the 3rd or even 2nd century AD, on the basis of the distinctive features and shapes of the letters, and they are, in fact, not only the earliest Sogdian rock inscriptions to have been found, but are also among the oldest Sogdian inscriptions that have been discovered. Based on the *nisbas* (an adjective that indicates a person's place of origin) of the inscriptions, scholars have been able to establish that the Sogdian authors of these inscriptions came from Maimargh (near Samarkand) and Chach (the modern Tashkent oasis).

The most recent Sogdian rock inscriptions (from the 9th–10th centuries AD) have been found in Kyrgyzstan. These rock inscriptions, along with other traces of Sogdian writing that have been discovered beyond the borders of Sogdia, provide convincing evidence about the prominent role of the Sogdian language and script, and about the routes Sogdian settlers travelled to reach the most distant corners of Inner Asia.

A large number of diverse Sogdian inscriptions have been found in the territory of Uzbekistan. However, the most significant of them is a 16-line vertical wall inscription in ink, discovered during excavations at the site of Afrasiab in 1965. It dates from the second half of the 7th century AD. The inscription, read by V.A. Livshits, describes a mission of envoys, led by the chief of the chancellery (*dapirpat*) Pukarzate, who were sent to the King of Samarkand, Avarkhuman, with gifts and a bride from King Turantash of Chaganian (Surkhandarya basin). A recent examination of specimens of Sogdian script from Chach has yielded some very interesting results. They include short inscriptions on coins, giving the title and name of the ruler, and sometimes the name of the region. Among the Chach coins are examples of earlier coins from the 3rd–4th century AD, and this suggests that the Sogdian script and, possibly, the language were already in use in Chach at this time.

A second group of coins dates from the 7th century and the first half of the 8th century AD. It is very diverse in terms of iconographic features: the coins depict images of rulers wearing crowns, solar (a sun) and lunar symbols, images of animals such as camels and horses, as well as *tamgas*. Each coin has a legend, often giving the name of a ruler: Shaniabag, Sochak, Tarnavch, Yazatpir (as read by V.A. Livshits). The study of the legends on Chach coins has allowed for a completely different interpretation of the early medieval history of this area.

We also know of several Sogdian inscriptions on silver vessels. Most of them are written in a regular cursive script characteristic of Sogdian texts from the 6th to the 9th century. The shape of letters of one of the inscriptions suggests it dates back to the 4th century. It is noteworthy because it mentions the title and name of a ruler from Chach (Tashkent oasis) and next to the inscription is a *tamga* which has exactly the same form as the *tamga* on many coins found in Tashkent province. These make up the earliest evidence of Sogdian script and language in Chach. Sogdian inscriptions have also been found on coins issued by kings and rulers of separate dominions of Chach in the 6th and early 8th centuries AD, with ancient Turkic names among the names of rulers.

Three other inscriptions on silver vessels are in a Bukharan variant of Sogdian script. Apparently Bukharan or Western Sogdia differed from Samarkand or Eastern Sogdia both in terms of political structure and in dialect.

In addition to the inscriptions on silver vessels, the Bukharan variant of Sogdian script has also been found on coins of rulers of the Bukhara oasis. The Bukharan Sogdian script differed from the common Samarkand Sogdian script only in the shapes of a few letters, and was apparently used only for official inscriptions.

An archive of Sogdian documents from the early 8th century AD, found during excavations of a castle on Mount Mugh, some 120 kilometres east of Samarkand, is of outstanding importance for the history and culture of Central Asia's peoples. Eighty-nine documents in Sogdian, Arabic and Chinese were found here. The vast majority of the manuscripts are in Sogdian language and script. These include private and diplomatic letters, contracts, a calendar and economic and accounting records. They were translated by a group of scholars from Leningrad (St Petersburg), including A.A. Freiman, V.A. Livshits, M.N. Bogolyubov and O.I. Smirnova.

Many of the documents originate from Penjikent and its surroundings, from the upper reaches of the Zarafshan river. They are connected with the name of the 'prince of Panch' (Penjikent), Devashtich, who is referred to in a number of documents as the Sogdian king, the ruler of Samarkand. Of particular interest is a report to Devashtich from his emissary Phatufarn, who was sent to Chach to negotiate a treaty with the rulers of Chach, Ferghana and the Turkic Khagan to form an alliance against the Arabs.

The documents from Mount Mugh contain valuable information on the socio-economic, military and cultural history of Sogdia. In particular, for the first time, they provided information on the existence of four categories of slaves in the region, on foundations of Sogdian family law, and on the participation of Turks in the urban life of Sogdia and its administration.

The **Bactrian language** and its script were the second most widespread and long used in Central Asia. During early medieval times the use of Bactrian spread over a vast territory from India to Xinjiang. Its importance is demonstrated by the fact that it was the official language in the two great states of the Kushans and Hephthalites, as well as in the smaller early medieval principalities and possessions of Tokharistan.

The name 'Bactrian' for the language and script was proposed by W.B. Henning. It became the most widely accepted name for this language, replacing the former names of 'Eteo-Tokharian', 'Kushan', 'Kushano-Bactrian' and 'Graeco-Bactrian'. However, the Kushan kings themselves called it 'Aryan', as we know from the edict of Kanishka on the Rabatak inscripton. It says: 'And he [i.e. King Kanishka] issued a Greek edict (and) then he put it into Aryan.' Research confirms that the Bactrian script is derived from the Greek cursive script, which was widespread in the Hellenistic states. Examples of this script can be seen, in particular, in parchments found in Avroman and Iranian Kurdistan. Bactrian script was created in Bactria and can be explained by the strong Hellenistic traditions and the use of the Greek alphabet and language in this region. In the early days of the Kushan empire the official script of the state was Greek, as we can see in the legends and Greek titles used on the coins of the first Kushan kings. Under the Kushan king Kanishka (probably during the first half of the 2nd century AD) Bactrian legends and the titles *shaonano shao kaneshki kushano* ('King of Kings Kanishka the Kushan') appeared on coins instead of titles in Greek.

For this reason, it was assumed that the Bactrian script had also been created during the reign of Kanishka. However, there have been several discoveries of inscriptions which suggest that the Bactrian script had been in use before Kanishka. For example, there are the rock inscriptions from Dasht-i Navur, which, according to G. Fussman, include a Bactrian inscription with the name of King Wima Kadphises II, who preceded King Kanishka, along with inscriptions in Kharoshthi and another, unidentified script. This view has since been challenged by J. Cribb, who believes that the inscription bears the name of Wima I Takto, an even earlier Kushan king.

It would appear that the Bactrian script and language, as known to us, had already been used on the coins of Tanlismaidates, which date from the end of the 1st century BC to the 1st century AD. The legend on these coins includes the female name Raggodeme, the first element of which is derived from the Iranian word *rang* (colour), with the combination of letters *ng* rendered in a typical Bactrian double consonant *g*. We should also note that attempts were made to use different combinations of letters to convey the phoneme /ʃ/ ('sh'), which is absent in the Greek alphabet, and which appear on the Heraeus coins. There are also ostraca with Bactrian inscriptions that may date from a time earlier than the time of Kanishka's rule (the first half of the 2nd century AD). This suggests that Bactrian script appeared in common use as early as the 1st century AD, i.e. when other scripts also emerged in Transoxiana, namely Khorezmian and Sogdian. Bactrian script and language became official under Kanishka, as revealed in the edict of the king and confirmed in the legends on coins.

The Bactrian alphabet probably contained 25 letters. At any rate, this is the number of letters indicated by the Buddhist monk Xuanzang, who visited Bactria-Tokharistan in the early 7th century AD, for the script of Tokharistan, which, all scholars agree, refers to the Bactrian alphabet. Xuanzang wrote: '... their language differs somewhat from that of other countries. The number of radical letters in their language is twenty-five; by combining these they express all objects (things) around them. Their writing is across the page, and they read from left to right. Their literary records have increased gradually, and exceed those of the people of Su-li [Sogdia]...'

However, none of the known Bactrian manuscripts contains examples of the letters *psi* and *xi*. A distinctive feature of the Bactrian script is the introduction of the special character *san* to indicate the hushing sibilant, which graphically was rendered in a similar fashion to the letter *rho*.

There are two types of Bactrian script – monumental or lapidary, and cursive. The first type is characterised by separate letters, a combination of rounded and angular forms, the absence of capitalisation or sentence case, and words written together (not split). The cursive script is characterised by a wide range of writing styles and very complex letter-signs, often with combined letters.

The chronology of Bactrian written language covers a period of about 800 years (from the 1st/2nd centuries AD to the 8th/9th centuries AD). The Bactrian inscriptions we know of today can be divided into three groups: 1) epigraphic – inscriptions on rocks and stone slabs, pottery and potsherds (ostraca), gems and other objects; 2) numismatic – inscriptions on coins; 3) handwritten documents – inscriptions on papyrus, palm leaves, paper and birch bark. The techniques include graffiti inscriptions, carved on rocks, walls and stone slabs, as well as inscriptions scratched or made in black ink with a thin brush, on potsherds, papyrus or other materials.

Up to the mid-1950s, the number of specimens of Bactrian script that had been discovered, especially from the Kushan period, was very small: they consisted mainly of brief inscriptions on coins, seals and gems. It was only the discovery of Bactrian inscriptions on limestone slabs made by French archaeologists during excavations of a temple complex on the hill of Surkh Kotal in Baghlan province (northern Afghanistan) in 1954–1959 that really initiated research into the Bactrian language and writing. In the 1960s and 1980s, many Bactrian inscriptions were discovered during excavations in various parts of Bactria but they were all shorter than the inscriptions from Surkh Kotal.

Bactrian inscriptions from the Kushan period have been found only in Bactria and at two sites outside it – a stone slab with a trilingual inscription in Bactrian, Kharoshthi and an undeciphered script found at Dasht-i Navur (Kabulistan); and rock inscriptions found at Wakhan (present-day Afghanistan).

In Northern Bactria, Bactrian inscriptions have been found at the following major sites, going from west to east: the Kara-Kamar cave complex (graffiti inscriptions on the rock surface); the site of Kampyrtepa (black ink inscription on a clay vessel, inscriptions on potsherds using black ink, handwritten specimens on papyrus); Zartepa (inscriptions on potsherds); Old Termez; at the Karatepa Buddhist monastery (graffiti inscriptions on cave walls, inscriptions on sherds and vessels) and at the Fayaztepa Buddhist monastery (inscriptions in black ink on sherds and vessels, and an inscription in black ink on a sherd near a dump); Mirzakultepa (a sherd with an incised inscription); Airtam (a stone sculpture with a six-line Bactrian inscription on the base); Yalangtushtepa (incised inscriptions on a *khum* and black ink inscriptions on potsherds); Shahtepa (an incised inscription on a fragment of a vessel rim) and Dushanbe (an inscription on the rim of a *khum*).

In Southern Bactria, inscriptions have been found at the following major sites, going from north to south: Dilberzhin (inscriptions in monumental script on stone slabs and ostraca with inscriptions in black ink and graffiti inscriptions); Balkh (a fragment of a clay vessel with a cursive inscription); modern Rui in the province of Samangan (the royal archive of the kingdom of Rob); Surkh Kotal (the most extensive Bactrian inscription that we know of, consisting of 25 lines carved on a limestone slab; two shorter copies of this inscription also carved on limestone slabs have also been found here); Rabatak (a monumental inscription on a stone slab); Uruzgan (rock inscriptions); and Jagatu (rock inscriptions).

There have only been a few discoveries of Bactrian inscriptions on the territory of Bactria/Tokharistan from the early medieval period. These are of legends on coins found scattered between the Hissar Range in the north and the Hindu Kush in the south. Coins with Bactrian character countermarks in Northern Tokharistan were mainly produced in the Chaganian region, occasionally in Kuftan, and possibly in other regions. In addition, copper coins with a square hole and a Bactrian cursive legend were probably produced in Kobadian.

Among other specimens of Bactrian script, we should mention a sherd with an inscription in black ink from Zangtepe and finds from Kala-i Kafirnigan. Coins with Bactrian legends were produced in many areas of Southern Tokharistan, but also beyond it, in Kabulistan, Zabulistan, Gandhara and even in Northern India.

In contrast to those from the Kushan period, Bactrian inscriptions from the early medieval period have been found beyond the borders of Bactria/Tokharistan proper. Thus, Bactrian rock inscriptions have been found to the south of the Hindu Kush, in Jagatu, to the west of Ghazni, and in Uruzgan (Afghanistan), as well as in the Tochi river valley and at Shatial (Pakistan).

A Bactrian wall inscription in black ink, possibly made by natives of Chaganian, was found in a palace building on the site of Afrasiab. The specimens of Bactrian inscriptions that were found here are, for the most part, very short. They give the names and titles of kings and gods on coins, and on gems the names of their owners and their social status (e.g. 'Varahran satrap') and sometimes a religious formula. The most interesting inscription, on a bulla, is in the Ashmolean Museum in Oxford, but it is very difficult to make out. It has been translated by V.A. Livshits as reading: 'Moon-Kanishka, *yabghu*, son of the king of Hindustan'. W.B. Henning believed that Moon-Kanishka was the full name of the great Kushan king, which he bore before ascending the throne while still a prince of Tokharistan. Inscriptions on vessels and potsherds, or ostraca, are mostly hard to read because they are so fragmentary. They contain the names of the contents of the vessels, personal names and sometimes religious formulas. An example of this is a bilingual inscription, in Bactrian and Kharoshthi, on a vessel found at an excavation site at a Buddhist monastery in Old Termez. It reads: 'The gift of Buddhashira, preacher of the law dharma'. (From the original Russian translation by G. Grek and V.A. Livshits). This votive inscription suggests that Buddhashira, a preacher of dharma, i.e. the law, presented this vessel as a gift to a Buddhist temple.

Another interesting Bactrian inscription is one found on the rim of a *khum* at the site of Zartepa; it translates as '...god Shiva-Visha'. The inscription on a large *khum* found at the excavation of a Buddhist temple in Dalverzintepa is quite different. Here, the beginning of the phrase has survived and reads: 'This is written by me...'.

'Graffiti' inscriptions on the walls of the caves of the Karatepa Buddhist monastery in Old Termez are very well known. They have been studied by V.A. Livshits, H. Humbach and J. Harmatta. The inscriptions were discovered by B.J. Stavisky's expedition while carrying out an in-depth study of this outstanding monument of Buddhist culture in Central Asia from 1960 onwards. These inscriptions are mainly visitors' inscriptions, giving the names of Bactrians (e.g. Borzomiro, Oromazdo) who came to worship at the Buddhist shrines. In some cases they begin with the words *ΚΑΛΔΟ ΜΑΛΟ (Α)ΓΑΔΟ...*, which mean 'When (they) came here'. However, J. Harmatta read one of the inscriptions giving the name of this Buddhist monastery as *CΑΔΟ ΓΑ(Β)Ο*, which means 'the Hundred Caves'. This reading was not accepted by other scholars of Buddhist inscriptions from Karatepa. Another significant Bactrian inscription was discovered by B. Turgunov during excavations at the site of Airtam. A stone relief with the figures of a standing woman and a seated man was found in one of the rooms. A six-line Bactrian inscription in monumental script was carved on its base. Unfortunately, only fragments of the inscription have survived because the surface of the base has been destroyed. It originally had about 350 to 360 letters. Each of the first five lines contained 60 to 65 letters, while the sixth line had 51 letters (260 letters have survived fully or partially).

The best-preserved line is the sixth line, as most of it had been buried in the earth. We were able to decipher the final phrase of the inscription when we first examined it, and made out the following words: '...and this was written by Mirozado by order of Shodiya'. Later, in spite of its poor condition, we were able to reconstruct the content of the inscription and identify a number of previously unknown Bactrian words. The inscription tells us that, in the fourth year of the Kushan king Huvishka's rule, a certain Shodiya was sent to Airtam to restore a Buddhist monastery which had fallen into disrepair.

The inscription was read by V.A. Livshits and E. Rtveladze; its latest translation is as follows:

1. [It was] King Huvishka's fourth year of reign, when …a city/land… The king presented(?) this *sangha* and (??) city…
2. …this [that is, the *sangha*] was established by Shodiya and… …who put the temple in order/decorated.
3. …The sanctuary(???) which the king named after Kanishka(?) and in addition Shodiya(?) had erected a large gate in the acropolis for the gods(?).
4. …The flowing water/ was waterless(?) that is why Shodiya dug in(??).
5. …Shodiya dug and both(?) deities(?) were brought/came.
6. …And this was written by Mirozado by order of Shodiya.

This is the first and most extensive monumental Bactrian inscription to have been discovered in Central Asia, and the first Bactrian inscription accompanying a sculpture. It is of major importance for understanding the creation and dating of the Airtam religious complex, and contributes to our knowledge of the Bactrian lexicon and its dialects. For example, a number of Bactrian words ending in an *omicron* in the Surkh Kotal inscriptions are rendered with a final *alpha* in the Airtam inscription. It is possible that this is indicative of different Bactrian dialects spoken by people on the left and right banks of the Oxus river.

Fragments of papyrus manuscripts found during excavations of Kampyrtepa, in a structure located in the eastern part of the site, are of particular interest for the study of the history of Bactrian written language. Fragments of manuscripts were unearthed from almost the entire area of the structure both under and in the rubble. Altogether about 30 fragments of various sizes (2.8 × 6 cm; 2.8 × 1 cm; 1.8 × 1.2 cm) were found, as well as several intact, thin sheets, stuck together and rolled up into a tube, which disintegrated into several fragments when they were removed. The sheets are approximately 15.0 centimetres wide and 0.1–0.2 centimetres thick, with left margins of up to 1.5 centimetres. There are inscriptions on both sides in black ink, in straight lines of three to four or even more lines, with a line spacing of 2.0–2.5 centimetres and a letter height of 3.0–5.0 millimetres.

The inscriptions are in cursive Bactrian script and the language is Bactrian. The word *ABO* appears on two fragments. This is either the preposition 'in', 'on', 'at' or the noun 'water'. One fragment bears the word *BIΔO* ('chief'; cf. the Bactrian word *asbarobido* for 'chief of the cavalry', which was found on a gemstone). The other fragment has remnants of words and prepositions but, on the whole, none of the fragments provides a coherent text. The fragments of manuscripts found here date from the reign of Kanishka, i.e. the first half of the 2nd century AD.

Bactrian manuscripts from Kushan times were unknown in Central Asia before the Kampyrtepa excavations. Palaeographic and archaeological data indicate that the oldest (supposedly 4th century AD) Bactrian manuscript was the 'London' or 'Loulan fragment' found by Sir Aurel Stein in Xinjiang and since lost.

Seven manuscript fragments, known as the 'Berlin Hephthalite fragments', date from the 8th–9th centuries AD.

Evidently, discoveries at Kampyrtepa put back the date of the Bactrian manuscripts by several centuries and indicate that the use of Bactrian cursive script for writing documents perhaps began at the same time as the inscriptions on coins, stone slabs and potsherds.

Archaeological research in recent years has led to the discovery of a new script known as the **'unknown script'**. It came to the attention of scholars after G. Fussman determined that the trilingual inscription from Dasht-i Navur included writing in an unidentified script along with Kharoshthi and Bactrian. He also identified similar inscriptions on a limestone slab from Surkh Kotal and a potsherd from Khalchayan.

Later, V.A. Livshits noted the presence of inscriptions in a similar script on ostraca from Fayaztepa and Old Merv. He believed a more archaic version of the same script appeared on a silver cup from the 5th century BC found at Issyk Kurgan. In 1980 P. Bernard produced an inscription on a silver ingot from Ai-Khanum with characters similar to those of the Issyk inscription and the unknown script.

V. Vertogradova published several inscriptions on clay fragments from Karatepa and Khatyn-Rabad. New inscriptions in the unknown script from Koshtepa, Kampyrtepa and Old Termez were published in 1998 by E. Rtveladze.

Several hypotheses have been made about the language of this script. For example, based on the Dasht-i Navur inscription, G. Fussman believed that the inscription reflected the language of the ancient peoples of Jaguda (Zabul) – Kamboji, perhaps even akin to proto-Ormuri. However, the discovery of this script far beyond the areas where these languages were used makes it difficult to accept this assumption. P. Bernard believed that the language of the Ai-Khanum inscription is Bactrian, and this hypothesis is more plausible.

V.A. Livshits suggested that the Issyk inscription was a more archaic variant of this script. Having compiled the data from all these different findings, V. Vertogradova came to the conclusion that we could now speak of two types of unknown script: an early one, represented by the Issyk and Ai-Khanum inscriptions, and a more complex one consisting of several variants, and that later versions of this writing system evolved at the very beginning of the Christian era. She believed that the overall structure of the unknown script is close to Aramaic and Kharoshthi.

More than ten specimens of this script have been found in Bactria, which was the main area where it was used. Only three inscriptions have been found outside Bactria: at Issyk Kurgan (the archaic version), Dasht-i Navur and Old Merv.

Furthermore, the new findings add three new characters to the alphabet of the unknown script, extending it to 15 characters so far. Significantly, there are four examples of a word beginning with a character that was either a very common vowel or consonant in the language represented by this script. The available evidence suggests that there were two types of script – rounded and geometric. As far as its linguistic identity is concerned, we should consider the indisputable fact that Bactria was the main centre of the unknown script, and that it was also one of three officially recognised scripts of the Kushan state.

If this is correct, then the unknown script must reflect the language of a people who made up a significant part of the population in Bactria and the Kushan state, and who also played an important role in religious and administrative life, or it must be the language of the ruling dynasty and a privileged segment of the population.

The bulk of the autochthonous population in Bactria were Bactrians, a people of Eastern Iranian origin whose script and language are reflected in many inscriptions, including that of Surkh Kotal. Another significant but allochthonous ethnic group in Bactria were Greeks, who had been a privileged class in this area in the not-so-distant past, and who probably survived during the Kushan period, and also had their own language and script.

Indian inscriptions in Kharoshthi and Brahmi, which were used to write Prakrit and Sanskrit, provide convincing evidence of the deep penetration of Indian ethnic groups into the ethnosphere of Bactria. So we know that three major ethnic groups of Bactria had their own scripts. Two of them – Bactrian and Kharoshthi – are used in the inscriptions from Dasht-i Navur, and this makes sense as the first of these reflected the language of Bactria's indigenous population, while the second was the language of colonies of Indian settlers and of the Buddhist religion that played an extremely important role in life in the Kushan state. The third script then, must reflect the language of one of the other major ethnic groups that inhabited Bactria. In addition to the ethnic groups mentioned above, we should note three waves of migration of nomadic peoples who came to Bactria: the Saka, Yuezhi, Asii, Pasiani, Tokharians and Sakarauli.

Of these, the most important place in the history of Bactria was occupied by the Yuezhi and Tokharians. The dominant role of the Tokharians is reflected in the name Tokharistan – land of the Tokharians, which replaced or was used alongside the former name Bactria, probably from the 1st century BC onwards. It is possible, however, that the Yuezhi and Tokharians are one and the same ethnic group, as some researchers suggest. The Yuezhi were immigrants from Inner Asia and a foreign ethnic group, and, hence, had no connection with the autochthonous Bactrian language. However, to date, we have no information about the origin of the Yuezhi language itself. No written sources have survived with even a single word in the Yuezhi language. It may be fair to argue then that since the Yuezhi, and primarily the Kushans, played a major role in the history of the Kushan state, and since the unknown script in the Dasht-i Navur trilingual inscription appears to be official, along with Kharoshthi and Bactrian, the unknown script may convey the Yuezhi/Tokharian language, although it is not yet proven.

Identifying the language of the unknown script would finally settle the argument. At any rate, identifying it as Yuezhi would explain both its widespread distribution and the diverse range of its use. Judging by inscriptions on pottery from rural settlements in Bactria, it was not only the script of an official language, but also used in everyday life. However, we should emphasise that our main task now is to collect material and compile a full alphabet of the unknown script.

Yet another local script used in Central Asia was **Khorezmian**, which, unlike Sogdian and Bactrian was prevalent mainly in ancient Khorezm.

Examples of ancient Khorezmian script were discovered in the 1930s, and their discovery is wholly to the credit of the Khorezm archaeological and ethnographic expedition headed by S. Tolstov. He was also a key figure in deciphering legends on coins executed in this script. A true understanding of the script itself became possible after an archive of Khorezmian documents on leather, wooden sticks and plaques was discovered during excavations at Toprak-Kala in 1948–1949. However, many of the documents on leather were decayed, leaving only fragments with faint traces of letters or imprints on clay. Only eight documents on leather remain available for reading. Also, more than 20 complete and fragmented documents on wooden sticks and plaques survived. They were first deciphered by S. Tolstov, and the interpretations were later amended and corrected by W.B. Henning. Still later, V.A. Livshits published them in full, together with a reading and translation. A number of other Khorezmian inscriptions on pottery and ossuaries from Tok-Kala were discovered in the following years. At the same time, work continued on clarifying the Khorezmian legends on coins. V.A. Livshits made an outstanding contribution to their reading, translation and interpretation. Analysis of the legends has shown that they reflect the Khorezmian language, which belongs to the Eastern Iranian group of languages.

The study of the language of these inscriptions was facilitated by the fact that Khorezmian words and phrases survived in Arabic texts dating from the 12th to the 13th century, especially in the book by the Khorezmian jurist al-Zahidi al-Ghazmini, *The Acquisition of the Object of Desire, for the Completion of the Sufficiency* (about 3,000 words in total). Further, *The Chronology of the Ancient Nations* by al-Biruni (973–1048 AD) records Khorezmian names for days, months, constellations and holidays, and some Khorezmian words are mentioned by Arabic and Persian geographers of the 10th century, namely al-Maqdisi, Istakhri and Ibn Fadlan. All of these medieval records of the Khorezmian language were studied in detail by A. Freiman and, somewhat later, by W.B. Henning and D. MacKenzie.

Khorezmian script was developed from Aramaic and, like Sogdian, retained the Aramaic ideograms that were used only in writing and not in speech. For this reason, Khorezmian script, like other scripts based on Aramaic, is often called ideographic. The Khorezmian script runs from right to left in horizontal lines. The exact number of letters in the alphabet is unknown. Vowels, as in other scripts of Aramaic origin, were only rarely indicated in writing.

According to V.A. Livshits, a total of 20 letters out of the Aramaic script of 22 were used, and three letters appear as ideograms, along with two additional letters. Consequently, only about 15 letters were used in the Toprak-Kala documents to render the words of the 'living' ancient Khorezmian language. The documents on leather were lists of receipts, particularly for wine and flour received from individuals, presumably destined for state repositories.

Of particular interest, however, are the documents on wood, among which three categories stand out:

1. 'Household lists', listing the names of free men and domestic male slaves who made up a large family.
2. Revenue documents, listing the delivery and issue of wheels and other items.
3. Labels, probably bearing proper names.

The most interesting of these are the 'household lists', which were deciphered by S. Tolstov and W.B. Henning, with V.A. Livshits making a particularly significant contribution to their understanding. These documents reflect the composition of large and small families and provide insights into the nature of slavery in ancient Khorezm.

For example, document No.1 contains the names of 21 men, of whom one name is that of the householder, two other names are those of his sons, another name is that of his son-in-law, and 17 of the names are those of slaves, with 12 slaves belonging to the householder, his sons and son-in-law, two to his wife, two to his grandchildren, and one more slave being the property of a concubine's son.

The documents from Toprak-Kala are unique records of their kind, and the most valuable sources of information about family composition during this ancient period of Central Asian history. For the sake of clarity, let us take a look at the text of document No.1 as translated by V.A. Livshits: 'House of Γawnasami: Γawnasami; (sons) – first present M…, first present *Friyaxwas, son-in-law Γawfarnak; slaves: Satayoδak, Katfanak, Δusitanak, Xwasak, Fraβoδak, Marti(y)asak, Mihraβirtak, Xwarzβanak, Pandkasak…, Sawβaγdak, βewarsawak, Wax(u)smari; these are slaves of the wife (of the house owner) – Razmβewarak, Pitanak; slaves of children – Kak, Farnaβγawak; slaves of a son of a concubine – first present Δarteγanak…'. 'First present' means 'present for the first time in a census or 'listed for the first time'.

Other ancient Khorezmian inscriptions are very short: legends on coins and inscriptions on clay fragments of vessels. The inscriptions from the 7th–8th centuries AD from Tok-Kala are of special interest: they are executed in black ink on the lids and walls of ossuaries. The inscriptions were made vertically in one or several lines and contain, as V.A. Livshits established, proper names and dates with an indication of days and years from the ancient Khorezmian era which began in the mid-1st century AD. Another group of Khorezmian inscriptions from the 7th and 8th centuries AD has been identified on silver vessels found in the region of the Kama river, on a trade route used for transporting furs. These inscriptions contain dates: day, month, year, as well as the name of the owner, and indications of weight.

At the beginning of the 8th century, Qutaiba ibn Muslim's campaign against Khorezm caused enormous damage to ancient Khorezmian written documents. As al-Biruni writes, whole libraries were destroyed on his orders. However, according to V.A. Livshits, although ancient Central Asian scripts were beginning to be replaced by Arabic, and despite the subsequent widespread use of Arabic, the Khorezmian alphabet continued to be used here in the early 11th century.

In southern Central Asia, predominantly in northern Bactria/Tokharistan, in ancient and early medieval times, in addition to local writing systems, the Indian writing systems of **Kharoshthi and Brahmi** were also in use. They were the heritage of the Buddhist community or *sangha* and of the Indian colonies that emerged in southern Central Asia as a result of trade and the introduction of Buddhism into the region.

The study of these writing systems began in the late 1930s when a fragment of a stone slab with a partially preserved inscription, identified by V.M. Masson as Kharoshthi, was found at the Old Termez site.

Subsequent years of research at Karatepa and then at Fayaztepa in Old Termez revealed a significant number of Indian inscriptions on fragments and complete vessels, as well as graffiti and *dipinti* inscriptions painted. Inscriptions on pottery made in several alphabets were also found here, which included Brahmi-Bactrian, Brahmi-Bactrian-Kharoshthi and Brahmi-Kharoshthi. Finds of Indian inscriptions outside Old Termez are quite rare and have consisted mainly of inscriptions from Kushan times on clay fragments from the Dalverzin hoard. Manuscripts on birch bark in Brahmi from Old Merv and Zangtepa, and a rock inscription in Kharoshthi found in the eastern Pamirs, date from the early medieval period. There have also been (as yet unverified) reports of rock inscriptions at Zarautsai (present-day Uzbekistan), near the famous rock paintings here. Most of the Indian inscriptions that have been found are either etched on clay or written in black ink, while inscriptions on gold bars are punch-marked.

The earliest inscriptions in Kharoshthi from Karatepa date back to the 1st–2nd centuries AD, although J. Harmatta has ascribed the Kharoshthi inscription from the eastern Pamirs to the 3rd–2nd centuries BC. The latest Brahmi inscriptions date from the 7th–8th centuries AD.

There is almost no information about the presence of medieval Indian inscriptions in Central Asia, with the exception of one inscription from Mount Takht-i Suleiman in Osh, which apparently dates from the 16th century. Indian and Central Asian systems of writing, including Parthian, Sogdian and Khorezmian, were all based on Aramaic. T. Grek, M. Vorobyova-Desyatovskaya, J. Harmatta, and especially V. Vertogradova, who published a monograph about Indian inscriptions from Karatepa, have all made significant contributions to the deciphering and study of Indian inscriptions found in Central Asia.

The Indian inscriptions on pottery found at Karatepa and Fayaztepa all relate to the giving of offerings. They include parts of votive formulas, as well as proper names, the rank or office of Buddhist monks, the names of vessels and, most importantly, the names of Buddhist schools and monasteries.

They often include a formula, reconstructed by V. Vertogradova, which in several fragments defines the purpose of the offering as being 'For the good and happiness of all living beings', and include names with epithets such as 'Buddhashira-dharmakathika', i.e. 'the Buddha who teaches good deeds', and other names, such as, Buddhamitra, Sanghanala, Asvahahara. In one of the inscriptions, Vertogradova found the name apparently given to the Buddhist cave monastery of Karatepa, 'Khadevaka (king's) vihara'.

An equally important achievement has been the determination, from the inscriptions, of the affiliation of the Termez Buddhists to the Mahasanghika school, one of the main schools in the Mahayana Buddhist tradition. This assumption, first made by J. Harmatta, was confirmed by subsequent studies of inscriptions from Karatepa. In 2007, Kharoshthi inscriptions of quite different content (that is, 'secular' content, not religious), were found at Kampyrtepa. These inscriptions were inscribed on the entrance arches of the portal leading to the gate of the citadel. Six of these inscriptions are short, according to G. Fussman, and contain only the name 'Da-ma-sya'. The other two are longer and are still being interpreted. The excavations here are ongoing, but a tentative date for the inscriptions could be the 2nd or 1st century BC.

3.2

CENTRAL ASIA'S ROLE IN THE SPREAD OF RELIGIONS IN EASTERN TURKESTAN (XINJIANG) AND THE FAR EAST

Central Asia has had a major role in the diffusion of world religions such as Buddhism, Islam, Zoroastrianism and Christianity, as well as Judaism and Manichaeism, in the countries of Inner Asia and the Far East. The missionaries who introduced the ideas of these religions included immigrants from the Near East, Arabs, Byzantine Greeks, Syrians and Jews, as well as the inhabitants of Central Asia, Bactrians, Sogdians, Parthians, and also representatives of various ethnic groups of the Indian subcontinent.

The emergence of these religions in Central Asia meant that the region was home to several states where one religion or another was dominant – Buddhism in the Kushan state, Islam in the Arab Caliphate, and Zoroastrianism in the Achaemenid, Parthian and Sassanian states. Alongside missionary activity, there was religious persecution (of Nestorianism, Manichaeism and Judaism), disagreements among supporters of one or another religion (for example in Nestorianism), military action and holy war or 'jihad' against infidels (by supporters of Islam). After a period of adaptation and integration into the life of Central Asian peoples, and following similar processes to their introduction in Central Asia, these religions spread to the Far East. But the significance, continuity and extent of dissemination of these different religions, from the time of their introduction to the present day, varied greatly. Buddhism occupied the most significant place in the religious systems of the Far East. It spread (largely peacefully) from the Kushan period onwards, mainly through the mediation of Central Asian peoples.

Chinese sources list the Buddhist monks Kang Senghui and Baoyi or Pao-i (Ratnamati), who were Sogdians, Dharmaraksha (Zhu Fahu) and Dharmamitra, who were Bactrians and An Shigao, a Parthian, as the most prominent figures in the dissemination, propagation and development of Buddhist beliefs. The first translations of Buddhist works into Chinese were made by immigrants from India and Bactria/Tokharistan (Yuezhi). To this day, Buddhism continues to be the dominant religion in the countries of the Far East in one form or another.

Christianity was introduced into Central Asia in the first centuries AD (Saint Thomas the Apostle played a major role in its dissemination in India, as did Bishop Barshabba in Central Asia), and its position was consolidated by the Nestorians. Nestorian adherents took their religion as far as Chang'an, in China, to the Turks (especially the Uigurs) and the Mongols. Nestorianism continued to be practised among them and played an important role until the 13th–14th centuries. The last Christian communities in Central Asia were destroyed by Ulughbeg. The return of Christianity to the countries of the Far East and Central Asia is associated with the colonisation of these countries and the activities of Portuguese, Dutch, Italian and Russian missionaries.

Significant activity through the mediation of Central Asian missionaries succeeded in spreading Manichaeism (its founder, the prophet Mani, is said to have claimed that 'my religion is of the kind that it will be manifest in every country, and in all languages, and it will be taught in far-away countries'.). It was particularly widespread among the Uigur Turks in areas of Eastern Turkestan (Xinjiang), where it became the state religion. Manichaean communities also existed in China. It is well known, for example, that in 719, the governor of Chaganian (a region in the Surkhan Darya valley) asked the Chinese emperor to receive a great Manichaean teacher (Mozhag) and allow him to build a Manichaean temple in the Chinese capital. With the introduction of Islam in Xinjiang, Manichaeism effectively disappeared as a religious system, although its ideas

Fresco. Dura-Europos 1st century BC.

survived among various sects in the Near East and Europe (for example, among the Paulicans and Albigenses) for a long time.

The role of Judaism in the religious life of Inner Asia and the Far East is less clear; in Central Asia, especially in the Merv region, Judaism seems to have been introduced in the first centuries AD and then penetrated into Xinjiang. An early Judaeo-Persian document was found in Khotan by Sir Aurel Stein, testifying to the penetration of Judaism into this area.

The spread of Zoroastrianism in Xinjiang and China is most likely attributable to the Sogdians, who founded numerous colonies along the routes of the Silk Road. Zoroastrianism was evidently practised only by the Sogdian diaspora and did not have any influence in the countries of the Far East. The presence on Okinawa Island of clay funerary monuments with decorations in relief, reminiscent of Central Asian ossuaries, is, however, intriguing.

Zoroastrianism

Zoroastrianism is an ancient religion. It takes its name from its founder, Zarathushtra, which in Old Iranian translates as 'possessing a golden (or old) camel'. Most scholars believe that Zarathushtra was a historical and not a mythical figure.

The Zoroastrian tradition defines the time of Zarathushtra's life as '258 years before Alexander' (that is, Alexander the Great). Taking into account this date and drawing on other indirect evidence, many scholars believe that Zarathushtra (Zoroaster in Greek) lived during the end of the 7th and beginning of the 6th century BC. According to Zoroastrian tradition, Zarathushtra began preaching the new religion at the court of Kavi Vishtaspa, the ruler of Bactra (present-day Balkh in northern Afghanistan), where he had arrived from his homeland, Airyanem Vaejah. What is the essence of the religion of Zarathushtra, or to be more precise, of the religious reforms he introduced, in that it replaced the old polytheism of the Iranian-speaking peoples, while also borrowing much from it?

The time when Zarathushtra started preaching his ideas was an extremely important one in the history of Central Asia and Iran. Early communal relations were being dismantled and new class-based ones were becoming established. The new religion reflected these changes and served the needs of the newly emerging class-based society. It called for political unification, the creation of a strong centralised authority and determined military action against the nomadic peoples, who in that period came to be seen as the true 'scourge of God' by the inhabitants of the agrarian oases.

In religious as well as social terms, Zarathushtra's reforms were focused on belief in the one god, Ahura Mazda (literally, the 'Wise Lord') and the struggle against the *asuras* and *daivas*, the former tribal deities, who were henceforth declared enemies of Ahura Mazda. From then on, a permanent and irreconcilable war between good and evil, truth and falsehood, light and darkness was proclaimed. This struggle acquired cosmic proportions and became the basis of Zoroastrian dualism, with Ahura Mazda leading the forces of light and Angra Mainyu ('Destructive Spirit') or Ahriman leading those of darkness.

All the diverse rituals of the pagan pantheon were henceforth transferred to a peculiar collection of six so-called *amesha spentas* or 'beneficent immortals'. These were not deities of flesh and blood in the pagan sense but abstract entities fleshed out symbolically and they were, essentially, only functions of one single deity. The ancient pagan rituals, in particular the use of *haoma*, a sacred liquor, were categorically revered.

Thus, as time passed, the religion of Zarathushtra gradually spread among the Iranian-speaking peoples and although it retained its fundamental basis, it also underwent change. Zoroastrianism, one of the most important religions of antiquity, was gradually formed as it incorporated the religious and philosophical dualism of Zarathushtra, together with old Iranian beliefs and historical legends.

Zoroastrianism assumed its definitive shape under the Sassanians (3rd–7th centuries AD), a time when Zoroastrian literature also began to be disseminated. It is worth noting that the first sacred texts of the Zoroastrian religion were originally passed on orally from generation to generation and were compiled into a single text and written down only a few centuries after the death of Zarathushtra.

The Avesta, the sacred book of the Zoroastrians, was then created. It is believed that the first codification of the Avesta took place in the 1st century BC, but on the basis of the Zoroastrian tradition, several scholars consider the event to have taken place during the time of the first Sassanian kings (3rd–4th centuries AD). The term 'Avesta' (from Middle Persian *apastak*, meaning 'basis', 'groundwork', i.e. the basic or foundational text) also appeared around this time. The Avesta is a collection of religious texts of the Zoroastrian religion, similar to the Koran for Muslims or the Holy Scriptures for Christians. It was composed at different times and in different places. The main part of the Avesta was destroyed after the adoption of Islam, and only the texts that were necessary for everyday religious practice survive today.

Zoroastrianism developed a complex and distinctive funerary ritual. It is based on the strict injunction of the Avesta that neither earth, nor fire, nor water should be defiled by contact with a corpse. According to the Avesta, any person who buried the corpse of a man or a dog in the ground would be committing a grave sin and was liable to 500 lashes of a 'horse whip'. Moreover, a plot of land where a man or a dog was buried could not be irrigated or sown for a year. But how were they to go about burying the dead? Zoroastrian priests worked out a strict sequence of complex burial rites, outlined in the *Vendidad* (a section of the Avesta). It stipulated that a corpse should first be placed in a *kata*, a small building, and then taken to a *dakhma* (a natural elevation or a special structure) where birds, predators or specially trained dogs could devour the corpse. And only after the bones had been cleaned in this way could they be placed in a designated ossuary, built of stone, clay or lime, or rock-cut. In the *Vendidad*, these ossuaries are called *uzdana*, and in later Pahlavi texts *astodan*. The exact translation of these terms remains ambiguous: some scholars believe that the term *astodan* stood for the clay ossuary receptacles, which were very common in Central Asia, while others, in particular the well-known German Iranist W.B. Henning, have translated the word as referring to a crypt or tomb made of earth. The burial was carried out by dedicated people, the so-called *ristokasha*, who were considered unclean. They were forbidden to be closer than 30 paces from fire, water or a *baresman* (a cult object made up of a bundle of rods), or to approach people closer than three paces.

In addition to Avestan terms, the term *naus* (derived from the Greek word naos) was widespread among Zoroastrians of the Sassanian period and the first centuries of Islam to designate a burial structure for keeping the purified bones of the dead.

Zoroastrian funerary monuments, such as the *uzdana, dakhma, kata* and temples, as well as ossuaries have been discovered and studied in many places in Central Asia, including Bactria, Margiana, Parthia and Khorezm.

Khorezm and Bactria had a particular role in the formation of Zoroastrianism. The recent discovery of various Buddhist monuments in Bactria, with their magnificent works of art, has eclipsed the indisputable fact that Zoroastrianism was the main religion of this region. Buddhism in Bactria was based in urban areas and was sustained by immigrants, who settled widely in the territory at the time of the Kushan state; while Zoroastrianism was the religion of the indigenous population of Bactria, and its traces remain in several archaeological sites.

The spread and persistence of this religion here has been verified by a whole range of sources, written testimonies, epic traditions, archaeological, epigraphic and numismatic data. In the *Vendidad*, which was codified in the 1st century BC, Bactria (Bahdi) is listed among the righteous Zoroastrian countries, and described as the beautiful country 'crowned with flags'. The secular historical tradition, based on the Sassanian *Khudaynama* ('Book of Kings'), preserved an earlier notion of the Bactrian king, Kavi Vishtaspa, the patron of Zarathushtra, at whose court the prophet began to preach the new religion. The king of Balkh (Bactra), Hystaspes, the patron of

Zardusht, was described by Tabari, al-Maqdisi, Firdawsi, Daqiqi, al-Biruni and other medieval authors.

The indisputable connection between Zarathushtra and Zoroastrianism and Bactria was also established by Graeco-Roman authors, beginning with Ctesias of Cnidus (5th century BC); in several fragments of his works Zarathushtra is referred to as a magus and a king of the Bactrians. The tradition associating Zarathushtra with Bactria was echoed in later Graeco-Roman sources, for example in the *Res Gestae* of Ammianus Marcellinus (4th century BC), writing about the 'Bactrian Zoroaster' (XXIII, 6, 32), as well as in the works of early Christian authors writing about Zarathustra as the founder of Bactra, from where the 'new law' spread 'over the entire world'.

Contrary to the scepticism of earlier scholars such as W.B. Henning, there is striking evidence of the existence of Zoroastrian burial rites in the accounts of Onesicritus, a Macedonian who accompanied Alexander the Great on his campaigns in Asia, and stated that: 'Those who are disabled by disease or old age are thrown alive to be devoured by dogs kept expressly for this purpose, and whom in the language of the country they call "entombers". The places on the exterior of the walls of the capital of the Bactrians are clean, but the interior is for the most part full of human bones' (Strabo, XI, 11, 3). Scattered human bones found by myself and A.S. Sagdulaev in settlements dating from the Achaemenid period in Northern Bactria and in Southern Sogdia support this account. B.A. Litvinsky established that the Oxus Temple at Takht-i Sangin was Zoroastrian, and apparently built at the end of the 2nd century BC.

There is considerable and unequivocal evidence of the existence of Zoroastrianism in Bactria during the Kushan period. In particular, there is the Rabatak inscription published by N. Sims-Williams and J. Cribb. Lines 7–11 of this inscription state that King Kanishka gave orders to Shafar the *karalrang* to build a sanctuary and to make and place in it images of gods '(of) whom the … glorious Umma leads the service here, (namely:) the lady Nana and the lady Umma, Aurmuzd, the Gracious One, Sroshard, Narasa, (and) Mihr'. Moreover, above the names of these Zoroastrian deities the names of the Hindu deities Maaseno (Mahasena) and Bizago (Vishakha) were inscribed in smaller letters.

Thus, the Rabatak inscription establishes the primary role of Zoroastrian deities in the religious beliefs of King Kanishka I and, accordingly, in Bactria, as the above-mentioned sanctuary was built in Baghlan, within the territory of this region. The name of the deity Sraosha is recorded in one of the caves of Karatepa. The names of other Zoroastrian deities, Pharro and Mao, have been found in inscriptions at the Buddhist temples of Fayaztepa and Dalverzintepa. This may indicate some fusion of Zoroastrianism and Buddhism or assimilation of Zoroastrian deities into the pantheon of bodhisattvas (the incorporation of deities from other religions is a distinctive feature of Mahayana Buddhism, one of the two branches of Buddhism).

The depiction of deities on the coins of Kanishka and Huvishka, many of which, as Sir Aurel Stein has shown, are of Zoroastrian origin, is equally important evidence of the prevalence of Zoroastrianism in Bactria and in the whole of the Kushan state. Bactrian onomastics, found in epigraphic monuments of Bactria, is further confirmation of the prevalence of Zoroastrianism in this region. The use of composite names was very common. One of their components inevitably used a name of the great Zoroastrian *yazata* (divinities) – Mithra (Mihr), for example, in the names Mihrzad, Borzomihr and Dharmamitra.

An inscription found at Airtam contains the word *iazado* appearing in combination with a word meaning 'both'. This, incidentally, is the earliest and only evidence (not taking into account a later example from the 7th century, i.e. the name Yazatpir on a Chach coin), of the existence of the cult of *yazatas* in Central Asia, which until now had only been considered hypothetically.

Finally, the most striking evidence of the existence of Zoroastrianism in Bactria is funerary structures, whose Zoroastrian features have been established by B.A. Litvinsky and this author. Examples of all the different kinds of funerary structures mentioned in the *Vendidad* (*kata, dakhma, uzdana, naus*) have been discovered and excavated in Northern Bactria. They have been studied at the Dalverzintepa, Old Termez, Yalangtushtepa and Shahtepa sites, and especially at Kampyrtepa. Evidence of other Zoroastrian rites of purification and protection from defilement, in particular of the rite of *bareshnum*, have also been noted here (with some displaying variations from the relevant parts of the *Vendidad*).

From Central Asia, Zoroastrianism penetrated into China and Serindia, possibly together with Buddhism. The Sogdians played a significant role in the spread of Nestorianism and Manichaeism in Xinjiang and China. There is less information about the spread of Zoroastrianism in these countries. The vast majority of Sogdians practised Zoroastrianism in its local Central Asian version, which some scholars refer to as Mazdaism.

The Chinese probably first became acquainted with Zoroastrianism as early as before the time of Christ. In any case, the travels of Zhang Qian (second half of the 2nd century BC) and regular Chinese embassies in the 1st century BC to Bactria, Sogdia and Parthia, where Zoroastrianism was a dominant religion, clearly suggest that the Chinese must have been aware of this religion. Zoroastrians were also inhabitants of the Sogdian colonies established in the first centuries AD along the eastern section of the Silk Road, as well as Bactrians living in the cities of Xinjiang.

According to Chinese written sources, the first Iranian fire temple was built in Chang'an in AD 621. Zoroastrian temples – *xianmiao* (the Chinese called the religion *xianjiao*, 'the religion of Heaven') – also existed in other Chinese cities such as Luoyang and Kaifeng and, no doubt, in the cities of Xinjiang, under Chinese rule. Moreover, Sogdian fire temples appeared here much earlier than in China proper, and it was Sogdian Zoroastrians who brought the religion to this state before the Persians. One of the earliest Zoroastrian monuments in China is the Anyang funerary bed with fictive gateposts bearing an image of a Sogdian fire altar found in Northern Henan, at Zhangdefu (near Anyang), bearing an image of a Sogdian fire altar. No Zoroastrian texts have as yet been found here, but it is believed that fragments of the Sogdian manuscripts which record part of the Avestan text and of an epic tale about the hero Rustam, found in the vicinity of Dunhuang, were created by Zoroastrians. One of the fragments preserved in the British Museum mentions 'the perfect, righteous Zarathushtra', and the first two lines contain a Sogdian version of the Avestan hymn *Ashem vohu*. We can therefore say with some certainty that the Sogdians played a key role in the spread of the great religions of the East, Buddhism, Christianity, Zoroastrianism and Manichaeism, to Inner Asia.

Buddhism

In both antiquity and early medieval times, Buddhism played an exceptionally important role in the spiritual life of the peoples who lived along the routes of the Silk Road.

It is one of the world's most widespread religions, originating in India in the 6th century BC. Its founder, Shakyamuni ('the sage of the Shakya clan'), was a historical figure, Prince Siddhartha, from the noble Gautama family. He is said to have lived in North India in the years 566–476 or 563–473 BC.

According to Buddhist legend, the future Buddha (in Sanskrit 'Buddha' means 'The Enlightened One') came to earth, embodied as Prince Siddhartha, in order to show humankind the path of salvation from suffering. After leaving home on a pilgrimage, he sought the means to escape suffering and one day, meditating under a sacred Bodhi tree, he achieved enlightenment through the 'four noble truths' and became the Buddha. He gave his first sermon near Benares to five men who were to become his future disciples, and then, for over 40 years, he travelled about spreading his teaching. Those who followed were originally called 'followers of the Dharma'.

The Dharma is one of the basic concepts of Buddhism, comprising the teachings and practices of the Buddha, construed as universal truth. It was only later that this teaching became known as Buddhism after its founder.

In addition to the various schools of Buddhism that exist, there are two main directions of thought – the Hinayana and the Mahayana. The Hinayana, or the 'Small Vehicle', is the 'narrow path of salvation', and is associated with the complete renunciation of worldly life. It was popular in early Buddhism and played a major role in the kingdom of Magadha. In Hinayana Buddhism, the role of the bodhisattvas is relatively insignificant; they are not objects of veneration and play no role in the salvation of human beings. A person's salvation depends on themselves, and on following the path shown by the Buddha.

Mahayana, the 'Great Vehicle', became the most widespread school of Buddhism after the Fourth Buddhist Council convened by King Kanishka in Kashmir. Unlike in Hinayana Buddhism, in Mahayana Buddhism the bodhisattvas are supernatural and celestial beings, who are different incarnations of the Buddha himself. They have voluntarily given up their right to enter nirvana so that they can help people. They are characterised by love and compassion for people and are therefore highly revered in the Mahayana tradition.

The pantheons of bodhisattvas were constantly being extended with more deities, especially with those taken from Shaivite and Vaishnavite traditions, but also included deities of peoples who had fully or partially embraced Buddhism. These deities, according to A.N. Kochetov, 'were not particularly mythologised, and were mostly reduced to stories about their conversion to Buddhism'.

During the reign of the Emperor Ashoka (273–236 BC) Buddhism became the official religion of the vast Indian kingdom of the Mauryas (322–184 BC) and from here it spread to Bactria, Sogdia, Serindia (Xinjiang) and China.

According to B.A. Litvinsky Buddhist missionaries appeared in what is now Afghanistan and then in Central Asia in the middle to end of the Graeco-Bactrian period (i.e. in the middle of the 2nd century BC). Then, local adherents of the Buddha's teaching appeared, and in the Kushan period (1st–2nd century AD) Buddhist influence intensified further. P.C. Bagchi proposed an even earlier date for the penetration of Buddhism into Bactria, namely the Ashoka period.

E. Zürcher dated the arrival of Buddhism in southern Central Asia to the 1st century BC. T.K. Mkrtychev and other scholars share a similar view. According to A. Foucher, Buddhism could not have existed in Bactria before the end of the 1st/beginning of the 2nd century AD. B.J. Stavisky believes Buddhism appeared in Central Asia and only in Northern Bactria or Tokharistan during the 2nd and 3rd centuries AD. According to G.A. Pugachenkova and Z.I. Usmanova, Buddhist communities appeared in Merv (Margiana) in the 4th century AD and the first Buddhist monument here dates, in their opinion, from the 3rd–4th centuries AD, although G.A. Koshelenko dated it to the first centuries AD.

In this author's opinion, the history of early Buddhism in Central Asia (up to the 4th century AD) can be divided into three periods:

I. The introduction of Buddhism and construction of the first Buddhist structures in Northern Bactria/Tokharistan at Airtam, Karatepa, Fayaztepa (1st century BC–1st century AD)
II. The establishment and consolidation of Buddhism in Northern Bactria, and its spread to Sogdia, Margiana and Chach (2nd century AD–first half of the 3rd century AD)
III. The temporary decline of Buddhism along with the destruction and neglect of a number of Buddhist complexes in Northern Bactria/Tokharistan (second half of the 3rd century AD to the 4th century AD).

Buddhism spread to China along two paths: first, directly from India and second, from a number of historical and cultural areas of Central Asia, where Buddhism already occupied a strong position by the time it first appeared in China.

According to E. Zürcher, Buddhism appeared in China between the first half of the 1st century BC and the middle of the 1st century AD. This view is also shared by other scholars. For example, P.C. Bagchi attributed great importance to the role of Tokharistan in spreading Buddhism and Indian culture. E. Zürcher, H. Maspero, E. Chavannes and others have all written about the significance of the spread of Buddhism from Central Asia to China. B.A. Litvinsky repeatedly emphasised the important role of Buddhism in Central Asia in his work. However, by contrast, V.M. Stein, for example, wrote that we should not exaggerate the role of Central Asian Buddhism and of the Yuezhi in its dissemination in China. Again, a contemporary scholar of Buddhism, B.J. Stavisky, has expressed doubt that Central Asia was a re-transmitter of Buddhism to China.

Chinese textual sources provide two main accounts of the introduction of Buddhism to the Chinese. Both of them are associated with the Yuezhi, a people who settled in Northern Bactria in the second half of the 2nd century BC, and who later spread throughout this area.

According to the first version, the preface to the 'Sutra in Forty-Two sections' describes how the Han emperor Mingdi sent a group of envoys to the land of the Yuezhi to procure sacred texts. Different dates are given for this mission: AD 60, 61, 64 and 68. After three or, according to one version, 11 years, the envoys returned with the text or translation of the 'Sutra in Forty-Two sections'.

The envoys were accompanied by the first foreign Buddhist missionaries to China, Kashyapa Matanga and Dharmaratna. Following this the emperor built a Buddhist temple in Luoyang, the Pi-ma-sai (meaning 'White Horse Temple').

There are several interpretations of this account. For example, the famous Chinese scholar T'ang Yung-t'ung does not dismiss the possibility of this version reflecting historical fact. By contrast, H. Maspero considered this version to be a piece of fiction, a story of propaganda, full of anachronisms, which he believed originated in the 3rd century AD and which was further elaborated on in the 4th–5th centuries AD.

In the second version, in accordance with a tradition that developed in the early 3rd century AD, a Chinese envoy to the Yuezhi court, a student of the imperial academy called Ching Lu (there are different spellings of his name), was taught the Buddhist sutras by a Yuezhi crown prince in the year 2 BC. This story first appears in a very distorted passage about India from the account known as *Hsi-jung chuan* in the *Wei-lüeh* ('Brief History of Wei'), which was compiled around the middle of the 3rd century AD. The completed passage reads as follows: 'Anciently, under the Han emperor Ai, in the first year of the period *Yüan-shou* (2 BC), the student at the imperial academy Ching Lu received from I-ts'un, the envoy of the king of the Great Yüeh-chih, oral instruction in (a) Buddhist sūtra(s).'

E. Zürcher believes that most likely Ching Lu received this instruction from a Yuezhi envoy in the Chinese capital. E. Chavannes has suggested a correction to the text of this passage based on two later parallel versions of the story: '…the student of the imperial academy Ching Lu obtained a mission to the Great Yüeh-chih. The (Yüeh-chih) king ordered the crown prince to instruct him orally in the Buddhist sūtras', i.e. as E. Zürcher pointed out, E. Chavannes' version completely reinterprets the passage from the *Wei-lüeh,* by suggesting instead that Ching Lu did not learn the Buddhist sutras in China at the court of the emperor from I-ts'un, the Yuezhi envoy, but instead that Ching Lu was sent as an envoy from the Chinese emperor to the Great Yuezhi, and that he learned the sutras from the Yuezhi crown prince in the land of Yuezhi. It is worth noting that these versions of how the Chinese first became acquainted with sacred Buddhist texts have not been presented in Russian scholarship with any great precision.

There is also debate about the historical evaluation of the second version, some scholars considering it unreliable, others believing it to be historically accurate. E. Zürcher pointed out there is no evidence to support this version in the official chronicles of the Han dynasty, the *Han Shu,* which provides no information either about a Chinese envoy being sent to the Yuezhi in 2 BC, nor about a Yuezhi envoy sent to China in the same year. In fact, information about this embassy does not appear until the 3rd century AD when this tradition 'after more than two centuries of silence turns up in some seven versions, which are partly unintelligible and in which neither the name of the Chinese scholar nor the function of the Yüeh-chih nor the place of action appears to be fixed'. Zürcher therefore concludes that it cannot be used as reliable material for historical research. He then draws attention to the fact that the tradition about the introduction of Buddhism to China doggedly associates this major event with the Yuezhi, and consequently with Bactria/Tokharistan, where, according to P.C. Bagchi, Buddhism may have emerged as early as the 3rd century BC at the time of Ashoka. However, even if we do not have confirmation of this event in the *Han Shu*, it does not rule out that the Yuezhi contributed to the introduction of Buddhism into China, because the tradition, whatever it may be, is based on real facts.

The significant role played by some of the regions of Central Asia, namely Parthia, Bactria and Sogdia, in the spread of Buddhism is supported by the information in Chinese textual sources. The scholars P. Pelliot, E. Chavannes, H. Maspero, O. Franke, E. Zürcher and other Western, Chinese and Japanese scholars have all made reference to these texts in their work.

Buddha. Impression from a mould. Sogdia. Takhtakaracha Pass.

Parthia

Chinese texts mention five Parthians who facilitated the spread and propagation of Buddhism in China. Two of them, An Shigao and An Xuan, were active during the reign of the Eastern Han dynasty (AD 25–220); two others, Tan(wu)di (Dharmasatya?) and An Faqin, were active during the Wei dynasty (AD 220–265); and the calligrapher monk An Hui-tse lived in the 4th century AD. The most famous is An Shigao. He became famous primarily for being the first translator of Buddhist sutras into Chinese and for establishing a school of translators of Buddhist texts, from which famous figures later emerged.

According to tradition, An Shigao was a crown prince who gave up his throne to devote himself to religious life. H. Maspero believes that An Shigao was a member of the ruling family from one of the small kingdoms that collectively made up the Parthian state under the Arsacids.

L. Wieger sought to link An Shigao with a Parthian prince who appears in Western sources, but this idea was not supported by other scholars. From Parthia, An Shigao went to China and in AD 148 settled in Luoyang, where he lived for more than 20 years. H. Maspero suggested that An Shigao founded a special Parthian school of translators in Luoyang. Some 30 to 176 works were ascribed to him by later bibliographers. An Shigao had a profound influence on the development of Buddhism and the system of Buddhist philosophy and practice in China.

The second Parthian to spread Buddhism in China, the *upāsaka* An Xuan, was originally a merchant. He arrived in Luoyang in AD 181 and joined the Buddhist community headed by An Shigao. Together with the first known Chinese monk, Yan Fotiao, who described himself as a disciple of An Shigao, they translated into Chinese the Buddhist scripture *Ugradattaparipr̥cchā* – about the path of a bodhisattva's life.

Chinese texts mention one other Parthian, An Faqin, who played an active role in the dissemination of Buddhism during the Western Jin dynasty (AD 265–316). He translated five Buddhist works into Chinese, including the *Ashokarajavadana*, the legendary history of the Emperor Ashoka.

Another native of Parthia, Tan(wu)di (Dharmasatya?), also contributed to the propagation of Buddhism in China at the same time, but there are no further details about him in the sources.

The last Parthian Buddhist monk mentioned in Chinese textual sources is An Hui-tse. In addition to his religious functions, he was a famous calligrapher, who created miniature manuscripts of the sutras as well as a copy of the *Pañca-vimśati-sāhasrikā-prajñā-pāramitā*.

Major academic research on the history of Buddhism in China, including the role of scholars from Central Asia, was undertaken at the end of the 19th century and the first half of the 20th century, at a time when no Buddhist sites had as yet been discovered on the territory of Parthia. In the early 1960s, new discoveries revealed that Old Merv, the capital city of Margiana, had been a major Buddhist centre during the first half and beginning of the second half of the 1st millennium AD. Two Buddhist sites were discovered here: a large, above-ground monastery located in the south-eastern corner of the city, where a Buddha's head and Indian manuscripts were found; and a Buddhist stupa that had been erected outside the eastern wall of the city.

There is no doubt that the stupa was built in the 6th century AD, during the Sassanian period. However, there are different opinions about the date of the Buddhist monastery. Initially it was dated to the first centuries AD, but recently it has been suggested that it dates from the end of the 3rd to the beginning of the 4th century AD.

This hypothesis is problematic. Archaeological studies have shown us that the Sassanians, who conquered Northern Tokharistan in the second half of the 3rd century AD, destroyed many Buddhist monuments there. At that time, the Buddhist complex in Airtam, the cave monastery of Karatepa, the above-ground monastery of Fayaztepa, and the Buddhist structures of Dalverzintepa had all fallen out of use.

And at the same time, according to this hypothesis, a major above-ground Buddhist monastery is supposed to have been built in Merv, which was controlled by the Sassanians. This makes no sense. The original dating of the site is more likely to be correct, and at the time of the Sassanian campaign against Buddhism, this monastery must have been undergoing major decline.

All the Buddhist teachers mentioned in Chinese textual sources were directly or indirectly connected with Merv and Margiana – first a Parthian and later a Sassanian region, which had Buddhist structures.

Sogdia

This region of Central Asia played a prominent role in the establishment of trade and cultural ties with China. Sogdians were also instrumental in the dissemination of Buddhism in China. Chinese textual sources name about 20 Sogdian Buddhist monks, among whom the more well-known are Kang Ju, Kang Mengxiang, Kang Senghui, Kang Sengkai (E. Zürcher gives his Indian name as Sanghavarman, while according to P.C. Bagchi it is Sanghamar) and Baoyi or Pao-i (Ratnamati). Kang Ju was a contemporary of the famous Yuezhi monk Lokakshema and was active in China after AD 190. He was born in Luoyang and later moved to Chang'an, which had a large Buddhist community with a group of translators working on translating Mahayana texts into Chinese. Another Sogdian, Kang Mengxiang, who worked on translations of works from the life of the Buddha, is mentioned in the same group of translators.

The ancestors of Kang Senghui (he died in AD 280) migrated from Sogdia to India and then moved to Chiao-chou, on the Gulf of Tonkin (present-day Hanoi, Vietnam), where Senghui was born in the first quarter of the 3rd century AD. After his father's death he renounced the world and became a monk. In AD 247 he moved to Chien-yeh (modern Nanjing), where he built a monastery and founded a Buddhist school. Kang Seng hui was the first Buddhist teacher in southern China. He is credited with converting the Emperor Sun Hao to Buddhism, building many monasteries and stupas and translating several Buddhist texts and commentaries into Chinese, some of which have survived to this day.

Another Sogdian monk, Baoyi (family name Kang, Indian name Ratnamati), whose ancestors migrated from Sogdia to India, arrived in China between 454 and 456 AD, where he stayed in the Waguan temple in the southern capital. He was an accomplished connoisseur of Buddhist sutras and the Vinaya, and various kinds of incantations and divinations, and was known by his contemporaries as the 'Mentor in Tripitaka'.

Additionally, Chinese textual sources mention another two individuals from the 4th century AD who were directly associated with the propagation of Buddhist teachings in China. The first is Kang Fa-shih, who was not only an exegete, but also the first known calligrapher-monk of Buddhist texts in Chinese history. He worked closely with the greatest calligrapher of this time, Kang Hsin, who, judging by his name, was also a Sogdian. The Buddhist sutras produced by these two men were highly prized.

Thus, Sogdians, as well as Parthians, played a significant role in the spread of Buddhism in China. However, most of them originally came from (i.e. were born in) India or China, but not from Sogdia.

We still know little about the spread of Buddhism in Sogdia. Apart from a Buddhist shrine in the Sanazar river valley, no Buddhist monuments have as yet been discovered in the region that was Sogdia. However, we do know of the discovery of the head of a Buddha near Samarkand and of Buddhist statuettes found in Southern Sogdia.

Bactria/Tokharistan

Chinese tradition relates this region with the first contact of the Chinese with the Buddhist creed. People who came from Tokharistan played an active role in the dissemination and propagation of Buddhism in China.

The very first of them, the monk Zhi Loujiaqian or Zhi Chen, whose Indian nickname was Lokakshema, arrived in China from the Yuezhi land some 20 years after An Shigao, during the period AD 168–188, according to E. Zürcher, while P.C. Bagchi has pointed out that Lokakshema arrived in Luoyang in AD 147. Lokakshema is credited with translations of 12–14 Buddhist texts into Chinese, in addition to having the distinction of being the first translator of the *Śūraṃgamasamādhisūtra*. Lokakshema was particularly instrumental in translating the Mahayana sutras and introducing Mahayana Buddhism to China.

Another Yuezhi *upāsaka* monk, Zhi Qian (first half of the 3rd century AD), also called Chih Yüeh (*tzu* Kung-ming), was a disciple of Zhi Liang, who himself had been a disciple of Lokakshema. He is described as having been a lean and shrunken man, with very light eyes and golden pupils (incidentally, this is the first and only description of the physical appearance of a Yuezhi person). From Luoyang he moved first to Wuchang, then to Chien-yeh (Nanjing), where he lived until the mid-3rd century AD and translated Buddhist writings. Zhi Qian was a man of remarkable knowledge, and it is no wonder that he was described as having a frail body but a mind like a palace. He knew many languages and had studied the 'barbarian writing(s)', meaning non-Chinese scripts from South and Central Asia. Between AD 222 and 253 he translated 49 Buddhist texts into Chinese in a refined literary style. He is said to have composed the first Chinese Buddhist hymns, and wrote a commentary on the *Liao-pen sheng-ssu ching* (*Śālistambhaka Sūtra*).

The 3rd-century Buddhist monk Zhu Tanmoluocha, known as Dharmaraksha (Chinese name Zhu Fahu), came from a Tokharian family who settled and continued to live in Dunhuang for generations. He was a very important figure in the spread and propagation of Buddhism in China and his activities explain his other nickname:

'the Bodhisattva of Dunhuang'. He travelled to Chang'an and Luoyang alternating trips with periods at home. Dharmaraksha is said to have possessed remarkable knowledge and a phenomenal memory and also knew 36 languages. He is credited with translating more than 150 Buddhist texts into Chinese and founding a monastery in the suburbs of Chang'an, where several thousand monks were trained. His most outstanding quality is said to have been his understanding of 'the idea of the end of the cycle of rebirth – nirvana'. He died at the age of 77.

All the facts referred to above testify to the prominent role of Buddhist monks from Central Asia in spreading Buddhism in China in the first half of the 1st millennium AD, in translating Buddhist works into Chinese, establishing Buddhist schools and accustoming the Chinese with the Buddhist faith.

Let us now turn to an important feature of early Buddhist structures that shed light on the nature of Buddhist beliefs in Central Asia. Airtam is one of the earliest and main centres of Buddhism in Northern Bactria but no images of bodhisattvas were found among the sculptures discovered here. The sculpted images of the Airtam frieze show musicians of the *pancha mahashabta* – the five sacred sounds. According to P. Bernard, the sculptural block found at this site with a six-line Bactrian inscription shows the Hindu god Shiva and his consort, Parvati. According to J. Harmatta, they are in fact Pharro and Ardoxsho. The Buddha or bodhisattvas are not mentioned in the inscription itself. There are no images of bodhisattvas among the paintings and sculptures discovered at Karatepa either. Nor are they mentioned in the numerous Brahmi and Kharoshthi inscriptions found there. There are also no images of bodhisattvas in the paintings of Fayaztepa or among the sculptures found there.

There are no images of bodhisattvas even among a large number of secular and religious figures found in the first Buddhist temple at Dalverzintepa, built outside the city. By contrast, during excavations of the second Buddhist temple, located in the centre of Dalverzintepa, a number of sculptural images of bodhisattvas were found.

I believe that such clear-cut differences show us that Buddhist centres such as Airtam, Karatepa, Fayaztepa and the first Buddhist temple of Dalverzintepa were created in a pre-Kanishka period where the Hinayana tradition was dominant and bodhisattvas were not worshipped.

It is significant that the depiction of bodhisattvas in comparatively large numbers appears only in the second Buddhist temple at Dalverzintepa, the construction of which has been dated by archaeological findings to the 2nd–3rd centuries AD.

The following observations are also significant. In a painting found at Fayaztepa, a cursive Bactrian inscription behind the head of one of the male figures gives the name of one of the main deities from the Kushan pantheon – Pharro – the deity of good fortune. During excavations at the second Buddhist temple at Dalverzintepa a fragment of a vessel wall was found with a one-line Bactrian inscription in black ink which clearly reads Mao – the name of the moon deity in the Kushan pantheon.

Thus, the presence of Buddhist and Avestan deities in the Buddhist temples of Northern Bactria has been recorded in two places so far. The image of Mithra was also discerned in the Buddhist paintings at Bamiyan. These findings are not coincidences. We know that Mahayana Buddhism readily absorbed deities of other religions into its own pantheon, which could be attributed to the greater accessibility and ease with which Buddhism could prevail over other religions. On this basis, we can assume that the Buddhists of Bactria included the ancient Avestan deities Pharro and Mao in their pantheon and possibly others too.

Two inscriptions from Fayaztepa and some, possibly in Kharoshthi, from Karatepa, mention the Mahasanghika Buddhist school. Manuscripts found in a Buddhist stupa in the suburbs of Old Merv are a compilation based on the sutras of teachings of the Shravakayana, i.e. the vehicle of the Shravakas, belonging to the Sarvastivadin school. Mahasanghika and Sarvastivada were the principal early Buddhist schools.

Christianity

Representatives of various branches of the Christian Church initially appeared in Central Asia having migrated mainly from Persia and Syria, and then made their way along the routes of the Silk Road to Xinjiang and China. They made a significant contribution to the establishment of cultural contacts between the West and the East. They arrived in Central Asia in the early centuries AD for a number of reasons: some were missionaries, others were fleeing persecution from, or disagreements with, adherents of other religious movements in their countries of origin.

Among them were Christian Orthodox Melchites and Jacobites, representatives of one of the branches of the Western Syrian Church, which took its name from its founder, Jacob Zanzalus (also called Baradaeus), but most of them were Nestorians, followers of Nestorius (AD 380–440). Their presence and role in the spread of Christianity in the aforementioned countries is associated with political and, more particularly, religious activities.

In the 4th century and early 5th century AD, as their own position grew stronger, the Orthodox Church in Byzantium and the government supporting it intensified their battle against heretics, including the Nestorians.

Disagreements about the interpretation of the Holy Scripture, religious rituals and the nature of Christ that had arisen in the previous centuries within the once-united Orthodox Church eventually led to a schism and the formation of several sects and different movements.

Nestorianism emerged definitively in the first half of the 5th century AD as a result of fierce disputes among Christians about Christ's single or dual nature, divine and human. Nestorianism, represented by its spiritual leader Nestorius, was condemned as heresy at the Council of Ephesus in AD 431. Nestorians stressed the distinction between the two natures of Christ, admitting only an external connection between them; they also refused to accept the Virgin Mary as the Mother of God. This movement, known as Dyophysitism, mainly had followers in the Eastern Syrian ('Nestorian') Church, whereas the followers of another movement, Monophysitism, recognised only the divine nature of Christ, and considered His human nature to be merely a part of Him, which had no value in and of itself. Among the supporters of Monophysitism were the Armenian, Egyptian and Western Syriac churches. In the struggle between the Monophysites and the Dyophysites the former prevailed, and the Nestorians, who constituted the majority of the second trend, fled to Iran. It should be noted, that by this time, both of these movements had split from the Orthodox Church. In Iran, the majority of the Orthodox Christians adopted the Nestorian doctrine. Nestorians played an important role here, occupying positions in the government and in trade, and they included skilled doctors, scientists and craftsmen.

It should also be noted that before the mass influx of Nestorians into Persia, large Christian communities had already existed here, and been recorded as early as the 2nd century AD. The positions enjoyed by Christians had become especially strong in the Sassanian state under Shah Yazdegerd I (399–420), when the Christian Church in Persia declared itself independent of Byzantium. After settling in Persia, under Shah Peroz (459–484), the Nestorian Church received even more support and was recognised there as the official Church, while the position of the Melchite Orthodox Church diminished considerably, primarily for political reasons. Sassanian Iran was almost permanently at war with Byzantium and, having been driven out from there, the Nestorians had no sympathy for Byzantium. Nevertheless, the Nestorians, as well as other Christian movements, periodically also suffered persecution in Persia, and the Zoroastrian priesthood, afraid of losing its position, played a part in this.

This was one of the reasons for the mass exodus of Nestorian Christians from Persia to Central Asia and further to the East from the end of the 5th and into the 6th century AD, although the missionary activity characteristic of this religion should not be ignored either. However, Christianity had made its way to Central Asia long before the arrival of the Nestorians.

In the Christian tradition, the spread of Christianity to the East, to India and neighbouring countries, particularly Bactria, is associated with the name of Thomas the Apostle, who was given India when the Apostles drew lots to divide up the parts of the world where they would go to preach Christianity. Thomas, however, did not want to go to India, so the Lord sold him for 20 pieces of silver to Habban (or Nabban), a merchant of the 'King of India', Gondophares, who was searching for a skilled carpenter. When Thomas arrived in India at the court of Gondophares, he began preaching Christianity and converted the king, his brother Gad, and many others in the towns and villages. He then arrived in another kingdom, that of King Mazdai (in Greek, Misdaeus), and converted his wife, Tertia, and other noble women and men to the Christian faith. His activities aroused suspicion and he was killed by four soldiers, after which he was allegedly buried in the burial place of the kings, from where his body was secretly removed and sent westwards.

This legend of the Acts of Thomas may, of course, not be credible, but the historical person mentioned in it did exist – the 'King of India', Gondophares, is known from other sources. According to Christian tradition, Thomas the Apostle visited Gondophares in AD 29, so on this premise we can date the king's reign back to the second quarter of the 1st century AD. The Indo-Parthian dynasty of rulers to which Gondophares belonged did not last long and was apparently abolished by the Kushans in the second half of the 1st century AD.

There are more reliable sources than the Acts of Thomas that testify to the early spread of Christianity in Central Asia and neighbouring countries. One is the Syriac *Book of the Laws of Countries*, which, according to one version, was attributed to Bardaisan of Edessa (AD 154–222), and according to another, was composed by his pupils, allegedly in the middle of the 3rd century, in Bactria. At this time, the Christian Gospel was already widespread in Persia and Lydia. The *Book of the Laws of Countries* also mentions the presence of Christians in Kushan, i.e. in the territory of the Kushan state. The Armenian historian Elishe also wrote about the presence of Christians in Bactria and in the country of the Kushans up to the Indus during the reign of Shapur II (309–379). According to O. Hansen's research, another stage of Christian migration to this region took place during the reign of the Sassanian shah, Yazdegerd II (438–457).

According to Christian tradition, Barshabba, the legendary bishop of Merv and founder of the Christian Church in Eastern Iran, also played a prominent role in the Christianisation of Central Asia. Barshabba was one of the Christians deported from Syria to Iran by the Sassanian king, Shapur II, where he converted Shapur's sister and wife, Shirran, to the Christian faith. In order to free her from Barshabba's influence, Shapur sent Shirran to Merv; however, Barshabba soon followed her. In Merv, he became the first Christian bishop. After his death and burial, Barshabba is said to have risen miraculously and lived for another 15 years. A Sogdian version of a Syriac text found near Turfan claims that Barshabba founded churches in an area stretching from Fars to Gorgan, Tus, Abarshahr, Sarakhs, Merverud, Balkh, Herat and Sistan.

Al-Biruni's celebrated work *Vestiges of the Past* notes that the liturgical calendar of the Melchite Christians in Khorezm included on 21 June the commemoration of the priest Barshabba, 'who brought Christianity to Merv about 200 years after Christ'.

The synodical lists of the Eastern Syriac Church mention a bishop of Merv attending the Synod of Dadisho in 424 AD. This fact testifies to the existence of a Christian parish here large enough to justify a bishop, an important figure in the Church's hierarchy. It is also evidence that Christian ideals and their bearers had penetrated Merv long before AD 424.

Bodhisattva. Kampyrtepa. 1st century AD.

Thus, Christianity was already widespread in Central Asia, especially in Merv and Bactria, in the early centuries AD. However, it is equally clear that its position was strengthened by the mass influx of Nestorians. Before this event, we can probably say that the spread of Christianity in this region was more likely to have been spontaneous; with the arrival of the Nestorians the process took on a more deliberate character.

In the 6th–7th centuries AD, Nestorian Christianity in Central Asia became so firmly established, and Christian communities grew so large, that metropolitans had to be established in a number of cities. According to Syriac chronicles, under Patriarch Isho'yahb II (628–643), metropolitans were established in Samarkand and Herat, as well as in India and China. According to other sources quoted by V.V. Bartold and E. Sachau, the metropolitan of Herat was created in the second half of the 6th century, and a metropolitanate of Samarkand, allegedly, during the patriarchy of Ahai (410–416). Apparently, a metropolitan was also founded in Merv in the 6th century and in the 7th century the metropolitans of Kashgar and Navekat were established. As is well known, in AD 644, Elia, metropolitan bishop of Merv, converted Turks living beyond the river Oxus (Amu Darya) to Christianity. Some Turkic tribes had probably adopted Christianity even earlier. According to Theophylact Simocatta, in AD 591, when the rebellious Sassanian general Bahram

Chobin was defeated, many of his Turkic allies who had fought with him had a sign of a cross on their foreheads. They claimed that such a sign was placed on the foreheads of newborns, on the advice of Christians, to ward off all manner of misfortune.

It is likely that there were also some Christians among the Hephthalites, a powerful tribe who established one of the most significant states in Central Asia in the late 5th and early 6th century AD. According to accounts by Elishe, when concluding a treaty of alliance with the Armenians the Chuni-Hephthalites 'took a Christian oath to keep a firm alliance with them'.

In addition to Nestorian Christians, there were probably many Orthodox Christians in Central Asia. Based on a study of an 8th-century document, S.P. Tolstov believed that the metropolitan of the Khazars also included a special Khwalis (i.e. Khorezmian) Christian diocese. According to al-Biruni, the city of Merv was the seat of the metropolitan of Khorasan, and this implied the existence of a very large Christian community of Orthodox Melchites here. Before attaining the highest religious office of metropolitan, Melchite priests first had to pass through several other offices such as chorister, acolyte (or reader), subdeacon, deacon, priest and bishop.

Chach ruler with a cross. Coin. 7th century AD.

The Melchite calendar of al-Biruni, given in *Vestiges of the Past,* includes a Feast of Roses, which was also celebrated in Khorezm on the fourth day of the month of Ayyar (May) –'The Feast of Roses according to the ancient rite, as it is celebrated in Khwarizm. On this day, they bring Juri-roses to the churches, the reason of which is this, that Mary presented on this day the first roses to Elizabeth, the mother of John.'

Historical data on the widespread dissemination of Christianity in pre-Muslim Central Asia are supported by material evidence. These include churches and monasteries, Christian religious objects, funerary monuments and coins bearing Christian symbols.

Churches and monasteries occupy a special place in this list. Few of them have been discovered in Central Asia, but records show that they existed in Merv, Samarkand, Khorezm, Taraz, Merke, Semirechye and other places, which had Christian communities.

Many of them were destroyed after the arrival of the Arabs, while others were replaced by Muslim mosques. Abu Bakr Narshakhi wrote, 'On entering the town through the Gate of the Bazaar, "the street of the drunkards" (Kū-i- Rindān) was on the left; behind it was the Christian Church, which was subsequently converted into the Mosque of the Banū Ḥanzala tribe.' Narshakhi also reports that when Ismail ibn Ahmad took Taraz in AD 893 and converted many of its inhabitants to Islam, the Christian church of this city was turned into a Grand Mosque.

In 1938 M.E. Masson surveyed the ruins of a monastery near the Urgut district in the Samarkand Region. In the 1950s, a team of the South Turkmenistan Archaeological Complex Expedition (YuTAKE) investigated the remains of a structure known to locals as Kharoba Koshuk, which lay 15 kilometres to the north of Old Merv. G.A. Pugachenkova identified it as a Christian church on the basis of architectural analysis and dated it to the 5th–6th century AD. Subsequent investigations confirmed her assumption.

A small monastery believed by G.Y. Dresvyanskaya to belong to Melchite Orthodox Christians was investigated by YuTAKE/STACE in the north-eastern corner of the Gyaur-Kala site in Old Merv. A Christian church dating from the 7th–8th century AD was found on the site of Ak-Beshim in the Kyrgyz Republic.

A rectangular building with a round hall from the Koshtepa I site in the Urgut District in the Samarkand Region, dated to the 7th–8th century AD, is yet another example of a Christian building. This assumption is based on its architectural features, which it to some extent shares with Byzantine Christian churches, and also on a fragment of the wall of a large storage jar, a *khum*, with seal impressions that probably depict a baptismal ceremony.

The Arab geographer Ibn Hawqal (10th century) gave an interesting account of the Christian village of Wāzkard (Wazkird), which was published by V. V. Bartold. According to Ibn Hawqal: 'Al-Sāwadār [Shāwdār mountains] is a mountain to the south of Samarkand…On al-Sāwadār [there is] a monastery of the Christians where they gather and have their cells. I found many Iraqi Christians there who migrated to the place because of its suitability, solitary location and healthiness. It has inalienable properties, and many Christians retreat to it; this place towers over the major part of Sogd and is known as Wazkird.'

V.V. Bartold believed that this Christian village was situated in the district of Urgut, south of Samarkand. Several dozen examples of Syriac graffitti inscriptions and images of the cross have also been found here, in an area south-west of Urgut, in the gorge of Gulbogh. All these findings suggest that for several centuries the Urgut area was a major centre of Christianity in Central Asia.

Ibn Hawqal's accounts also indicate that a Christian village called Winkard existed on the bank of the Syr Darya river in what is now the Tashkent Region.

Central Asian coins with Christian symbols, discovered only recently, also make for very interesting evidence. In the centre of the reverse side of one of these coins, found in

Penjikent, is a straight, four-pointed cross with broad ends similar to a Nestorian cross, with a dynastic sign of a Sogdian ruler placed next to it. The obverse of the second coin, which comes from the site of Varakhsha, has an image of a beast of prey moving right, and a Nestorian cross in the centre of the reverse side. O.I. Smirnova believes that these coins were most likely issued by Sogdian Christian princes or the head of a Christian community or monastery. Bronze coins depicting the Nestorian cross were issued by Rokhanch IV (7th century), the ruler (*afshin*) of Ustrushana.

A 7th-century bronze coin discovered at Afrasiab is particularly interesting. On the obverse is a bust of a ruler with Mongolian features, wearing a tall *bashlyk*-shaped headdress. To the right of the head is a large cross, with a vertical bar is longer than the horizontal one, and to the left is a small Nestorian-type cross. This arrangement of crosses is typical of the coins of Christian Byzantium, in particular of those of Justinian I (527–565). Findings of such coins in Central Asia are not uncommon and they are probably copies of the latter. The profusion of Christian symbols on this coin suggests that the Turkic ruler who issued it was a Christian, most likely a Nestorian. A. Musakaeva identified about a dozen bronze coins with an image of a beast of prey or deer on the obverse and a Nestorian cross on the reverse in the collection of coins assembled by V.A. Shishkin's expedition in Varakhsha.

In addition to coins, many objects with Christian symbols and motifs dating from early and late medieval periods have also been found in Central Asia. One of the most interesting discoveries is a hoard of early Christian objects found in the 1920s at the Geoktepa site in southern Turkmenistan. The partly preserved hoard from the 6th century includes round plaques and medallions with holes around the edges, designed for sewing onto cloth. They bear images of a ram or lamb, an early Christian symbol for Christ, which was in use until the end of the 7th century, when the Council in Trullo banned the practice in AD 691–692, and Christ was thereafter depicted 'in his human form'. Other plaques depict a phoenix, an early Christian symbol of immortality and resurrection.

The most interesting motifs are depicted on the gold medallion. On one side is an image of a ram standing on a pedestal of three horizontal lines, above these is a small cross, and behind the ram's head is a staff with a fluttering banner attached to its top end. On the other side is a standing human figure behind whom is a flagstaff. M.E. Masson demonstrated that these motifs represent Christian iconography and symbols: the ram is a lamb, the human figure is an image of Christ the Shepherd, the staff with the fluttering banner represents the *khorugv* or banner of the Christian Church, and the three horizontal lines represent Mount Golgotha, where Christ became a martyr.

The rim of a *khum* with three seal impressions and an image of two male figures was found at Koshtepa I. One of the figures is wearing a long robe and a tall headdress, and stands at full height. In his left hand he is holding a book, possibly a Gospel, in his raised right hand he holds a cross, as if he were blessing the man kneeling before him, who is dressed in rich robes and wears what may be a crown. It is possible that this is a depiction of a baptismal ceremony, and, judging by the crown and the rich vestments, the convert was a person of noble lineage.

The Urgut district has yielded a number of other Christian religious objects, in particular, a bronze censer, with scenes from the New Testament depicted on its surface: the Annunciation, the Meeting of Mary and Elizabeth, the Nativity, Baptism, Crucifixion and Women Coming to Embalm the Body of Christ. According to V.N. Zalesskaya, the censer is of Syriac origin and can be dated to the 8th or 9th century AD.

The so-called 'Ampoule of Saint Mina', which is in the Hermitage Museum in Saint Petersburg, comes from Samarkand. It is a small vessel with a flat body and two handles attached to the neck. Both sides of the body are covered with stamped medallions with full-length images of Saint Mina with outstretched arms. At the top left and right are images of crosses and on the bottom are two camels. Ampoules of this kind were made in the 4th–7th centuries AD in the Coptic monastery of Saint Mina, west of Alexandria, Egypt. They were filled with water from the monastery's healing spring and were taken from the monastery by pilgrims travelling beyond Egypt's borders. A ceramic tile depicting a Nestorian cross is kept in the local history museum in Osh (Kyrgyz Republic). Several similar images have also been found here on the slopes of the holy Mount Takht-i Suleiman. Other kinds of Christian objects have also been found in Central Asia. Christian burials with bronze crosses worn on the body have been discovered at the Jamukat and Navaket necropolises. A similar cross was found in one of the graves of the Dashti-Urdakon necropolis in Penjikent district. A.I. Terenozhkin reported the discovery of a Nestorian bronze cross at Afrasiab. A Nestorian pectoral cross made of nephrite and dating from the 8th or 9th century was found at the Krasnaya Rechka site in the Kyrgyz Republic. The walls of ossuaries discovered at Afrasiab and Mizdakhkan, and in some regions of Sogdia, Khorezm and Chach, all have depictions of Nestorian crosses.

There is no doubt that Byzantine coins played a significant part in introducing Christian iconography to the local population. A considerable number of those coins, as well as bracteates, have been found in Central Asia, beginning with those of Constantine the Great and later emperors. All of them bear images of crosses from simple to patriarchal.

Christian written records have also provided evidence of Christianity in Central Asia. The earliest of them (dating from no later than AD 740) is a fragment of a vessel from Penjikent with a Syriac text – a fragment of psalms included in the Peshitta, the Syriac version of the Bible. There are a lot of Syrian rock inscriptions, probably of Christian content, in the Urgut district, but they are barely legible due to their poor state of preservation. Several Sogdian Christian inscriptions from the Kyrgyz Republic dating from the 9th and 10th centuries AD have been deciphered and translated by V.A. Livshits.

One of them, made on the rim of a *khum* found at the Krasnaya Rechka site (ancient Saryg), reads: 'This *khum* is intended for the teacher of Yaruk-Tegin. Master-Pastun. Let it [khum] be full, amen, amen.' Based on the inscription, V.A. Livshits believed that the notable Turk Yaruk-Tegin was probably a Christian leader from Saryg. Another Sogdian inscription, originating from the Yakalyg site in the Chu valley, consists of a clerical title and typical Sogdian name, 'Bishop Shirfarn.' Syriac and Sogdian Christian inscriptions have been found in Taraz. A short vertical Sogdian inscription on the wall of a *khum* gives a clerical title and Turkic name, 'Presbyter Il-tag.'

Another Syriac inscription on a vessel is of particular interest. It has two Christian names, Peter and Gabriel who, according to A.Y. Borisov, were Jacobite Christians.

A significant number of Nestorian Christian tombstones with Syriac inscriptions and images of crosses dating back to the 13th and 14th century have been found in Semirechye. Also of interest are Nestorian gravestones (*kayraks*) with epitaphs in Syriac script. The earliest of these gravestones were found in the excavations of the citadel of the Krasnaya Rechka site, which date back to AD 789 and 909. Among many funerary monuments that have been excavated in Central Asia, it has been possible to distinguish Christian graves, for example, in the necropolises of Old Merv, Taraz, Ak-Beshim, Navaket, Jamukat, and so on. Judging by these, it would seem that Christians in Central Asia practised burial in *khums*, ossuaries and crypts as well as burial in graves in the ground. In particular, evidence of a burial in a *khum* with an engraving of a Nestorian cross was found in the necropolis at Ak-Beshim.

The Church of the East or Nestorian Christianity probably penetrated the regions of Xinjiang before the 6th century AD, but it had taken firm root there by the following century. Its emergence in these areas seems to be connected with the activities of Nestorian missionaries and Sogdian merchants, Christians by birth, who promoted Christianity not only here, but also in neighbouring Tibet. This is eloquently demonstrated by an inscription found in Ladakh, on the border of Kashmir and Tibet. It was written in Sogdian vertical script, with images of crosses carved on a free-standing rock. The inscription reads: 'Year 210. I have arrived from the interior [i.e. from Eastern Turkestan]. A Samarkand slave (of God) Noshfarn will go to the khagan of Tibet' (based on V.A. Livshits' Russian translation). The inscription is dated in accordance with the Persian era of the Sassanian king Yazdegerd III, and this would correspond to the year 841/842 AD.

There are very few surviving written sources relating to the spread of Christianity in Xinjiang. However, texts of Christian works written in the Sogdian language but in the Syriac alphabet, known as Estrangelo, found here, testify to the widespread presence of Christianity in this region. In addition, the Sogdians, who translated Christian works into their own language, also used Sogdian script.

Nestorianism made its way from the oases of Xinjiang along the Silk Road to China. According to Chinese chronicles, a Nestorian Syriac family called Mar Sargis, whose ancestors came here from the West, were living in Gansu province as early as the 6th century. Patriarch Isho'yahb II (AD 628–643) is credited with establishing the first metropolitanate in this country. The intensive missionary activity of the Nestorians played a major role in the spread of Christianity here. For example, according to Syriac chronicles, during the reign of Patriarch Timothy I (AD 780–819), Shubḥa-lïshō', one of the most prominent propagandists of Nestorianism, who came across Central Asia from the Caspian region, arrived in China having converted pagan Turks, fire worshippers, Manichaeans and Marcionites to Christianity along the way.

But the most striking evidence of the Nestorian presence in China is the famous stone stele from Chang'an, erected in AD 781 by the Chorepiscopus of Khumdan, Yazedbouzid, son of Milis, a priest of Balkh in Tokharistan. It gives a brief history of this doctrine in China. The inscription on the stele is in two languages – Chinese and Syriac. The author of the Syriac version was Adam (or Jingjing in Chinese), a Persian Christian monk, who was responsible for the translation of some 30 Christian texts into Chinese.

The first mission of the Church of the East to China, led by Bishop Alopen, arrived in Chang'an in AD 635. In China the Nestorians founded several monasteries: four of them in Chang'an, one in Luoyang and four in Sichuan, Wu-chün (in present-day Zhouzhi County, Shaanxi) and Lingwu (in Ningxia).

In China, Nestorianism was mainly practised by the non-Chinese; there is no data on its dissemination among the Chinese themselves. According to A. Nikitin, Nestorianism in China enjoyed special patronage under the Tang dynasty emperors, who were interested in trade contacts with the West and whose guides were mostly Nestorian Sogdians, Persians and Syrians.

However, later, as the political situation changed, Nestorians began to be persecuted, and an imperial edict of AD 845 ordered Christians, as well as Manichaeans and Buddhists, to leave China. By the end of the 10th century AD, Christianity in China had completely disappeared. Despite the relatively short existence of Nestorianism in China, it left a lasting trace in the form of monasteries, translations of Christian texts into Chinese, and in its influence on Chinese philosophy. The Japanese scholar P.Y. Saeki believes that the writings of some Chinese philosophers include sayings borrowed from the Gospels.

In addition to Syrian missionaries, Tokharian and Sogdian priests, natives of Central Asia, as well as Sogdian merchants, played a prominent role in the spread of Nestorianism in China.

Passing from one country to another, persecuted by the followers of other religions, Nestorian Christians traversed the difficult Silk Road, all the way from distant Syria and Byzantium to Chang'an in China. Many of them became martyrs, but nothing could make them abandon their beliefs. They carried with them the Word of God to spread it in other lands.

Manichaeism

The Manichaeans, 'tormented by the vicissitudes of fate', 'persecuted by official authorities', 'destroyed and despised….' Authors, ancient and modern, have devoted many lines to writing about their history and the spiritual essence of their faith. However, most of these remain inaccessible to a wide range of readers.

The Manichaeans made their mark not only on the cultural history of Central Asia, but actually all along the Silk Road. They set out from the cities of Iran, and eventually made their way as far as the steppes and deserts of Inner Asia.

The basis of this 'world religion' founded by Mani is a dualistic concept of a world that consists of two opposing forces: Light and Darkness (good and evil, spirit and matter), locked in a continuous struggle with each other. The Manichaeans believed that before the creation of the Cosmos there were two eternally opposed natures or gods – the Father of Greatness, that is, the original Light itself, and the King of Darkness. The First Man – Ohrmizd (Middle Persian *ohrmizdbay*) – had been sent to fight the King of Darkness. To help the First Man, the God of Light gave him five sacred elements (also called the Five Sons of the First Man): clean air or ether, a warm wind, light, water and purifying fire. The struggle ended in failure and the First Man asked God of Light for help, so Ohrmizd was sent the Living Spirit. However, in spite of this, his soul remained in the grip of Darkness. According to the Manichaean doctrine, the soul, like the body, of every human being is also born of evil, and the only thing that is in man from the divine good is the 'spark of godly light'. The task of every true Manichaean lies in its liberation, which can be achieved through moral perfection. For this reason, laymen or 'Hearers' were not to kill their own kind or animals, and had to abstain from eating meat. Further prohibitions were imposed on the so-called category of the 'Elect', who were forbidden to marry or even to harvest plants that were used as food for animals. The main tasks of the 'Elect' were to pray for the remission of sins committed by Hearers and to preach the Manichaean religion. In return for this, the 'Elect' would immediately be admitted to the New Paradise, while Hearers had to undergo a series of rebirths, appearing on Earth in ever new bodies before they could enter purified into the New Paradise.

The high moral standards preached by the Manichaeans and their social message – 'He who is rich will be poor, will beg for alms and will suffer great torments' – attracted the poor and ordinary people. With its well-organised propaganda, Manichaeism began, still during the lifetime of Mani, to spread not only in Iran, but also in Mesopotamia, Asia Minor and the Roman Empire and even made its way to the East and Central Asia. Mani claimed 'my religion is of the kind that it will be manifest in every country, and in all languages, and it will be taught in far-away countries'.

The Manichaeans created an extensive literature, which was mainly of a religious nature. Mani himself wrote extensively in an East Aramaic dialect and in Middle Persian, and used the Estrangelo variant of Syriac script, which made it possible to convey the vowel sounds of Persian (with vowel diacritics), making reading and writing much easier. Moreover, according to many accounts, Mani was an outstanding artist who also illustrated his works – in fact an artist who was considered unequalled in the world. Until recently, the people of Central Asia and Iran associated Mani's name with great artistry.

The success of Mani's teaching along with certain elements of social protest, however passive, could not but cause concern to the ruling class and the Zoroastrian priesthood of Persia. Consequently, during the reign of the next Sassanian king, Varahran (Bahram) I (AD 273–276), Mani was imprisoned and executed, and the followers of the Manichaean religion were brutally persecuted. Large numbers of Manichaeans fled to Central Asia.

The Arab historian Ibn al-Nadim wrote: 'The first of the sects in addition to the Samanïyah [Buddhism] to enter the Land beyond the River (Transoxiana) was the Manichaeans. The reason for this was that, after Chosroes [Bahram I] had executed and gibbeted *Mānī* and forbidden the people of his kingdom to dispute about the religion, he began to slay the followers of Mānī wherever he found them. So they did not stop fleeing from him until they had crossed the River of Balkh [Amu Darya] and entered the realm of the Khan, with whom they remained.'

Manichaean communities were established in Central Asia during Mani's lifetime. One of the most notable figures of the Manichaean Church, Mar Amo, a highly educated man who was well versed in the Parthian language and script, played a pivotal role in the spread of Manichaeism here. Mani himself had sent Mar Amo to Central Asia to preach Manichaeism. Mar Amo came first to Abarshahr, then went to Merv, and from there to the former Kushan territory, where he also founded a Manichaean community.

After Mani's death, Mar Amo was active in missionary work along the middle reaches of the Amu Darya, where he founded a Manichaean community in the city of Zamb (medieval Zamm, modern Kerki).

Two important documents that were discovered in the Turfan oasis in Xinjiang attest to Mar Amo's activities in Central Asia. One is a letter sent from Merv by Mani's first successor, Mar Sisin (Greek and Latin Sisinnios), to Mar Amo in Zamb. The letter urges Mar Amo to conduct vigorous propaganda activities, and to patiently and persistently expound the fundamental principles of the Manichaean faith. Later, Manichaeism was to spread widely in many cities and regions of Central Asia, but its main centres were Merv, Samarkand and Chaganian.

At one time, Samarkand was the residence of the supreme head of the Manichaeans, while the Sogdian language became the official language of the Eastern Manichaean Church by the end of the 6th century.

The position of Manichaeism was also strong in Chaganian, whose king sent a *mozhag* (*mozak*) teacher, i.e. a Manichaean priest of the highest rank, to the Chinese emperor in AD 719 as an ambassador and preacher of the religion. He wrote to say that this man was skilled in astrology and possessed profound wisdom and that there was no question to which he could not provide an answer. The king particularly asked that the *mozhag* be allowed to build a chapel where he could perform services according to the precepts of his religion.

All this suggests that Manichaeism was not only an officially recognised but possibly also the predominant religion in Chaganian. A Sogdian inscription on a fresco discovered in one of the buildings at Afrasiab and deciphered by V.A. Livshits is of particular interest in this respect. It tells of the embassy of Turantash, King of Chaganian, to the King of Samarkand, Varkhuman (Avarkhuman), and, more specifically, states that Chaganians arriving in the capital of Sogdia would not proselytise and attempt to spread their faith among the residents of Samarkand, which very probably referred to Manichaeism.

It is well known that the Manichaean religion was widespread among Turkic tribes. Many Manichaean manuscripts were written in Old Turkic and it was in Xinjiang that a large number of richly illustrated Manichaean writings were discovered, among them the Uigur text the *Xuāstvānīft* ('Confessional Prayer') one of the fundamental texts of the Manichaean religion, discovered by the British-Hungarian explorer Sir Aurel Stein in the Mogao Caves of Dunhuang.

In AD 762/763, in the Chinese city of Luoyang, the Uigur Tengri Khagan Bogu met the Manichaean Elect, after which he and his close associates adopted Manichaeism, which was then declared the state religion of the Uigur Khaganate. Manichaeism retained this status here until AD 840.

Manichaeism made its way into China from Central Asia via Eastern Turkestan. According to W.B. Henning, it was mainly propagated by Sogdians. Many Manichaean texts were translated into Chinese, and Manichaean churches were built in the city of Luoyang, the capital of the Tang empire, and also in Taiyuan in AD 807.

In Eastern Turkestan and other areas of Inner Asia, Manichaeism continued to retain its importance for a long time. Finds in Xinjiang, especially in the Turfan oasis, attest to the fact that for several centuries, Manichaeism played an important role in the development of architecture, fine and applied art. Manichaeans played a particularly significant role in the development of music, frescos and miniatures used to illustrate books. Richly illustrated Manichaean books were highly prized by the people of this time. Manichaean monasteries are also thought to have been the prototype of the later Muslim *khanqah* – buildings specially designed for spiritual retreat.

The issue of differentiating Manichaean antiquities from the heritage of the many and varied cultures of Central Asia remains a difficult one for researchers to resolve. However, with the discoveries of Manichaean texts, paintings and miniatures, as well as monasteries, this question has been resolved to a greater or lesser degree for Xinjiang. But so far there has been no convincing scholarly evidence of the Manichaean identity of any particular monument in Central Asia proper.

Several scholars consider the temples excavated in Penjikent to be Manichaean, associating some types of ossuaries and terracotta objects with the Manichaeans.

In the late 1970s, an unusual burial ground was investigated at Bittepa, located in the spurs of the Babatag mountains on the left bank of the Surkhan Darya river. It consisted of several vaults that had been carved out of conglomerates at a height of 15–20 metres. The crypts contained skeletons lying on their backs, accompanied by a number of grave goods. This necropolis probably belonged to the inhabitants of the early medieval capital of the Chaganian region (with the same name), now the site of Budrach, which is located 4 kilometres from the above-mentioned burial ground, and directly opposite it, on the other side of the river.

Archaeological studies have shown that necropolises were usually located close to a town or village. Here, however, it is situated at some distance from the site and in such a secluded spot, as to suggest that those buried in the Bittepa cemetery belonged to a separate religious community.

Analysis of particular aspects of funeral rites at the Bittepa burial ground indicates that it might have belonged to a Manichaean community. In particular, no ceramic vessels have been found. It is possible that these were replaced by wooden ones, but they are also absent, and their absence cannot be accounted for by a poor state of preservation of the wood, since a wooden pyxis box found at this site has been perfectly preserved. It is fair to assume that the absence of vessels with food and water in the graves is related to a change in funeral rites. From the Bronze Age onwards, the people of Chaganian cared for their dead by placing several vessels with food and water in the graves. Food offerings in the form of bones of sheep, and occasionally of cattle, have often been found in ancient burial sites. One possible interpretation of this change in practice is that among the inhabitants of Chaganian, a soul on the way to the afterlife was no longer considered to need food. With the exception of *astragali* (game pieces made of bone), no animal bones have been found in early medieval Chaganian graves, although, grains of various cereals had been placed in some of them.

This evidence, then, suggests a rejection of the use of meat, but not of food in general, for use in funeral rites. In this respect it is significant that the prohibition of eating meat was one of the main precepts of the Manichaean religion, whose priests and adherents were expected to eat only plant-based foods. But how did the Manichaeans bury their dead and did they have any specific funeral rites? Unfortunately, this aspect of the Manichaean religion remains a puzzle for scholars, as very little information about these practices has survived in written sources. Individual fragments of Manichaean texts indicate that one of their funeral rites probably did include burial. A passage in a Parthian Eyewitness Account of Mani's Death (M 5569) says:

> ...like a lord, who lays aside (takes off) his weapons and his clothes and puts on another royal garment, thus the Apostle of Light laid aside the warlike dress of the body, and took place in a ship of light, and he took the divine garment, the diadem of light and the beautiful garland. And in great happiness he flew with the light-gods, who went on (his) right and on (his) left, with (music of) harp(s) and song(s) of happiness; he flew by divine, miraculous power like a swift lightning and a bright sight hastening to the radiant path of light and to the moon-chariot, the assembly(-place) of the gods, and he remained with the Father, the god Ohrmizd.[1]

It would seem that the Manichaeans did not have any canonically approved funeral rites, at least not in those regions of Central Asia and Xinjiang where the Manichaean religion had established itself. Its adherents appear to have adapted to the funeral practices that already existed in these areas, slightly modifying them according to the requirements of their religion. Moreover, the newly converted brought to the funeral rites elements of local customs and beliefs, which had existed there for a long time.

Living alongside Christians in the same towns and regions, having much in common and often sharing the same vagaries of fate through victimisation and cruel persecution, the Manichaeans might have adopted both Christian symbolism and Christian objects for their own rituals.

The small, round, lidded wooden box found at Bittepa contained a part of a phalanx of a finger. Similar boxes – pyxides – are widespread in the Christian world and were an essential article in Christianity. Made from silver, gold, bone and wood, they were often decorated with Christian motifs and symbols, but examples without such decoration have also been found. They were originally intended for keeping relics of the 'True Cross' and later relics of various saints. Pyxides have been found in many Christian burials. Researchers believe that in this case, the box was a personal item, and was worn and stored like a medallion or amulet, fulfilling a magical healing function. The discovery of the pyxis in the Bittepa burial ground is so far the only one of its kind in Central Asia.

Another interesting religious object found here is a miniature bronze amulet in the form of a jug with a cross-shaped 'Tree of Life' growing out of it. This amulet may well be unrelated to Christianity, as the Tree of Life motif is common to many religions including Manichaeism, but in Christian dogma there is a direct link between the concepts of the cross and the Tree of Life. The images of the Tree of Life in Christian art are therefore often interpreted as images of the cross.

Another extremely important find has been made in recent years. The archaeologist K.A. Sheiko discovered a small ceramic vessel covered in writing, in ink, from the rim to the base. According to him, the vessel was found in the Sariasiya district of the Surkhan Darya region, at the Afghantepa site.

The writing on the vessel is in Syriac script, which was used in Inner Asia mainly by Christians and to some extent by Manichaeans. Before a reading of the inscription on this vessel is complete, it is of course difficult to say whether it belonged to Christians or Manichaeans. In either case, however, it has great significance for the cultural history of Central Asia. Firstly, it is the first Syriac inscription from Tokharistan to have been discovered; secondly, it is the most important of all those previously found in Central Asia; and thirdly, it is one of the earliest. Christianity and Manichaeism played an important role in the history of Inner Asia and left a lasting mark on the cultural history of the peoples and countries along the routes of the Silk Road. They brought the spiritual values of their respective faiths to many countries and peoples, in spite of suffering and persecution.

Mithras slaying the bull (Tauroctony).

Mithraism

'Milites Mithrae' ('the soldiers of Mithras') is one of the names of the adherents of the once great but now forgotten world religion, Mithraism.

From the 1st to the 4th century AD, Mithraism spread across the vast expanse of the Roman Empire, from its borders with Parthia to Britain. Mithras Tauroctonos ('Mithras the Bull-Slayer') was worshipped by many segments of Roman society – by legionaries, sailors, slaves and the *coloni* (tenant farmers), the highest nobility and even emperors such as Nero, Commodus, Diocletian, Licinius and especially Julian (AD 361–363), who entered the history books under the nickname Julian the Apostate – an ardent enemy of the rising forces and power of Christianity.

'If the growth of Christianity had been arrested by some mortal malady', wrote Ernest Renan, 'the world would have been Mithraic.' There was a time when Mithraism was just one step away from finally overcoming Christianity. And yet Christianity prevailed. The reasons for this, aside from socio-economic ones, are to be found in the nature of the human psyche. The militant religion of Mithras (it is no accident that one of his main epithets was *invicto Mithrae* – 'invincible Mithras') called for eternal struggle and the destruction of evil, whereas the religion of Christ the Messiah, by contrast, demanded endurance, the acceptance of suffering and redemptive atonement. While Christ is a god of suffering, Mithras is a god of victory.

Mithraic symbols. Relief from Ptuj (Slovenia).

Indeed, the vast majority of humankind is by nature inclined to suffer and endure hardships in a never-ending struggle against evil, rather than to overcome it. Ousted (in favour of Christianity) but still unconquerable, Mithraism became permanently fixed in human consciousness: the two most important symbols of Christianity – the birth of Christ in a cave and the first day of great celebration (Christmas), on 25 December (for Catholics), are most likely borrowed from Mithraism – it is the same day that Mithraists celebrated the birth of Mithras.

Mithra, known as Mithras in the Roman Empire during the first centuries AD, who gave the religion its name, was the god of the Sun, the treaty and the union. Mithra was originally a deity of the Indo-Aryan peoples and had the auxiliary status of *yazata*. The earliest mention of Mithra (mid-second millennium BC), along with the deities Varuna, Indra and Nasatya, is in a treaty between the Hittites and the Mitanni recorded on the so-called Boghaz Keui tablets.

Later, the image of Mithra (Mihr, Miiro) entered the religion of Zarathushtra, where it became one of the main deities of many great empires of the East: the Achaemenid, Kushan and Sassanian. However, Mithraism, which was widespread in the Roman Empire in the first centuries AD, had very little in common with the cult of Mithra of the Indo-Aryan peoples and Zoroastrianism.

Sources relating to Mithraism are mainly lapidary inscriptions: dedications of zealous worshippers to the god Mithras, found in large numbers especially in the Pannonia area on the Danube, surviving examples of Mithraic art, and Mithraic temples (*Mithraeum/Mithraea*). No Mithraic sacred texts have survived, and the nature of the religion or cult has to be inferred from individual texts on Mithraism, contained in the essays of Roman and Christian authors.

There are two main hypotheses about the provenance of Mithraism. According to the first, proposed by the Belgian scholar Franz Cumont, Mithraism had its roots in an ancient Iranian religion. His hypothesis suggested that Mithraism originated in Syria, and its dissemination westwards to Rome and Pannonia was facilitated by 'Hellenised Magi'. The soldiers of the Legio XV Apollinaris are considered to have played an important role in this process. This legion was sent from Pannonia in AD 62 to fight the Parthians and then returned. There is evidence to suggest that it was in this legion that Mithraists first appeared in the Roman army. We shall turn to the fate of one of the soldiers of the legion later.

Proponents of the second hypothesis, the 'Danube hypothesis', posited by the Swedish Indologist S. Wikander, believe that Mithraism originated in the region of Pannonia, where it was formed and established as a religion, and from there penetrated into Rome and other parts of the empire. For example, according to P. Beskow and E. Francis, an important role in the dissemination of Mithraism in Syria and, in particular, in Dura-Europos, was played by Palmerian mercenary troops, who were stationed on the Danubian frontier of the Roman Empire in the early 2nd century AD, and who then returned home to Syria. The same role is attributed to the Legio XV Apollinaris, whose soldiers allegedly brought Mithraism to the Near East from its place of origin – Pannonia.

There has been increasing support for the hypothesis of the Danubian origin of Mithraism and its unique religious mysteries because it was in Pannonia, in the famous Mithraeum in Carnuntum, that the earliest known dedication to Mithras was found on an altar, which, judging by the inscription on it, was erected by a centurion of the Legio XV Apollinaris.

In simple terms, Mithraism is based on the eternal struggle between good and evil, with Mithras embodying the forces of good, and Ahriman the forces of evil. The legend has it that Mithras was born from a rock in a cave with a dagger in one hand and a torch in the other, and a Phrygian cap on his head (hence one of his nicknames – *theos ek petras* 'the god from the rock').

Shepherds who happened to be nearby at the time were the first witnesses to his birth, and they presented him with the first-born of their cattle and fruits. After some time, following his earthly mission to destroy evil, Mithras began to wrestle with a mighty bull, who represented the evil, coarse and dark forces of the universe. The fierce and violent struggle between them ended in victory for Mithras, who succeeded in wounding the bull with a dagger. Mithras then dragged the wounded bull to the cave. This rite of passage, full of dangers and obstacles, came to be known in Mithraism as the *transitus dei* ('the transit of the god'), and is an allegory for the difficulties and vagaries of human life. However, the battle between Mithras and the bull did not end there, as the bull escaped. The Sun sent a message through the raven, ordering Mithras to kill the bull, and he managed to do so with the help of his dog. Following this, a great miracle occured, as the death of the bull revived the good forces of nature, and Mithras was transformed into the giver of all good things for man: health-giving plants and herbs grew out of the bull's body and tail, and vines from the bull's blood. The scene depicting tauroctony ('the slaying of the bull') became the main symbol of Mithraism and was erected in all Mithraic temples; it often also depicted Mithras' main companions: a serpent representing the Earth and drinking the bull's blood, a dog biting the bull and a scorpion attacking the bull's testicles.

With his propitiatory bull sacrifice, Mithras delivered mankind from universal evil. Hence another of his most important epithets – *salutaris* (the saviour).

Having accomplished this feat, Mithras summoned his worshippers to a Last Supper where the main Mithraic sacrament took place – consecration of the wine that embodied the sacred blood of the vanquished bull. After this, Mithras ascended to heaven.

However, this mission of Mithras on Earth is still not complete. When the forces of evil in the person of Ahriman send humankind many misfortunes and catastrophes, heralding the end of the world, Mithras will come to the aid of humankind and perform several feats until he destroys evil in an all-consuming fire, symbolising the purification and renewal of the whole world. At Mithras' word, the dead will rise again and assemble in one great gathering, where he, the god of justice, will separate the good from the evil and offer the good communion with the blood of the sacred bull and grant them immortality.

Thus, it is in Mithraism that the idea and formation of the ceremonial aspect of Resurrection took shape – one of the main dogmas of the Christian Church.

In their service of God, the worshippers of Mithras (*mystes*) had to pass through seven grades of initiation, ascending a ladder of spirituality as they advanced. These grades were known as: Raven (*Corax*), Bridegroom (*Nymphus* or, 'One who is shrouded' – *Cryphius*), Soldier (*Miles*), Lion (*Leo*), Persian (*Perses*), Runner of the Sun (*Heliodromus*) and Father (*Pater*). At the top of the last and highest grade, which required particular moral purity, was the 'Father of (the) Fathers' (*Pater Patrum*), in whom some researchers see a prototype of the future Roman Pope. The 'Father of the Fathers' presided over the entire religious community, whose members called one another 'brothers' (*fratres*).

In a special ritual to purify their souls from corruption, they addressed each other with the words 'dear brother', ate four cross-shaped loaves of bread, and drank wine and water. The religious mysteries of the Mithraists included music, prayers to the Sun, fires lit on altars, and on 25 December Mithraists observed their main celebration: the birth of Mithras. The rituals were performed by special persons – 'priests' (*sacerdos*) who performed the three obligatory prayers at dawn, midday and dusk, as well as the daily liturgy.

Another, specific ritual was performed when an initiate passed from one grade to the next. For example, an initiate claiming the grade of a soldier was presented with a wreath on a sword, which he would then place on his shoulder, saying: 'Mithras alone is my wreath.' After the rite had been performed he could not, under any circumstances, either at a feast or for military exploits, lay the wreath on his head, and would instead say to its bearers: 'My wreath rests in my god.'

Mithraic ethics demanded from its followers continuous moral improvement and the attainment of virtue, which were to be proved by passing tests requiring great courage. According to one Christian author, an initiate joining a Mithraic community would have his eyes bandaged, his hands tied with the entrails of chickens, and would then be made to jump over a moat filled with water. The ritual ended with the appearance of a 'liberator' who would cut the fetters with a sword. Other tests were no less severe, including participation in a simulated murder. Moral purification, improvement, prolonged abstinence, strength of mind and, finally, bravery were the chief virtues of Mithraic ethics.

Mithraic symbolism was complex and full of profound meaning, embodied primarily in the various depictions of Mithras represented in examples of this religion's art. These are depictions of Mithras 'the bull slayer' (*tauroctonos*), Mithras 'born from rock' (*petrogen*), and a lion-headed Mithras (*leontocephalus*), showing a lion-headed god with a serpent entwined around him, a scorpion on his chest, holding a staff and an axe. At his feet are a raven, a staff wrapped in serpents, tongs and a hammer (as seen in a relief from Ostia Antica).

Key Mithraic symbols include a seven-pointed star, various solar signs, the Phrygian cap, a bow and sword, a dog, a lion, a serpent and a scorpion, the latter representing the main virtue of Mithraism – bravery. A relief discovered in Ptuj (Slovenia) shows many of these symbols combined in a single image. It has a star at the top, below which is a raven gripping a bow in its talons, and a Phrygian cap placed on a dagger.

The Felicissimus Mithraeum in Ostia Antica (Italy) has an example of a truly remarkable mosaic with images of symbols reflecting the seven stages of initiation into Mithraism.

Mithraists performed their religious rites in dedicated temples – Mithraea. They were underground (inscriptions refer to them as *crypta* or *spelaea*) in the form of caves with a vaulted ceiling artificially cut out of the rock, or they were above-ground, artificially erected structures imitating the appearance of caves. Along the walls of these constructions were benches made of stone or bricks, on which the *mystes* sat. These cave-like structures were illuminated by lamps, often placed in special niches in the walls. At the back of the structure, some Mithraea had a sanctuary room (*cella*) with steps leading up to it. Here there was an altar of fire and a sculpture of Mithras, the 'bull slayer'. The tauroctony and the main symbols of Mithraism were usually depicted on the wall opposite the entrance to the sanctuary.

Most of the Mithraea that have been discovered are small, about 5–6 metres long. However some are as big as 15 and even 23 metres long (for example, the Mithraeum III at Carnuntum) and were probably intended for use by hundreds of worshippers.

The architecture of a Mithraeum is now well known as so many have been excavated. A map drawn up by M. Vermaseren demonstrates that Mithraea have been discovered in North Africa, Syria, Mesopotamia, Asia Minor, Italy, Austria, Romania, Hungary, Spain, France, England and Scotland – in other words in practically every part of the erstwhile Roman empire. Of particular importance for the history of Mithraism are those excavated at Dura-Europos (Syria), Carnuntum (Austria), Altenburg (Germany) and Klagenfurt (Austria), and the Mithraeum of Santa Prisca (Rome, Italy).

Until recently, no Mithraea had been known of in the area east of Dura-Europos. Today, however, there is some evidence of the existence of this type of structure on the territory of ancient Uzbekistan.

Ten years ago, the team of the Uzbekistan Art History Expedition, led by this author, investigated the Kara-Kamar area in the far south of the Surkhan Darya region of Uzbekistan, bordering Turkmenistan. Here, the Sherabad valley gives way to the low spurs of the vast Kalif-Sherabad ridge of sandstones and conglomerates from the Tertiary period. Several artificial caves have been carved into this thick rock.

The name Kara-Kamar (literally 'Black Cave') itself suggests that these caves pre-date the Islamic era, as the word *kara* (black) is usually applied to archaeological sites from this era not to designate the colour but to mean 'impure', 'un-Islamic'.

Kara-Kamar was first investigated in 1877 by N.A. Maev during a road survey in eastern Bukhara. He noted the presence here of three caves on the eastern side, covered inside with crude images of people, horses, dogs, hands and heads, made, in his opinion, by shepherds who had driven their flocks into the cave for the night.

In 1940, the Kara-Kamar caves were studied by the archaeologist G.V. Parfenov, who believed they were a Buddhist cave monastery, similar to Karatepa in Old Termez, although no clear traces of Buddhist identity were found. His conclusions were based mainly on the similarity between the architectural appearance of the Kara-Kamar and Karatepa caves and on the alleged presence of images of a 'lotus' and 'stupa' in the former. However, the results of this research were never published.

Our detailed research, which led to the discovery of inscriptions in ancient Latin and other languages, has allowed for a completely different interpretation of this cave complex, unique in Central Asia. It has a U-shaped courtyard (55 × 30 m), which is open from the north-east and is enclosed on the other three sides by a sandstone wall between 2–3 metres and 8–10 metres thick, in which the cave structures are arranged on two levels. The lower tier contains the largest and best-preserved caves, and the second tier contains small niches (2 × 1 and 2 × 1.8 m) at a height of 5–6 metres above the courtyard. Part of the courtyard, above the entrances to the cave structures, was covered by a 'rock overhang', which later collapsed from weather and wind erosion. The inscriptions and the cave structures have also been damaged as a result.

Three well-preserved cave structures (Nos. 1–3) and one that was badly destroyed (No. 4) have been identified in the lower tier. They are rectangular (with a significant rounding of corners), with a longitudinal axis, and vaulted and were cut into the sandstone with the help of narrow metal tools, traces of which are clearly visible on the walls and ceilings of the structures. They are 9–11 metres long, 4.5–5.5 metres wide and about 4 metres high. The entrances to the structures are in the form of arches with projecting thresholds, now almost destroyed. There used to be an adjoining archway with a rounded ceiling between structures 1 and 2. In the rear facing wall at a height of 1.6–1.7 metres, two triangular niches (15 × 20 cm) were cut one above the other, and there are similar niches in the side walls of structure No. 3. They were probably intended for lamps and incense burners.

What could these structures have been used for?

The features of the structures suggest that they could not have been used for habitation or any other similar purpose. It is more likely that they were used as places of worship, which is also consistent with the content of the inscriptions found here. Many images and inscriptions, both ancient (1st–2nd centuries AD) and modern, have been found on the surfaces of the rocks and walls here. The images include depictions of a two-humped camel, a horse, a predator, a scorpion, palms, a bow with arrows, swords, and complex *tamga*-type symbols.

The inscriptions are in Arabic, Bactrian, Greek and Latin, with later inscriptions in Uzbek and Russian.

The medieval Arabic inscriptions are very short and contain only the year according to the Islamic calendar: 584 AH (1187–1188); 837 AH (1433–1434) and 949 AH (1542–1543). In addition, there are Arabic inscriptions from the 19th to the early 20th century containing religious formulas such as *basmalla* and *kalimah*.

Among Bactrian inscriptions from the first centuries AD, only one is well-preserved, which is a name, 'Larziokhsho' or 'Arziokhsho'. 'Arziokhsho' includes the component 'Ochsho', the name of the ancient Bactrian deity of the Amu Darya river, the Oxus. According to V.A. Livshits, this inscription means 'Given (by the god) Okhsho' or 'precious' to (the god) Vakhsh'.

The Latin inscriptions found here are dedicatory (*tituli sacri*). While the presence of Bactrian and Arabic inscriptions at these places is understandable, the discovery of ancient Latin inscriptions here came as a complete surprise. They were studied by the distinguished classicist Y.G. Vinogradov (from photographs) and his student

Y.B. Ustinova, who visited Kara-Kamar in 1988. However, the author of this book had already identified them as Old Latin during the first study of the site, with the name Gaius Rex clearly legible.

Both Latin inscriptions were to the left of the entrance to structure No. 3, and one of them was 1.5 metres higher than the other.

The first inscription consists of three short vertical lines which have been read as:

PAN
G. REX
AP. LG.

Let us begin with the third line of this inscription, containing the standard abbreviation for the Legio XV Apollinaris – the name of the famous Roman legion mentioned earlier. In the second line, the letter *G* is the initial of the name Gaius, and Rex is the nickname of this Gaius of the XVth legion. A reading of these lines makes clear the first line, where the abbreviation PAN from *Pan(nonici)* is given – the name of the area on the Danube and the place of the main location of the Legio XV Apollinaris, from where in AD 62 it was transferred to the kingdom of Armenia to fight against the Parthians, where the Romans suffered a crushing defeat. Later this legion took part in the suppression of the Judean revolt and accompanied Emperor Titus to Alexandria, before being transferred back to Pannonia in AD 112. One of the symbols of this legion was a hand placed at the top of the staff of a banner. It is worth noting at this point that we found similar images at Kara-Kamar.

No less interesting is the second inscription, which in the lower line contains two letters, 'IM', which was the standard Roman Mithraic abbreviation for *invicto mithrae* ('invincible Mithras'), often also used in the phrase *deo invicto mithrae* ('the invincible god Mithras'). It is evident, therefore, that the Latin inscriptions in Kara-Kamar, one of which contains a dedication to the god Mithras, were made by the soldiers of the Legio XV Apollinaris. It is entirely possible that they were captured during the Roman–Parthian Wars and were banished to the far east of the Parthian empire, which, as we now know, included the region of Kara-Kamar. Incidentally, the same fate had befallen soldiers of Marcus Crassus 100 years earlier, when he suffered a terrible defeat in the battle with the Parthians in Mesopotamia in 53 BC, following which 10,000 Roman legionaries were exiled to Margiana (the name of the Murghab river region in Turkmenistan), from where Kara-Kamar is a mere 300 kilometres. Could it be that this territory (Margiana and the valley of the middle course of the Oxus river) had been a traditional place of exile for captive Roman legionaries?

The content of the inscriptions and the architecture of the structures which are similar (even in the details) to Mithraea, particularly the Mithraeum in Caesarea (Israel), suggests that the Kara-Kamar structures were originally part of a Mithraeum. It was probably built in the late 1st century AD by captive Mithraic legionaries of the Legio XV Appolinaris on the eastern border of the Parthian state, which they may have been guarding.

However, the historical significance of the discovery of Kara-Kamar is not only the fact that it represents the first Mithraeum to have been found in Central Asia, but also the fact that the Latin inscriptions from here are the most easterly Old Latin inscriptions to have been discovered. Until now, the first such Latin inscription was the one discovered in Kabristan (present-day Gobustan in Azerbaijan, 4 km west of the Caspian Sea), carved on a rock by Julius Maximus, centurion of the Legio XII Fulminata under the Emperor Domitian, Caesar Domitianus Augustus Germanicus (81–96 AD).

The renowned scholar of religion Prof. I.A. Borichevsky is known to have made the extraordinary observation that 'The forgotten rival of Christ has now risen from the ashes.' In a number of European countries Mithraic readings are regularly held, and journals, collections of articles and books on Mithraism are published – and hundreds of millions of Christian Catholics and Protestants celebrate Christmas on 25 December, perhaps not realising that this was originally a day to pay homage to the sun god, the uncompromising fighter against evil, the invincible Mithras.

PART IV

MIGRATIONS OF CULTURES

4.1

THE SILK ROAD

The Silk Road is one of the most remarkable achievements of civilisation. A transcontinental route, it meant that for the first time in human history the West and the East were connected: the Mediterranean countries with the Far East, the ancient classical civilisations with that of the Chinese.

The emergence of this route can be traced back to the second half of the 2nd century BC when the Chinese envoy and traveller Zhang Qian first opened up the Western Regions (the Chinese name for the countries of Central Asia) for China. In this way, two great routes to previously unknown lands came to be connected. The first ran from west to east, from the Mediterranean to Central Asia, and was scouted and traversed by the Hellenes and Macedonians during the campaigns of Alexander the Great and the Seleucid general Demodamas. The second, running from east to west, from the Han empire to Central Asia, was the route taken by Zhang Qian as he crossed these regions, moving from north to south through Dayuan (Ferghana), Kangju (Transoxiana) and Bactria.

The Sogdians had a prominent role in the development of the Silk Road as they moved eastwards to settle elsewhere following the conquest of Sogdia by Alexander the Great. Later, Sogdian trading stations appeared all along the eastern part of the route, stretching from Central Asia to Chang'an in China and, possibly even as far away as Japan. At the end of the 6th century BC, the Sogdian merchant Maniah, having skirted the Caspian and crossed the Black Sea, arrived in Constantinople, thereby establishing a new route for the silk trade – the 'Caucasian Silk Road'. There is evidence that the Sogdians also traded along the maritime routes of the Silk Road, which went from Arabia to India and thence further east to China.

The term 'Silk Road' – *Seidenstrasse* or *Seidenstrassen* ('Silk Roads', since there were many routes), in German – was first coined and introduced into academic circles by the German scholar Baron F. von Richthofen in 1877 in his seminal book on China. His choice of the name was entirely justified, for it was silk, as another German scholar A. Hermann noted, which, at the end of the 2nd century BC, was the main commodity responsible for bringing together the two different worlds of the West and the East. It would be wrong, however, to reduce the significance of the Silk Road in the history of world civilisation solely to the silk trade. Its role was much broader and more complex, as caravans on the route did not only carry a variety of Eastern and Western goods, but also spiritual values, ideas and religious philosophies. Between 10,000 and 9,000 BC, in the south-west of Anatolia, in Upper Mesopotamia and in the Levant, the first centres of the future ancient civilisations of the East began to emerge, with the transition from economies based on hunting and gathering to productive ones based on early irrigation methods for farming and on cattle breeding.

The great civilisations of antiquity formed a vast belt in a geographical area between latitudes 20 and 50, between the South and East China Seas and the Atlantic Ocean.

Initially, during the Neolithic period, the first farming cultures, the bases of later ancient civilisations, occupied separate isolated territories (the Southern Balkans, Asia Minor, Mesopotamia, the Eastern Mediterranean, south-western Central Asia, the Indus Valley and the lower reaches of the Huanghe or Yellow River) separated by vast uninhabited spaces, and these were in fact almost unconnected to one another. The first permanent settlements, prototypes of future cities, emerged at this time – Jericho and Chatal-Huyuk. During the Chalcolithic and Bronze ages, when the first civilisations and early state-like entities emerged, a trend towards the expansion of territories began. Thus, the territories of the Cretan-Mycenaeans, Egypt, Mesopotamia and Luristan were established, along with the civilisations of Transcaucasia and the northern Caucasus, the Namazga civilisation, which spread widely in southern Central Asia, the Harappan or Indus Valley Civilisation, and the Yin civilisation of China. Trade began to take place across several thousand kilometres of land.

At the beginning of the 3rd millenium BC, in Lower Mesopotamia and Egypt, the first societies with state-like structures in the history of humankind, the so-called *nomes*, emerged – city-states established by the Sumerians and ancient Egyptians. They traded with, and pursued a policy of colonisation over, neighbouring regions, in particular Elam with its capital, Susa.

In early 3000 BC, the Elamites migrated even further, thereby expanding the range of cultural influences and trade relations. Proto-Elamite tablets, impressions of cylindrical seals and unique specimens of pottery have been found at sites on the Iranian Plateau, in Tepe-Hissar, near the border with Turkmenistan, and in Shahr-i Sokhta on the border with Afghanistan – i.e. thousands of kilometres north-west of Elam itself.

In turn, a stream of cultural influences was flowing southwards and south-west from southern Turkmenistan, home to the thriving and well-developed Namazga culture at that time. Pottery and other articles from this culture have been found at Shahr-i Sokhta in present-day south-eastern Iran, and at the Nosharo and Sibri sites in present-day Pakistan. In the Indus valley, in the first half of the 3rd millennium BC, one of the most remarkable civilisations of the ancient East emerged – the Harappan civilisation, which was to last until its collapse in the middle of the 2nd millennium BC.

In the 1970s, in the Amu Darya valley at the confluence of the Kokcha and Amu Darya rivers in northern Afghanistan, French archaeologists discovered six settlements with materials from the Harappan civilisation, and one of these sites, Shortugai, was excavated in full. These discoveries suggest that the Harrapan people had found a way north from the Indus valley, through the Khyber Pass to the Amu Darya valley in the second half of the 3rd and the first half of the 2nd millennium BC. It has been suggested that Harappan colonies existed here for the mining of Badakhshan lapis lazuli deposits, which were then transported to Harappan settlements.

At the same time, a sea trade route connecting the Indus valley with Mesopotamia was also established. Mesopotamian texts make frequent references to the inhabitants of Meluhha (most likely referring to the Indus valley) and speak of items such as gold, tin, silver, lapis lazuli, carnelian and timber being exported from Meluhha.

A hoard of precious objects, including gold and silver vessels made in Mesopotamian artistic styles, was found in the area of Fulol in northern Afghanistan. Of particular interest are the items made of lapis lazuli, a semiprecious stone, which was highly prized in the East from ancient times. The main deposits of lazurite are in Badakhshan, in the upper Amu Darya basin, and the earliest findings of lapis lazuli items in Central Asia, Iran, Mesopotamia, Egypt and West Asia date from the 4th–3rd millennia BC.

The mapping of these finds, comparing them with a report about the mineral made by an Assyrian agent who had been sent by his king to the mountainous region of Badakhshan to acquire lapis lazuli, together with a number of Sumerian texts, led V.I. Sarianidi to propose the existence of a 'Great Lapis Lazuli Road' between the countries of the Near East and Badakhshan. Thus, as early as the 3rd to the 2nd millennium BC, a system of overland and sea routes connecting the most remote cultures and civilisations in the vast region of the Middle East extending from west to east, from the plains of Mesopotamia to the Indus valley, and from north to south, from the deserts of Central Asia to the Arabian Sea, was established. In time, these roads became one of the major parts of the Silk Road. This established system of roads can rightly be called Mesopotamian–Harappan, given the most important contribution of these two civilisations to its formation.

During this period, migrations of different peoples also increased. Especially significant was the migration of Indo-Europeans westwards (Celts, Italic peoples, Etruscans), to the south (Achaeans, Dorians, Hittites), and south-eastwards (through Central Asia). This led to major changes in the ethnic map of Eurasia.

For the first time in the history of the world, Egypt and Assyria had conquered territories that lay on different continents to theirs: North-East Africa and West Asia. At the same time, the Phoenicians from the Eastern Mediterranean made their first journey around the African continent and founded colonies on its northern coast.

Thus, by the beginning of the 1st millennium BC, a large part of Eurasia had already been subjugated, and people began to explore vast expanses of the sea.

At the end of the first half of the 1st millennium BC a momentous event occurred in human history, as the Achaemenid empire established itself as the largest empire the world had ever seen. It stretched from India in the east and Central Asia in the north-east to Greece in the west and Egypt in the south-west.

It brought together for the first time territories that spanned the three continents of Asia, Africa and Europe, and encouraged all manner of human exploration of new territories – in trade, culture and ethnic interactions. It gave the Hellenes their first contact with India and Central Asia and enabled them to establish the first Greek settlements in Bactria. It was on the territory of the Achaemenid empire that a 2,400 kilometre-long state road, the so-called 'Royal Road', running from Ephesus to Pasargadae and Susa, was built. The road had caravanserais and post stations (*angareion*) every 25–30 kilometres, about whose messengers (called *angaros*) Herodotus wrote: 'Now there is nothing mortal that accomplishes a journey with more speed than these messengers, so skilfully has this been invented by the Persians.'

By the end of the 1st millennium BC through to the 1st millennium AD, the vast geographical areas from the Pacific to the Atlantic Ocean (encompassing the Han empire, the Kushan kingdom, Kangju, the Parthian state and the Roman empire) formed a continuous belt of civilisations, states and cultures. It could be said that this was the first time that the world had been divided in such a manner, since it was the first time in human history that the borders of a number of states were immediately adjacent to each other along a length of 11,400 kilometres stretching from east to west. It is no accident that the Silk Road, the first transcontinental road of its kind, emerged at this time. The need for it arose out of the political, economic and cultural events that had been experienced by the peoples of Eurasia in the preceding eras. The first itineraries also appeared.

The first detailed guidebook covering an area extending from the Syrian city of Hierapolis in the Eastern Mediterranean to 'Sera Metropolis', the capital of Seres (China), was compiled by a Macedonian merchant called Maes. This information can be found in Ptolemy's *Geographia*; Ptolemy in turn had derived his information from the writings of Marinus of Tyre, probably written between AD 107 and 114, which have not survived. According to these accounts, the entire route was divided into two large sections: the first, from Hierapolis to the Stone Tower (which, in

Ptolemy's accounts, marked the mid-point of the Silk Road), and the second, from the Stone Tower to Sera Metropolis. The Central Asian section of the road began in Aria, an ancient region that was located in the most southerly part of modern Turkmenistan and north-west Afghanistan. From Aria, the road turned north to Antiochia of Margiana (today marked by the ruins of the ancient city of Merv near Bairam-Ali), and then turned eastwards and went to Bactra, the capital city of Bactria (Balkh in present-day northern Afghanistan). From Bactra the road went north, crossing the Amu Darya near Termez, and then it bifurcated: the northern route led through the Iron Gate (a narrow mountain pass between Bactria and Sogdia near the Derbent village in the Surkhan Darya region) to Maracanda (Samarkand), the capital of Sogdia, while the southern route ran along the Surkhan Darya valley to the mountainous region of Comedi, which some scholars believe is located in Kara Tegin. The northern route from Sogdia passed further on through Ferghana to arrive at the Stone Tower and the so-called Merchants' Station, while the southern route reached the same point via Kara Tegin and the Alay valley (in present-day Kyrgyzstan).

The Stone Tower was, most probably, the terminus of the Silk Road through Central Asia. Most scholars believe it to correspond to the Daraut-Kurgan area of the Alay valley. After the Stone Tower, the road went beyond Central Asia through Xinjiang, where the so-called Merchants' Station was situated near Irkeshtam.

The Central Asian section of the Silk Road described above became the primary trade route for a long time, right up to the 4th–5th centuries AD. Minor branches passing through Bukhara and Khorezm probably also existed. In the early medieval period (5th–8th centuries AD), the northern segment of the road, which ran through Semirechye to Chach (the Tashkent oasis) and Sogdia, and then through Paikend (in the Bukhara region) to Merv, and further on to northern Khorasan, became particularly important.

If you look at an ancient map, it is easy to see why Central Asia's location along the belt of the great civilisations of antiquity was so important. The distance from the Yellow and East China Seas to its eastern boundary was approximately 4,200–4,300 kilometres, and from the Atlantic Ocean to the Caspian Sea, 5,100–5,200 kilometres.

It is precisely this geographic location that has contributed to Central Asia's major ethnic movements, such as the migrations of Near Eastern, Dravidian, Indo-European, Indo-Iranian and Turkic peoples; the dynamic intercultural interaction (between Old Eastern, Eastern and Western Iranian, Hellenistic, Indian, Turkic and Chinese cultures); and the long-distance trade operations along the Silk Road and the signing of diplomatic treaties and military alliances. Central Asian peoples played a significant role in the spread of alphabetic scripts and the ideas of the major religions of the world (Buddhism, Christianity, Zoroastrianism, Manichaeism and

Islam), as well as many cultural and technical achievements in the countries of Inner Asia and the Far East.

From the above, it is clear that the Silk Road was not merely a road for caravan trade, but a unique phenomenon in Eurasian history with many aspects, which clearly had a considerable influence and impact on the history and culture of Eurasia.

It is generally accepted that the Chinese discovered the secret of making silk from silkworm cocoons some 5,000 years ago. A.A. Tikhomirov, a well-known expert on sericulture, has even provided an exact date for this discovery – 2698 BC, although others have suggested even earlier dates, claiming silk production began as early as 6,000 to 7,000 years ago.

According to a Chinese legend, the discovery of the first silk thread is attributed to the Empress Xi Ling-Shi, the wife of Emperor Hoang-Di. The legend has it that while she was drinking tea, the cocoon of a mulberry silkworm fell into her cup. Xi Ling-Shi is said to have pulled the cocoon by its protruding thread, which kept on unravelling. Thus was the first silk thread obtained, and in gratitude Empress Xi Ling-Shi was exalted as a goddess of the Heavenly Empire. Annual festivals are still held in her honour in many parts of China.

Some scholars believe that the cultivation of silkworms originated in the province of Shan Dun as early as 2255 BC, when the province paid a tribute to the Chinese emperor in the form of silk fabrics. Many years later it spread to the rest of China. Sericulture was especially widespread in the 2nd half of the 1st millennium BC, when silk was used in the manufacture of money, for fabrics, for the payment of tributes, and as currency in trade transactions.

Other scholars believe that sericulture originated in the mountains of India, still others think it originated in the Western Himalayas or even Iran. It is most likely, however that the origins of *Bombyx mori*, the silk moth, were in Northern China, home to its closest relative, the *Theophila mandarina*, the wild silk moth.

From China, probably in the 4th century BC, silkworm cultivation spread to India, and by the 1st–2nd centuries AD it came to Hami, the easternmost oasis of Xinjiang. In the 3rd century AD it reached Korea, and at the beginning of the 5th century AD it arrived in the Turfan oasis and Khotan. The beginnings of the manufacture of silk in Central Asia are commonly believed to have been in the 5th–6th centuries AD, when one of the largest centres of silkworm cultivation was established – in Sogdia. However, judging by the finds of locally produced silk fabrics at Kampyrtepa (Northern Bactria), dating from the late 2nd to early 3rd century AD, it is possible that the manufacture of silk had appeared here much earlier. In Rome, silk fabrics were already being used in 46 BC, and for some centuries silk still remained a commodity of trade there.

A number of cities of the Roman Empire, especially the coastal cities of the Eastern Mediterranean, had numerous weaving workshops which produced silk fabrics, but from raw silk, known as *metaxa*. In the 5th century, silk-weaving workshops appeared in Alexandria (Egypt). According to the historian al-Masudi, silk weaving began in Iran under the Sassanian Shah Shapur II (AD 309–379), who employed skilful craftsmen from Nestorians Posh.

However, all these workshops worked with raw silk, which, according to N.V. Pigulevskaya, was supplied here from India and Ceylon along the maritime routes of the Silk Road or by overland routes from Central Asia to Iran.

The art of sericulture spread to Merv, probably in the 5th century AD, and from there it spread to the south-east coast of the Caspian Sea via Eastern Iran. In the 6th century AD, as mentioned above, Sogdia emerged as one of the biggest centres of silk production in the East.

It is worth recalling an interesting story about the introduction of sericulture in Byzantium. According to a number of historical accounts, it was a group of monks, or according to other sources, Persians, who, around AD 550, on the orders of Emperor Justinian (527–565), brought silkworm eggs to Byzantium, by hiding them in hollowed-out staffs. Thereafter, the Byzantine Empire began to produce its own silk, and from here it spread to the southern Mediterranean.

Although sericulture reached other countries along the routes of the Silk Road, this took place later in the history of silk production. Revealing the secret of making silk was initially considered a crime in China, punishable by the death penalty. Once sericulture began to spread, China no longer had a monopoly on silk production. As the cultivation of silk spread to Central Asia and the Mediterranean countries, silk was no longer the main commodity on those routes, as many other goods were also traded.

Historical records are unable to give us the name of the first person to travel along the entire length of the Silk Road from China to Rome – it may have been a Roman soldier driven by the vicissitudes of fate, an enterprising Sogdian merchant, a Chinese diplomat, or a Nestorian heretic bringing the religion of Christ from distant Byzantium to Inner Asia.

However, a number of Chinese texts provide information about men (without naming them specifically) who travelled along the length and breadth of this road. Thus, in Du You's (AD 735–812) commentary in the *Tongdian* (AD 801), a historical encyclopaedia, he writes about a time when the Han emperor Wu di sent envoys to Anxi (Parthia), and two magicians were sent to him from Anxi in return as a gift. The magicians were dwarfs, originally from Li-kan, the Chinese name for the Egyptian city of Alexandria. According to H. Dubs, an embassy from Parthia with the Alexandrian magicians arrived in China between 110 and 100 BC. We also know for a fact that an envoy of the Roman empire sent by Emperor Marcus Aurelius (AD 161–180) arrived in China in AD 166, having travelled along the entire length of the Silk Road, covering the thousands of kilometres from Rome to the capital of the Chinese empire.

No doubt two-humped Bactrian camels accompanied the envoy on this journey. The camel's endurance and ability to locate underground springs and to sense approaching sandstorms, which could be lethal, as Edward Schaefer relates, helped travellers to cross the vast deserts of Asia.

4.2

THE HELLENES AND HELLENISTIC CULTURE IN CENTRAL ASIA

The Greeks had come into contact with the East, in particular with western Central Asia, long before the campaigns of Alexander the Great. According to Herodotus, the Persians under Darius I (522–486 BC) had already threatened to resettle the daughters of the rebellious Ionians in Bactria if they did not stop their uprising. Under Darius I some of the inhabitants of the Greek city of Barca had been forced into servitude and sent to Bactria.

The Branchidae also met with a tragic fate. After 150 years of power, the declining Achaemenid kingdom, riven by internal strife, recurring rebellions and a separatist aristocracy, led by a reluctant king, was unable to withstand the first blows inflicted by Alexander the Great. In the spring of 330 BC Alexander was already in Bactra – then the capital of one of the most important Achaemenid satrapies, usually ruled by members of the ruling dynasty. From there he set out in pursuit of the Bactrian satrap Bessus, who, after the assassination of Darius III, had proclaimed himself king of the Achaemenids. Bessus and his allies, the Sogdian Spitamenes and the Bactrian Oxyartes, burned all the ships at the crossing over the Oxus (Amu Darya) river and left for Nautaca.

According to Quintus Curtius Rufus, sometime after crossing the Oxus, Alexander came to a small town inhabited by the Branchidae. Although it had been many years since they had been resettled here, they continued to observe Greek customs and spoke two languages, although their Greek had mutated. They greeted their compatriots joyfully, but Alexander ordered the city to be razed to the ground and the inhabitants slaughtered. At the end of his account Quintus Curtius Rufus sorrowfully concludes: 'so the descendants expiated the guilt of their forefathers, although they themselves had never seen Miletus'. The Greek historian Strabo believed that Alexander destroyed the city out of his abhorrence for treason and sacrilege.

Where the town was actually located remains a mystery. Some scholars have suggested it was on the site of Kalif in south-eastern Turkmenistan, which in ancient times had one of the most convenient crossings over the Amu Darya, while others locate it in Sogdia. This author believes it was located in Southern Sogdia, in the present-day Kashka Darya province.

At any rate, long before the arrival of Graeco-Macedonian troops in Bactria and Sogdia, Greeks had already settled in these regions by the 5th–4th centuries BC. Some trade and cultural contacts existed between the Greeks and these areas, especially with Bactria, which took place through the territory of Iran. Coins from Greek cities from the mid-5th century BC, especially those minted in Athens depicting an owl on the reverse, have often been found in the territories of present-day Afghanistan and Pakistan corresponding to the ancient regions of Arachosia, Bactria and Gandhara. Many such coins were found in the so-called Kabul hoard, discovered by chance during works being carried out in the Kabul area. Even more interesting examples can be seen in the Amu Darya hoard discovered by local people in 1877–1878 in the ruins of an ancient fortified settlement which has since been identified with Takht-i Sangin or Takht-i Kuvad in southern Tajikistan. The hoard contained many coins including those minted in the Greek cities of Acanthus, Athens and Byzantium in the early 5th and mid-4th centuries BC. It included coins from the Greek cities of Asia Minor from the late 5th and early 4th centuries BC, as well as gold and silver coins from Achaemenid Iran and the Achaemenid satraps of Asia Minor. Scholars were also able to distinguish objects from Greece and Asia Minor in the hoard.

Naturally, contact between these regions was not one-way. We know that people from Central Asia, especially Sakas and Bactrians, served in the armies of the Achaemenid kings and took part in military campaigns against Greece. They were also garrisoned in the distant possessions of the Achaemenid kingdom. According to one account found on the island of Elephantine on the Nile river, a Khorezmian warrior, Dargaman, served there in the late 5th century BC.

Alexander the Great's campaign into Central Asia in 329–327 BC had a major impact on the social, political and cultural life of the region. It resulted in the incorporation of the southern regions of Central Asia into large Hellenistic states. It also led to the introduction of a new political and administrative system in these regions, giving rise to changes in the social structure, the introduction of certain forms of slave-owning economy that were common in the Hellenistic world, the emergence of a new economic level and the development of money and commodity relations.

There were notable innovations in spiritual and artistic life: the introduction of Greek and the emergence of a local Bactrian script based on the Greek alphabet, the influence of Hellenistic culture in town planning, architecture and the fine arts, and the spread of Greek beliefs in religious life.

This was a significant moment, marking the beginning of the Hellenistic era in the history of Central Asia. Many scholars use the terms 'classical' and 'antiquity' to define this chronological period in Central Asian history, but others have argued that these terms should only be applied to Greece and Rome.

This period is characterised by a general process in which many countries of the ancient world entered a new phase of social development, which was also manifested in the socio-economic and general cultural environment. This phase varied from country to country and was not identical or equivalent. However, whether it was Han China or Arsacid Parthia, Sako-Parthian-Kushan India, Graeco-Bactria or Kushan Bactria, changes took place in all these regions in all aspects of social life. It was one of the convergent processes of world history that affected all the countries of the ancient world. It is therefore appropriate to speak of 'the world of antiquity'. In European languages, the word antiquity refers to 'the distant past' or an 'ancient time', and is not necessarily connected only with the Graeco-Roman regions.

The death of Alexander the Great, in Babylon in 323 BC, altered the political situation considerably. The unified empire, created by the will and talent of a remarkable man, crumbled in the fierce battle over his legacy between the Diadochi, the rival generals, families and friends of Alexander, who continued fighting for several decades. These battles affected the western regions of Alexander's empire to a greater extent, but those of the east, in particular the Central Asian satrapies, were not spared.

During this time, Greeks and Macedonians made up the ruling class in Central Asia. Even before Alexander's death, it is well known that the satrap of Bactria and Sogdia was a Macedonian called Philip. His successor was a Greek from the island of Cyprus, called Stasanor, who took an active part in the war between two of the Diadochi – Eumenes and Antigonus I Monophthalmus. Stasonar took the side of Eumenes and sent him a contingent of Bactrian troops. For a time, Antigonus managed to seize most of Alexander's empire, but his hold on power was short-lived. In 312 BC, in a violent struggle against other Diadochi, the talented general Seleucus captured Babylon, the capital of Alexander's empire, thereby founding what came to be known as the Seleucid kingdom.

In the years that followed, Seleucus subdued the eastern satrapies and, probably in 306 BC, the eastern regions of Bactria, Margiana, Sogdia and Parthia. According to Appian, Seleucus came to rule over the Parthians, Bactrians, Sogdians and Hyrcanians after waging a series of wars with the Macedonians and barbarians.

The Battle of Ipsus, in Phrygia in 301 BC, in which the combined armies of Seleucus and Lysimachus inflicted a crushing defeat on the armies of Antigonus, marked the end of the wars between the Diadochi. The Hellenistic states of the Seleucids (including Mesopotamia, Syria, Iran, Afghanistan, the southern regions of Central Asia) and the Ptolemids (Egypt) were now established on the territory of Alexander's former empire.

Under Seleucus I and Antiochus I the Seleucid states included Bactria, Margiana, Parthia and Sogdia, while Khorezm was an independent state, and other areas of Central Asia were possessions of the Sakas, Parni and Dahae, who at that time were actively challenging the Seleucid dominions in Central Asia.

A number of historians believe that the military expedition undertaken by Demodamas was aimed against the Sakas. Seleucid domination began to be threatened not only by the Sakas, Dahae, Parni and other peoples of Central Asia, but also by the growing power and aspirations for independence of the Greek governors. Around the middle of the 3rd century BC, two of the most important eastern satrapies, Bactria and Parthia, seceded from the Seleucid kingdom. According to the Roman historian Pompeius Trogus (in Justinus' *Epitome*), the Parthians broke away under Seleucus II Callinicus (246–225 BC) and at the same time 'Diodotus, the governor of the thousand cities of Bactria, defected and proclaimed himself king; all the other people of the Orient followed his example and seceded from the Macedonians [i.e. the Seleucids].'

While in Bactria, and possibly also in Sogdia, the reign of Greek kings had been established for a long time, the situation in Parthia was different. The Parthian state had emerged here at about the same time as Bactria, in the mid-3rd century BC, as a result of the fighting between the nomads of the Parni confederation, led by Arsaces, and the Seleucid satrap Andragoras.

Although the Greeks no longer had any influence in the political life of the state, Hellenistic influences nevertheless continued to be evident in the cultural life of the country for a long time. The Parthian kings themselves acknowledged this by using Greek inscriptions on their coins. Greek titles, names and epithets such as 'philhellene' – lover of Hellenes – continued to be used for a long time.

Thus, from the second half of the 3rd century BC to the mid-2nd century BC, Greek rule continued only in areas of Central Asia such as Northern Bactria and Sogdia. Greek power was completely diminished after the Graeco-Bactrian kingdom came to an end as an independent state between 141 and 128 BC.

The long chronological period characterised by the political domination of the Graeco-Macedonian dynasties in several countries of the Near and Middle East, including the southern regions of Central Asia, is usually referred to as the Hellenistic era. There are several ways of describing it. For example, to the classical historian K.K. Zelin, Hellenism represented a specific historical phenomenon determined by the combination and interaction of Hellenic (Greek) and Eastern elements in economic, social and political spheres, ideology and culture.

At that time, the Hellenistic world itself covered a vast area stretching from mainland Greece to the Indus valley, within which scholars distinguish three zones, depending on the degree of Hellenisation: Hellas (Greece) itself; Asia Minor, Syria and Egypt; and the areas east of the Euphrates river. These areas are included in the widely accepted concept of the 'Hellenistic East', which includes Mesopotamia, Iran, the southern regions of Central Asia, Afghanistan and parts of the territories of Pakistan and India conquered by Alexander the Great.

The Hellenistic period in the history of the East began to come to an end from the beginning of the 4th century BC, but at different times in different parts of the Hellenistic world, depending on the political circumstances. In Eastern Mediterranean countries the period ended at the beginning of the 2nd half of the 1st century BC, as a result of the end of the Seleucid dynasty following its conquest by Rome. In the southern regions of Central Asia, it happened at the beginning of the 2nd half of the 2nd century BC, when the Graeco-Bactrian kingdom collapsed.

Hellenistic culture spread widely in the southern regions of Central Asia in this period and ultimately merged with indigenous cultures. Hellenism played a particularly prominent role in Bactria, Parthia and Sogdia, facilitated by a policy of intensive Graeco-Macedonian colonisation of those areas, which had been launched by Alexander the Great. According to a number of classical sources, in some areas of Central Asia, Alexander founded a number of cities named after him as well as smaller towns. The latter had probably started out as *katoikia* – military colonies with permanent Graeco-Macedonian garrisons. Three cities called Alexandria emerged on the territory of Central Asia: Alexandria in Oxiana, Alexandria in Margiana and Alexandria Eschate.

Later, with the establishment of Seleucid domination in Central Asia, they were renamed as Antiochia after King Antiochus I (281–261 BC), who continued Alexander's colonial policy. One of these cities, Antiochia in Margiana, was located on the site of Gyaur-Kala in Old Merv.

According to Pliny the Elder, 'In Margiane … the city Alexander had founded bearing his name was destroyed by the barbarians, but Antiochus son of Seleucus re-established a Syrian city on the same site, intersected by the river Murghab, which is canalised into Lake Zotha; he had preferred that the city should be named after him'.

According to Strabo, when Antiochia in Margiana was founded, Antiochus ordered a wall about 250 kilometres long to be built around the Margiana oasis, to protect it from raids by nomads. Many scholars associate the foundation of the city at the site of Old Termez with the names of Alexander and Antiochus. W. Tarn believed that the city was the site of Alexandria in Oxiana, mentioned by Ptolemy, which was destroyed by nomads in around 293 BC, and then rebuilt by Antiochus I who named it Antiochia Tarmita. However, according to P. Bernard, Antiochia Tarmita was built because of an active policy of urbanisation pursued by Antiochus I between 293 and 281 BC.

Excavations carried out in recent years at the citadel of Old Termez revealed habitation layers 2.5 metres thick with architectural remains and a variety of finds dating back to the 3rd–2nd centuries BC. In addition, more than 40 Seleucid and Graeco-Bactrian coins, starting with those of Seleucus I and Antiochus I and ending with Heliocles coins, were found in Old Termez in different years.

These finds confirm the existence of a significant settlement on the site of Old Termez in the 3rd–2nd centuries BC and make a strong case for considering Tarn's hypothesis that this was the location of Antiochia Tarmita. Yet another hypothesis put forward by the author of this book is that Alexandria in Oxiana was located at the site of Kampyrtepa, though the site has been insufficiently investigated by archaeologists for evidence of the Hellenistic period. Another city set up by the Greeks in Central Asia was Alexandria Eschate, which is identified by scholars as Khodjent.

These are the three cities originally called Alexandria and supposedly founded by Alexander the Great but there is archaeological evidence to suggest that settlements at the sites of Old Merv, Termez and Khodjent, with which the three cities are associated, were in fact established in the first half or middle of the 1st millennium BC, i.e. long before the arrival of the Greeks.

Archaeological expeditions in Central Asia and adjoining areas in the 1930s–1980s made some unique discoveries. The most interesting of them are the sites of Ai-Khanum, Takht-i Sangin, New Nisa, Old Nisa and Kampyrtepa. In the second half of the 2nd century BC, the Graeco-Bactrian kingdom succumbed to the attacks of the Saka and Yuezhi tribes, and more than a century later, the vast Kushan kingdom was established here.

Although many decades had passed since Greek rule in Bactria, and the Greeks themselves had apparently 'melted' into the local population, Hellenistic culture continued to play a significant role in material, artistic and spiritual life. Hellenic gods such as Heracles, Hephaestus, Dionysus and Athena were highly revered. They were included in the official pantheon of Kushan deities, and their images were reproduced on the reverse of Kushan coins and in sculpture. The Bactrian script based on the Greek alphabet remained in use. Hellenistic traditions lived on in the visual arts, in sculpture and monumental mural painting, and in other ways too. Studies at the sites of Dalverzintepa, Kampyrtepa and Khalchayan in the Surkhan

Darya region of Uzbekistan, undertaken by the Uzbekistan Art History Expedition in the 1960s–1980s, revealed the depth of Hellenistic traditions in Kushan urban culture. In fact, Heracles continued to be widely venerated in Kushan Bactria and some other areas of Central Asia well after the end of Greek rule.

The depiction of Heracles as a bearded, stocky athlete carrying a club on his left shoulder appears on one group of copper coins of the Kushan king Huvishka (mid–late 2nd century AD). An image of Heracles sitting on a rock or *omphalos* after one of his labours was used on silver imitations of Euthydemus tetradrachms, minted in the Bukhara oasis between the 2nd century BC and the 2nd century AD. A clay statue of a naked Heracles was found at the site of Dilberzhin in present-day northern Afghanistan. Terracotta images of Heracles have also been found at several sites in Northern Bactria, at Barattepa, Kara-Pichok and Sar-i Band. An image of a bearded Heracles in profile on a carnelian gem-intaglio was among the golden jewellery found in the Dalverzintepa hoard. Numerous finds from the Dalverzintepa site attest to the syncretic nature of the culture of this town, which included aspects of Indo-Buddhist and Hellenic cultures along with local Bactrian elements. Objects that had been imported from different regions of the Near and Middle East were also found here. This is no coincidence, as Dalverzintepa was situated on one of the most important branches of the Silk Road, which ran from ancient Tarmita along the Surkhan valley to the land of the Comedi and from there to the Stone Tower.

During the Kushan period, Hellenistic traditions were preserved not only in large towns such as Dalverzintepa, but also in small provincial towns. The finds from the Kampyrtepa site attest to this. The pottery that was found here is of particular interest, especially a large two-handled black clay vessel decorated all over with palmettes, leaves, wavy lines and rectangles with dots in the corners. Its shape is that of a typical Greek amphora. The palmette-leaf ornamentation is also a Hellenic borrowing. In Greece, amphorae were generally used for storing oil and wine.

Other typically Greek forms of pottery have also been found at Kampyrtepa: for example an *oinochoe,* a single-handled wine jug with three spouts, which allowed wine to be poured into three receptacles at once. Similar vessels with one, two and three spouts have been found in Khatyn-Rabad, Old Termez and other sites in Northern Bactria and Sogdia. Vessels similar to Greek *kraters* with wide necks and large bodies, which were used for diluting wine with water in Greece, have also been found here.

Other interesting finds include iron keys in the form of a long rod with a four-toothed ending, between 5 and 7.5 centimetres long. Their shape is similar to that of keys found in mainland Greece and the Greek cities of the northern Black Sea area. They were made in the Kushan period, and the tradition of making them was in all likelihood inherited from Greek settlers in Bactria.

Other objects that have been found include pyramid-shaped weights of different values and sizes made of unfired and well-hardened clay, probably of Greek origin. They were used as weights for looms and fishing nets.

No such objects dating from the pre-Hellenistic period have been recorded in Central Asia, but they are characteristic of Greek cities and settlements. This seems to indicate that they began to be used in Central Asia after it became subject to Hellenistic influence.

At the same time, the culture of Kampyrtepa had many aspects typical of all towns and settlements located along the trade routes. Moreover, Kampyrtepa was a fortress guarding the crossing over the Amu Darya river on one of the most important sections of the Silk Road that went northwards from Bactra and then to Sogdia, through the Iron Gate. It is no coincidence that the objects discovered here came from different countries or were influenced by their cultures: pottery with distinctive circular ornamentation from Khorezm; metal and terracotta items; an ivory comb with motifs of Indian origin; a pottery kiln typical of Margiana; Parthian coins; glassware from the Eastern Mediterranean; Chinese-style mirrors; and a metal buckle made in the Saka style. Two statuettes found here are particularly unusual. One is made of wood and set in a silver case clamped with nails. It is a likeness of an elderly man wearing a knee-length kaftan and loose trousers, which is similar in style to a famous bronze statue of a Parthian prince found at Shami (Iran). The second terracotta statuette shows a man with a proud face and distinctive beard, wearing a tall headdress, similar to the images of some personages from the town of Hatra (Mesopotamia).

The number of coins found at the site of Kampyrtepa is an indication of the scale of trade along the Silk Roads. More than 600 coins, including four hoards of treasure, have been found here to date – a remarkable amount for such a small town. There is one other important circumstance connected with Kampyrtepa's role in trade. Within the densely built-up citadel were many storehouses (more than 20) containing 5–20 large storage jars (*khums*) more than a metre high, designed for storing grains and different kinds of liquids. In view of the estimated population of Kampyrtepa, the number of warehouses and *khums* and their large amounts of food supplies suggests that they were used mainly to serve the trade caravans passing through the fortress. The historical and geographical writings of Hafiz-i Abru (early 15th century) include an interesting description that has long attracted the attention of scholars. He wrote:

> Burdagui is a place on the bank of the Jayhun, near Termez. Some say that Burdagui was founded long before Termez, but according to others, it was also built by Alexander. According to the latter version the name Burdagui is Greek and was given to the place also in the time of Alexander: it means a hostelry. In antiquity, the chief boatmen, who

were in charge of the crossings over the Jayhun River, lived in Burdagui; it was also the place where the sultans crossed the river. The ancient kings granted protection to the inhabitants of that place and exempted them from taxes; for this reason, the place was a bustling commercial centre. Every traveller arriving here was treated with respect. The people were known for their generosity, which was so great that each traveller passing here was the object of competition among the Burdagui people: each of them wanted to take the guest to their own house. There was much rivalry between the people of Termez and Burdagui. Around Burdagui there is much vegetation where tigers live.

Fragment of a vessel decorated with grapes and vine leaves. Kampyrtepa.

W.W. Barthold believed that this point was located at the site of present-day Kalif, where one of the shortest crossings across the Amu Darya had been in use since ancient times. However, M.E. Masson attributed its location to the Chushka-Guzar ('Wild Boar Pass'), located near the present-day *kishlak* (village) of Khoshman in the Surkhan Darya region. In fact, according to some scholars, it was at this point that Alexander the Great's troops crossed in pursuit of the Achaemenid satrap Bessus, who, after the assassination of Darius III declared himself king, using the name Artaxerxes III. V.F. Minorsky continued to ponder this question and asked Henning to look into the etymology of the name of the crossing. According to Henning, the original name was of Greek origin, and sounded like *pandoxī*, meaning 'inn' or 'hostelry', and it later changed to become *pardāxwī* or *pardāγwī* (*Pardagvi*) (from which 'Burdagui' in Hafiz-i Abru's account is derived) in one of the Sogdian dialects. Minorsky thought that this crossing point, evidently one that was established by the Greeks given its Greek name, was located near Termez, at the confluence of the Surkhan Darya and the Amu Darya.

Research at Kampyrtepa by the Tokharistan archaeological expedition has confirmed that Kampyrtepa had been established at the end of the 4th century BC under the Greek rulers of Bactria and, as a fortress guarding the important crossing across the Oxus river, it may well have had a Greek name. Greek inscriptions – graffiti – made on fragments of small vessels and on a *khum* have been found here, suggesting the presence of a Greek population. Furthermore, Kampyrtepa was likely to have been a customs clearing post for trade caravans; Hafiz-i Abru mentions the importance of Pardagvi ('Burdagui') as a customs post.

Greek inscription on the wall of a khum. 3rd–2nd centuries BC. Kampyrtepa.

The first graffito was scratched pre-firing on the outer surface of a thin-walled vessel, covered with a light engobe. It consists of three signs that indicate 15 drachmas.

The second graffito was made after firing, on the inside of a thin-walled vessel covered with a light yellow engobe. This graffito consists of three characters, indicating 7 *hoi* (*hoi* is a Greek measure of liquid equivalent to 3.28 litres).

These two short graffiti inscriptions are extremely significant because, before these, no Greek inscriptions with monetary units and measures of liquids had been found in Central Asia.

One of the graffiti on the vessels had been etched on the outside of a thick-walled vessel after firing. Four letters are still visible: *kappa, lambda, epsilon* and a fourth that is unclear, but may be *theta* to make *KLEΘ*. V. Yailenko believes these letters could indicate a personal name. However, he does not exclude the possibility that it is a remnant of the word *KLEΘ*… (a Greek gloss in the lexicon of Hesychius of Alexandria, the author of the lexicographical dictionary of the 5th century AD, which explains rare Greek words and phrases); it could mean 'divination', 'rumour' or 'glory'.

All these inscriptions indisputably testify to the presence of a Greek population in Kampyrtepa. Palaeographic data suggest that the fragments can be dated to the 2nd century BC. However, although the Greeks ruled southern Central Asia for almost 200 years, few Greek inscriptions have been found, and most of them have been discovered in Northern Bactria, with only two on the site of Afrasiab in Sogdia.

A short Greek inscription scratched on the wall of a vessel with the Greek name Soziris was found at the site of the ancient settlement of Garav-Kala in southern Tajikistan.

Thus, we have documentary evidence of the existence of two settlements in Northern Bactria with a Greek population. As a cultural phenomenon, Hellenism left a deep impression on the material and spiritual life of the ancient peoples of Central Asia, which outlived for a considerable period of time the political domination of the Hellenes in this and neighbouring regions. The Greek language continued to be used here for at least another two hundred years, functioning rather like the lingua franca it had been in ancient Europe (an influence that endured into the Middle Ages despite the preponderance of Latin).

In any case, it was not until the mid-first century AD that the Younger Arsacids came to power in Parthia and removed Greek inscriptions and language from coins, replacing them with Parthian ones. Sometime later, a similar process took place in the Kushan kingdom when King Kanishka I initiated a reform of language and script, which is clearly reflected in Kushan coins where Greek titles such as *basileus basileon* were replaced by equivalent Bactrian *shaonano shao* ('King of Kings') and epithets such as *soter megas* disappeared altogether.

Yet even during this period, the Kushan kingdom was still home to highly skilled Greek craftsmen. An inscription discovered during excavations at Surkh Kotal, the largest temple of the Kushan dynasty built under Kanishka I (or Huvishka) in present-day Baghlan province (northern Afghanistan), bears witness to this. The inscription mentions a person with a typical Greek name, Palamedes, who may have been the architect or builder of the temple. It is possible that Palamedes was a descendant of Hellenes who had migrated to Bactria three or four centuries earlier.

Isolated pockets of Greek settlements continued to exist, particularly in the Hindu Kush and North-West India, even 100–150 years after the fall of the Graeco-Bactrian kingdom.

This statement is supported by discoveries of 'Indo-Greek coins' bearing their rulers' Greek names (Antialkidus, Zoilus, Dionysus, Strato and others), Greek titles, epithets and nicknames, and images of Greek rulers and gods.

A similar phenomenon, hitherto unknown, has now been revealed for Bactria. A copper coin found at the site of Kampyrtepa shows a ruler in a diadem on the obverse, whereas the reverse bears an eagle with open wings in a heraldic pose and the Greek inscription 'Heliocles'. Based on stratigraphy, the coin has been dated to not earlier than the 1st century BC, suggesting that decades after the fall of the Graeco-Bactrian kingdom a small dominion ruled by Heliocles continued to survive in the Amu Darya valley, not far from Termez, despite the fact that many years earlier, Bactria had been conquered by the Yuezhi/Tokharians, who gave rise to the Kushan dynasty – founders of the great Asian kingdom.

With the passage of time, the remaining Greek population was absorbed into the local populations of southern Central Asia, contributing to their ethnogenesis. However, the memory of the *Yavanas* (Ionians), as the Greeks in the East were known, and their great leader Alexander the Great – Iskander Zulkarnain – has survived to this day, living on in the geographical names and folk legends about the cities he established in Central Asia and the Hellenistic origins of the region's peoples.

4·3

CENTRAL ASIA AND THE APENNINE PENINSULA

ALTHOUGH IT MAY SEEM STRANGE TO SUGGEST A LINK BETWEEN THE ETRUSCAN civilisation and the civilisation of one of the regions of ancient Central Asia – Khorezm – closer examination of information available to us suggests this idea is not without merit.

We know from coins that the Etruscans inhabited the territory of the Apennine Peninsula in the early 5th century BC, but we still do not know where they originally came from. Several scholars believe that the Etruscans were the indigenous inhabitants of the peninsula, although others, in particular V. Georgiev, believe that they migrated there from Asia Minor at the end of the 2nd and beginning of the 1st millennium BC.

Scholars seeking their origins rely, apart from various kinds of historical and linguistic documents, on the accounts of Herodotus, according to whom the Etruscans, whom he refers to as Tyrrhenians, migrated to the Apennine Peninsula from Lydia in western Asia Minor. The Etruscans occupied the area on the peninsula between the Arno and Tiber rivers, which came to be called Tuscany, from the Latin *Tusci* or *Etrusci*.

Some scholars associate the ethnonym *Tusci* not only with the Etruscans, but also with the name of the *Tursha* or *Teresh* people, mentioned as being among the 'Sea Peoples' who are supposed to have waged maritime campaigns against ancient Egypt.

However, Asia Minor may not have been the original homeland of the Etruscans: they may have lived even further east initially and only later moved into this region. In this regard, any parallels between Urartians, Caucasians and Etruscans are both interesting and difficult to explain.

It is equally difficult to provide an explanation for the similarities this author noticed between the statuary ossuaries from Khorezm and Etruscan funerary vessels, or *kenops*. The statuary ossuaries of Khorezm are unique, and have no counterparts in other Central Asian regions. They consist of round-based vessels topped with a sculpture, usually an anthropomorphic one, such as a woman sitting on a throne, a cross-legged man or a horseman. The ossuaries date from the 4th–3rd centuries BC.

Head of a goddess. Er-Kurgan 2nd–3rd century AD.

The question of whether Khorezmian ossuaries of this type originated locally or came from another country is yet to be settled.

Y.A. Rappoport noted that statuary ossuaries arose out of a combination of a funerary mask and a vessel and are of local origin. He mentions the similar development of Etruscan *kenops,* which initially consisted of an ordinary vessel to which a funerary mask was attached. Later the neck of the vessel was turned into a head, while the body of the vessel took the form of a human body and garments. Ultimately, an anthropomorphic figure was created.

However, while all the stages of the development of *kenops* in Etruria can be traced, we know correspondingly little about Khorezmian ossuaries, and their sudden appearance suggests they are a 'foreign' phenomenon.

As we know, the earliest ossuaries of this type in Khorezm were found in a manor house near Koi-Krylgan-Kala and date from the 4th–3rd centuries BC. They reflect the completed classical type: a funerary vessel in the form of a standing woman and a funerary vessel in the form of a man seated on a round base. Nothing comparable to this type of ossuary has been found elsewhere in Khorezm or in Central Asia and adjacent countries, or in monuments of earlier or contemporaneous times.

In this connection I would like to draw attention to the distinct similarities between the statuary ossuaries of Koi-Krylgan-Kala and Etruscan funerary urns or *kenops,* especially those from the Etruscan cities of Caere and Veii from the 6th–5th centuries BC. One of the similarities is the feature on top of the funerary vessel of a seated anthropomorphic figure. With regard to this, the *kenops* from Caere (late 7th century BC), with a male figure sitting on a rectangular bench, is very similar to an ossuary found at Koi-Krylgan-Kala.

These are also other similarities, such as the headdress of the male figure on the statuary ossuary from Koi-Krylgan-Kala, which looks like a flat cap with the edge and ear flaps turned up. A statue of Hermes from the temple in Veii dating from around 500 BC has a similar headdress. Clearly, such similarities could not have come about through the convergent evolution of the Khorezmian statuary ossuaries and Etruscan *kenops*.

Most likely, long before the Christian Era, Khorezm was part of the network of roads connecting the Mediterranean Sea and Central Asia, and the vicissitudes of fate meant that its peoples travelled to different parts of the *oikumene*. It is well known that in the 5th century BC, Khorezmians had lived in Egypt, perhaps for several generations, on the island of Elephantine, located on the lower Nile.

Thereafter Central Asia's ties with the Apennine Peninsula, and especially with the Roman empire, became stronger and more active. Rome, the capital of the Roman empire, was one of the starting points of the Silk Road. From here and from the other Roman cities, trade caravans moved eastwards by land and sea, along with diplomatic embassies and military legions sent to fight Rome's ancient rival, the powerful Parthian kingdom (mid-3rd century BC–AD 226).

The Romans had varying degrees of success in their wars with the Parthians, and the battles contributed to the existence of large numbers of Roman prisoners in Central Asia, although it is likely that some Romans arrived here even earlier. The Parthian kingdom served as an obstacle to the passage of Roman goods to the East along the

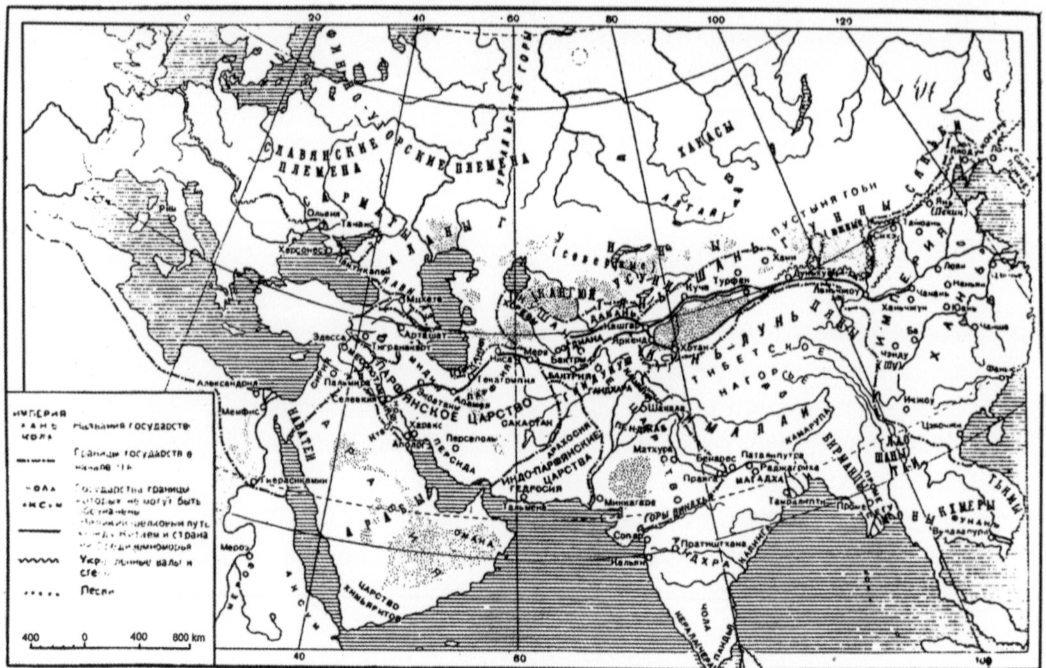

Map of the ancient world in the 2nd century AD.

main route of the Silk Road, through the territory of present-day Iran. The chronicle ('The History of the Former Han Shu Dynasty') explicitly describes how 'The king of this country always wanted to send envoys to Han, but Anxi [Parthia], wishing to control the trade in multi-coloured Chinese silks, blocked the route to prevent [the Romans] getting through [to China].'[2] Scholars addressing this particular problem believe that the main path for the flow of Roman goods was along the northern route from the ancient cities on the northern coast of the Black Sea via the lower Volga to Central Asia and further east, and also along the southern sea route from Roman-ruled Egypt to the ports situated on the west coast of India, especially the port of Barygaza (Baruch). It is no mere coincidence that large numbers of Roman coins have been found in India. From here, Roman goods went northwards to Bactria, which was under the control of the Kushans, and then eastwards to the countries of the Far East.

At the same time, it would appear that goods of Roman origin or from countries controlled by Rome, such as Egypt, did still manage to reach Central Asia via the main artery of the Silk Road or via the northern route.

It is also possible that goods travelled via Egypt and via the Roman-controlled region of Transcaucasia around the Caspian Sea, with the help of Sarmatian tribes who regulated those routes. Many Romano-Egyptian objects have been found in North Caucasian Sarmatian burial mounds. According to the Greek historian Strabo (1st century AD) the Aorsi, one of the Sarmatian tribes, controlled a road running along the Caspian Sea and 'were thus enabled to transport on camels the merchandise of India and Babylonia, receiving it from the Armenians and Medes' (Strabo, XI, V, 8). Trade and diplomatic and cultural contacts between the peoples of Central Asia and Rome became particularly strong with the emergence of the Kushan kingdom in the first half of the 1st century AD.

Like Rome, the Kushan empire also had hostile relations with Parthia, which contributed to the establishment of diplomatic relations between the Kushans and Rome. According to historical sources, Indian emissaries, who may have been from the Kushan court, arrived in Rome in AD 106 or 107 to participate as guests of honour in the triumph of Emperor Trajan who had defeated the tribes of Dacians (the ancestors of the Romanians). We also know that Emperor Hadrian (AD 117–138) received an embassy of 'Bactrian kings' and Antoninus Pius (AD 138–161) received 'Indian, Bactrian and Hyrcanian' emissaries.

Several items of Roman origin have been found in Central Asia, including coins. The first to start recording such finds here was M.E. Masson, who noted that no Roman gold coins had ever been found, and finds of silver coins were also rare. Between the Zarafshan valley and Lake Issyk-Kul, Masson discovered coins of the Roman emperors Vespasian (AD 69–79), Domitian (AD 81–96), Trajan (AD 98–117), Antoninus Pius

(AD 138–161) and Marcus Aurelius (AD 161–180), as well as some coins from the 3rd century AD, among them those of Aurelian (AD 270–275).

In the 1920s, a hoard of several hundred Roman silver coins was found near the town of Uratube in Khujum, northern Tajikistan, of which only 21 denarii survived. They were donated to the Hermitage Museum by a Dr Tarzi. These coins were discussed by E.V. Zeimal, who identified among them denarii of Vespasian, Trajan, Hadrian, Antoninus Pius, Marcus Aurelius and Lucius Verus, and Marcus Aurelius Commodus (AD 177–192). Zeimal originally suggested that the denarii from this find were a small part of the influx of Roman silver arriving from the south to the markets of the Kushan empire, and continuing north to areas that did not have their own regular coinage. However, he did not rule out the possibility that the introduction of Roman coins into the area may have been connected to trade along the northern section of the Silk Road.

Roman coins have also been found in the Surkhan Darya province. A sesterce of Emperor Nero (AD 54–68) was found at Khairabadtepa, and a copper coin of Emperor Constantine I (AD 306–337) at the site of Old Termez. Roman coins were also found in the collection of the priest Zampaev, which was based mainly on finds from Old Termez. Other items of Roman origin found in the area are also notable. The marble head of a male was discovered at the site of Ilontepe, near the town of Shurchi. The facial features and style of the hair have much in common with images on Roman reliefs from the 1st century BC–1st century AD, and bear some similarity to images of Emperor Augustus.

Another notable specimen is a marble head of a mascaron found at the site of Shahr-i Gulgul on the western bank of the South Surkhan Darya Reservoir. Fragments of different glassware brought to Bactria from Egypt and other Roman provinces have been found in Khalchayan and Kampyrtepa, and a carnelian intaglio from the Kushan period with an image of the goddess of fortune was found at Dalverzintepa.

A great many Roman objects have been found in Afghanistan, especially in Begram, 60 kilometres north of Kabul. Here, excavations of a palace building unearthed a considerable amount of glassware from the cities of Tyre and Sidon on the Phoenician coast of the Mediterranean Sea under Roman control. The finds include vases, goblets, plates and bottles, many of which are covered with stunning paintings. A glass goblet from the 1st century AD depicting Roman soldiers in battle on foot and horseback is especially intriguing. Amid other finds of Roman origin found at Begram are bronze counterweights with depictions of Athena and Mars, alabaster vessels, and plaster casts with scenes from Graeco-Roman mythology.

A significant number of Roman coins have also been found in Afghanistan, especially in the reliquaries of Buddhist stupas. Three Roman gold aurei of the emperors Domitian and Trajan and Emperor Hadrian's wife Sabina (AD 117–138) were found in the Ahin Posh stupa, along with Kushan coins. In Shewaki, near Kabul, an aureus of Emperor Trajan was found, along with a gold coin of Wima Kadphises. Finds of Roman coins in northern Afghanistan are less common. The excavation of the now famous Tillyatepa burial mounds near the town of Shaburgan unearthed a gold coin of Emperor Tiberius, minted in Lugdunum in Gaul (Lyons) between AD 16 and 27.

Roman influences contributed to the formation of the Kushan coinage system and the iconography of early Kushan coins. According to some scholars, the image of the head of the king in a laurel wreath on the coins of Kujula Kadphises was copied from a Roman imperial coin, possibly from the obverse of the aureus of Augustus, issued from 27 to 24 BC. Similarly, the depiction of a figure with a conical headdress sitting in a 'curule chair' on the reverse side of the same coins may also have been copied from Roman coins, especially those of Augustus, which have an image of the emperor sitting in such a chair on the reverse.

Under the monetary reform introduced by the Kushan king Kadphises II, monetary units were no longer based on silver, as they had been in the Graeco-Bactrian kingdom and in other Central Asian dominions, but gold. The new gold coins were based on the weight of the Roman gold aureus. Gold coins weighing 8.13 grams were issued most frequently, but also, more rarely, double staters weighing 16.07 grams and quarter staters weighing 2.01 grams.

With regard to Romano-Central Asian contacts, objects imported into Central Asia from Roman-ruled Egypt are of special interest. The most numerous among these items are objects made of blue Egyptian faience, which were produced in the Egyptian cities of Alexandria and Naucratis. However, some scholars believe that they could also have been made in the ancient towns situated north of the Black Sea.

Egyptian items have been found almost everywhere in sites and burial grounds in Central Asia from the Kushan period, especially in the territories of Khorezm, Sogdia and Northern Bactria. The most common objects include amulet-protectors in the shape of a fist (a fig sign), a frog, a turtle, sacred scarab beetles and bunches of grapes, as well as various forms of beads. Finds of statuettes of gods are less common, but the most popular among these are images of Harpocrates, Bes, Ptah-Sokar and Osiris.

In Egyptian mythology, Harpocrates or Hor-Pa-Kherd is one of the embodiments of Horus, the son of Isis and Osiris, the Sun God, who was depicted as a boy with the side-lock of youth and with a finger on his mouth. This gesture was interpreted by the Greeks as a sign of 'silence'. In Central Asia, a statuette of Harpocrates was found at Munchaktepa, situated on the Syr Darya bank near Khodjent, in northern Tajikistan. Another Egyptian deity, Bes, was much revered in the ancient world as a symbol of fertility and the life-giving forces of nature. He was depicted as an ugly, naked dwarf with prominent genitals. Statuettes of Bes have been found in Khorezm (at Bazarkala) and at Afrasiab (Samarkand), and in the territory of Northern Bactria (at the Tupkhana burial ground).

Figurines of a bald, naked man made of blue faience have been found in a number of burial grounds and ancient sites in Central Asia (e.g. Tupkhana and Rabat). Scholars believe they are amulets depicting Ptah-Sokar, a god combining two hypostases – that of Ptah, guardian of the ruling clan in the sacred Egyptian city of Memphis and creator of the world; and Sokar, the god of the dead in Memphis.

Phallic pendants and amulets in the form of the sacred scarab beetle have often been found here. The veneration of the phallus – a symbol of fertility and the life-giving force of nature – was widespread in ancient times (and continues to be so in many parts of the world today), particularly in Central Asia, where different kinds of depictions of the phallus have been found in burial sites dating back to the Bronze Age. However, there is no evidence of veneration of the beetle in Central Asia, unlike in Egypt. The renowned Egyptologist V.A. Korostovtsev provided an excellent description of the scarab beetle's importance in the life of the ancient Egyptians. According to him, 'through the ages, this insect played a major role in the religion and mythology of Egypt, and represented life and self-renewal'. Egyptian Scarab amulets spread throughout the Near and Middle East, southern Russia, Transcaucasia and Central Asia. They have even been found in Xinjiang.

Among the items of Egyptian blue faience, amulet-pendants in the shape of a fist (a fig sign) or a hand with outstretched fingers found in ancient sites and burial grounds are particularly noteworthy. The ritual use of the 'fig' gesture has been regarded as a symbol of protection from evil spirits by many peoples around the world from earliest times. It also had other meanings: for example, according to F. Petrie, in ancient Egypt, similar amulets were thought to increase sexual potency.

The other type of amulet, the one in the form of a hand with outstretched fingers, was also widely

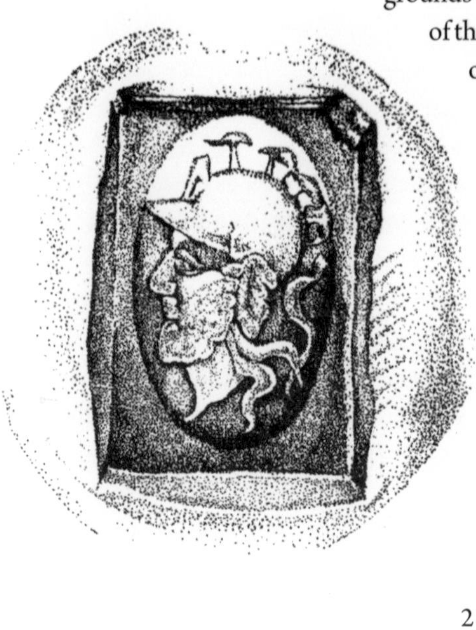

Head of a Roman legionary. Gemstone. Central Asia.

Fragment of a column
Oburdon, 9th century AD
Wood, H. 103 cm; D. 41 cm
Tashkent, State Museum of History of Uzbekistan
179/1

Bracelet
Dalverzintepa, 1st century AD
Gold, 98.5 × 76.4 mm, end diameter 22.1 mm
Tashkent, Agency for precious metals under the Central Bank of the Republic of Uzbekistan
KP-85 MAuЮИ

Bracelet
Dalverzintepa, 1st century AD
Gold, 69.2 × 51.4 mm, end thickness 43.6 mm
Tashkent, Agency for precious metals under the Central Bank of the Republic of Uzbekistan
KP-86 MAuЮИ

Bracelet
Dalverzintepa, 1st century AD
Gold, 74.2 × 83.6 mm, end diameter 17.5 mm
Tashkent, Agency for precious metals under the Central Bank of the Republic of Uzbekistan
KP-87 MAuЮИ

Part of bracelet
Dalverzintepa, 1st century AD
Gold, 75 × 37.2 mm
Tashkent, Agency for precious metals under the Central Bank of the Republic of Uzbekistan
KP-88 MAuЮИ

Bracelet
Dalverzintepa, 1st century AD
Gold, 83.9 × 71.2 mm, twisted wire diameter 9.7 mm
Tashkent, Agency for precious metals under the Central Bank of the Republic of Uzbekistan
KP-92 MAuЮИ

Bracelet
Dalverzintepa, 1st century AD
Gold, 63.3 × 56.2 mm, twisted wire diameter 7.7 mm
Tashkent, Agency for precious metals under the Central Bank of the Republic of Uzbekistan
KP-93 MAuЮИ

Ingot
Dalverzintepa, 1st century AD
Gold, 51.1 × 50.2 mm, thickness 25.2 mm
Tashkent, Agency for precious metals under the Central Bank of the Republic of Uzbekistan
КП-94 МАuЮИ

Hoop
Dalverzintepa, 1st century AD
Gold, 69.5 × 68.3 mm, thickness (with a ledge) 19.3 mm
Tashkent, Agency for precious metals under the Central Bank of the Republic of Uzbekistan
КР-95 МАuЮИ

Bracelet
Dalverzintepa, 1st century AD
Gold, 78 × 82.2 mm, maximum width 42.1 mm
Tashkent, Agency for precious metals under the Central Bank of the Republic of Uzbekistan
КП-96 МАuЮИ

Hoop
Dalverzintepa, 1st century AD
Gold, 46.8 × 42.5 mm, thickness 14 mm
Tashkent, Agency for precious metals under the Central Bank of the Republic of Uzbekistan
КР-97 МАuЮИ

Hoop
Dalverzintepa, 1st century AD
Gold, 46.8 × 42.5 mm, thickness 14 mm
Tashkent, Agency for precious metals under the Central Bank of the Republic of Uzbekistan
КР-97 МАuЮИ

Disk
Dalverzintepa, 1st century AD
Gold, 87 × 86 mm, thickness 6.2 mm
Tashkent, Agency for precious metals under the Central Bank of the Republic of Uzbekistan
КР-101 МАuЮИ

Disk
Dalverzintepa, 1st century AD
Gold, 61 × 59 mm, thickness 6.1 mm
Tashkent, Agency for precious metals under the Central Bank of the Republic of Uzbekistan
КП-102 МАuЮИ

Disk
Dalverzintepa, 1st century AD
Gold, 86 × 68 mm, thickness 61.8 × 7.4 mm
Tashkent, Agency for precious metals under the Central Bank of the Republic of Uzbekistan
КР-99 МАuЮИ

Wall painting
11th–12th century AD
310 × 180 cm
Samarkand, Gulyamov Institute of Archaeological Studies

Beads *(top)*
Dalverzintepa, 1st century AD
Gold
Tashkent, Agency for precious metals under the Central Bank of the Republic of Uzbekistan
KP-44 МАиЮИ

Armour of a soldier *(above)*
Shahrukhiya, Tashkent, 14th–15th century AD
Metal, L. 156 cm
Tashkent, State Museum of History of Uzbekistan
301/97;98

Monetary bearers
Fayaztepa, Surkhan Darya, 2nd century AD
Wall painting, 81 × 78 cm
Tashkent, State Museum of History of Uzbekistan
274/3

Fragment of painted decoration of the palace (two elements)
Varakhsha, 6th–7th century AD
Wall painting, 183 × 195.5 cm; 184 × 191.5 cm
Bukhara, Bukhara State Museum-Reserve
КП-15 14413/22

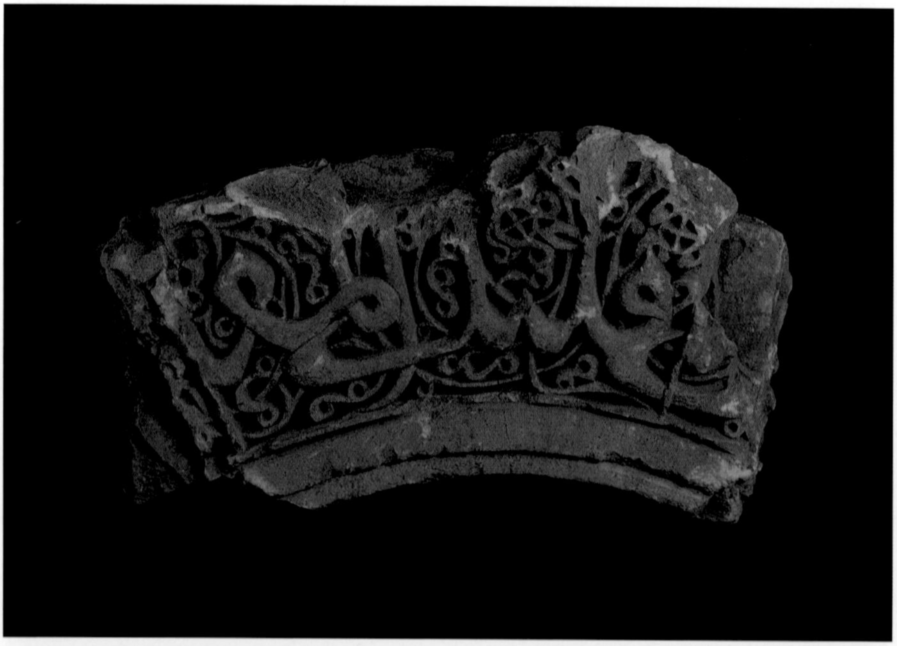

Fragment of architectural decoration with inscription *(top)*
Palace of Termezshahs, 11th century AD
Stucco, 56 × 26 × 18 cm
Termez, Archaeological Museum of Termez

Carved fragment from furniture *(above)*
Akchakhan-Kala, 1st century AD
Wood or ivory, L. 32.9 × D. 10 cm
Nukus, Institute of History, Archaeology and Ethnography of Karakalpakstan

Pin (front and back)
c. 1st century AD
Bone
Tashkent, Fine Arts Institute of the Academy of Sciences

Pin (front and back)
c. 1st century AD
Bone, L. 11.9 cm × W. 1.9 cm
Tashkent, Fine Arts Institute of the Academy of Sciences

Pin (front and back)
c. 1st century AD
Bone, L. 12 cm × W. 1.5 cm
Tashkent, Fine Arts Institute of the Academy of Sciences

Portrait from the Kings Gallery
Akchakhan-Kala, 1st century AD
Wall painting, H. 142 × W. 84 cm
Nukus, Institute of History, Archaeology and
Ethnography of Karakalpakstan
No. 1

Portrait from the Kings Gallery
Akchakhan-Kala, 1st century AD
Wall painting, H. 178 × W. 75 cm
Nukus, Institute of History, Archaeology and Ethnography of Karakalpakstan
No. 2

Panel from the Termez Palace ***(top)***
Tavka, 7th century
Wall painting, 16 × 9 cm
Termez, Archaeological Museum of Termez
SVAM 3179/6

Panel from the Termez Palace ***(above)***
Tavka, 7th century
Wall painting, 17 × 11 cm
Termez, Archaeological Museum of Termez
SVAM 3179/8

Panel from the Termez Palace
Tavka, 7th century
Wall painting, 14.5 × 9 cm
Termez, Archaeological Museum of Termez

Panel from the Termez Palace
Tavka, 7th century
Wall painting, 30 × 11 cm
Termez, Archaeological Museum of Termez
SVAM 3179/9

Panel from the Termez Palace
Tavka, 7th century
Wall painting, 18.5 × 12.5 cm
Termez, Archaeological Museum of Termez

Banquet scene
Balalyktepa, 7th century AD
Wall painting, 90.5 × 72 cm
Termez, Archaeological Museum of Termez
SVAM 31733

used. Depictions of it crowning particular objects, especially pins, from as early as the Bronze Age have been found in Central Asia at sites such as Sapallitepa, dating from the middle or second half of the 2nd millennium BC.

Along with amulets made of blue Egyptian paste, individual, relatively large representations of these hands, made of well-fired clay and marble, have been found in Central Asia. They have also been found crowning particular objects made of bone, in the form of a staff with a sharp end, referred to by some scholars as *styli* – a kind of 'rod' for writing.

The ritual significance of such symbols was various. They were amulets protecting against evil forces, symbols of power and strength, and of healing and fertility. For many peoples of the Caucasus, especially the Tushins and Khevsurs, the severed hand of an enemy was a trophy of honour, and it would have been nailed above the entrance to a house. In ancient Egypt and Mesopotamia, these symbols originally represented the 'heavenly hand', and were associated with sun worship; this symbolism then penetrated into Christianity where it has a prominent role, for example the Hand of Mary.

The hand symbol was also a representation of Sabazios – the Thracian god of fertility – whose cult first came to Phrygia from Asia Minor and then spread throughout the Roman empire from Spain to the ancient cities north of the Black Sea. Many such symbols made of bronze have been found here and have been interpreted as votive offerings to the god Sabazios. It is also possible it was Roman legionaries who brought the cult of this deity to Central Asia, where it merged with other cults of fertility, nature and the Sun, which had similar significance.

An object of particular interest is a cast bronze hairpin (12.6 × 0.4 cm) from the Kavatkal oasis of Khorezm (1st–2nd centuries AD) topped with a hand holding a ball between the thumb and index finger, and a snake on the wrist in relief. This image is similar to the top of a Roman banner from the 2nd century AD, found in the Dnieper river area. This consists of a bronze hand 11.5 centimetres high, with the fingers pointing upwards and a similar ball between the index finger and thumb. Below the hand is dedicatory inscription – 'The commander of the First Cohort of the Spanish Legion dedicates this to Great Jupiter Dolichenus'. Jupiter Dolichenus was a supreme god of the Syrians. The similarity of these two objects suggests a similar religious association. However the Roman banner includes a dedication by an individual, i.e. it was a personal votive object to a god worshipped by an individual devotee. The Khorezmian hairpin is most likely related to the cult of Sabazios. Several aspects of the pin attest to this: in addition to the symbol of the hand, the ball most likely symbolises the cone of a pine tree (the cone is an essential attribute of Sabazios); the snake is also often present in symbols associated with the cult of Sabazios.

Worship of deities from Asia Minor had spread all the way to the East. A silver plaque found at the site of Ai-Khanum, bearing an image of Cybele, a significant mother-goddess from Asia Minor, standing on her chariot drawn by lions, is direct evidence of this.

Items excavated at Kampyrtepa include a statuette of a musician playing multi-fluted pipes, the so-called *syrinx* or 'pan flute'. This musical instrument is associated with a variety of different figures, but it is noteworthy that numerous figurines of the god Attis playing a *syrinx* have been discovered in the territory of Asia Minor and north of the Black Sea. In the Hellenistic period, Attis was depicted wearing long trousers, a short-sleeved, pleated tunic with a belt and a Phrygian hat. The figure of the statuette from Kampyrtepa has the same attire, but unfortunately, the Phrygian cap, the most important attribute of Attis, is absent, as the head of the figure is missing.

It is quite probable that the cult of Attis, and of his wife Cybele, had spread to Central Asian territories, as the veneration of deities associated with death and renewal in nature, embodied in the cult of Siyavush in particular, had a long tradition in these regions. Fragments of ancient Bactrian manuscripts found at Kampyrtepa, written in black ink on the finest papyrus and dating from the first half of the 2nd century AD, provide further evidence of links between Kushan Bactria and Roman Egypt. Papyrus was invented in ancient Egypt where it was cultivated, just as it was in Palestine. The Egyptian rulers had exclusive rights to sell it abroad and they prohibited its export if it became necessary. The city of Alexandria was the main centre of papyrus trade in the world. It may have been from here that papyrus was brought to Bactria and later used as material for Bactrian manuscripts. The papyrus manuscripts discovered at Kampyrtepa were the first to be found in Central Asia and adjacent countries. The first Roman (Latin) and other inscriptions in Central Asia were found in Kara-Kamar in the far south-west of Surkhan Darya province.

Several short Bactrian inscriptions contain the personal names of visitors to this site. One of them, 'Arziokhsho', includes the component 'Ochsho', the name of the ancient Bactrian deity of the Amu Darya river, the Oxus, and, according to V.A. Livshits, could be translated as 'Given (by the god) Okhsho' or 'precious' to (the god) Vakhsh'. This inscription gives us an idea of how ancient the Kara-Kamar caves are, as the Bactrian script that became prominent under King Kanishka (in the first half of the 2nd century AD) had probably emerged under his predecessor, King Kadphises II, who ruled in the late 1st or early 2nd century AD, and continued to be used on the territory of Bactria (Tokharistan) until the 11th century.

We can say that Bactrian inscriptions are 'native' to this area. However, two three-line Latin inscriptions have also been found here. The discovery of these inscriptions caused a real sensation. Their presence here is especially surprising because Bactria was never part of the Roman empire.

Until this discovery, the most easterly Latin inscription to have been found was that left by centurion Lucius Julius Maximus of the Legio XII Fulminata under Emperor Domitian (AD 81–96), discovered in 1947 near Baku, on the shore of the Caspian Sea.

According to a number of experts who studied the inscription from Kara-Kamar, the name 'Gaius Rex' and possibly the name of one of the Roman legions, the Legio XV Apollinaris, are recognisable. This legion was transferred from Asia Minor to the Parthian border in AD 62 and took an active part in the Roman–Parthian wars.

The presence of the Roman inscription, together with other data, may give us an idea of what the caves of Kara-Kamar were used for. Several features suggest that they were not used for dwelling but were most probably some kind of sanctuary. Buddhist cave temples are well known, but they do not resemble the Kara-Kamar caves, where no Buddhist symbols have been found among the other depictions. However, both naturally occurring and artificial caves were frequently used as temples in Mithraism, an ancient religion that was widely practised in the Roman Empire.

The Latin inscriptions at Kara-Kamar may have been left by former soldiers of the Legio XV in the last third of the first century AD and one of them represents a dedication to Mithras, while the caves themselves were most probably used as a Mithraeum. However, how a Roman legionary came to be in Bactria remains unclear. It is possible that the so-called Gaius Rex was part of one of the Roman trade or diplomatic missions sent to Kushan Bactria, although it is more likely that during the frequent wars between the Romans and Parthians, Roman legionaries were taken prisoner. Of the 40,000 troops who marched with the triumvir Marcus Crassus in his ill-fated expedition against the Parthians in 53 BC, perhaps fewer than a quarter survived, and 10,000 captive Romans were, according to Pliny the Elder, sent to Margiana (the region in the lower reaches of the Murghab river in modern Turkmenistan) to guard the north-eastern borders of the Parthian kingdom.

There is no mention of the subsequent fate of these prisoners in Roman and Greek historical sources. The American sinologist H. Dubs drew attention to an account in the *Han Shu*, which was possibly related to these legionaries. The pretender to the Hun throne, the *shanyu* Zhizhi, having murdered a Chinese envoy, fled to Sogdia, having been invited there by the local governor in order to repel the nomadic tribes who had invaded the area. Zhizhi planned to establish a new Hun empire in Central Asia and built his capital on the Talas river.

Chen Tang, the deputy of the Chinese governor of the western border regions, was determined to eliminate a potential threat to China's interests. In 36 BC he took the risk of setting off with an army composed of Chinese and auxiliary troops from the local states.

After marching for several thousand miles, the troops approached Zhizhi's capital, and took it by storm. The account of this event sent to the imperial court by Chen Tang states that at the beginning of the attack, near the city, there were 'more than a hundred foot soldiers lined up on either side of the gate in fish-scale formation'.[3]

H. Dubs demonstrated that this kind of military formation was characteristic only of the Roman legionaries, claiming that a 'fish-scale formation is such an extraordinary affair that it naturally raises questions concerning the nature and nationality of troops who could execute so complicated a maneuver. These soldiers must have been drawn up in such a manner that they crowded together and overlapped their shields.' The execution of this required a high degree of discipline and organisation, typical of professional armies. At that time only the Greek and Roman armies would have been capable of this. The nomadic tribes did not have any kind of organised military formation. However, while Macedonian phalanx soldiers had small and round shields, Roman soldiers had oval and rectangular shields, which, when linked together, protected close rows of soldiers from arrows (incidentally, a terracotta plaque found at Kampyrtepa bears the image of just such a shield). Thus, Dubs concluded, there was 'considerable evidence that the "more than a hundred foot soldiers" were actually Roman legionaries' almost certainly they included some of the legionaries of Crassus, serving as mercenary soldiers for the *shanyu* Zhizhi.

It is also noteworthy that the city, which was stormed by the Chinese, had a double wooden palisade fortification. Such fortifications were used by the Romans, especially in front of gates. The vagaries of fate had led the Romans along the Silk Road and further east. Evidence for this comes from a short inscription bearing the typically Roman name 'Titus' found on one of the Miran frescoes in the Turfan oasis in Xinjiang. Perhaps this Titus was a descendant of the Roman legionaries of Crassus?

We must assume that further thorough archaeological and historical research in Central Asia and Xinjiang will eventually discover traces of Crassus' Roman legionaries.

4.4

CENTRAL ASIA AND SPAIN

Despite the great distance between Spain and Central Asia, the historical fortunes of the two regions have seen episodes of brief ties and some longer-lasting connections.

Strange as it may seem to the reader, the first evidence of contact between Spain and the peoples living on the territory of Central Asia is connected with the Alans, ancestors of the Ossetians, after whom the modern Republic of North Ossetia-Alania is named.

However, it is an established fact that, in antiquity, the Alans inhabited the area adjacent to the Aral Sea, where they even had their own state, which the Chinese called Yancai. Even in the 10th century, some Alans were still living in their ancient habitat and, as al-Biruni testified, at that time 'their language combined the languages of the Khorezmians and Pechenegs'. Under pressure from the Huns and other nomadic peoples, some Alans migrated to the Black Sea region and the North Caucasus in the first centuries AD.

In the 4th century AD, the new wave of Hun invasions once again displaced the Alans from their homes on the Don river and the Black Sea coast, and together with the Germanic tribes of the Visigoths, Ostrogoths and Vandals they moved to Europe and the Iberian Peninsula, i.e. Spain. The Alans and Vandals then crossed over to North Africa, from where their combined armies, led by Gaiseric, attacked Rome and plundered it mercilessly. This 'sack of Rome' provides the origin of the word 'vandal' and its derivative 'vandalism', denoting extreme acts of destruction of material and cultural wealth.

At the beginning of the 8th century AD, Spain and Central Asia were united under the aegis of one state – the Arab Umayyad Caliphate, which pursued an extremely aggressive policy of conquering new territories. In AD 711, while Qutaiba ibn Muslim was brutally suppressing the resistance of the peoples of Sogdia, Khorezm and Ferghana, another Arab commander, Tariq ibn Ziyad, crossed the straits separating Africa and Europe and began his conquest of the Iberian Peninsula. The straits have since been called 'Gibraltar', from the Arabic *Jabal al-Tariq* – 'Tariq's mountain'. Some evidence of this unification can be seen in coins of the 8th century AD unearthed in Central Asia from time to time that were actually minted in al-Andalus, which is how the Arabs referred to Spain. On the obverse of these coins is the Arabic inscription 'This dinar was struck in al-Andalus in the name of Allah' and on the reverse the Latin inscription 'This solidus was struck in Spain'. For almost half a century Spain and Central Asia were part of a single state, which ended with the creation of another Arab state, the Abbasid Caliphate, in the mid-8th century. About the same time, Abd al-Rahman, a member of the Umayyad dynasty, who had fled the persecution of the Abbasids, established the Caliphate of Córdoba on the territory of Spain, which took its name from the capital, the city of Córdoba.

The merging of these countries into one state, and particularly the domination of a single religion, Islam, contributed to cultural convergence. Mosques, madrasahs, minarets and mausoleums acquired similar features in keeping with local architectural and building traditions. The design of buildings shared many ornamental features, including vegetal and geometric décor.

There are also many common elements in the decoration of ceramics from Spain and Central Asia, including what is known as lustre (painting in gold on the surface of a vessel) and in the choice of textile designs. One of the central elements of these was the motif of birds facing the Tree of Life, which had its origins in Sassanian tradition.

During this period, the city of Córdoba became one of the centres from which the science and culture of the East spread to the other countries of Europe. The University of Córdoba was particularly famous, and it was during this time that the names and works of the great scholars of Central Asia, Ibn Sina, al-Khorezmi, al-Ferghani and Imam al-Bukhari, became known in Spain. Córdoba and later Toledo became established as important centres for the translation and transcription of the works of great Eastern thinkers, and there is every reason to believe that these cities contributed greatly to the fame and renown of the great scholars of Central Asia in Europe. For example, the main astronomical work of al-Khorezmi, *Zij* ('The Astronomical Tables'), is known to scholarship only by its Latin translation produced in Spain in the 12th century. The work was undertaken by Adelard of Bath and Petrus Alfonsi, who translated and edited a version by Maslama al-Majriti, an astronomer who lived in Córdoba in the 10th and early 11th centuries.

The first translation into Latin of the work of the great astronomer al-Ferghani, known in Europe as Alfraganus, *Kitab fi usul 'ilm an-nujum* ('Book about Elements of the Science of the Stars'), was completed in 1135 by John of Seville. Al-Biruni, the distinguished scholar born in the suburb of Kath in Khorezm (Uzbekistan), knew Andalusia well and in his work *Athar al-Baqiya* ('Vestiges of the Past') he identified a number of its geographical features. People from Uzbekistan and Spain travelled between the two countries for a number of reasons during this period, despite the distance separating them.

The Tashkent scholar S. Kamaletdinov has revealed a curious fact. At the end of the 10th century, amir Faiq al-Hassa, a prominent military leader, who owned vast territories and had constructed many buildings in Bukhara and other cities, played a significant role in the political life of the Samanid state. It was Faiq who actually wielded power in the state, much like another Amir, Bektuzun, did under Amir Mansur ibn Nukh. Previously it had been assumed that Amir Faiq was descended from Turkic *ghilman* (mercenaries), but on the basis of the Persian scholar al-Nasafi's manuscript, Kamaletdinov has established that one of his *nisbas* (an adjective indicating a person's origin) was in fact *al-Andalusi*, the Arabic name for Spain, as well as the region in modern southern Spain. Hence, Faiq was in fact of Spanish descent and had come to Bukhara via Baghdad for some reason. It is possible that he had been sold as a child to Rum (Byzantium) – his second *nisba*, mentioned in the same source, was *al-Rumi*. Faiq may have reached Baghdad from Rome, and in Baghdad the caliph of that time gave him to the Samanid ruler Nukh ibn Nasr. Nukh ibn Nasr encouraged him to adopt Islam and then passed him on as a personal servant to his son, the future Samanid ruler, Amir Mansur ibn Nukh, better known as Mansur I (AD 961–976). During the reign of Mansur I's son, Nukh ibn Mansur (AD 976–997), Faiq was entrusted with the most important affairs of state, alongside Hajib Tash, although in the last years of Nukh ibn Mansur's reign Faiq opposed him and for a time was even an ally of the Qarakhanids. He died in AD 999, when his full name was Amir Amid al-Dawla Abu-l Hasan Faiq ibn Abdallah al-Hasan al-Andalusi al-Rumi.

Direct diplomatic relations with Spain were established under Amir Timur (also known as Tamerlane) at the beginning of the 15th century. This came after a series of important military and political events connected with Turkish expansion into Europe. In a number of battles, especially at the Battle of Kosovo in 1389 and the Battle of Nicopolis in 1396, the Turkish army crushed the allied forces of several European countries and went on to conquer nearly the entire Balkan Peninsula. The rulers of many European countries turned to Amir Timur for help, as they believed he could save them from the Turks. Spain, which was keeping a close eye on the perilous events in Asia Minor and on the Balkan Peninsula, was also involved in this. At this time, Castile and Leon, under Henry III of Castile (1390–1406), represented the most powerful of the three alliances that emerged out of the *Reconquista*. On the eve of the decisive Battle of Ankara in 1402 between Amir Timur and the Turkish Sultan Bayezid, Castilian ambassadors Pelayo de Sotomayor and Fernando de Palazuelos arrived at Amir Timur's camp on a mission to learn more about his power. They were among the first to congratulate him on his great victory over Bayezid and, in turn, Amir Timur sent his envoy Haji Muhammad al-Qazi with gifts and letters. Henry III sent a return embassy to Samarkand, headed by his chamberlain Ruy González de Clavijo, to further strengthen the alliance with Amir Timur and establish trade relations. He was accompanied on the long journey by Fray Alfonso Paez de Sánta María, Master of Theology, and Gomez de Salazar, the king's security guard.

They set off from the port of Santa Maria near Cadiz on 22 May 1403 and after a long voyage Ruy González de Clavijo and his companions arrived in the territory of present-day Uzbekistan on 21 August the following year, having crossed the Amu Darya near Termez. From Termez they passed through the Iron Gate and arrived in Kesh (Shahr-i Sabz) on 28 August. The Spaniards spent two days in Kesh, visiting Ak Sarai, the majestic palace of Amir Timur, and the Timurid tombs.

On 8 September 1404 Amir Timur received the envoys of the Spanish king in his palace in Samarkand. After enquiring after the king's health, Amir Timur is said to have turned to those present saying: 'Look at these envoys sent to me by my son, the King of Spain, the first of all the kings among the Franks, who live at the edge of the world. They are indeed a great people and I bless my son, the King [of Spain]. It would be enough if he had sent you only with a letter, without gifts, as I am very glad to learn of his health and affairs…' The Spanish envoys remained in Samarkand for almost three months, and only left the city on 21 November.

Upon his return to Spain, Ruy González de Clavijo completed his diary of the journey to Samarkand, which he had apparently kept throughout the voyage; some believe, however, that he only wrote it after his return to Spain. The diary is one of the most important sources for the history of Amir Timur's era as it contains a wealth of information that is absent from other descriptions. It was first published in 1582 in Seville by Gonzalo Argote de Molina under the title *Historia del gran Tamorlan* ('The History of the Great Tamerlane') and it was frequently published in Spain and in other countries such as Argentina and Japan.

The most popular edition of Clavijo's diary was translated by I.S. Mirokova from its first Spanish edition, and published in Moscow in 1990. This translation has a commentary that takes into account contemporary scholarship and is one of the best editions of Clavijo's diary in the world.

4·5

SOGDIAN WAYFARERS

It is no exaggeration to say that the Sogdians, among the earliest peoples of Central Asia, were the creators of a great civilisation whose influence was felt across the vast expanses of Eurasia – from the Caspian Sea to the Pacific Ocean. Their presence in Xinjiang and China, along with other Central Asian peoples, is noted in many textual and epigraphic sources. Unfortunately, we do not have clear evidence about the date of their migration eastwards through Chach, Ferghana and Semirechye. There is no evidence of their presence in these areas prior to the first centuries AD.

However, according to many scholars, in particular W.B. Henning and G. Haloun, the eastward migration of the Sogdians began soon after Alexander's invasion of Central Asia. We know that Alexander's war with the Sogdians, who were led by Spitamenes, was marked by the destruction of many settlements and towns and the annihilation of the Sogdian population. According to the Greek historian Arrian, whose account was probably exaggerated, around 70,000 Sogdians were massacred. Henning believes the Sogdians had already come into contact with China between the 4th and 3rd centuries BC. However, there is no direct evidence to support such an early date. According to W. Eberhard, Chinese accounts first make reference to Sogdians in the 2nd century AD. It appears likely that there were other reasons that prompted Sogdians to establish trading stations in Xinjiang and China. Among them were the discovery of the Western Regions by Zhang Qian, the emergence of the Silk Road, and the consequent establishment of diplomatic relations with Parthia and Rome, as well as trade in a variety of commodities, particularly silk, between China and these countries. The Sogdians, through whose lands the most important routes of the Silk Road passed, were the main middlemen in this trade.

Over time, Sogdian merchants, who were very experienced with trade and interested in increasing profits, must have sent their own commercial agents to, and then set up trading stations in, the cities and oases of Xinjiang, with the aim of consolidating their control over larger sections of the Silk Road. Hence, the migration of Sogdians eastwards probably began in the 1st century BC, along with the beginning of regular traffic along the routes of the Silk Road.

Thereafter, Sogdian colonies were established along the entire eastern section of the Silk Road and remained in existence until the 9th and 10th centuries AD. Especially large colonies of Sogdians existed in such Chinese cities as Chang'an, Lanzhou and Dunhuang, where Sogdians lived in isolated communities. The Sogdian community in Dunhuang alone numbered about 1,000 at the beginning of the 4th century.

Apart from Sogdian communities in China, there were also settlements that the Sogdians founded and governed themselves. Based on an analysis of Chinese textual sources, the French scholar P. Pelliot established that between AD 627 and 644 several Sogdian settlements grew up around the lake at Lop Nor. One of these settlements was founded on the site of an abandoned Chinese city by a great leader from the kingdom of Kan (Samarkand) called Kang Yandian, who had arrived with many Hu – the Chinese name for Sogdians. Soon after, three fortified Sogdian settlements were established here, one of which was Putao-cheng: 'city of vineyards'.

It would appear that Sogdians reached Mongolia and southern Siberia via China, as items of Sogdian origin have been found in the Altai and Transbaikalia regions. It is possible that they also reached Korea and Japan, although there is no direct evidence of this; Sogdia and its capital Samarkand were, however, well known in these countries. This can be seen, in particular, in paintings found during excavations of the palace at Afrasiab. They depict the arrival of embassies from different countries coming to meet the Sogdian Ikhshid Varkhuman (AD 696), with one of the panels showing envoys from Japan or Korea.

Among the most interesting relics of the early period of Sogdian exploration of the Silk Road are the so-called 'Ancient Letters'. This name came to be used in academic circles to designate a group of private letters discovered in 1907 by the British scholar Sir Aurel Stein during excavations of the watchtower of the Great Wall of China to the west of Dunhuang in Xinjiang.

In addition to Chinese documents, five complete and several fragmentary letters on paper and silk, written in Sogdian cursive script in the Sogdian language, were found here. Their significance for scholarship lies not only in the wealth of previously unknown information about Sogdian colonies in Xinjiang, but also in the fact that they constitute the earliest known specimens of Sogdian writing, and are several centuries older than the documents discovered at Mount Mugh.

The date of the Ancient Letters is still a matter of debate. Stein dated them to the first half of the 2nd century AD and was supported in this view by the German scholar

H. Reichelt, who first published the letters in 1931, along with detailed descriptions and transliterations. The French scholars R. Gauthiot, P. Pelliot and F. Rosenberg also made significant contributions to the study of the letters.

Pelliot, in particular, highlighted that one of the letters contained information about the destruction of the Chinese capital Luoyang by nomads, which took place on three occasions, in AD 190, 311 and 535, as historical evidence indicates. W.B. Henning undertook a detailed, comparative analysis of the contents of the letters and historical data. He came to the conclusion that the letters had been written in AD 312–313, and that one of them reflected events known of from other textual sources related to the capture of the Chinese capital Luoyang by Huns. Henning's dating has been widely accepted in academic circles, although the Hungarian scholar J. Harmatta recently attempted to prove that the Sogdian letters were written in 196 AD, while the Japanese researcher A. Fujieda believes they date from the 6th century AD. A more recent close examination of the letters conducted by F. Grenet and N. Sims-Williams, taking into account archaeological, historical and numismatic evidence, has corroborated Henning's dating.

Some of these letters were written by natives of Samarkand and were destined for their city. One was written in Kucha, two in Dunhuang, the rest probably in Luoyang. The large Sogdian settlements with trading stations were all situated along the route of the Silk Road south of the Great Wall of China.

The letters also mention other Chinese cities where Sogdian merchants and their families lived: Jincheng and Chanban (Khumdan), among others. The commercial operations carried out in these places by Sogdian merchants were subsidised by wealthy Samarkand merchants, who provided credit and managed negotiations. The content of the letters is diverse. In particular, they mention various peoples who lived in the oases of Xinjiang: Indians, Huns, Chinese and Sogdians; they give names of people, mostly Iranian, and the names of cities and settlements. They tell of the dramatic events related to invasions by nomads and of trade transactions involving the sale of silk, fabrics, pepper and perfumes, and the purchase and sale of silver. Important details about the Sogdians are included, such as in the second letter, which mentions a hundred noble men from Samarkand who came to live in Dunhuang.

The letters also contain Indian terms related to trade, such as words for caravan or price. The second letter, in particular, has come to be known as 'Nanai-vandak's Report' in academic circles, and provides fascinating details on the phonology, morphology and syntax of the Sogdian language. The author of the letter, a Sogdian called Nanai-vandak, which means slave, or servant, to the goddess Nana, addressed it to Nanai-thvar, the head of the merchants in Samarkand. It contains a detailed account of the life of Sogdian settlers and the hardships they endured through the Hun invasion. The writing is filled with bitterness '…and, sir, if I were to describe to you all the details of how China was faring, you would have a (tale of) debt and misery'. In other parts of the letter, Nanai-vandak describes the tragic fate of Sogdians who died of starvation through famine.

The presence of a significant number of Sogdians in the towns and villages along the Silk Road is also supported by numerous Sogdian manuscripts from the 7th to the 10th centuries found in Xinjiang. They are in Sogdian script and language and their content is mainly religious, including translations of Buddhist sutras, Manichaean prayers and hymns in verse, and Christian essays, including fragments of psalms, Gospels, and parts of the Old Testament. The tales of Sogdian Manichaeans found in the Turfan oasis are also noteworthy: they include such stories as 'A Pearl Borer', 'Kar Fish', 'The Monkey and the Fox'. As Henning established, some of these tales are known of from the Arabic version of *Kalila and Dimna* and the Indian animal fables known as the *Panchatantra*. Sogdian texts of secular content have also been found. Apart from the 'Ancient Letters', these include the 'Legend about Rustam and His Battle with the Daevas' and a text describing the properties of various stones and the beliefs and rituals associated with them.

The role of Sogdians in introducing to China various writing systems, including Sogdian itself, as well as Parthian, Syrian (Estrangelo) and Manichaean, is no less important. The runic script of the ancient Turks was directly influenced by the Sogdian script.

Central Asians, in particular Sogdians and Bactrians, contributed greatly to the introduction into China of new musical instruments and many elements of musical culture, in particular the lute, harp, transverse flute and *syrinx* (pan pipe). Sogdian musicians and dancers were particularly popular in the Tang dynasty (7th–8th centuries). They included natives of Bukhara, Samarkand, Chach, Kabudan, Khumdeh, Maimargh and Khuttal. Musicians from Kabudan (a region near Samarkand), who were known as Cao in China, outnumbered all the musicians from other countries put together. Music from Samarkand was part of the official court repertoire. The dance performances by young boys and girls from Chach, particularly the 'Western Galloping Dance' performed by boys and the 'Dance from Chach' performed by two girls, were much admired by the Chinese. A poem, 'The Singer from Chach' by the Chinese poet Bai Juyi (AD 774–846) is particularly famous.

Purple net shirts are set in motion – the Chach dancers come!
Girdles droop from gilded thighs, flowered waists are heavy
Hats revolve with golden bells, snowy faces turn.

I watch – too soon the tune is done, they will not be detained;
Whirling in clouds, escorted by rain, they are off to the Terrace of the Sun.

Bai Juyi
quoted in *The Golden Peaches of Samarkand* by E. Schafer, 1963

Some crops and species of domestic animals were introduced to China from western Central Asia. According to Sima Qian's *Shiji* ('Records of the Great Historian'), 'The regions around Dayuan make wine out of grapes, the wealthier inhabitants keeping as much as 10,000 or more piculs stored away. It can be kept for as long as twenty or thirty years without spoiling. The people love their wine and the horses love their alfalfa. The Han envoys brought back grape and alfalfa seeds to China and the emperor for the first time tried growing these plants in areas of rich soil ... grapes and alfalfa for as far as the eye could see.'

Thus, the cultivation of alfalfa and grapes from Ferghana was introduced to China as early as the end of the 2nd century BC. Berthold Laufer is the author of the classic work *Sino-Iranica* about plants borrowed from ancient Iran which were cultivated in China. In one of his essays on the grapevine, he traces all stages of this crop's introduction to China, which the Chinese first came to know of following Zhang Qian's visit to Ferghana and Sogdia in 128 BC. When the Sogdian Kang Yandian established Sogdian colonies south of lake Lop Nor in the first quarter of the 7th century, he established four towns – the (so-called) 'towns of vines'.

The drinking of wine became very popular in China during the Tang dynasty. The Chinese word for the grape and vine, *p'u-t'ao, *bu-daw,* comes from the Iranian **budawa* or **buδawa* and was apparently borrowed by the Chinese in Sogdia and Ferghana and later entered the Japanese language. On the orders of Emperor Wudi (140–87 BC), the famous Ferghana *argamaks,* believed to be descended from a breed of 'heavenly horses', were brought from Dayuan/Ferghana to China. Researchers believe that the cultivation of pistachios, which were known as the 'nuts of western foreigners' in China, also began here under the influence of Central Asia and Persia.

Central Asians had an exceptional role in the manufacture of glass in China, where it began to be produced in the late Zhou period. However, the two kinds of glass produced had many imperfections. According to the Chinese chronicle the *Beishi* ('History of the Northern Dynasties') (4th–7th centuries AD):

> During this time of the emperor Tai Wu [424–452 CE], traders came to the capital of wei from the Da Yuezhi country [Central Asia, the territory of the former Kushan Empire], who said that by fusing certain minerals they could make the five colours of

liuli glass. They then gathered (materials) and dug in the hills, and fused the minerals at the capital. When ready, the material so obtained was of even greater brilliancy than the *liuli* glass imported from the West. An edict was issued that a movable palace should be made of this material, and when it was done it held more than a hundred people. It was bright and transparent so that all who beheld it were astonished and thought it was made by magical power. After this, articles made of glass became considerably cheaper in China than they had been before, and no one regarded it as particularly precious.'[4]

According to the Tang annals, in the mid-7th century AD the ruler of Tokharistan sent the Chinese emperor two 'agate lamp-trees', and in AD 718, the ruler of Sogdia sent him various gifts including a cup made of rock crystal and an agate bottle.

According to E. Schafer, there is evidence of objects made of carnelian being exported to China from Samarkand and Tokharistan in AD 718; raw, unworked carnelian often came from Tokharistan. Lazurite (lapis lazuli) was very popular in China, and pieces of it were considered 'luxury gifts'. It was used for making jewellery and decorating sacred objects such as amulets. The main ancient deposits of lazurite were in Badakhshan, but the main supplier of it to China via Khotan was Chach. In AD 750, when the Chinese army conquered the region under its Korean commander, Gao Xianzhi, he took from there gold, camels, thoroughbred horses, as well as a considerable amount of lapis lazuli.

While China exported silk and silk products to the Western Regions, peoples from Central Asia passed on to China the secrets of processing flax and wool, and also carpets and tapestries. Woollen carpets were gifted to the Tang emperor from such Central Asian dominions as Maimargh, Kesh and Chach. Khatun, the queen of Bukhara, made a gift of two large coverlets and an 'embroidered carpet' to the Chinese empress.

Semi-precious stones were supplied to China as raw materials and finished products from various regions of Central Asia, in particular from Badakhshan, Chach and Tokharistan. Central Asia was also one of the main sources of medicinal plants for China. For instance, according to the historical work the *Tan Shu* ('Old Book of Tang'), in the period AD 713–755 up to 200 species of rare medicinal plants were sent to China from Tokharistan, along with fine horses and red and emerald glass. Among them was the Indian wonder drug *citragandha,* which was a mixture of all kinds of remedies for treating wounds and haemorrhages. It was brought to China not only from India but also from Tokharistan, and on one occasion was brought here by a combined embassy from Badakhshan, Chach, Kesh, Maimargh and Kapisa.

Furthermore, in addition to the famous 'blood sweating' heavenly horses from Ferghana, other animals such as hunting and pet dogs, leopards, cheetahs and lions were brought to China as gifts from various regions of Central Asia. A lion was sent from Samarkand as a gift to Emperor Taizong in AD 635. The Chinese were so impressed by the animal's power and majesty that two poems were dedicated to it. One of these, composed by Yu-Shih-nan, is a *fu* poem or 'rhapsody':

It glares its eyes – and lightning flashes.
It vents its voice – and thunder echoes.
It drags away the tiger,
Swallows down the bear,
Splits the rhinoceros,
Cleaves the elephant.
It crushes the mighty guar between gums and palate,
It bends the boa snake between finger and palm.

from *The Golden Peaches of Samarkand,* E. Schafer, 1963

Lions were delivered to China from Tokharistan in the 7th–8th centuries AD. According to M.E. Masson, lions were part of the local fauna in Tokharistan from ancient times. The most ancient reference to these beasts in this region is in an account of the time of Alexander the Great's conquest in 328 BC, when he is said to have gone hunting in the Sogdian region of Basista, not far from Samarkand. He was apparently attacked by an enormous lion, which he killed 'with a single blow'.

According to the *Beishi,* lions used to inhabit the 'Tashena' mountains south of Samarkand and were brought to the court of the Chinese emperor from there. There are many depictions of lions on artefacts and in examples of fine art from Central Asia, and coins from Southern Sogdia dating from the 4th–7th centuries AD are particularly noteworthy in this respect. The reverse of these coins includes an image of a lion standing on its hind legs and a warrior striking it with a sword. M.E. Masson believed that unlike tigers, which inhabited the greater part of Central Asia up to the beginning of the 20th century, lions had already disappeared from the local fauna by the time of the Arab conquest of this region.

There is considerable evidence of close contacts between Central Asia and the civilisations of China and Xinjiang. Central Asia's contribution can be summed up in two ways: its direct influence on particular aspects of the civilisations of Xinjiang and China, and its role as a mediator in trade and cultural contacts along the Silk Road from the Far East through Central Asia to the Mediterranean.

4.6

SOGDIAN SEAFARERS

> Captain Ismailawayh told me that these species of fish are often found in the sea of Zanj and in the ocean of Samarkand.
>
> Buzurg ibn Shahriyar, 10th century AD

TEXTUAL SOURCES, HISTORICAL WORKS AND TALES AND LEGENDS OF THE peoples of Central Asia have all provided details of the sea and ocean voyages undertaken by Sogdians, and of the role of navigation, in ancient and medieval times along the Amu Darya, which was undoubtedly a wider, deeper and more full-flowing river than it is today.

During these periods, there were numerous large and small rivers and lakes in Transoxiana. The Avesta hymn dedicated to the goddess of water and fertility Ardvi, whose epithets were Sura ('strong') and Anahita ('pure, untainted') says:

'All the shores of the sea Vouru-Kasha are boiling over, all the middle of it is boiling over, when she runs down there, when she streams down there, she, Ardvi Sura Anahita, who has a thousand cells and a thousand channels … .'[5]

Nineteenth-century scholars believed this passage described the delta of the Amu Darya (ancient Oxus), and they equated the sea of Vouru-Kasha with the Aral Sea, and the goddess Ardvi with the goddess of the Amu Darya. These assumptions are still more or less valid, although there are different views about the location of the places.

A rock painting showing a sailing vessel. Beshtobe (near Nukus).

Here, it is worth noting that an English envoy called Jenkinson, who had visited Khorezm in 1558, wrote of the river Ardok, the main channel of the Amu Darya. The name has a clear etymological link to the name of the river Ardvi and the eponymous deity mentioned in the Avesta. Depictions of different kinds of vessels on monuments found in Transoxiana dating from the ancient and medieval periods provide further evidence for this view.

The divine protector of this river – albeit more likely only of its upper courses – was the great Bactrian deity Okhsho, appearing on gold coins of the Kushan king Huvishka as a stately male figure in long robes, holding a staff in his right hand and a large fish in his left. The Tajik name for the Amu Darya, Vakhsh, is derived from this deity. In antiquity, people built temples to the great river deity (one was discovered at the Takht-i Sangin site), erected statues and altars, and made votive offerings to the deity.

The component Vakhsh (Oxus) was part of the theophoric names of many Bactrians, the most famous among them being Alexander's father-in-law, Vakhshuvas Oxyartes. After the death of his son-in-law, he was the first in the history of Central Asia to issue gold coins in his own name with Aramaic legends conveying the Bactrian pronunciation of his name – Vakhshuvar – which, according to V.A. Livshits, means 'chosen or protected by the god Vakhsh'. This name has survived to this day in southern Uzbekistan in the name of the small *kishlak* (village) of Vakhshuvar located in the foothills of Baisuntau (in the Denau district of Surkhan Darya province), where the ancestral shrine of this famous Bactrian ruler was located.

A number of different textual sources that mention Bactrians and Khorezmians suggest that they were making sea voyages as early as the 6th and 5th centuries BC. Among them was Dargaman, a Khorezmian, serving in a military garrison on the island of Elephantine in the lower Nile in 464 BC. An inscription discovered at Pergamon mentions a Bactrian called Orontes, who rebelled against King Artaxerxes and took possession of Pergamon. None of these people could have reached these places unless they had travelled via the Mediterranean or the Aegean seas.

The first Sogdian seafarer known to us was probably the father of the famous Kang Senghui, the first Buddhist teacher in south-eastern China. His ancestors lived in India, to where they migrated from Sogdia, and then Kang Senghui's father moved to Jiaozhi, i.e. present-day northern Vietnam, where he was involved in trade. In all likelihood, Kang Senghui reached China via the well-travelled and easier sea route, travelling across the Indian Ocean around the Malay Peninsula to the ports of south-eastern China.

Although we can only speculate about the above, we do know with some certainty that at the beginning of the second half of the 6th century AD, a Samarkand merchant called Maniakh and his Sogdian companions reached the Black Sea after a long journey, and sailed across it from Sebastopolis (Sukhumi) to Constantinople on a Byzantine ship. Here they engaged in negotiations with the Byzantine emperor for the delivery of Sogdian silk to Byzantium. Maniakh was accompanied by a Central Asian Kholiatai. According to P. Lerch, the Kholiatai (Choalitoi) were Khorezmians.

Later, the Sogdians repeatedly crossed the Black Sea on Byzantine ships to conduct a mutually beneficial trade in silk and other merchandise. The scholar V.I. Abaev has made the interesting observation that the name *Sudak*, a town still located on the eastern coast of the Crimean Peninsula, must have originally sounded like *Sogdak*, which means 'small Sogdian colony'. It is possible that the appearance of such a name reflected the prominent role of Sogdians not only in trade by caravan, but also in the maritime trade with Byzantium on the Black Sea.

Recent finds in China and Japan seem to point directly to Sogdian involvement in maritime trade in the Far East as well. Among them are two sandalwood fragments with Pahlavi and Sogdian inscriptions, found hidden in the Horyu-ji temple in Nara, the ancient capital of Japan. The Pahlavi inscription gives the name of the owner of items or an intermediary in their sale. The Sogdian version has two words, apparently referring to a measure of weight. The date that these objects arrived in Japan, indicated in one of the inscriptions, is AD 761.

In the first half of the 1980s, during archaeological excavations in Canton Province, near the Vietnamese border, Chinese scholars unearthed a clay vessel containing drachmas of the Sassanian King Peroz (AD 459–484) along with other silver and gold items, indicating the date of the burial of these items as the first half of the 6th century AD. However, the most important find was a silver vessel with an inscription that was originally described as Pahlavi or East Iranian. The Japanese scholar and Sogdologist Yotaka Yoshida has established it as being of Sogdian origin. He also translated the inscription as follows: 'This vessel belongs to (…) from the Chach people, (weight) 42 staters.' There is also a *tamga* seal in the middle of the inscription. Chach (Shash in Arabic) is the name of the area of present-day Tashkent and adjacent areas. Notably, yet another silver vessel, found in 1908 in the village of Kerchevo in the Urals, and now held by the State Hermitage Museum in St Petersburg in Russia, also has a Sogdian inscription dating from the 4th century AD indicating that it belonged to the ruler of Chach.

As a result of the discovery of these objects, a number of Chinese and Japanese scholars have suggested that they point to the involvement of Sogdian merchants in maritime trade between India and China in the early medieval period.

For example, the Japanese scholar Yajima Hikoichi believes that Sogdian merchants used this route as early as the 7th–8th centuries AD for selling sandalwood to China.

The biggest seaport on the south-east coast of China was Guangzhou, where a large Perso-Arab colony already existed in the 7th–8th centuries AD and engaged in trade by sea. It is possible that people from Central Asia, often referred to as Persians, were among its population.

There are echoes of the ancient traditions of Sogdian traders travelling by sea in the accounts of the Arab geographer al-Muqaddasi (10th century), according to whom merchants from Samarkand first came to Iraq and then went on to India and China by sea. The famous *Kitab Aja'ib al-Hind* ('Wonders of India'), created in the second half of the 10th century, written by Buzurg ibn Shahriyar, is based on stories from sailors and merchants on their way to India, China, Indonesia and Africa. It includes an entertaining tale about the capture of a whale off the coast of the Arabian Sea in 300 AH (AD 912–913). 'Captain Ismailawayh told me that these species of fish are often found in the sea of Zanj and in the ocean of Samarkand.' The sea of Zanj is part of the Indian Ocean off the east coast of Africa, and the name Zanj was used by the Arabs to refer to native East Africans.

As for the 'ocean of Samarkand', scholars have different opinions as to its location. It is clear, however, that this is the name given to the rest of the Indian Ocean, apparently from the Persian Gulf to India. This name did not appear by accident; it comes from the ancient traditions of Sogdian navigators. Apparently, by this time, the natives of Samarkand were so active in maritime trade and appeared so frequently on the sea routes that the eastern half of the Indian Ocean began to bear the name of this city.

In another part of his book, Buzurg ibn Shahriyar writes: 'A captain told me that it is said that the great Sea of Samarkand adjoins the Herkend, and that they say it is called the Sea of Samarkand because the river Samarkand flows into it, and that he saw many *fals* [whales] in the sea.' The Samarkand river, according to some scholars, is the Indus, which has its source in the Himalayas, directly abutting the Pamirs. It appears that in ancient and medieval times this river was used by merchants coming from Central Asia to ship their goods, and therefore for some time it was called the Samarkand river. Many Greek authors wrote about the existence of a river route from India to Central Asia, and still further to Transcaucasia and the Black Sea. This route ran along the Indus, the Kunduz Darya or the Balkhab river, and then along the Amu Darya and the Uzboi before reaching the Caspian Sea.

The earliest image of a ship in Central Asia can be seen on the petroglyphs of Beshtobe, 20 kilometres from Nukus. Here, carved into the surface of the rock, is an image of a flat-bottomed vessel with a single mast, quadrangular sail, high, rounded prow and a relatively low stern. On either side of the sail are two stylised human figures holding onto it. It is interesting to note that a bone plaque from Sparta dating from the beginning of the 1st millennium BC has a similar image of two (more realistic) figures holding up a sail on either side of a mast. The carving from Beshtobe appears to portray the same process.

According to S.P. Tolstov, the ship in the petroglyph from Beshtobe dates from the 3rd millennium BC to the beginning of the 1st millennium AD, i.e. the Bronze Age. He notes that the vessel's construction differs markedly from that of contemporary barges on the Amu Darya known as *kayuks* and is in fact reminiscent of one of the images of vessels found on ancient Egyptian monuments. This type of rudimentary, single-sail vessel was widespread in Egypt, Mesopotamia and the Eastern Mediterranean. For example, the world's oldest depiction of a sailing ship is the one on a ceramic vessel from pre-dynastic Egypt, i.e. from the 5th–4th millennia BC. It shows a similar, simple, sailing vessel with a high stern and prow and a quadrangular sail, placed not in the centre, but closer to the bow of the ship.

In order to navigate the Aral Sea and the Amu Darya, the ancient Khorezmians created single-masted sailing vessels, which they used for fishing, among other things. The bone plaque from Sparta mentioned above, which shows fishermen fishing directly from the boat, is a vivid example of the use of the vessel for such purposes.

Fishing had always had a significant role in the lives of people from Khorezm. Its Neolithic, Kelteminar culture, which flourished there between the 5th and mid-2nd millennium BC, was a civilisation based on hunting and fishing. It is possible that this type of sailing ship emerged in Khorezm under the influence of the ancient civilisations of West Asia, with which Khorezm had close ethno-cultural links, as S.P. Tolstov and L.S. Tolstova have demonstrated.

There are even more striking analogies with Phoenician ships, such as the trading vessel depicted on an 8th-century-BC bas-relief in the palace of Sargon II. Like the ship in the petroglyph from Beshtobe, it has a single sail and a single mast supported by two ropes: one attached to the prow, and the other to the stern. Moreover, the bow of the Phoenician ship is finished with a steep stem in the shape of a horse's head, while the stern, which is lower, looks like the tail of a horse. The steep, rounded stem on the Beshtobe vessel suggests that its bow may also have been shaped like the head of an animal, and the stern shaped like a tail.

The earliest mention in textual sources of riverboats on the Amu Darya is in the description of the campaign by the Achaemenid king, Cyrus the Great, against the Massagetae queen, Tomyris, in 538 BC. In Herodotus's account, Cyrus ordered pontoon bridges to be built across the Amu Darya (Araxes) to enable his army to cross, and had towers erected on the vessels to make the bridge.

The second account featuring the presence of ships on the Oxus River is by Arrian in 330 BC. In this account, Bessus, having learned about the approach of Alexander the Great's army, 'crossed the river Oxus, and having burnt the boats upon which he had crossed, he withdrew to Nautaca in the land of Sogdiana' (Arrian, III, 28). Strabo (1st century AD) maintained that the river Oxus was navigable and was the largest river, except those in India, which he had seen in Asia (he borrowed his information from Patrocles (3rd century BC)).

The same is stated in the Chinese chronicle the *Shiji* (1st century AD) according to which, 'along the river Gui (Amu Darya) live merchants who carry their goods by river and overland for many thousands of li'. All these sources suggest the extensive exploration of river navigation on the Amu Darya in ancient times. Unfortunately, little is known about the types of vessels used to navigate the river. Most likely, they included both rowing and sailing vessels. However, thanks to the discovery of a unique bulla with an imprint of a gemstone in habitation layers dating from the late 4th or early 5th century AD at Karatepa (Old Termez), we do have reliable information about one of the vessels.

According to B.G. Peters, who published a description of the bulla, it shows a rowing warship and a pilot boat with two sailors sailing in front of the warship under the stem. The warship has a rounded bottom, the sides are made of wicker and covered in skins, and it has a high bow reminiscent of a dragon's head with rams facing forward. Five horizontal lines running from stern to bow, intersected in turn by ten vertical lines, are inscribed on the side of the vessel. A large steering oar can be seen on the stern, and below it are 18 rowing oars, indicating that the boat had 36 rowers and a helmsman. In addition, there are images of five warriors with spears standing at the side of the boat. According to Peters, the construction of the ship depicted on the bulla has many similarities to surviving images of a *kuphar*, a type of round boat (from the Arabic *quffa* meaning a basket woven from reeds and leaves) used for transport in Babylon (beginning of the 1st millennium BC). The design of the vessel depicted on the bulla from Karatepa also bears significant resemblance to an Assyrian round vessel from the 8th century BC, depicted on a relief from Nimrud. The rounded outlines of both vessels and the division of their sides into rectangular compartments are entirely similar. However, the Assyrian vessel does not have a high stem finished with a ram, which suggests the vessels had different purposes – the vessel on the bulla from Karatepa, as correctly noted by B.G. Peters, looks like it was used for military transport.

From the available data, it is evident that two types of ships were used in ancient times for navigating the Amu Darya: single-masted, keeled, sailing ships and 'round' (wicker) rowing boats. The origins of both are probably linked to the countries of the Eastern Mediterranean and Mesopotamia, from where their designs were borrowed, although it remains unclear when this borrowing took place. It is possible that this

A Chinese embassy crossing the Syr Darya. Afrasiab. Late 7th century AD.

was in the 6th–5th centuries BC, when, according to historical sources, Khorezmians lived in Egypt on the island of Elephantine, and in the Hellenistic era, when Central Asia, Mesopotamia and the Eastern Mediterranean were connected to each other by strong cultural and political ties.

A visual representation of the third type of vessel used on the Amu Darya in ancient times can be seen on the wall paintings in the palace of the Sogdian Ikhshid Varkhuman (end of the 7th century AD), at Afrasiab. The northern wall of the palace shows a scene of a group of women crossing a river in a large boat, possibly as part of a Chinese embassy. Judging by the number of people in it, it is a rather capacious boat, as it is capable of carrying ten women, who are led by a princess.

This is also clear from the broad shovel-shaped oar at the stern used to steer the boat, and from the construction of the boat itself. It has a rounded bottom and relatively high sides, made of three wide panels of wood. The prow of the boat is crowned with the head of a griffin, and the stern is slightly bowed and has a ring on it for mooring.

At the front of another boat are two horses and a man swimming beside them. Horses were used to control the movement of a vessel to prevent it from being swept away too far from its destination by the current. The method of steering a river craft using an oar and horses was widely practised for crossing the Amu Darya right up to the beginning of the 20th century, in particular in conjunction with a certain type of rowing boat known as a *kime*, and this was remarked on by many travellers to Turkestan in the second half of the 19th century.

The design of the *kime* or *kema*, the system of steering by using a stern oar and horses, its size, and the number of passengers it could carry, all make it very similar to the vessel depicted in the painting from Afrasiab.

Furthermore, judging by a sketch by N.A. Karazin from 1888, the type of oars used on ships and rafts in the Khiva Khanate was similar to the type of oars used in early medieval Sogdia. All of this suggests that the design of the *kime* is derived from the type of vessel depicted in the wall paintings of Afrasiab. It is this type of vessel, unlike the first two mentioned above, that is of local origin.

Rafts and inflatable skins have probably been in use on the rivers of Transoxiana, both for crossings and longer voyages, since ancient times, and more specifically, individual, inflatable floats or *burdyuks*, made from the skins of a variety of animals, were also in use. The earliest evidence of their use dates from 330–329 BC, when Alexander the Great's army crossed the Oxus, probably in the region of Kalif or Chushka-Guzar. According to Arrian, when Alexander reached the river, he realised that the crossing was impossible because at this point the river was 6 stadia wide (almost 1.2 km), very deep, and with a current so strong that it pulled out stakes driven into the riverbed.

He ordered the hides used as tent covers to be gathered, packed with dry grass and carefully sewn up to keep out the water. Using these, Alexander's army crossed the Oxus in five days (Arrian, III, 29, 2). Such inflatable skins were widely used for crossing the Amu Darya, especially in its upper reaches, even in later times.

In addition to individual floats, rafts using inflatable skins, often of cowhide, were also made. Two inflatable skins were used with parallel poles placed across them, fastened together with rope. This produced a raft capable of carrying at least four people, or perhaps even more. A similar method for river crossings was described by the Arab traveller Ahmad ibn Fadlan in the early 10th century.

Sketches by Karazin from 1885 suggest that more conventional rafts, without skins and made of beams placed in longitudinal and transverse rows, were widely used on the Amu Darya and Syr Darya. The rafts would have been steered by oarsmen with long oars standing at the front and back of the raft. The capacity of these rafts was variable – some could carry several people and cargo in addition to the oarsmen, others could only take one passenger with their possessions. In the Middle Ages, Termez was the largest river port on the Amu Darya – or Jayhun, as it was known in Arabic. The 10th-century geographers Istakhri and Ibn Hawqal noted that the city of Termez served as a port for the Jayhun. According to al-Maqdisi, writing at the end of the 10th century, Tirmidh (Termez) was the largest city on the Jayhun and had docking facilities for ships on both sides of the river. To describe the ships and boats, al-Maqdisi uses the Arabic word *al-sufan*, which translates as 'vessel, ship' and not 'boat', suggesting that vessels on the river were of different sizes and designs.

M.E. Masson suggested that boatmen – *keshtabanan* – lived in the southern part of Termez closer to the embankment, and later, in the 15th century, west of the citadel. He also believed that alongside the boatmen lived craftsmen whose main occupation was making and equipping river vessels. The wood from local elm trees, known as *karagach*, and mulberry trees were used for making and equipping river craft, and reeds and cotton were used to caulk the seams.

Clavijo's records dating back to 1404 also note the importance of the crossing at Termez. At the time, boats ferrying people from one bank to another and along the Amu Darya could only do so if they had a special document or decree authorising the route.

Boats on the Amu Darya were used not only for crossing it, but also for extended voyages along the river. Thus, the Moroccan explorer Ibn Battuta's accounts from 1334 tell us that in summer, ships from Khorezm sailed along the river to Termez bringing wheat and barley. It was a ten-day journey downstream. By contrast, the overland route to Termez from Khorezm, which went through Bukhara and Karshi, took about a month. It was thus three times faster to go by river. The distance from Termez to Khorezm by river was approximately 600 kilometres, suggesting that ships had to cover a distance of 60 kilometres per day.

Another major Central Asian river, the Syr Darya (Seyhun in Arabic), was also widely used, although there is much less information about it. Yaqut al-Hamawi's book *Mu'jam al-Buldan* ('Dictionary of Countries') from the 13th century was a compilation of geographical details known to the Arab world at this time. According to the book, ships sailed to Khodjent and Ferghana on the river Shash, and the city of Nudjent or Nudjaket was home to boatmen (*keshtabanan*) working on the rivers Park (the Chirchik) and Hashart (the Syr Darya). Masson identified the city of Nudjent or Nudjaket as the site of Khanabadtepa on the south-eastern outskirts of Tashkent, and Y.A. Buryakov believed it to be the city-site in the settlement of Gul at the confluence of the Chirchik and Syr Darya.

The main crossings over the Syr Darya were near Khodjent, in the Benakent (Shahruhia) area at the confluence of the Ahangaran and Syr Darya rivers, and in the Chinaz area, where the town of Chinachket, i.e. 'the town of Chinese merchants', existed in medieval times.

In ancient and medieval times, large settlements at major crossings over the Amu Darya and Syr Darya were home to specific groups of individuals who specialised in ferrying people across the rivers. They had their own way of life and customs and, apparently, had some kind of guild or organisation based around their particular occupation.

The accounts of Hafiz-i Abru provide interesting information about one such crossing. This was referred to as the 'Greek' crossing, Burdagui – a distortion of the Greek word πανδοχεῖον (*pandocheion*, 'hostelry'), which we identified as the sites of Kampyrtepa and Shurob-Kurgan, which lie 30 kilometres to the west of Termez. To quote Hafiz-i Abru:

> Burdagui is a place on the bank of the Jayhun, close to Tirmidh… And in olden times the more important boatmen responsible for the crossing of the Jayhun were in this 'Burdagui'. And the passage (*gudhargah*) of the sultans who were crossing this stream was there, and the kings of old protected its inhabitants because of their guarding of the crossing of the river, and freed them from taxes (*tarkhan*). For that reason the population there was numerous and the masters (*khuvajagan*) were opulent and served well every traveller who went there.

The extract makes it clear that a number of people lived at the crossing of Burdagui and that there were many ships, and if there were owners of large ships, there were likely to be even more owners of smaller vessels who engaged exclusively in ferrying people across the river. The *Mu'jam al-Buldan* also provides the same information.

At the time of the Russian conquest of Central Asia, navigation on the Amu Darya and Syr Darya continued to play an important role in the life of the peoples of that region, but the ships themselves were becoming simpler and less diverse.

The nature of navigation on the Amu Darya was described in detail by a staff captain, A. Bykov, during reconnaissance surveys of this river in 1876–1878. According to Bykov's report, the crossings at Kobadian, Patta-Hissar, Shurob and Chushka-Guzar had two vessels – *kimas* – on either bank, while the larger crossings at Kalif and Kerki had six and four boats respectively. Each *kime* was operated by a number of boatmen or *kimechi*: a large *kime* had 6–7 boatmen, a medium one had 3–4 or 5 boatmen. The number of *kime* at each crossing depended on the importance of the passing trade route or on the number of people living on either side of the river.

Moreover, all the money earned from the crossing went to the Emir of Bukhara via the rulers of the provinces, except for 25 per cent which was given as payment to the boatmen. The main income of up to 12,000 *tangas* annually came from the Kalif crossing: from caravans with goods from Bukhara and Karshi and salt from the settlement of Kampyrtepa (in the Kugitang mountains) bound for the cities of Akhchi, Balkh and Khulm in the territories of present-day northern Afghanistan.

In the summer of 1878, Bykov also undertook a reconnaissance of the river between the mouth of the Vakhsh and the village of Khoja-Jambas 50 kilometres from Kerki, and provided detailed information about the vessels used for navigating and crossing the Amu Darya. One type of rivercraft in various sizes was used here: the flat-bottomed *kime*. He noted that the *kime* resembled the Khiva *kayuks* but was much wider, heavier and more difficult to steer.

The wood used to build the *kime* was *tal* or *pat* – local varieties of poplar. Tetrahedral timbers joined by tenons were used to construct the vessels. The bottom of the *kime* was flat and reinforced with transverse planks nailed to it for greater stability.

Large *kime* were as much as 20 metres or more in length, from bow to stern, more than 5 metres wide in the middle, and 1 metre high on the sides. Inside, the vessel was divided into compartments by beams laid across from one side to the other and fastened with strips of iron. There were two compartments for the boatmen (*kaikchi* or *kimechi*) on the stern and bow, and three more in the middle of the boat. The average *kime* was about 5 metres long and more than 3 metres wide. Large *kime* could carry up to 16–18 camels, or 18–20 horses, or 200 sheep or 700–800 poods (approximately 11.5–13 tonnes) of grain, while medium-sized *kime* could carry 10–12 camels, or 12–14 horses, or 150 sheep and up to 400 poods (6.5 tonnes) of grain.

The *kime* were rowing vessels with no sails, steered by short, triangular, heavy oars. However, according to Bykov, the main means of propulsion were horses, tethered to beams on the vessel by rope. Two horses were usually used: one was tied to the front and one to the stern, on the side opposite to the current, so that the spine of the horse was 60–70 centimetres below the sides of the boat. In deep water, the horses would swim across, but in shallow water and on the shore they would pull the boat along while tethered to a strong rope by means of a harness and a shaft. As Bykov noted, this method of steering the vessel through shallow water and by land was exactly the same as the one used in Russia at the time.

The *kime* was used not only to cross the river, but also to sail on it, as can be seen from the calculations provided by Bykov, according to which, with a tow rope, upstream, a *kime* could cover 25 versts (nearly 27 km) at most per day, while further down the river in deep water it would cover 80 versts (just over 85 km) per day, which was equivalent to a three- or four-day journey by land. Thus, a *kime* could cover the distance from Termez to Khorezm in eight to ten days.

As a reconnaissance officer, Bykov was primarily interested in the use of these vessels for military purposes. According to his preliminary calculations, two large *kime* were needed to transport one company of infantry of no more than 160 bayonets, without cargo.

During the same period, two kinds of vessels were widely used in the lower reaches of the Amu Darya: *kayuks* and *kemas*. The scholar G.P. Snesarev has been able to provide us with some useful ethnographic details. The *kemas* were large, flat-bottomed vessels propelled by both oars and sails, which were used for transporting agricultural produce, fabrics and other cargo. They sailed down the Amu Darya as far as the Aral Sea and up to Termez, while the journey from Khorezm (from Kanka) to Termez overland took a month.

The crew of a large *kema* consisted of a captain (*darga*), his assistant (*yarim-darga*), who acted as helmsman, as well as 15 sailors. They were all members of a collective group or association and jointly hired a vessel, usually for a period of

12 months. Once a contract was agreed and sealed with vermilion wax (*kizil*), they paid the vessel owner a deposit.

The captain of the vessel would negotiate an amount with merchants for carrying their freight. Once the journey was completed and they had been paid by the merchants, part of the earnings was paid to the owners of the vessel, and the rest was distributed among the crew. As we can see, this system of payment in Khorezm was somewhat different to that used at crossings on the middle courses of the Amu Darya and as recounted by Bykov, where the bulk of the money earned went to the state coffers. In the villages near the rivers, the profession of boatman was considered hereditary and passed down from generation to generation. The same kind of professional communities of *kimechi* boatmen were documented by B.H. Karmysheva in Kalif.

According to Snesarev, before becoming a sailor a novice underwent a long period of training lasting several years, acquiring many skills for handling a ship. Snesarev also discovered a number of ritual practices that were followed. Sacrifices to the Amu Darya deity were made, including animal sacrifices followed by a ritual meal, throwing salt into the water, and immersing the captain in the river before the launch of a vessel. Snesarev's research revealed that the bow of a *kema* (known as *bosh* in Uzbek) would have been decorated with long braids of horsehair, with one or two mirrors imitating eyes placed in their centre, and coins, shells and amulets sewn onto strips of cloth were attached to the sides of the braids. He thinks that some kind of image of a female head was placed on the bow, which in his opinion must have been the river goddess Ardvi Sura Anahita. This is only a hypothesis, however, although the notion of bows of ships being adorned with figures is supported by the wall painting of Afrasiab dating from the 7th–8th centuries AD, depicting a ship's bow crowned with the head of a griffin. Of course, in antiquity, any of a wide range of images could have been used, including the head of Anahita.

Thus, even though these are cursory accounts, the importance of sailing on the river and its impact on the lives of the people of Transoxiana in ancient and medieval times is evident. It provided a steady income to the rulers controlling the crossings, sustained the major caravan trade and smaller trade operations, and supported a significant segment of the population who were engaged in fishing, ferrying and shipbuilding, and providing services to the passing merchant caravans.

Moreover, the wealth of experience accumulated during voyages along the Amu Darya and on the Aral Sea over the centuries allowed the Sogdians to go on to explore the wider expanses of the seas and oceans.

4·7

CHINA AND CENTRAL ASIA

From the second half of the 2nd century BC after the voyage of Zhang Qian, a new geographical concept – the Western Regions – was introduced in the Chinese world to designate Central Asia and Eastern Turkestan (present-day Xinjiang).

Trade, cultural and diplomatic relations between China and the Western Regions had developed over many centuries and were intricately connected with the exploration of new routes, roads and geographical regions previously unknown to the Chinese.

Formidable geographical barriers between China and Central Asia had to be overcome, such as the Taklamakan desert, the Kunlun and Tien-Shan mountains and the Pamirs, and there were thousands of kilometres of challenging routes. Surmounting these natural obstacles required considerable physical effort and will, especially in the initial stages of trying to establish contact between civilisations as different from each other as the Chinese and Central Asian.

China probably had already established trade relations with Khotan, from where famous Khotan jade came to China, as early as the first half of the 1st millennium BC.

China had probably also established relations with Altai in the same period. It was in this region that unique specimens of Chinese silk embroidery and multicoloured fabrics imported from the kingdom of Chu were found in Pazyryk *kurgans* (burial mounds). Going by archaeological finds and information from Chinese textual sources, it would appear that networks of routes were developed in Central Asia as early as the 1st millennium BC to connect the region to China. Before the establishment of the Han empire, China mainly consisted of the north-eastern part of the country between the Huanghe (Yellow River) and Yangtze rivers. It was not until the rise of the great Han empire in 206 BC that China emerged as a powerful state, wielding considerable influence over its neighbouring peoples and actively pursuing policies of territorial expansion. Diplomatic missions, military contingents, merchants and artisans streamed westwards along the roads opened up by Zhang Qian and his followers.

Meanwhile, Han China gradually pushed west of the Huanghe river and adopted a policy of the systematic colonisation of new territories and of their settlement by the Chinese. Prior to this, these territories were likely mainly inhabited by Indo-European peoples such as Tokharians and tribes speaking Turkic and Mongolian languages. According to the chapters on the Western Regions from the *Han Shu* ('History of the Former Han Dynasty'), as compiled for example by Ban Gu:

> By the time of the first Ch'in emperor, the Jung and the Ti were driven away and the long walls were built to form a boundary for China. However, in the west, these did not extend further than Lin-t'ao. The Han dynasty arose, and we come to the time of Emperor Hsiao Wu; he undertook the task of subduing the various barbarian peoples and of spreading [Han] prestige, whereas Chang Ch'ien for the first time opened up a way in the Western Regions. Thereafter, the general of cavalry on the alert (*P'iao-Chi*) attacked and vanquished those lands of the Hsiung-nu that lay to the right [i.e. to the west], [in 121 BC]. He forced the kings of K'un-yeh and Hsiu-ch'u to surrender and thereupon had those territories evacuated.
>
> *For the first time* [the italics are mine E.R.] fortifications were built at Ling-chu and further west; and once Chiu-ch'uan had been founded, members of the [Han] population were gradually removed there to fill that area. This was then divided; Wu-wei, Chang-i and Tun-huang were founded to form a line of four commanderies based on the two barriers.[6]

According to the Chinese texts, there were two main routes that led to the Western Regions from China – a southern one and a northern one. The southern road (Nan Dao) went from Yumenguan (the Yumen Pass) and Yangguan (the Yang Pass) through Shanshan, skirting the northern edge of the southern mountains (the Kunlun mountains) and proceeding along the course of the river west of Shache (the Yarkand oasis in Kashgar). The road then led to the Wakhan Corridor, where it forked – going westwards to the country of Great Yuezhi (Bactria) and Anxi (Parthia), and south to India.

The northern road (Bei Dao) began from the royal court of Nearer Jushi, running alongside the northern mountains and following the course of the river west to Kashgar, and then through the Onion Range (Pamirs), west to Dayuan (Ferghana) and Kangju, and then northwest to Yancai (near the Aral Sea).

Zhang Qian's journey and the advance of the Chinese to Xinjiang, the main roads leading to the Western Regions came under the control of the Han and were accordingly lined with defensive fortifications. According to Chinese texts, several government posts were established from Dunhuang to the Salt Marsh (Lop Nor) and 'a complement of several hundred agricultural conscripts was stationed at both Lun-t'ai and Ch'u-li. A colonel [for the assistance of imperial] envoys was established to protect them and to provide supplies for the Han envoys who were proceeding to the outer states. At first, Han only protected the southern road, but subsequently took over the northern road, too, completely. The two routes were managed by a special official, who was given the title of "protector general". This officer kept under observation the activities of the various outer states such as Wu-sun and K'ang-chu, and when an incident occurred he submitted a report to the throne.'

Some of these roads had specific names. For example, the road from Dunhuang through Khotan to the south circumventing the Pamirs along the Wakhan Corridor was called the 'Jade Road'. The road through the Terek-Dayuan Pass was known as the 'Silk Road'. There was also an 'Imperial Highway' via the Gansu Corridor, and a 'Road of Merchants, Wanderers and Missionaries', which ran between Kunlun and Tian Shan. All these roads began in the city of Chang'an, the capital of Han China, to the west of Beijing. The most important junction was at Dunhuang (in modern Gansu province), where the roads diverged. The strategic importance of Dunhuang can be seen in the fact that the final sections of the Great Wall, which protected the city from raids by nomads, ran along the city's north and north-west borders. Caravans passing from China to the West or, vice versa – those coming from the West, stopped in Dunhuang before tackling the final section of the Silk Road leading to Chang'an; peoples from different countries, including Sogdians, made their permanent homes here. It was near Dunhuang that Sir Aurel Stein found the famous Sogdian Ancient Letters in a watchtower of the Great Wall of China.

As time passed, the number of main roads linking the 'Celestial Empire' with the West increased. The *Wei Shu* ('Book of Wei') describes Dong Wan and Gao Ming's mission to the Western Regions in the second quarter of the 5th century AD. According to the description in the *Wei Shu*, there used to be two roads leading to the Western Regions, and then these increased to four. The first road went from the Yumen Pass, crossed the Flowing Sands, and after 2,000 li to the west came to Shanshan. The second road went from the Yumen Pass, crossed the Flowing Sands, and after going north 2,200 li, reached Jushi (Cheshi); the third road went from Shache (Yarkand) to the west, and after 100 li reached the Pamirs (Ts'ung-ling or Congling), and after another 1,300 li to the west reached Wakhan (Jiapei or Ch'ieh-pei); the fourth road went from Shache to the south-west and after 500 li reached the Pamirs, and after a further 1,300 li to the south-west reached Bolu (Bolor).

The desertion of many once-inhabited oases as a result of climate change and invasion by nomadic tribes led to adjustments to some of these routes.

The Chinese geographer Pei Ju (end of the 6th–beginning of the 7th century), the author of the *Maps of and Notes about the Western Regions*, of which only fragments have survived, described three main roads leading from Dunhuang to the Western Sea [Mediterranean Sea]. The northern road now followed a slightly different route through Hami, Lake Barkul, the base of the Turkic Khagan at Lake Issyk-Kul, the steppes of southern Kazakhstan, the Volga region, and then, probably, through the northern Caucasus to Byzantium and the Mediterranean Sea.

The second, middle road, began at Turfan and went via Karashar, Kucha and the Pamirs to Ustrushana and Samarkand, and then on through Bukhara, Merv and Sassanian Iran to the Mediterranean Sea. The third, southern road from Dunhuang went around the salt lake at Lop Nor, crossed the Taklamakan desert, passed through the Wakhan Corridor, and went through Tokharistan along the Hindu Kush through Sassanian Iran to the Mediterranean Sea. Pei Ju added 'from each country roads also branch off, and in turn intersect other roads in the south and north. Thus, by following (those roads) one may reach anywhere. Therefore, it is known that Qu, Gaochang and Shanshan are the gateways to the Western Regions.' Thus, over the centuries, after Zhang Qian's journey, a network of roads connecting the East and the West was established, which became known to scholarship as the Silk Road.

The Chinese and Hellenic, Iranian- and Turkic-speaking peoples all played a significant role in its creation. Two Chinese figures, Zhang Qian and Gan Ying, were instrumental in bringing together the civilisations of the Far East and the West.

Zhang Qian had discovered the Western Regions (Central Asia) for China, and Gan Ying, the Eastern Mediterranean – the civilisations of the ancient Near East, ancient Rome and Greece. It is assumed that somewhat earlier, at the end of the 4th to the 3rd century BC, Sogdians had begun to move to the oases of Xinjiang along roads familiar to them. These roads might have connected Central Asia and this region since the Bronze Age, and possibly even earlier.

At about the same time, the Hellenes had reached the far north-eastern borders of Central Asia; it is possible that they had already heard about the country of the 'Seres-Chinese' from the locals. Only one more step was needed to connect the roads coming from the West and the Far East and transform them into one long transcontinental route. This step was taken by Zhang Qian.

The journeys of Gan Ying

Zhang Qian had paved the way to Central Asia – the Western Regions. More than two hundred years later, another Chinese pioneer, Gan Ying, first made his way further west to the countries of the Eastern Mediterranean.

The Chinese chronicle the *Hou Han Shu* ('History of the Later Han Dynasty') tells us that 'in the ninth year [97 BC], Ban Chao sent his Subaltern Gan Ying, who probed as far as the Western Sea [i.e. the Mediterranean], and then returned. Previous generations never reached these regions. [...] No doubt he prepared a report on their customs and investigated their precious and unusual [products].' Gan Ying tried to reach Rome, but a shortage of funds forced him to return to China.

Gan Ying's journey was a natural consequence of the gradual exploration of the roads from Central Asia going west by the Chinese. Although Gan Ying was the first Chinese person to reach the Eastern Mediterranean, the Chinese had in fact received their earliest knowledge about the countries near the Eastern Mediterranean from Zhang Qian, who had gathered much information while in Bactria. Zhang Qian's reports are quoted extensively in Sima Qian's *Shiji*, and used in particular in Fa Ye's (AD 398–445) *Hou Han Shu*, where he writes 'Going southwest more than a hundred days further on horseback, you reach Tiaozhi [Upper Mesopotamia – E.R.]. In the kingdom of Tiaozhi there is a town on the top of a hill [...] It borders on the Western Sea [Mediterranean Sea]'.[7]

Soon after Zhang Qian's journey, under the same Emperor Wu di (140–87 BC), a constant exchange of embassies with Dayuan and other states of Central Asia was established, with at least a dozen Chinese embassies being sent each year. In 113 BC, for the first time, the Chinese established diplomatic relations with Anxi (Parthia). An embassy was sent to visit the town of Ctesiphon, which was at that time the capital of Parthia, a few thousand kilometres from the Chinese capital Chang'an.

Following this, between 111 and 105 BC the Parthian ruler sent his envoys 'to see China', as textual sources say, with presents for the Chinese court of eggs of large birds (ostriches) and conjurers from 'Li-kan'. Researchers have established that Li-kan, or Lixuan, corresponds to the city of Alexandria, founded by Alexander the Great in Upper Egypt. Thus, the period between 111 and 105 BC is a crucial date in the history of the Silk Road, as documentary evidence from this time is the first proof of its existence over the formidable distance from Egypt in the West to China in the East.

Diplomatic envoys were perhaps the first to travel along the route, and trade caravans probably followed.

The conjurors from Alexandria occupy a special place in this exchange because, as Chinese sources testify, before their arrival in China, the art of illusion was unknown here. A renowned scholar of cultural links between China and Africa, V.A. Velgus, believed that the arrival of the conjurers from Alexandria at the end of the 2nd century BC may have been the impetus not only for the introduction of this art form in China, but ultimately also for the evolution of traditional Chinese theatre.

The art of illusion appears to have originated, like many other art forms, in the countries of the Eastern Mediterranean. Egyptian and Chaldean magicians were particularly famous for it, and Alexandria was the centre for these arts in the Hellenistic world. In later times, Chinese sources recorded the arrival in China of illusionists from the countries of the Eastern Mediterranean that were part of the Roman empire, which the Chinese called Da Qin. They could transform things, breathe fire, disarticulate their limbs, replace the heads of bulls with those of horses (and vice versa), and juggle up to ten balls at a time.

The jugglers themselves are claimed to have said: 'We are people of (from) Haixi [the country west of the sea]'. Haixi is Da Qin, if we are to believe the account in the *Xiyu juan* ('Chapter on the Western Regions') from the *Hou Han Shu*.

Most of the cultural exchange and trade between the Eastern Mediterranean and Parthia on the one hand, and China on the other, was conducted overland through Central Asia, although there was also a sea route linking these countries, used mainly by Chinese and Malay seafarers. Yet the Chinese themselves did not undertake their first sea voyages to Mesopotamia until the 9th and 10th centuries AD.

Thus, in the 200 years following the discovery of the Western Regions by Zhang Qian, the Chinese had decisively and methodically become masters of all the roads that led there, and had established regular diplomatic relations and trade with several Central Asian dominions, and also made repeated attempts to gain political control over them, as evidenced by their wars with Dayuan (Ferghana). All this activity paved their way to the Mediterranean Sea and to contact with the civilisations of Rome and ancient Greece.

Chinese goods probably began to enter Central Asia in the second half of the 2nd to the 1st century BC, after the discovery of the Western Regions by Zhang Qian, and the establishment of various relationships with the peoples of Central Asia along with the beginnings of the Silk Road.

However, there is also some evidence of the earlier arrival of Chinese articles here. For example, during Zhang Qian's time in Bactria, he reported having seen bamboo staffs from Qiong and cloth from Shu. According to the people of Bactria, these items were purchased by their merchants, who went to trade in Shendu. Contemporary research suggests that 'Shu' corresponds to China's Sichuan province, while Shendu covers north-western India, Burma and Yunnan province in south-western China.

Thus, even before the beginnings of the Silk Road, Chinese and Bactrian merchants were carrying goods to their respective countries. Coins, mirrors, objects of jade, silk fabrics and other Chinese objects have all been found in Central Asia.

Coins

It is possible to distinguish two major periods of the ingress of Chinese coins into historical and cultural areas of the eastern and central parts of Central Asia.

The first period is of wu zhu (wu shu) coins issued between 118 BC and AD 618 and Hou ch'uan (Huo Quan) coins from the time of Emperor Wang Mang (AD 9–23).

The second period, from the 7th–8th centuries AD, includes bronze coins of the Tang dynasty, which had a significant influence on the formation of monetary systems in some regions in the eastern and central parts of Central Asia, especially Sogdia.

Discoveries of coins from other Chinese dynasties are extremely rare. In fact, we only know of one – a bronze coin with a square hole, from the Northern Zhou dynasty (AD 557–581), issued in AD 579. It was discovered at the Budrach site, the capital of the ancient Chaganian region, 6 kilometres from the town of Denau in today's Surkhan Darya province in Uzbekistan.

Bronze wu zhu coins were produced in China for over 700 years. Their first official issue was under the Emperor Wu di in 118 BC and they continued to be struck until the establishment of the Tang dynasty in 618 AD. Wu zhu coins are round, with a square hole in the centre. Both the obverse and reverse sides always have an outer rim; the inner rim, applied along the edge of the square hole, is present only on the reverse. The legend on wu zhu coins consists of two characters for 'Wu' and 'zhu' placed on the obverse, on either side of the square hole, and they are read from right to left. Coins weigh 1.5–3 grams, and have a diameter of 25–30 millimetres, with some variations on either side.

Initially, the casting of wu zhu coins was not confined to official government mints, but was also undertaken by individual, provincial mints and small workshops. When mint regalia (the right to mint coins) was established in 113 BC, it became the prerogative solely of the central government.

Wu zhu coins are quite common in the eastern and central parts of Central Asia. They have been found particularly in Ferghana, where, by 1988, 42 such coins had been found in 32 graves at 16 burial sites. In addition, two wu zhu coins were discovered more recently during excavations of Mugkhona in the Gava region of Northern Ferghana. Two similar coins were also found during excavations of the Munchaktepa burial site near the town of Pap in the Ferghana valley. Finds of wu zhu coins are also known in other areas. In particular, four degraded coins were found in Penjikent. Thirteen wu zhu coins, three of them from a habitation layer, were discovered during excavations at Munchaktepa I and II, located near the Farkhad Gate in Northern Tajikistan. Another, similar coin was found at the site of Kanka in the Ak-Kurgan district of the Tashkent region. In addition, such coins have also been found in the Alay mountains, in Kum-Aryk (Kyrgyzstan), in a child's grave in the

Almashik burial site in Tien Shan, and in a similar grave in the Mardan burial site at the Otrar oasis in Southern Kazakhstan.

Finds of bronze Hou ch'uan coins from the time of the Emperor Wang Mang have been rare. These coins appear to have been issued originally in AD 14, when the emperor undertook a monetary reform of the Han empire. They were officially in circulation only during his reign. One Hou ch'uan coin was found on the burial grounds of Khangaz I in Ferghana, one in Penjikent, and another at Afrasiab in Samarkand; such finds are also recorded at Kanka in the Tashkent region.

Most finds of ancient Chinese coins in the eastern and central parts of Central Asia have been in Ferghana and adjacent areas. Separate finds have been made in Sogdia, Chach, Ustrushana and the Otrar oasis, and probably mark the western border of the spread of ancient Chinese coins in this region.

The origin of wu zhu coins found in Ferghana is believed to be connected to the opening up of the Silk Road in the late 2nd century BC, as one of its routes went through this area. It has been suggested that wu zhu coins were not used as actual money here, but as ornaments, because the coins found in Ferghana have only been found in burial sites. However, it is probably premature to see the use of wu zhu coins as limited to this. More recently, such coins have been found not just in burial sites, but also in habitation layers of sites such as Penjikent, Munchak I and II, and Kanka. Unlike Sogdia and Bactria, ancient Ferghana did not issue its own coins and it is possible that wu zhu coins were used as a means of currency here.

The further spread of Chinese coins into the eastern and central regions of Central Asia was during the Tang dynasty, the coins of which gained even wider circulation there. Three kinds of bronze coins of the Tang dynasty have been found.

The most common are those with four Chinese characters, one along each side of the square hole on the obverse, that read *kai yuan tong bao*; the reverse side is smooth, without inscriptions, but sometimes there is a thickening in the shape of a semicircle or crescent to the left of the hole, which, according to Chinese tradition, was interpreted as the mark of the emperor's fingernail. They were issued from AD 621 to 907. The second type of Tang coin has the legend *da li yuan bao* on the obverse and was issued between AD 766 and 779. The third type of Tang coin has the legend *qian yuan zhong bao* and was issued from AD 758 to 760.

Going from east to south, Tang coins have been found in the following locations: Kitai-gorod (China town) island at Issyk-Kul – 2 specimens; Krasnaya Rechka – 8 specimens and 2 fragments; Balasagun – 1 specimen; Turtkul, near Novopavlovsk village near Bishkek – 1 specimen; Tashkent region, at the Kanka site – 3 specimens; Khanabad – 1 specimen; Afrasiab – several specimens; Penjikent – 1 specimen; Budrach – 1 specimen; Shurob-Kurgan – 2 specimens; Old Termez – 3 specimens (according to museum collection data); and 1 specimen found in a ditch at the Nadir-Diwanbegi madrasah in Bukhara.

In total, about 30 specimens of Tang coins have been recorded, but this register is probably far from complete, unlike the one of wu zhu coins. The overwhelming majority of these coins were found in habitation layers at sites and settlements, for example during the excavation of a dwelling at the site of Shurob-Kurgan. This suggests that Tang coins were used in a number of areas of the eastern and central parts of Central Asia as a viable form of currency.

The range of circulation of Tang coins includes Semirechye, Ferghana, Chach, Sogdia and Northern Tokharistan, and one coin was found in Bukhara. This distribution attests to the fact that one of the most important routes of the Silk Road went through these areas, along which Chinese goods were transported to Tokharistan (through the Iron Gate Pass) and further on to India (through the Hindu Kush mountain passes – there are known findings of Tang coins in northern Afghanistan and India). One example of a traveller along this road is the Chinese monk called Xuanzang, who took the route during his pilgrimage to Buddhist shrines in India about AD 630. The importance of Tang coins is evidenced by the fact that they had a marked influence on the development of coinage in a number of dominions of the eastern and central parts of Central Asia.

Bronze coins based on Tang coins, with a square hole and a Sogdian legend, were issued by Turgeshes of Semirechye and Chach and the Turkic rulers of Semirechye, Chach and Sogdia. Similar coins were also issued by the Sogdian Ikhshids, beginning with the reign of Shishpir (AD 642–not later than AD 655) and by local princes of Penjikent and other Sogdian principalities, and also in Paikend, a merchant city at the Bukhara oasis. Bronze coins with a square hole and glyphs were produced in Otrar (south Kazakhstan), and cast bronze coins with square holes and Sogdian legends were also issued in Vakhsh – one of the possessions of Northern Tokharistan. The same coins, but with a Bactrian legend as yet undeciphered, were circulating in the Kafirnigan river valley area (Northern Tokharistan). Finds of small coins with a square hole and remnants of Bactrian legends have also been found in Old Termez.

At some point, probably in the mid-7th century, Sogdia began to issue bronze coins with a bilingual Sogdian–Chinese legend: the obverse was similar to Tang coins and included the four Chinese characters *kai yuan tong bao*; the reverse had a symbol of the Sogdian Ikhshids and a Sogdian legend reading 'divine' on the right. Similar coins have been found in Penjikent and near the Bibi-Khanum mosque in Samarkand.

Apart from wu zhu, Hou ch'uan and *kai yuan tong bao* coins, one other type of Chinese coin has also been found in Central Asia. A hoard of knife-shaped coins, possibly from the time of Emperor Wang Mang, was found near the railway station in Bishkek, Kyrgyzstan.

The influence of Chinese coins on Sogdian coinage and that of a number of other areas of Central Asia can be seen by the Sogdian word *pny* meaning 'coin' found on Turgesh coins in combination with the title 'The coin of the Sovereign of Turgesh', on Chach coins with a camel, and on coins of the Chach possession of Benaket ruled by Shaniabag. In 7th-century China the word *fen*, from which the Sogdian *pny* was derived, denoted both a weight and a monetary unit.

Coins confirm information from textual sources about periods of the most intensive political impact and, consequently, of cultural relations and trade between China and Central Asia. Thus, while diplomatic embassies from various Central Asian dominions were being sent with gifts and tributes to the court of the Celestial Empire almost annually during the Han (206 BC–AD 220) and Tang (AD 618–907) dynasties, they were very infrequent during the period of the Northern and Sui dynasties. Typically, the following phrase is often repeated in the annals of the history of the Sui dynasty and its contact with Central Asian dominions: 'In the Sui dynasty in the sixth summer of the rule of Kai-huang [AD 586], a messenger with tributes was sent, and after that there were no more embassies.' This state of affairs was a result of the weakening position of the Chinese empire in Central Asia from the second half of the 5th to the first half of the 7th century because of the rising power of the Hephthalites and the subsequent domination of the Turks, who controlled the roads leading from China to Asia.

Mirrors

Mirror. Han period. 2nd–1st centuries BC.

Apart from coins, mirrors were among the most significant objects among Chinese imports to Central Asia. Specimens of mirrors have mainly been found in the Ferghana valley, in the foothills of the Tian Shan and Alay mountains, and at the Tashkent oasis.

The earliest mirrors of the *zhaoming* style (1st century BC) have been found in the Pskent burial ground and at Vrevskaya railway station. Mirrors of the *baiju* style (1st century BC–1st century AD) were discovered at Farkhadstroi (the Farkhad hydroelectric power station) and at the Kairagach burial ground in Ferghana. Chinese mirrors found at the Isfara, Karabulak and Turatash burial sites

(Western Ferghana) as well as in the Ketmen-Tyube and Kenkol valleys date back to the 2nd–3rd centuries AD. A total of 20 complete mirrors and some fragments of Chinese mirrors have been found in the Ferghana Valley. Chinese mirrors have also been found during excavations of the Munchaktepa burial ground near the town of Pap in the Ferghana valley.

Chinese mirrors have mostly been found in Chach (Tashkent oasis) in the burial site at the Vrevskaya station, the Pskent and Jun burial sites; in Semirechye in northern Kyrgyzstan at the Kenkol burial site, near Petrovka village, Kalininskoye, and the Kyzyl-sai burial site; and in Sogdia at the Buddhist structure in the Sanzar river valley. In Northern Bactria, in Tokharistan, the earliest find (1st century BC–1st century AD) is of an arched, bronze mirror from Barattepa, Gormalitepa (fragments). Most of the mirrors come from the Han period, but some are from the Tang period (e.g. the ones found in Sanzar and Adjinatepa, among other places).

The locations where mirrors have been found delineate an area of Chinese trade interests and cultural influence: Semirechye, Ferghana, Sogdia, Northern Bactria/ Tokharistan. Outside these areas, to the west of Sogdia, no Chinese mirrors have been found, so there have been no finds in the Bukhara oasis or Khorezm.

Inscriptions

Only a few Chinese inscriptions have been found in the eastern and central parts of Central Asia. One of them comes from Munchaktepa, where a pebble measuring 6.5 x 4.5 centimetres was discovered during the construction of Farkhadstroi. On one side are two Chinese characters meaning 'gold' and 'jewel', on the other side is a schematic representation of a man with a large beard. The inscription dates back to the first centuries AD.

On Mount Mugh near Penjikent (Tajikistan), eight paper documents in Chinese were found, along with Sogdian documents. Five of the Chinese documents have Sogdian text on the reverse. One of the documents includes a date corresponding to AD 706.

More than ten Chinese inscriptions were found in the Gilgit area in the upper reaches of the Indus, in an area directly adjacent to the Pamirs. Most of them are short and contain only Chinese names, possibly of merchants, diplomats or pilgrims passing through the region. One inscription is longer, with 12 Chinese characters conveying a message about Gu Wei-long, an envoy of the 'Great Wei', heading for the dominion of Mi-mi. Although two Wei dynasties are known of in Chinese history, the Cao Wei (AD 220–265) and the Northern Wei (AD 386–534), scholars believe that this embassy may have been sent from China between AD 443 and 453.

Mi-mi is the Sogdian dominion of Maimurgh, located south-west of Samarkand. Thus, the Chinese envoy mentioned in the inscription was heading for Sogdia, via a circuitous route through the Wakhan Corridor and probably going further through the Iron Gate (Derbent), through which the main route connecting Tokharistan with Sogdia passed. K. Jettmar and the Chinese scholar Ma Yong believed that such a circuit was chosen by the Chinese embassy because the direct routes from China through Xinjiang to Central Asia were probably blocked by nomads, possibly Hephthalites, who were active in the area at the time.

Silk fabrics and other objects

Silk fabrics made in China itself have been found at a number of sites of historical and cultural significance. Most of the finds come from the Tang period of the 7th–8th centuries AD and possibly from an earlier period.

The earliest find is probably from the 1st century BC–1st century AD. It consists of fragments of silk of Chinese origin found at Khalchayan (Northern Bactria), although some scholars believe classifying these as Chinese is not justified. The remaining finds of silk date back to early medieval times. Some of these were found in Northern Tokharistan: four fragments at the Bittepa burial ground, one in a mound in Old Termez, and one in Balalyktepa.

The fragments from the burial site of Bittepa (7th–8th century AD) are of a type of damask silk, which was exported in large quantities from China to the Western Regions in the early medieval period via the Silk Road. Chinese silks (plain, damask and multicoloured) have also been found on Mount Mugh in Sogdia, and in Ferghana during excavations of the Munchaktepa burial ground (5th–8th centuries AD), where the faces of the dead were covered with particularly valuable Chinese silk. Such face coverings made of Chinese silk have also been found at the Karabulak burial site in Southern Ferghana, and in Semirechye, at the Kenkol burial site.

The small quantity of Chinese silks found in the eastern and central parts of Central Asia can be explained by the fact that textiles are generally poorly preserved in the kinds of environmental conditions typical for Central Asia. It does not suggest that imports of silk from China were limited. The manufacture of silk in Central Asia itself only began in the 5th–6th centuries AD, although we cannot rule out that it took place earlier in Bactria/Tokharistan, as suggested by discoveries of silk objects at Tilyatepa (Southern Bactria) and Kampyrtepa (Northern Bactria) that are probably of local origin.

Lacquer tables and bowls are among other items imported from China that have been found. Fragments of such items have been found frequently in burials from the first centuries AD in the valleys of the Chu and Talas rivers of Semirechye. Nomadic peoples in Central Asia are known to have made objects, especially jewellery, based on and heavily influenced by objects imported from China.

The bronze handle of a small vessel in the form of a coiled dragon was found in a layer from the first half of the 2nd century AD at the citadel of Kampyrtepa, 30 kilometres to the west of Termez. Such handles were often used to decorate Chinese vessels.

A glazed ceramic drinking horn (*rhyton*) in the shape of a bull's head was found at the Khanabadtepa site located on the south-eastern outskirts of Tashkent. Its style and workmanship are typical of Tang art.

Among objects mostly found in eastern Central Asia are items such as a copper apothecary spoon, a Chinese dish, a copper lid from a vessel with a Chinese inscription, and a terracotta head of a Chinese man with high cheekbones, slanting eyes and a drooping moustache. He is wearing a cap with a cord, a kind of headdress characteristic of the Tang period in China.

Jade objects

A mineral mined in the mountains, light green jade was widely used in ancient times by many peoples around the world to make different kinds of tools and household objects, as well as objects used for ritual and magical purposes. Jade was believed to have special properties that could help in various situations, including childbirth and kidney trouble. It is no coincidence that its name was derived from the Greek *nephros* meaning 'kidney'.

Jade was especially prized in ancient and medieval China. However, there are no deposits of nephrite in China, or in eastern Central Asia. Khotan, situated on one of the routes of the Silk Road, had always been the main centre for its extraction and trade. Dark green and white jade was mined from the beds of two rivers, which merged at Khotan before flowing into the Tarim. Some jade was apparently finished locally in Khotan, but it was usually exported in its raw, unprocessed form. Jade was also highly valued in Central Asia, where it probably also arrived from Khotan. It is widely known that Timur's tomb in Gur-Emir was made of two large slabs of jade that were brought to Samarkand from the upper reaches of the Ili river on the orders of Ulugbek after his campaigns against the Mongol invaders in 1425. However, items of jade are rarely found on the territory of Central Asia, and most of them are items of jewellery dating back to the early and late medieval periods.

The earliest item of jade found in Central Asia is an article from a Chust site, dating from the beginning of the 1st millennium BC. This is also the earliest evidence of links between this region and Eastern Turkestan (present-day Xinjiang).

An oval seal stone with an image of a yak made of jade dating from the Achaemenid period was found in the ruins of a burial ground of the Kenkol type in the upper reaches of the Sokh river (in Ferghana). A jade bowl dating back to the period from the 2nd century BC to the 1st century AD was found in the Berkarin burial ground in Kyrgyzstan. There have been two finds of jade objects outside Ferghana and Semirechye: the hilt of an iron dagger and the detail on the fastening of a belt. They were found in barrow No. 2 of the Orlat burial mound at the site of Kurgantepa, located north of the town of Ishtykhan in Samarkand region, together with some bone plates (2nd–1st centuries BC). The head of a jade object with an image of a wolf dragon (3rd–2nd centuries BC) was found at Takht-i Sangin.

A pre-revolutionary museum in Tashkent contains a number of jade items but there are no dates and almost no information about where they were found. Among them are a seal and buckle of cream jade, a white jade ring, a greenish jade ring (found at the site of Eski-Akhsi, Chust district), two more rings, a seal without an inscription, a seal with a flower, a quadrangular seal with an inscription, and another seal (found at the site of Afrasiab). It is believed that some of these items date to the pre-Islamic period.

Archaeological data has substantially supplemented the information provided by Chinese chronicles about Chinese imports to the Western Regions. Although these texts provide detailed lists of goods and gifts exported to China from the Western Regions, they say almost nothing about the reverse process, and only provide information about Chinese envoys to the regions and the time of their sojourns.

The authors of the Chinese chronicles say nothing about the introduction of Chinese coins to the Western Regions and their subsequent influence on the coinage of these regions. The role and significance of Chinese money, especially from the Han period, in the history of money and commodity relations in this region has still not been sufficiently studied.

For example, it is thought that in the first centuries AD no money and commodity relations existed in Ferghana in the first centuries AD – the main area where Han coins penetrated Central Asia at that time – but that wu zhu coins were used similarly to Charon's oboli or as simple ornaments. This view is based on the preponderance of finds of Chinese wu zhu coins in burial sites. However, recent finds in habitation layers of archaeological sites, as well as a number of other considerations, raise questions about the validity of this hypothesis. In the last centuries BC to the first centuries AD,

Ferghana was a rich agricultural region with a well-developed economy, agriculture and crafts, and a significant number of cities, all recorded by Zhang Qian when he visited the region in the second half of the 2nd century BC. It was from Ferghana that the Chinese first brought crops such as alfalfa and grapes – and obtained the secrets of wine production – and the famous breed of heavenly horses.

Given these circumstances it is unlikely that only barter was used for trade in Ferghana. Unlike the other Central Asian regions – such as Bactria, Sogdia, Khorezm and Margiana – Ferghana had no coins of its own, and lay within the territory of Chinese money circulation using wu zhu coins as a unit of currency. Thus it is not inconceivable that Ferghana later produced its own coins based on Chinese coins – some examples of wu zhu coins found there do not give the impression of being genuine. Tang coins played an even more significant role. Along with Byzantine and Sassanian coins, they were an international currency used for trade on the Silk Road, as evidenced by discoveries of these coins far from their original place of issue. Archaeological data and textual sources indicate that the eastern and central regions of Central Asia were an area of Chinese political and commercial interest, while further to the west, Chinese influence, if any, was negligible. This was for political reasons. The western parts of Central Asia were either directly part of the Parthian state or were under its influence. The Parthians strictly guarded their trading interests, and prevented both Chinese goods from entering the West, and Roman ones from going to the East. Nevertheless, there were still many opportunities for exchanges between East and West.

4.8

ANCIENT KOREA AND ANCIENT CENTRAL ASIA

THE DISCOVERY IN 1965 OF WALL PAINTINGS OF GREAT SIGNIFICANCE TO scholarship in the palace at the site of Afrasiab made it possible to establish that historical and cultural ties had existed between ancient Korea (the Goguryeo state) and Sogdia. In the paintings, featuring many different figures and depicting embassies from many countries, L.I. Albaum, the first scholar to examine the murals, identified two of the figures as representatives from the ancient state of Goguryeo. They are portrayed wearing a distinctive headdress decorated with a plume of two feathers. An inscription of several lines on the robe of one of the figures was deciphered by V.A. Livshits, and suggests that the various figures in the wall paintings are ambassadors to the Sogdian Ikhshid Varkhuman, who, according to O.I. Smirnova, ruled in the period AD 650 or 655 until 696 at the latest. Several scholars, including B.I. Marshak, A.M. Belenitsky, A.M. Mode, Jan Bogin and S. Antonini among others, subsequently gave further interpretations of the paintings. A young Japanese scholar, E. Kageyama, pointed out that very similar images of Korean ambassadors can be found in 12 paintings in the Mogao cave temples in Dunhuang, which along with other paintings, are the narrative illustrations of the *Vimalakirti-nirdesa sutra*. A similar image of a Korean ambassador reproduced on the walls of Crown Prince Zhanghuai Li Xian's tomb led Kageyama to believe that all these representations follow a typical style of painting in the Chinese capital. For this reason, Kageyama suggested that the depictions of the Korean ambassadors in the paintings at Afrasiab are not evidence of a visit by them to Samarkand in the second half of the 7th century AD, but instead reflect a style of Chinese art. It should be noted, to her credit, that Kageyama has proposed this hypothesis with due caution ('if this argument is right') as there is no evidence to refute the claim that these paintings do indeed depict the actual presence of Korean ambassadors in Samarkand where, as I have suggested, they came with other ambassadors for the coronation of the Ikhshid Varkhuman. In this light, I would

Mural depicting Korean ambassadors. Afrasiab.

like now to turn to direct or indirect evidence, albeit limited, of contacts between the ancient regions of Central Asia and Korea.

The earliest evidence of this contact is most likely the bronze statuette of a warrior wearing a distinctive Athenian helmet found in southern Korea, dating from the 6th to 5th centuries BC. It is possible that the statuette came to Korea from Central Asia, where Hellenistic artefacts from this early period were found in the Amu Darya hoard (the Oxus Treasure) and where the first Greek settlement, of the Branchidae, emerged under the Achaemenid king Xerxes (486–465 BC). Finds in Korea dating from the 5th–6th centuries AD include glass vessels of Roman origin unearthed during the excavation of a burial site in Gwangju, South Korea. Korean scholars believe that they were made in the Eastern Mediterranean or in southern Germany and most likely came to Korea along one of the routes of the Silk Road crossing Central Asia. In the catalogue of a collection of masterpieces of ancient art from the National Museum of History in Seoul, which mainly consists of objects recovered by the Otani Japanese expedition led by Count Ōtani Kōzui in Xinjiang (1902–04), is a semi-spherical silver bowl from the 5th–6th centuries AD found in a burial site in Gwangju. The outer surface of the bowl is divided into three bands edged by concentric circles. In the upper band is a double row of palmettes, with similar palmettes decorating the lower band or base. The middle of the vessel is divided into roundels formed by twisted lines, and there is a scene showing an animal being chased, featuring dogs, birds and hares. One of the roundels contains an image of a reclining man wearing trousers and a shirt girded by a belt with a round buckle. The man's head is turned back unnaturally in relation to his torso. He has a straight nose, large eyes and a tall headdress. His left hand is raised and his right hand is resting on his elbow.

In terms of the style of depicting human figures and animals and the nature of the ornamentation, this bowl has many similarities with the paintings from Penjikent and images found on Sogdian vessels. In all likelihood, the bowl was made in Sogdia, from where it was transported through numerous Sogdian colonies along the routes of the Silk Road all the way to the capital of China, Chang'an, and possibly further to Korea. Given the prominent role of Sogdians in trade along the routes of the Silk Road, there is nothing extraordinary about the presence of Sogdian silver in the Far East. For instance, a silver bowl with a Sogdian inscription was found at a burial site near Canton on the border with Vietnam. The inscription was deciphered by Yotaka Yoshida and is evidence that the vessel belonged to the ruler of Chach (Tashkent oasis).

Professor Jeong Su-il, a well-known Korean scholar, has shown me a fax sent to him by a Korean journalist with a picture of a coin found near Vladivostok, which is near Korea. The coin belongs to a group of so-called imitation Bukharkhudat coins bearing the name of Caliph al-Mahdi (reigned AD 775–785), which were issued by Arab governors, modelled on the coins of rulers of Bukhara (Bukharkhudat), who had in turn imitated the Sassanian coins of Varahran (Bahran) V. The obverse of the coins has an image of Bukharkhudat encircled by a Sogdian inscription reading 'Ruler – King of Bukhara'. Coins from the time of al-Mahdi include a short legend in Arabic with the name of the ruler appearing behind the ruler's head. Bukharkhudat coins bearing the names of Harun al-Rashid and Suleiman have also been found. The discovery of imitation Bukharkhudat coins in the Far East is particularly interesting because it is the first time a coin of this type has been found so far from where it was minted. Moreover, there have been discoveries of objects of Sogdian origin, including those with Sogdian inscriptions, in Transbaikalia, Altai and Western Siberia.

Chinese textual sources provide some information on visits by persons of Korean origin to Central Asia. One of them is the Buddhist pilgrim, the monk Hyecho, who, like Xuanzang (albeit a century later), visited Sogdia, Chach and Huttal in AD 723 and provided interesting descriptions of these and neighbouring regions, noting the presence of Buddhist monuments there.

Buddhism made its way to Korea in the 6th century AD via China. Buddhist missionary monks from Sogdia, Tokharistan, Bactria and Parthia played an important role in its establishment here. Consequently, as far as Central Asian and Korean contacts are concerned, we may also note an indirect influence of Central

Asian Buddhism on the formation of this religion in Korea, in the states of Goguryeo and Silla.

Another person of Korean descent connected directly with the history of Central Asia, and indeed at one of its most pivotal moments, is Gao Xianzhi. He was an assistant to the governor of the Western Regions, the name given to Xinjiang and Central Asia by the Chinese. In AD 747 Gao Xianzhi undertook a campaign to Bolu (Tibet), and the following year he intervened in a conflict between the rulers of Chach (Tashkent) and Ferghana on behalf of the latter and invaded Chach with the Chinese army. In AD 749, he arrested the ruler of Chach and sent him to China, where he was executed.

After this, the son of the executed ruler turned to the Arabs for help. By the middle of the 8th century, the Arabs controlled almost the entire territory of Central Asia. By this time, all the actions of the Arabs in Central Asia were under the command of Abu Muslim, who headed the anti-Umayyad movement and was in fact instrumental in bringing to power a new dynasty in the Caliphate, the Abbasids.

Arab troops led by Ziyad ibn Salih were sent to fight the Chinese army led by Gao Xianzhi. A decisive battle between them took place at the Talas river near the city of Dzhambul (south Kazakhstan). The Chinese were defeated and the remnants of the army fled to China. The Battle of Talas (AD 751) was an event of great historical importance. On the one hand, it effectively put an end to Chinese encroachments into the eastern and central parts of Central Asia, which the Chinese had been striving to control for almost a millennium. On the other hand, it signalled the ultimate political and administrative control of the Arab caliphs in the region and the triumph of Islam. As fate would have it, it was a Korean military leader, Gao Xianzhi, who had a part to play in it.

The above information, although fragmentary, is nonetheless connected, and testifies to the longstanding and ancient cultural ties between Uzbekistan and Korea, to the direct presence of Koreans in Central Asia in the early medieval period, and possibly to the presence of Sogdians in Korea.

ENDNOTES

1 Turfan fragment M 5569. Translation from D.M. Gwynn, *Christianity in the Later Roman Empire: A Sourcebook* (London, 2014), p. 178.

2 Translation from *Through the Jade Gate to Rome: A Study of the Silk Routes during the Later Han Dynasty, 1st to 2nd Centuries CE,* trans. and annotated by John E. Hill (Charleston, SC, 2009).

3 Translation by J. J. L. Duyvendak cited and emended by Homer H. Dubs in 'A Military Contact between Chinese and Romans in 36 BC', *T'oung Pao,* 2nd Series, 36:1 (1940), pp. 64–80 (at p. 64 and n. 4).

4 Translation from Joseph Needham (ed.), *Science and Civilisation in China,* vol. 4, pt 1 (Cambridge, 1964), p. 108.

5 From 'Aban Yasht (Hymn to the Waters)', trans. James Darmesteter, in *Sacred Books of the East,* 23, ed. Max Müller (Oxford, 1883), p. 101.

6 Ban Gu, *China in Central Asia: The Early Stage: 125 BC – AD 23. An Annotated Translation of Chapters 61 and 96 of* The History of the Former Han Dynasty, publication et annotation A.F.P. Hulsewé (Leiden, 1979), p. 74.

7 Translation from *The Western Regions according to the Hou Han Shu,* The *Xiyu juan,* 'Chapter on the Western Regions', from *Hou Han Shu* 88, trans. by John E. Hill. Available online at https://depts.washington.edu/silkroad/texts/hhshu/hou_han_shu.html#sec11 [last accessed 16 September 2021].

BIBLIOGRAPHY

Part I: Civilisations

Аскаров А.А. Новые подходы к проблеме этногенеза тюркоязычных народов Центральной Азии.//Независимость и история: новые подходы к изучению истории Узбекистана. Ташкент, 1997.

Ахмад ибн Йахйа ибн Джабир ал-Балазури. Завоевание Хорасана (Извлечение из сочинения «Футух ал-булдан»)/Перевод с арабского, предисловие, комментарий и указатели Г. Гоибова. Душанбе, 1987.

Ахмедов Б.А. История Балха (XVI – первая половина XVIII в.). Ташкент, 1982.

Ахмедов Б.А. Значение письменных памятников в изучении этнической истории узбеков.//Материалы к этнической истории населения Средней Азии. Ташкент, 1986.

Бартольд В.В. Очерк истории Семиречья. Фрунзе, 1943.

Бартольд В.В. Туркестан в эпоху монгольского нашествия.//В. В. Бартольд. Сочинения. Т. 1. М., 1963.

Бичурин Н.Я. Собрание сведений о народах, обитавших в Средней Азии в древние времена. Т. 2. М.; Л., 1950.

Гамкрелидзе Т.В., Иванов В.В. Первые индоевропейцы в истории: предки тохар в древней Передней Азии.// ВДИ, 1989, № 1.

Гафуров Б.Г. Таджики. М., 1972.

Гоибов Г. Ранние походы арабов в Среднюю Азию (644–704 гг.). Душанбе, 1989.

Гумилев Л.Н. Древние тюрки. М., 1967.

Иванов В.В. Тохары.//Восточный Туркестан в древности и раннем средневековье. М., 1992.

История ат-Табари. Ташкент, 1987.

Калалы-гыр 2. Культовый центр в Древнем Хорезме (IV – II вв. до н.э.). М., 2004.

Кляшторный С.Г. Древнетюркские рунические памятники как источник по истории Средней Азии. М., 1964.

Литвинский Б.А. Борьба народов Средней Азии против греко-македонских захватчиков.//История таджикского народа. Т. 1. М., 1963.

Литвинский Б.А. Индийский фактор в цивилизации Центральной Азии.// Азия – диалог цивилизаций. М., 1996.

Литвинский Б.А., Соловьев В.С. Средневековая культура Тохаристана. М., 1985.

Массон В.М. Алтын-депе.//Труды ЮТАКЭ. Т. 18. Л., 1981.

Массон В.М. Средняя Азия в эпоху раннего железа: культурная и социально-экономическая динамика.//Раннежелезный век Средней Азии и Индии: Тез. докл. Ашхабад, 1984.

Рашид ад-Дин. Сборник летописей. Т. 1. М.; Л., 1960.

Ртвеладзе Э.В. Бактрийские города с индоарийскими названиями.//Города Центральной Азии на Шелковом пути. Самарканд, 1994.

Ртвеладзе Э.В. К истории евреев-иудаистов в Средней Азии (домусульманский период).// Верования и культы домусульманской Средней Азии. Тез. докл. М., 1997.

Ртвеладзе Э.В. Этюд по исторической географии Бактрии и Согдианы во время похода Александра Македонского (о местонахождении города Бранхидов).//ВДИ, 2000, № 4.

Ртвеладзе Э.В. К вопросу о субстратном языке юга Средней Азии (III – II тыс. до н.э.) // Тарих, мустақиллик, миллий ғоя. Ташкент, 2001.

Ртвеладзе Э.В., Лившиц В.А. Памятники древней письменности. Ташкент, 1985.

Ртвеладзе Э.В., Нефедов Н. Уникальная серебряная монета греческого правителя из Ер-Кургана (Южного Согда).//НЦА. Вып. 1. Ташкент, 1995.

Толстова Л. С. Исторические предания Южного Приаралья: к истории ранних этнокультурных связей народов Арало-Каспийского региона. М., 1984.

Толстов С.П. Древний Хорезм. Опыт историко-археологического исследования. М., 1948.

Ходжайов Т.К. Антропологический состав населения эпохи бронзы Сапаллитепа. Ташкент, 1977.

Ходжайов Т.К. Краткие итоги изучения антропологии Средней Азии в связи с проблемами этногенеза узбекского народа.// Материалы к этнической истории населения Средней Азии. Ташкент, 1986.

Bernard P. 'Fouilles d'Aï-Khanoum (Afghanistan). Campagnes de 1972 et 1973', *CRAI* (1974).

Fouilles de Shortugaï recherches, ed. H.-P. Francfort (Paris, 1989).

Gibb H.A.R. *The Arab Conquests in Central Asia* (London, 1923).

Henning W.B. 'The Inscriptions of Tang-i Azao', *BSOAS*, vol. 20, issue 1 (1957).

Henning W.B. 'The First Indo-Europeans in History' in *Society and History: Essays in Honour of Karl August Wittfogel* (The Hague, 1978).

Kelvan A. 'Hebrew Inscription in Ossuaries Found in Central Asia', *Qadmomiyyot*, vol. 12 (1979).

Livshits V.A., Usmanova Z.I. 'New Parthian Inscriptions from Old Merv', *Irano-Judaica*, vol. 3 (1994).

Margoliouth D. 'An Early Judeo-Persian Document from Khotan in the Stein Collection, with Other Early Persian Documents', *JRAS*, vol. 35, issue 4 (1903).

Minorsky V.F. 'A Greek Crossing on the Oxus', *BSOAS*, vol. 30, pt. 1 (1967).

Mukherjee B.N. *An Agrippan Source. A Study in Indo-Parthian History* (Kolkata, 1969).

Mukherjee B.N. 'An Inscribed Gem from Indo-Iranian Borderland', *BAI*, n.s., vol. 7 (1993).

Narain A.K. *On the 'First' Indo-Europeans: The Tokharian-Yuezhi and Their Chinese Homeland* (Bloomington, IN, 1987).

Neusner J. 'Jews in Iran' in *Cambridge History of Iran*, vol. 3 (Cambridge, 1983).

Rtveladze E.V. 'Découvertes en numismatique et épigraphie gréco-bactriennes à Kampyr-Tepe (Bactriane du nord)', *RN*, 6th series, vol. 150 (1995).

Shaked S. *Le Satrape de Bactriane et son gouvernour, Documents araméens du IV*[e] *s. avant notre ère provenant de Bactriane* (Paris, 2004).

Watters T. *On Yuan Chwang's Travels in India, 629–645 AD*, Oriental Translation Fund, n.s., vol. 14 (London, 1904).

Zand M. 'Bukharan Jews' in *Encyclopaedia Iranica*, vol. 4, fasc. 5 (London, 1989).

Part II: States

Абаев В.И. Надпись Дария I о сооружении дворца в Сузе.// Иранские языки. М. – Л., 1945.

Баженов Л. В. Древние авторы о Средней Азии (VI в. до н. э. – III в. н. э.). Хрестоматия / Под ред. Л. В. Баженова. Ташкент, 1940.

Беленицкий А.М. Зооморфные троны в изобразительном искусстве Средней Азии.//Известия отделения общественных наук АН ТССР, Вып. 1. Душанбе, 1962.

Бернштам А.Н. Проблемы древней истории и этногенеза Южного Казахстана.//Известия АН КазССР, серия археологическая, 1949, № 67. Вып. 2.

Бикерман Э. Государство Селевкидов. М., 1985.

Бирюков Д.В. У истоков денежного обращения Средней Азии (К проблеме ахеменидского влияния на генезис монетной формы денег в Среднеазиатском регионе).//НЦА. Вып. 1. Ташкент, 1995.

Бичурин Н.Я. Собрание сведений о народах, обитавших в Средней Азии в древние времена. Т. 2. М.; Л., 1950.

Вайнберг Б.Н. Некоторые вопросы истории Тохаристана в IV–V вв. (в связи с запустением Кара-тепе).// Буддийский культовый центр Кара-тепе в Старом Термезе. М., 1972.

Вайнберг Б.И. Монеты древнего Хорезма. М., 1977.

Вельгус В.А. Известия о странах и народах Африки и морские связи в бассейнах Тихого и Индийского океанов. М., 1978.

Воробьева-Десятовская М.И. Надписи письмом кхароштхи на золотых предметах из Дальверзин-тепе.// ВДИ, 1976, № 1.

Гафуров Б.Г. История таджикского народа. В кратком изложении. Т. 1. М., 1952.

Горбунова Н., Ивочкина Н. Монеты Ушу из могильников Ферганы.//СГЭ. Вып. 53. Л, 1988.

Грантовский Э.А. Ранняя история иранских племен Передней Азии. М., 1970.

Григорьев В.В. Поход Александра Великого в Западный Туркестан // ЖМНП. Ч. CCLXVII. 1881.

Давидович Е. А. Первый клад тетрадрахм Кушанца «Герая» // ВДИ, 1976, № 4.

Дандамаев М.А., Луконин В.Г. Культура и экономика древнего Ирана. М., 1980.

Довутов Д. Драхма Селевка с городища Шахри Мунк.// НЦА. Вып. 2. Ташкент, 1997.

Дьяконов И.М. История Мидии. М., 1956.

Дьяконов И.М. Языки древней Передней Азии. М., 1967.

Дьяконов И.М. Восточный Иран до Кира (К возможности новых постановок вопроса).//История иранского государства и культуры. М., 1971.

Дьяконов И.М., Дьяконов М.М, Лившиц В.А., Массон М.Е. Налоговые парфянские документы II века до н. э. из Нисы.//Материалы ЮТАКЭ. Вып. 2. М. – Л., 1951.

Дьяконов И.М., Зеймаль Е.В. Правитель Парфии Андрагор и его монеты.// ВДИ, 1988, № 4.

Дьяконов М.М. Сложение классового общества в Северной Бактрии.//СА, 1954, № 19.

Дьяконов М.М. Очерки истории древнего Ирана. М., 1961.

Живопись и скульптура Таджикистана. Л., 1984.

Зеймаль Е.В. Раннесогдийские монеты с изображением Геракла и Зевса.//СГЭ. Вып. 37. Л., 1973.

Зеймаль Е.В. «Варварские подражания» как исторический источник.//СГЭ. Вып. 40. Л., 1975.

Зеймаль Е.В. Политическая история древней Трансоксианы по нумизматическим данным.//Культура Востока. Древность и раннее средневековье. Л., 1978.

Зеймаль Е.В. Амударьинский клад: Каталог выставки. Л., 1979.

Зеймаль Е.В. Древние монеты Таджикистана. Душанбе, 1983.

Зеймаль Е.В. Начальный этап денежного обращения древней Трансоксианы.// Средняя Азия, Кавказ и зарубежный Восток в древности. М., 1983.

Зеймаль Е.В. Подражания оболам Евкратида.//Литвинский Б.А., Седов А.В. Культы и ритуалы Кушанской Бактрии. М., 1984.

Зограф А.Н. Монеты «Герая». Ташкент, 1937.

Зограф А.Н. Античные монеты.//МИА, 1951, № 16.

Зуев Ю.А. К вопросу о взаимоотношениях усуней и канцзюй с гуннами и Китаем в I в. до н.э.// Известия АН КазССР, серия истории, экономики и права, вып. 2, 1957.

История таджикского народа. Т. 1-2. М., 1963–64.

Кляшторный С.Г. Древнетюркские рунические памятники как источник по истории Средней Азии. М., 1964.

Культура и искусство древнего Узбекистана. Каталог выставки. Т. 1-2. М., 1991.

Левина Л.М. Древнехорезмийский памятник – Елхарас. М., 2001.

Левушкина С.В. Химический состав металла монет из Северной Бактрии.//Ртвеладзе Э.В., Пидаев Ш.Р. Каталог древних монет Южного Узбекистана. Ташкент, 1981.

Лившиц В.А. Общество Авесты.// История таджикского народа. Т. 1. М., 1963.

Лившиц В.А. К открытию бактрийских надписей на Кара-тепе.//Буддийские пещеры Кара-тепе в Старом Термезе. М., 1969.

Лившиц В.А. Документы из дворца Топрак-кала.//Топрак-Кала. Дворец. Труды ХАЭЭ, Т. 14. М., 1984.

Лившиц В.А., Кругликова И.Т. Фрагменты бактрийской монументальной надписи из Дильберджина.// Древняя Бактрия. Материалы Советско-Афганской археологической экспедиции. Вып. 2. М., 1979.

Лившиц В.А., Луконин В.Г. Среднеперсидские и согдийские надписи на серебряных сосудах.// ВДИ, 1964, № 3.

Лившиц В.А., Никитин А.Б. Ранний пехлевийский острак из буддийского храма в Дальверзин-тепе// ВДИ, 1990, № 4.

Литвинский Б.А. Орудия труда и утварь из могильников Западной Ферганы. М., 1978.

Литвинский Б.А., Седов А.В. Тепаи-шах (Культура и связи кушанской Бактрии). М., 1983.

Луконин В.Г. Культура Сасанидского Ирана. Иран в III–V вв. Очерки по истории культуры. М., 1969.

Малявкин А.Г. Танские хроники о государствах Центральной Азии. Новосибирск, 1989.

Мамбетуллаев М. Хум с городища Большая Айбуйир-кала с древнейшей надписью в Средней Азии.//Вестник Каракалпакского филиала АН УзССР. № 1. Нукус, 1979.

Массон В.М. Денежное хозяйство древней Средней Азии по нумизматическим данным.//ВДИ, 1955, № 2.

Массон В.М. Древнебактрийские монеты, чеканенные по типу тетрадрахм Гелиокла.//ЭВ. 1956. Вып. 11.

Массон В.М. Еще раз о геродотовой реке Акес.//Эллинистический Ближний Восток, Византия и Иран. История и филология. М., 1967.

Массон В.М., Ромодин В.А. История Афганистана. Т. 1. М., 1964.

Массон М.Е. Редкая среднеазиатская монета из собрания Государственного Эрмитажа.//ВДИ, 1953, № 3.

Пичикян И.Р. Культура Бактрии (ахеменидский и эллинистический периоды). М., 1991.

Пугаченкова Г.А. Три ахеменидские геммы из собрания Музея истории УзССР.//Труды Музея истории УзССР, 1956, вып. 3.

Пугаченкова Г.А. Халчаян. К проблеме художественной культуры Северной Бактрии. Ташкент, 1966.

Пугаченкова Г.А. Скульптура Халчаяна. М., 1971.

Пугаченкова Г.А. К открытию надписей кхароштхи на золотых предметах Дальверзинского клада.//ВДИ, 1976, № 1.

Пугаченкова Г.А. Еще о халчаянской скульптуре.//Центральная Азия. Новые памятники письменности и искусства. М., 1987.

Пугаченкова Г.А. Интерпретация одного из персонажей на Биянайманском оссуарии.//ИМКУ. Вып. 27. Самарканд, 1996.

Пугаченкова Г.А., Ремпель Л.И. Очерки искусства Средней Азии. М., 1982.

Пугаченкова Г.А., Ртвеладзе Э.В. и др. Дальверзинтепе – кушанский город на юге Узбекистана. Ташкент, 1978.

Пугаченкова Г.А., Ртвеладзе Э.В. Северная Бактрия – Тохаристан. Очерки истории и культуры. Ташкент, 1990.

Пьянков И.М. Сведения Ктесия о владениях Бардии на востоке Ирана.//ВДИ, 1961, № 4.

Пьянков И.В. Средняя Азия в известиях античного историка Ктесия (текст, перевод, примечания). Душанбе, 1975.

Пьянков И.В. Древнейшие государственные образования

Средней Азии (Опыт исторической реконструкции).//Древние цивилизации Евразии. История и культура. М., 2001.

Рапэн К. Эллинистическая сокровищница Ай-Ханум.//Городская культура Бактрии – Тохаристана и Согда. Ташкент, 1987.

Ртвеладзе Э.В. Рец. на кн.: Б. Я. Ставиский. Кушанская Бактрия: проблемы истории и культуры. М., 1977.//ВДИ, 1981, № 2.

Ртвеладзе Э.В. Бронзовый кинжал из Южного Узбекистана (Вахшувар).// СА, 1981, № 1.

Ртвеладзе Э.В. Денежное обращение в Северо-Западном Тохаристане в раннем средневековье.//Городская культура Бактрии – Тохаристана и Согда. Ташкент, 1987.

Ртвеладзе Э.В. Селевкидские монеты из Кампыртепа.// ОНУ, 1989, № 2.

Ртвеладзе Э.В. Из недавних открытий Узбекистанской искусствоведческой экспедиции (УзИскЭ) в Северной Бактрии – Тохаристане.//ВДИ, 1990, № 4.

Ртвеладзе Э.В. Модели генезиса монетной чеканки в среднеазиатском междуречье.//На среднеазиатских трассах Великого шелкового пути. Очерки истории и культуры. Ташкент, 1990.

Ртвеладзе Э.В. К интерпретации слов «Σαυαβ» и «Αυτειχ» на тетрадрахмах Херайя/Хиайя.//НЦА. Вып. 2. Ташкент, 1997.

Ртвеладзе Э.В. Бухара в древности и раннем средневековье.//Бухара. Жемчужина Востока. Ташкент, 1997.

Ртвеладзе Э.В. Новые данные к истории государства Кушан.//ОНУ, 1997, № 5.

Ртвеладзе Э.В. Китайский импорт в Центральную Азию в домусульманский период (по археологическим данным).// Санъатшунослик масалалари. Илмий мақолалар тўплами. Ташкент,1998.

Ртвеладзе Э.В. Великий шелковый путь. Ташкент, 1999.

Ртвеладзе Э.В. Эволюция художественной культуры и развитие государственности в Узбекистане (ранняя стадия).//Санъат, 1999, № 1.

Ртвеладзе Э.В. К истории становления Кушанского государства в Бактрии и Гандахаре.//Индия и Центральная Азия (доисламский период). Ташкент, 2000.

Ртвеладзе Э.В. Древние и раннесредневековые монеты историко-культурных областей Узбекистана. Т. 1. Ташкент, 2002.

Ртвеладзе Э.В. Александр Македонский в Бактрии и Согдиане. Ташкент, 2002.

Ртвеладзе Э.В. Монеты Кеша (Киша) III–II вв. до н. э. – VIII в. н. э.//ОНУ, 2002, № 6.

Ртвеладзе Э.В., Лившиц В.А. Памятники древней письменности. Ташкент, 1985.

Ртвеладзе Э.В., Мусакаева А.А. К истории денежного обращения в Западном Согде (Клад подражаний тетрадрахмам Евтидема из Бухары).// ОНУ, 1986, № 6.

Ртвеладзе Э.В., Пидаев Ш.Р. Каталог древних монет Южного Узбекистана. Ташкент, 1981.

Ртвеладзе Э.В., Саидов А.Х. Дипломатия стран Центральной Азии в древности (I в. до н. э. – V в. н. э.).//Московский журнал международного права, 1999, № 1.

Смирнова О.И. Заметки о среднеазиатской титулатуре (по монетным данным).//ЭВ, 1961, № 14.

Смирнова О.И. Каталог монет с городища Пенджикент (материалы 1949–1956 гг.). М., 1963.

Смирнова О.И. Очерки из истории Согда. М., 1970.

Ставиский Б.Я. Кушанская Бактрия: проблемы истории и культуры. М., 1977.

Ставиский Б.Я. Заметки об Амударьинском кладе.//Искусство Востока и античности. М., 1977.

Тарн В. Эллинистическая цивилизация. М., 1949.

Толстов С.П. Древний Хорезм. Опыт историко-археологического исследования. М., 1948.

Толстов С.П. По следам древнехорезмийской цивилизации. М.; Л., 1948.

Тургунов Б.А., Ртвеладзе Э.В,, Лившиц В.А. Открытие бактрийской монументальной надписи в Айртаме (Предварительное сообщение).// ОНУ, 1981, № 3.

Штейн В.М. Экономические и культурные связи между Китаем и Индией в древности. М., 1960.

Antiquities of Southern Uzbekistan (Sōka, 1991).

Aus den Schatzkammern Eurasiens Meisterwerke antiker Kunst, exh. cat., Kunsthaus Zürich, 29 January – 2 May 1993 (Zurich, 1993).

Bagchi P.C. *India and Central Asia* (Kolkata, 1955).

Bailey H.W. 'Languages of the Saka', in Spuler et al. (eds), *Handbuch der Orientalistik*, sect. 1, vol. 4: Iranstik, 1: Linguistik (Leiden and Cologne, 1958).

Bellinger A.R. 'The Coins from the Treasure of the Oxus' in *American Numismatic Society: Museum Notes*, vol. 10 (New York, 1962).

Bernard P. 'Fouilles d'Aï Khanoum. IV: Les monnaies hors trésors', *Questions d'histoire gréco-bactrienne* (Paris, 1985).

Bernard P., Rapin C. 'Un parchemin gréco-bactrien d'une collection privée', *CRAI*, vol. 138, no. 1 (1994).

Bopearachchi O. *Monnaies Gréco-Bactriennes et Indo-Grecques: Catalogue raisonné* (Paris, 1991).

Chavannes E. 'Les pays d'occident d'après le Wei lio', *T'oung Pao*, 2nd series, vol. 6 (Leiden and Boston, MA, 1905).

Cribb J. 'The "Heraus" Coins: Their Attribution to the Kushan King Kujula Kadphises, c. AD 30–80' in *Essays in Honour of Robert Carson and Kenneth Jenkins* (London, 1993).

Cunningham A. 'Coins of the Kushâns, or Great Yue-ti', *NC*, 3rd ser., vol. 12 (London, 1892).

Fussman G. 'L'inscriptions de Rabatak. La Bactriane et les Kouchans' in *La Bactriane au carrefour des routes et des civilisations de l'Asie centrale: Termez et les villes de Bactriane-Tokharest: actes du colloque de Termez 1997* (Paris, 2001).

Gardner P. *The Parthian Coinage* (London, 1877).

Ghirshman R. *Persia from the Origins to Alexander the Great* (London and New York, 1964).

Henning W.B. 'Mitteliranisch' in Spuler et al. (eds), *Handbuch der Orientalistik*, sec. 1, vol. 4: Iranstik, 1: Linguistik (Leiden and Cologne, 1958).

Henning W.B. 'The Bactrian Inscription', *BSOAS*, vol. 23, no. 1 (1960).

Herodotus, *The Histories*, trans. A. D. Godley, 4 vols, The Loeb Classical Library (London and New York, 1920–30).

Hirth F. 'The Story of Chang K'ien, China's Pioneer in Western Asia', *JAOS*, vol. 37, pt. 2 (1917).

Houghton A., Lorber C. *Seleucid Coins: A Comprehensive Catalogue*, parts 1–2, vols 1–2 (New York, 2002).

Lerner J.D. 'A Graeco-Sogdian Mint of Euthydemus', *RN*, vol. 151 (1996).

Maspero H. 'Le songe et l'ambassade de l'empereur Ming: Étude critique des sources', *Bulletin de l'École française d'Extrême-Orient*, vol. 10 (1910).

Mukherjee B.N. 'Imperial Cults in the Kushāṇa Empire' in *India and Central Asia in Pre-Islamic Period* (Tashkent, 2000).

Narain A.K. 'The Five Yabgus of the Yüeh-chih' in *India: History and Thought* (Calcutta, 1982).

Newell E.T. *The Coinage of the Eastern Seleucid Mints from Seleucus I to Antiochus III* (New York, 1938).

Pugachenkova G.A. 'Antiochus Commagenes et le Prince Kushans', *Annales archéologiques arabes syriennes*, vol. 21 (1971).

Pugachenkova G.A. *Les Trésors de Dalverzine-Tepe* (Leningrad, 1978).

Rapin C., Grenet F. 'Les inscriptions économiques de la trésorerie hellénistique d'Aï Khanoum (Afghanistan)', *Bulletin de correspondance hellénique*, vol. 107, no. 1 (1983).

Rea J.R., Senior R.C., Hollis A.S. 'A Tax Receipt from Hellenistic Bactria', *Zeitschrift für Papyrologie und Epigraphik*, vol. 104 (1994).

Robinson E.S.G. 'The Dates of the Earliest Coins', *NC*, 6th ser., vol. 16 (1956).

Ronca I. (Hrsg.). *Ptolemaios: Geographie 6, 9–21. Ostiran und Zentralasien.* Teil 1. IsMEO (Rome, 1971).

Rtveladze E.V. 'La circulation monétaire au Nord de l'Oxus à l'époque gréco-bactrienne', *RN*, 6th ser., vol. 26 (1984).

Rtveladze E.V. 'Découvertes en numismatique et épigraphie gréco-bactriennes à Kampyr-Tepe (Bactriane du nord)', *RN*, 6th ser., vol. 150 (1995).

Rtveladze E.V. 'Parthia and Bactria' in *In the Land of the Gryphones: Papers on Central Asian Archaeology in Antiquity* (Turin, 1995).

Rtveladze E.V. 'Pre-Muslim Coins of Chach', *SRAA*, vol. 5 (1997–98).

Rtveladze E.V. 'A Bactrian Seal Bearing the Name of an Unknown King (?) from Chaganian, Uzbekistan', *Circle of Inner Asian Art*, no. 18 (2003).

Schlumberger D., Le Berre M., Fussman G. *Surkh-Kotal en Bactriane*, MDAFA 25 (Paris, 1983).

Sims-Williams N. 'A Note on Bactrian Syntax', *Indogermanische Forschungen*, vol. 78 (1973).

Sims-Williams N., Cribb J. 'A New Bactrian Inscription of Kanishka the Great', *SRAA*, vol. 4 (1995–96).

Tarn W. *The Greeks in Bactria and India*, 3rd edn (Chicago, 1985).

Verma T.P. 'The Evolution of Kushana Titles', *Journal of the Numismatic Society of India*, vol. 53, pt. 1–2 (1991).

Wroth W. *Catalogue of the Coins of Parthia: With a Map and 37 Plates* (London, 1903).

Zeymal E.V. 'Coins from the Excavations of Takht-i Sangin (1976–1991)' in K. Tanabe, J. Cribb, H. Wang (eds), *Studies in Silk Road Coins and Culture: Papers in Honour of Professor Ikuo Hirayama on his 65th Birthday* (Kamakura, 1997).

Zürcher E. *The Buddhist Conquest of China* (Leiden, 1959).

Part III: Cultural and spiritual development and Part IV Migrations of cultures

Авеста в русских переводах (1861–1996). СПб., 1998.

Альбаум Л.И. Живопись Афросиаба. Ташкент, 1975.

Аршавская З.А., Ртвеладзе Э.В., Хакимов З.А. Средневековые памятники Сурхандарьи. Ташкент, 1982.

Бартольд В.В. Работы по исторической географии.// В. В. Бартольд. Сочинения. Т. III. М., 1965.

Бартольд В.В. Работы по источниковедению.// В. В. Бартольд. Сочинения. Т. VIII. М., 1973.

Бичурин Н.Я. Собрание сведений о народах, обитавших в Средней Азии в древние времена. Т. 2. М.; Л., 1950.

Боричевский И.А. Митраизм и христианство. М., 1929.

Бузург ибн Шахрияр. Чудеса Индии. М., 1959.

Буряков Ю.Ф. Историческая топография древних городов Ташкентского оазиса. Ташкент, 1975.

Быков А.А. Очерк переправ через реку Аму-дарью. Ташкент, 1879.

Гумилев Л.Н. Древние тюрки. М., 1967.

Дандамаев М.А., Луконин В.Г. Культура и экономика древнего Ирана. М., 1980.

Даркевич В.П. Аргонавты средневековья. М., 1976.

История Узбекистана в источниках: Известия путешественников, географов и ученых XVI – первой половины XIX в. Составитель Б.В. Лунин. Ташкент, 1988.

Кинк Х.А. Египет до фараонов. М., 1964.

Лившиц В.А., Луконин В.Г. Среднеперсидские и согдийские надписи на серебряных сосудах.// ВДИ, 1964, № 3.

Маршак Б.И. Согдийское серебро. М., 1971.

Массон М.Е. Городища Старого Термеза и их изучение.//Труды УзФАН СССР. Серия 1: История. Археология. Вып. 2: Термезская археологическая комплексная экспедиция 1936 г. Ташкент, 1941.

Массон М.Е. Ахангеран. Археолого-топографический очерк. Ташкент, 1953.

Петерс Б.Г. Изображение корабля на булле из Кара-тепе.//Буддийские комплексы Кара-тепе в Старом Термезе. Основные итоги работ 1978–1989 гг. М., 1996.

Пичикян И.Р. Культура Бактрии (ахеменидский и эллинистический периоды). М., 1991.

Путешествия Ибн Батуты. Арабский мир и Центральная Азия. Ташкент, 1996.

Римшнейдер М. От Олимпии до Ниневии во времена Гомера. М., 1977.

Ртвеладзе Э.В. К локализации «греческой» переправы на Оксе.// ВДИ, 1977, № 4.

Ртвеладзе Э.В. Кушанская крепость Кампыр-тепе (исследования и открытия).//ВДИ, 1984, № 2.

Ртвеладзе Э.В. Из недавних открытий Узбекистанской искусствоведческой экспедиции (УзИскЭ) в Северной Бактрии – Тохаристане.//ВДИ, 1990, № 4.

Ртвеладзе Э.В. Проповедники буддизма из стран Трансоксианы в Китае.//ОНУ, 1998, № 4–5.

Ртвеладзе Э.В. Согдийцы на Дальнем Востоке.//ОНУ, 1998, № 8–9.

Ртвеладзе Э.В. Великий шелковый путь. Ташкент, 1999.

Ртвеладзе Э.В. Александр Македонский в Бактрии и Согдиане. Ташкент, 2002.

Руи Гонсалес де Клавихо. Дневник путешествия в Самарканд ко двору Тимура (1403–1406). М., 1990.

Снесарев Г.П. Под небом Хорезма. М., 1973.

Снисаренко А.Б. Эвпатриды удачи. Трагедия античных морей. Л., 1990.

Толстова Л. С. Исторические предания Южного Приаралья: к истории ра̣нних этнокультурных связей народов Арало-Каспийского региона. М., 1984.

Толстов С.П. Древний Хорезм. Опыт историко-археологического исследования. М., 1948.

Устинова Ю.Б. Наскальные латинские и греческие надписи из Кара-Камара.// ВДИ, 1990, № 4.

Хуэй-Цзяо. Жизнеописания достойных монахов (Гао сэн чжуань). Т. 1. М., 1991.

Шумовский Т.А. Арабы и море. М., 1964.

Al-Biruni, *The Chronology of Ancient Nations, or The Vestiges of the Past*, trans. E. Sachau (London, 1879).

Al-Istakhri, Abu Ishaq Ibrahim ibn Muhammad / Goeje, M.J. de, Noldeke, T. (eds), 'Viae Regnorum descriptio ditionis Moslemicae auctore Abū Ishāk al-Fārisi al-Istakhri' in *Bibliotheca Geographorum Arabicorum*, vol. 1, 2nd edn (Leiden, 1927) [in Arabic and Latin].

Al-Muqaddasī, Muḥammad ibn Aḥmad Shams al-Dīn / Goeje, M. J. de (ed.), 'Descriptio imperii Moslemici auctore Al-Moqaddasi', in *Bibliotheca Geographorum Arabicorum*, vol. 3 (Leiden, 1877).

Arrian of Nicomedia, *The Anabasis of Alexander, or, The History of the Wars and Conquests of Alexander the Great*, trans. E.J. Chinook (London, 1984).

Ban Gu, *China in Central Asia: The Early Stage: 125 BC–AD 23: An Annotated Translation of Chapters 61 and 96 of The History of the Former Han Dynasty* (Leiden, 1979).

Beskow P. 'The Routes of Early Mithraism', *Etudes mithraiques* (Leiden, 1978).

Clauss M. *The Roman Cult of Mithras: The God and His Mysteries* (New York, 2001).

Daniels C.M. 'The Role of the Roman Army in the Spread and Practice of Mithraism' in Hinnells, J. (ed.), *Mithraic Studies*, II (Manchester, 1975).

Dubs H.H. 'A Military Contact between Chinese and Romans in 36 BC', *T'oung pao*, 2nd Series, 36:1 (1940), pp. 64–80.

Gordon R.L. 'Franz Cumont and the Doctrines of Mithraism' in Hinnells, J. (ed.), *Mithraic Studies*, I (Manchester, 1975).

Ibn Ḥawqal, Abū al-Qāsim ibn 'Ali / Goeje, M.J. de (ed.), 'Viae et regna, descriptio ditionis moslemicae auctore Abu'l-Kasim Ibn Haukal' in *Bibliotheca Geographorum Arabicorum*, vol. 2 (Leiden, 1873) [in Arabic and Latin].

Ibn Hawqal, *Ketāb ṣurat al-arż*, ed. M.J. de Goeje (Leiden, 1927); trans. J.H. Kramers and G. Wiet as *Configuration de la terre*, 2 vols (Beirut and Paris, 1964).

Jeong Su-il. *The Silk Road Encyclopedia* (Seoul, 2002).

Kageyama E. 'A Chinese Way of Depicting Foreign Delegates Discerned in the Paintings of Afrasiab' in Huyse P. (ed.), *Iran: questions et connaissances*, vol. I: *La période ancienne* (Paris, 2002).

Lerch P. *Khiva oder Kharezm: seine historischen und geographischen Verhältnisse* (St Petersburg, 1873).

Pliny the Elder, *Natural History*, 10 vols, trans. and ed. H. Rackham, W.H.S. Jones and D.E. Eichholz, The Loeb Classical Library (London, 1938–62).

Saeki Y.P. *The Nestorian Documents and Relics in China* (Tokyo, 1951).

Sima Qian, *Records of the Great Historian*, trans. B. Watson, rev. edn (New York, 1993), pp. 244–5.

Strabo, *The Geography of Strabo*, 3 vols, trans. W. Falconer and H.C. Hamilton (London and New York, 1903–6).

Teixidor J. 'Ahiram Inscription', *The Oxford Encyclopedia of Archaeology in the Near East*, ed. E.M. Meyers (Oxford, 1997).

Turcan R. *Mithra et le mithriacisme* (Paris, 1981).

Vermaseren M. J. *Mithra, ce dieu mystérieux* (Paris and Brussels, 1960).

Vermaseren M. J. *Mithras: The Secret God* (London, 1963)

Wikander S. *Études sur les mystères de Mithras*, Vetenskaps-societeten i Lund (Lund, 1950).

Xuan-Zang, *Record of the Western Region*, bk 1 of *Buddhist Records of the Western World*, 2 vols, trans. Samuel Beal (London, 1884).

Yajima Hikoichi. 'The Stamped Aromatic Woods from the Treasure House of Hōryūji and the Early Islamic Indian Ocean', *Journal of Asian and African Studies*, no. 37 (1989).

Yoshida Y. 'Additional Notes on Sims-Williams' Article on the Sogdian Merchants in China and India' in *Cina e Iran. Da Alessandro Magno alla Dinastia Tang* (Florence, 1996).

The following abbreviations are used in the list of references.

Abbreviations

ВДИ – Вестник древней истории. М.

ЖМНП – Журнал Министерства народного просвещения. СПб.

ИМКУ – История материальной культуры Узбекистана. Ташкент; Самарканд.

МИА – Материалы и исследования по археологии СССР, М.; Л.

НЦА – Нумизматика Центральной Азии. Ташкент.

ОНУ – Общественные науки в Узбекистане. Ташкент.

СА – Советская археология. М.

СГЭ – Сообщения Государственного Эрмитажа. Ленинград.

ХАЭЭ – Хорезмская археолого-этнографическая экспедиция

ЭВ – Эпиграфика Востока. М.; Л.

ЮТАКЭ – Южно-Туркменистанская археологическая комплексная экспедиция

BAI – Bulletin of the Asia Institute

BSOAS – Bulletin of the School of Oriental and African Studies

CRAI – Comptes rendus des séances de l'Académie des Inscriptions et Belles-Lettres

JAOS – Journal of the American Oriental Society

JRAS – Journal of the Royal Asiatic Society of Great Britain and Ireland

MDAFA – Mémoires de la Délégation archéologique française en Afghanistan

NC – Numismatic Chronicle

RN – Revue numismatique

SRAA – Silk Road Art and Archaeology

INDEX

This publication is translated according to the 2008 edition

This new translation first published in 2022 by
Scala Arts & Heritage Publishers Ltd
305 Access House, 141–157 Acre Lane
London SW2 5UA
www.scalapublishers.com

Distributed in the book trade by
ACC Art Books
Sandy Lane, Old Martlesham,
Woodbridge, Suffolk IP12 4SD
accartbooks.com

Special support: Saida Mirziyoyeva, Deputy Chairwoman of the Council of the Art and Culture Development Foundation of the Republic of Uzbekistan

Commissioning Editor: Gayane Umerova, Executive Director of the Art and Culture Development Foundation of the Republic of Uzbekistan

ISBN 978 1 78551 373 2

Edited by Violetta Tsilitsskaya
Designed by Matthew Wilson
Translation by Laila Friese with editing by David Price in association with First Edition Translations Ltd, Cambridge, UK

Printed and bound in Turkey